Plato's *Parmenides*

I saw eternity the other night
Like a great ring of pure and endless light,
    All calm as it was bright;
And round beneath it, time in hours, days, years,
    Driv'n by the spheres,
Like a vast shadow moved, in which the world
    And all her train were hurled.

        Henry Vaughan, "The World"

Plato's *Parmenides*

Translation and Analysis

R. E. Allen

University of Minnesota Press • Minneapolis

Copyright © 1983 by the University of Minnesota.
All rights reserved.
Published by the University of Minnesota Press,
2037 University Avenue Southeast, Minneapolis, MN 55414
Printed in the United States of America.

Library of Congress Cataloging in Publication Data

Plato.
    Plato's Parmenides.
    Includes bibliographical references and index.
    1. Reasoning. 2. Socrates. 3. Zeno, of Elea.
I. Allen, R. E. II. Title.
B378.A5A44   184   82-7051
ISBN 0-8166-1070-3   AACR2

The Northwestern University
Research Grants Committee has provided
partial support for the publication
of this book.
The University of Minnesota Press
gratefully acknowledges
this assistance.

The University of Minnesota
is an equal-opportunity
educator and employer.

To
Ann Branin Usilton Allen

Bibliographical Abbreviations

ACPA   H. F. Cherniss, *Aristotle's Criticism of Plato and the Academy*, vol. i., Baltimore, 1944.

AM   W. D. Ross, *Aristotle's Metaphysics,* Oxford, 1924.

DK   H. Diels, and W. Kranz, *Die Fragmente der Vorsokratiker* (8th ed.), Berlin, 1956.

HGM   T. L. Heath, *History of Greek Mathematics*, Oxford, 1921.

LSJ   Liddell and Scott, (ed. Jones), *A Greek-English Lexicon* (9th ed.), Oxford, 1951.

PC   F. M. Cornford, *Plato's Cosmology*, London, 1937.

PED   R. Robinson, *Plato's Earlier Dialectic* (2nd ed.), Oxford, 1948.

PP   F. M. Cornford, *Plato and Parmenides*, London, 1939.

Proclus   *Procli Philosophi Platonici: Commentarium in Platonis Parmenidem* (ed. Cousin), Paris, 1864.

PTF   R. E. Allen, *Plato's Euthyphro and the Earlier Theory of Forms*, London, 1970.

PTI   W. D. Ross, *Plato's Theory of Ideas*, Oxford, 1951.

PTK   F. M. Cornford, *Plato's Theory of Knowledge*, London, 1935.

REA   H. F. Cherniss, *The Riddle of the Early Academy*, Berkeley and Los Angeles, 1945.

SPM   R. E. Allen (ed.), *Studies in Plato's Metaphysics*, London, 1965.

TBEE   T. L. Heath, *The Thirteen Books of Euclid's Elements*, Cambridge, 1908; New York, 1960.

Preface

The aim throughout what follows has been to use the structure of the *Parmenides* as a control on the interpretation of individual passages, to solve the dialogue as one might crack a code, in order to obtain within such limitations as the subject-matter may admit results which are provably true. The *Parmenides* has been read as everything from a joke to an exercise in the detection of fallacies to a revelation of the Unknown God. In actual fact, the dialogue is aporetic, akin to Beta of Aristotle's *Metaphysics* rather than Lambda, let alone the *Enneads*, and in no sense a budget of fallacies.

Since aporetic analysis is fundamental to what follows, it may help to indicate its relation to previous literature. Richard Robinson, in his admirable treatment of the *Parmenides* in the second edition of *Plato's Earlier Dialectic*, observed that the initial objection to Ideas in the *Parmenides*, the Dilemma of Participation, is restated in the *Philebus* (15b-c)—the only such argument which Plato directly repeats. Robinson inferred that Plato regarded the objection as serious but not fatal. The inference seems fair enough—but what does it mean? In philosophy, as a rule, an objection that is not fatal is not finally serious.

The answer was suggested by Joseph Owens' fine Avicennean interpretation of Aristotle in *The Doctrine of Being in the Aristotelian Metaphysics*. Dealing with Aristotle's aporematic treatment of the causes in *Metaphysics* B, Owens remarked that not only Aristotle's vocabulary but his concepts of *aporia* and *euporia* were anticipated at *Philebus* 15b-c. They are indeed, and this is the solution to Robinson's problem: an objection is serious but not fatal if it is an *aporia*, a puzzle or perplexity, a knot that binds the intellect and needs to be untied. But if the first objection to Ideas in the *Parmenides* is aporetic, it is reasonable to think that other objections are aporetic as well.

Robinson and Owens connect with Ryle's review of Cornford's *Plato and Parmenides* and Ryle's own subsequent articles on the *Parmenides* in *Mind* of 1939. Ryle's work exhibits the empiricist and broadly Aristotelian prejudices that later commentators in the tradition of linguistic analysis have characteristically betrayed, and his comparison of the hypotheses about Unity to Russell's Paradox is on the face of it absurd. And yet, and yet . . . The comparison reveals a profoundly original and important point, which Ryle saw, or half-saw, by attending specifically to structure: the hypotheses about Unity have this in common with Russell's Paradox, that they involve a double *reductio ad absurdum*, disproving both a proposition and its denial; and the structure that exhibits this is consciously marked and cannot be dismissed as accidental or "merely ostensible." There is some sense, then, in which Ryle has to be right, and thanks to Robinson and Owens it is possible to specify that sense: The structure of the third part becomes intelligible if the hypotheses about Unity form a massive, reticulated aporia; and at the same time, the second and third parts of the *Parmenides* are brought into structural relation.

In respect to this final section of the *Parmenides*, it should be added that Aristotle's *Physics* is an indispensable source for understanding the physical deductions of the *Parmenides* with respect to place, time, motion, and infinity; and this implies that the *Physics* continues a professional academic tradition in physics and mathematics that is also represented by various arguments in the *Parmenides*. Those arguments exhibit a high degree of technicality and professionalism, which is why they have not been understood by scholars unaware of the tradition they represent. I am happy to say that on this point I have been anticipated by results obtained by G. E. L. Owen. My own understanding of many of the issues involved has been much deepened by the patient instruction of Marshall Clagett and Harold Cherniss.

If the account here offered is true, a Platonic dialogue that has resisted interpretation for several thousand years can now be read and understood. The dialogue has not been exhausted; no interpretation can do that. It has only been solved in the sense that it is now possible to begin to learn what it has to teach. Yet it is not in principle a difficult thing to read a book, and the interpretation of classical texts is in the final analysis only reading. The sole merit of the present study, if it is accurate, is that it makes accessible what has always been there to be seen.

With solution of the *Parmenides* there will come, in the fullness of time, a clearer understanding of later dialogues such as the *Theaetetus, Sophist, Politicus,* and *Philebus,* which are far more aporetic than they are usually taken to be, and this will involve close consideration of the method of collection and division announced in the *Phaedrus,* but used as early as the *Gorgias.* That method aims at cleaving nature at the joints; but though the metaphor of cleaving fits species and genera, it does not fit terms unrestricted by reason of their generality, and this fact introduces considerable metaphysical complexity. We need to learn how these methods of inquiry are related to Plato's earlier dialectic, and specifically to Socratic elenchus and the method(s) of hypothesis. This would be to continue work that Richard Robinson has so excellently begun.

In addition, it is now possible to reconstruct Plato's interpretation of Parmenides, Zeno, and by derivation Heraclitus and the Pluralists: all rest on an implicit nominalism which tacitly confuses naming with meaning.

The *Parmenides* also puts at issue the works of Aristotle, and this in respect not only of testimony and criticism concerning Plato, with which Harold Cherniss has so nobly dealt in *Aristotle's Criticism of Plato and the Early Academy* and *The Riddle of the Early Academy* (which latter, by the way, the Library of Congress once catalogued under Games), but of the development of his own metaphysics out of the *Parmenides*, and in particular his account of substance, form, and universality. It is now become clear that the main criticisms that Aristotle directs against Plato's theory of Ideas are derived from Parmenides' objections to Socrates' theory: Aristotle did not think the knots could be untied. It is further clear that the assumption on which Parmenides' objections rest, namely, the reality of sensibles independently of Ideas and the reality of independent Ideas that are yet conceived to participate in each other, and the resulting inconsistencies that the hypothesis of separate Ideas then entails, is the foundation of Aristotle's own metaphysical views. Aristotle's testimony about the One and the Indefinite Dyad, or the Great and Small, turns out to be an interpretation of substrate doctrines offered in the hypotheses about Unity in the *Parmenides*. No wonder Aristotle and Hermodorus and others had trouble: they had to interpret the *Parmenides* too—a sufficient refutation in itself of claims of an 'esoteric' teaching.

This study, then, provides the basis for fresh inquiry into the later Platonism, into Aristotle's criticisms of Plato, his testimony about Plato, and the origins of his own positive doctrines.

Very little in this book is new: almost everything has been said before, except that it needed to be connected a little differently. F. M. Cornford is the foundation of it all. Other commentators, rarely, have had greater weight of learning. Other commentators have had keener analytic ability, though this is true less often than it is pretended, as is evidenced by clarity of style. But Cornford, by reason of his constant humility in the face of the text, his clarity of mind, his transparent honesty of purpose, his judiciousness and tact, and constant good sense, is and remains the teacher of all who wish to learn. There is a morality of inquiry, a virtuousness in search, which Cornford in his use of evidence constantly shows. Robinson and Ryle, who have each contributed so much to this study, could not, I think, have written without him. Certainly I could not, and if I have seen further, it is because I have stood on the shoulders of a giant.

I have been asked why I have not considered at greater length the pamphlet literature in the journals. There are many reasons, including the obvious stylistic one that with a long and complicated argument to get through, wandering along by-ways bogs you down. But it is also true that while articles can have an important place in advancing discussion, the treating of limited topics in abstraction from context is a constant inducement in the study of Plato to oversimplification, artificial technicality in matters remote from the text, and scholarly impressionism. The literature on what is called "the Third Man" is a case in point: that literature is at this point very large; as it happens, there is a Third Man argument in Aristotle, who answered it, and no Third Man argument in the *Parmenides* at all, except in a derivative and adjectival sense.

Many of the essays in *Studies in Plato's Metaphysics* will provide a helpful background, often by way of contrast, for the argument of this book. More complete bibliography will be found in Harold Cherniss's articles in *Lustrum* (4 1959) 5-308; 5 (1960) 321-615), which mention the main contributions to the literature on the *Parmenides* in this century. For more recent bibliography one may consult W. K. C. Guthrie's *A History of Greek Philosophy: V. The Later Plato and the Academy*, Cambridge, 1978. Professor Guthrie's own valuable discussion of the *Parmenides* provides an index of present understanding of the dialogue.

I am aware that the book which follows is not easy reading, a fact which no amount of hard writing could change. But if the reader will take time to follow the argument, there is a reward. Beneath the surface complexity of the *Parmenides* there is an underlying simplicity, a rhythmical, dynamic beauty like that of music. I count myself fortunate to have been able to live, for brief periods of time, in the presence of such great beauty, and in the presence of an intellectual power which is awesome.

Contents

**Plato's *Parmenides*
Translation**

Introductory Conversation (126a-127a)

The narrator is Cephalus of Clazomenae.

126a   When we arrived at Athens from our home in Clazomenae, we met Adeimantus and Glaucon in the Agora. Adeimantus took my hand and said, Welcome, Cephalus. If you need anything here that we can provide, please say so.

Well really, I replied, we are here for just that very purpose — to ask something of you.

You have only to state it, he said.

b   What was the name, I said, of your half-brother on your mother's side? I do not remember. He was just a boy, the last time I came here from Clazomenae, but that was a long time ago now. His father's name, I think, was Pyrilampes.

Quite so, he said, and his own is Antiphon, but why do you ask?[1]

These gentlemen here, I said, are fellow-citizens of mine, much interested in philosophy. They have heard that your Antiphon used to associate with a certain Pythodorus, a companion of Zeno's, and that he can relate from
c   memory the arguments that once were discussed by Socrates, Zeno, and Parmenides, having heard them from Pythodorus.

True, he said.

Well, I replied, that is what we want, to hear those arguments.

No difficulty there, he said. When Antiphon was young he used to rehearse them diligently, though now, like his grandfather of the same name, he spends most of his time on horses. But if you will, let us call on him. He just left here for home, but he lives nearby, in Melite.

127a   So we set out to walk, and found Antiphon at home giving directions to a smith for making some sort of bit. But when he dismissed the fellow, his brothers told him why we were there, and he recognized me from my previous visit and greeted me warmly. When we asked him to go through the arguments, he at first hesitated—he said it was a difficult task.[2] But finally, he complied.

Characters and Setting (127a-d)

  According to Antiphon, Pythodorus said that Zeno and Parmenides once
b came to Athens for the Great Panathenaea. Parmenides was then well along in years and quite grey, a distinguished-looking man of perhaps sixty-five. Zeno was about forty, handsome and tall. It was said that he had been Par-
c menides' favorite. They stayed at Pythodorus' house in Ceramicus, outside the city walls, and Socrates came there with a number[3] of other people, eager to hear a reading of Zeno's treatise, which Zeno and Parmenides had brought to Athens for the first time. Socrates was then quite young. Zeno himself read to them, but Parmenides, as it happened, was out. Pythodorus
d said he came in with Parmenides and Aristoteles, who was later one of the Thirty Tyrants, when the reading of the arguments was very nearly finished, and they heard only a small part of the treatise remaining. As for himself, however, he had heard Zeno read it before.

Part I.
Zeno's Paradox
and the Theory of Forms (127d-130a)

Zeno's Paradox (127d-128e)

e   When the reading was finished, Socrates asked to hear the hypothesis of
the first argument again. When it was read, he asked, What does that mean,
Zeno? If things are many, then it follows that the same things must be both
like and unlike; but that is impossible; for unlike things cannot be like or
like things unlike. Isn't that your claim?

It is, said Zeno.

Now, if it is impossible for unlike things to be like and like things unlike,
it is also impossible for there to be many things; for if there were, things
would undergo impossible qualifications. Isn't that the point of your arguments, to contend, contrary to everything generally said, that there is no
plurality? And don't you suppose that each of your arguments is a proof of
just that, so that you believe that you have given precisely as many proofs
that there is no plurality as there are arguments in your treatise? Is that what
you mean, or have I failed to understand you?

128a   No, said Zeno, you have grasped the point of the whole treatise.

I gather, Parmenides, said Socrates, that Zeno here wishes to associate
himself with you not only by other marks of friendship, but also by his
book. He has written to much the same effect as you, but by changing
tactics he tries to mislead us into thinking he is saying something different.

b   In your poem, you say that the All is one, and for this you provide fine and
excellent proofs. He, on the other hand, says it is not many, and he also
provides proofs of great multitude and magnitude. So you say unity, he says
no plurality, and each so speaks that, though there is no difference in what
you mean, what you say hardly seems the same at all. That is why what
you've said appears to mean something quite beyond the rest of us.[4]

Yes, Socrates, said Zeno. But you have not wholly perceived the truth

about my treatise. To be sure, you pick up the scent of the arguments and
c   follow their trail like a young Spartan hound,[5] but you overlook this at
the outset: the book is not so thoroughly pretentious as to have been written with the motive you allege, disguised for the public as a great achieve-
ment. What you mention is incidental. The real truth is that it is a kind of
defense of Parmenides' argument, directed against those who ridicule it
d   on the ground that, if it is one,[6] many absurd and inconsistent consequences follow. This book is a retort to those who assert plurality, and
pays them back in kind with interest; its purpose is to make clear that their
own hypothesis, that plurality is,[7] when followed out far enough, suffers
still more absurd consequences than the hypothesis of there being one. I
wrote it when I was young, in a spirit of controversy, and when it was
written someone stole it, so that I was not allowed to decide whether
e   or not it should see the light of day. That is what you overlook, Socrates:
you suppose it was written by an older man zealous of reputation, not by
a young man fond of controversy. Though as I said, you did not misrepresent it.

Socrates' Solution to Zeno's Paradox (128e-130a)

I accept that, said Socrates. What you say is no doubt true. But tell me:
do you not believe that there exists, alone by itself, a certain character of
129a likeness, and again, another character opposite to it, what it is to be unlike;
and that you and I and the other things we call many get a share of these
two things? Things that get a share of likeness become like in the respect
and to the degree that they get a share; things that get a share of unlikeness become unlike; and things that get a share of both become both. Even
if all things get a share of both, opposite as they are, and by reason of having a share of both it is possible for them to be both like and unlike themselves, what is surprising in that? If someone were to show that things
b   that are *just* like become unlike, or *just* unlike like, no doubt that would be
a portent. But I find nothing strange, Zeno, if he shows that things which
get a share of both undergo both qualifications, nor if he shows that all
things are one by reason of having a share of the one, and that those very
same things are also in turn many by reason of having a share of multitude.
But if he shows that what it is to be one is many, and the many in turn one,
c   that *will* surprise me. The same is true in like manner of all other things. If
someone should show that the kinds and characters in themselves undergo
these opposite qualifications, there is reason for surprise. But what is surprising if someone shows that I am one and many? When he wishes to show
that I am many, he says that my right side is one thing and my left another,
that my front is different from my back, and my upper body in like manner

different from my lower; for I suppose I have a share of multitude. To show
that I am one, he says I am one man among the seven of us, since I also have
d   a share of the one. The result is that he shows that both are true. Now, if
someone should undertake to show that sticks and stones and things like
that are many, and the same things[8] one, we shall grant that he has proved
that something is many and one, but not that the one is many or the many
one; he has said nothing out of the ordinary, but a thing on which we all
agree. But I should be filled with admiration, Zeno, said Socrates, if someone were first to distinguish separately alone by themselves the characters
I just mentioned—likeness and unlikeness, for example, multitude and the
e   one, rest and motion, and all such similar things—and then show that these
things in themselves can be combined and distinguished. You have do doubt
dealt manfully with the former issue. But as I say, I should admire it much
more if someone should show that this same perplexity is interwoven in
130a   all kinds of ways in the characters themselves—that just as you and Parmenides have explained in the things we see, so it proves too in what we
apprehend by reflection.

Part II.
Parmenides' Criticisms
of the Theory of Forms (130a-135d)

The Extent of Separate Ideas (130a-e)

As Socrates was speaking, Pythodorus said he expected Parmenides and Zeno to be annoyed at every word. Instead, they paid close attention, and from time to time glanced at each other and smiled as if in admiration. When Socrates finished, Parmenides expressed this. Socrates, he said, your impulse toward argument is admirable. Now tell me: do you yourself thus distinguish, as you say, certain characters themselves separately, and separately in turn the things that have a share of them? And do you think that likeness itself is something separate from the likeness that we have, and one and many, and all the others you just heard Zeno mention?

Yes, I do, said Socrates.

And characters of this sort too? said Parmenides. For example, a certain character of just, alone by itself, and of beautiful and good, and all such as those in turn?

Yes, he said.

Well, is there a character of man separate from us and all such as we are, a certain character of man itself, or fire, or even water?

I have often been in perplexity, Parmenides, he said, about whether one should speak about them as about the others, or not.

And what about these, Socrates—they would really seem ridiculous: hair and mud and dirt, for example, or anything else which is utterly worthless and trivial. Are you perplexed whether one should say that there is a separate character for each of them too, a character that again is other than the sorts of things we handle?[9]

Not at all, said Socrates. Surely those things actually are just what we see them to be, and it would be quite absurd to suppose that something is a

7

character of them. Still, I sometimes worry lest what holds in one case may not hold in all; but when I take that stand, I retreat, for fear of tumbling undone into depths of nonsense. So I go back to the things we just said have characters, and spend my time dealing with them.

e   You are still young, Socrates, said Parmenides, and philosophy has not yet taken hold of you as I think it one day will. You will despise none of these things then. But as it is, because of your youth, you still pay attention to what people think. Now tell me this: do you think, as you say, that there are certain characters, and that these others here, by reason of having a share of them, get their names from them? As for example, things

131a   that get a share of likeness become like, of largeness large, of beauty and justice beautiful and just?

Yes, certainly, said Socrates.

The Dilemma of Participation (131a-c)

Then does each thing that gets a share get a share of the whole character, or of a part? Or could there be any kind of sharing separate from these?

Surely not, Socrates replied.

Well, does it seem to you that the whole character, being one, is in each of the many?

What prevents it, Parmenides? said Socrates.

b   Therefore, being one and the same, it will be present at once and as a whole in things that are many and separate, and thus it would be separate from itself.

No, it would not, he said, at least if it were like one and the same day, which is in many different places at once and nonetheless not separate from itself. If it were in fact that way, each of the characters could be in everything at once as one and the same.

Very neat, Socrates, he said. You make one and the same thing be in many different places at once, as if you'd spread a sail over a number of men and then claimed that one thing as a whole was over many. Or isn't that the sort of thing you mean to say?

c   Perhaps, he said.

Now, would the whole sail be over each man, or part of it over one and part over another?

Part.

Therefore, Socrates, he said, the characters themselves are divisible, and things that have a share of them have a share of parts of them; whole would no longer be in each, but part of each in each.

Yes, so it appears.

Well, Socrates, are you willing to say that the one character is in truth divided for us, and yet that it will still be one?

Not at all, he said.

The Paradox of Divisibility (131c-e)

d   No, for consider, he said: if you divide largeness itself, and each of the many large things is to be large by a part of largeness smaller than largeness itself, won't that appear unreasonable?[10]

Of course, he said.

Well then, suppose something has a given small part of the equal. Will the possessor be equal to anything by what is smaller than the equal itself?

Impossible.

e   But suppose that one of us is to have a part of the small. The small will be larger than this part of itself, because it is part of it, and thus the small itself will be larger. But that to which the part subtracted is added will be smaller, not larger, than before.

Surely that could not happen, he said.

Then in what way, Socrates, will the others get a share of characters for you, since they cannot get a share part by part or whole by whole?

Such a thing, it seems to me, is difficult, emphatically difficult, to determine, he said.

The Largeness Regress (131e-132b)

Really! Then how do you deal with this?

What is that?

132a   I suppose you think that each character is one for some such reason as this: when some plurality of things seem to you to be large, there perhaps seems to be some one characteristic that is the same when you look over them all, whence you believe that the large is one.

True, he said.

What about the large itself and the other larges? If with your mind you should look over them all in like manner, will not some one large again appear, by which they all appear to be large?

It seems so.

Therefore, another character of largeness will have made its appearance alongside largeness itself and the things that have a share of it; and over and above all those, again, a different one, by which they will all be large. And b   each of the characters will no longer be one for you, but unlimited in multitude.

Ideas as Thoughts (132b-c)

But Parmenides, said Socrates, may it not be that each of these characters is a thought, and that it pertains to it to come to be nowhere else except in minds? For in that way, each would still be one, and no longer undergo what was just now said.

Well, he said, is each of the thoughts one, but a thought of nothing?

No, that is impossible, he said.

A thought of something, then?

Yes.

c   Of something that is, or is not?

Of something that is.

Of some one thing which that thought thinks as being over all, that is, of some one characteristic?

Yes.

Then that which is thought to be one will be a character, ever the same over all?

Again, it appears it must.

Really! Then what about this, said Parmenides: in virtue of the necessity by which you say that the others have a share of characters, does it not seem to you that either each is composed of thoughts and all think, or that being thoughts they are unthought?[11]

But that, he said, is hardly reasonable.

Ideas as Paradigms (132d-133a)

Still, Parmenides, he said, this much is quite clear to me: these charac-
d   ters stand, as it were, as paradigms fixed in the nature of things, and the others resemble them and are likenesses of them; this sharing that the others come to have of characters is nothing other than being a resemblance of them.

Well, Parmenides said, if something resembles a character, is it possible for that character not to be like what has come to resemble it, insofar as it has become like it? Is there any way in which what is like is not like what is like it?

There is not.

Rather, what is like must have a share of one and the same character
e   as what it is like?

True.

But will not that of which like things have a share so as to be like be the character itself?

Certainly.

Then it is not possible for anything to be like the character, or the char-acter like anything else. For otherwise, another character will always appear alongside it, and should that character be like something, a different one
133a   again. Continual generation of a new character will never stop, if the char-acter comes to be like what has a share of it.

You are quite right.

Then the others do not get a share of characters by likeness. It is necessary to look for something else by which they get a share.

So it seems.

Separation and Unknowability (133a-134e)

Do you see, then, Socrates, how great the perplexity is, if someone should distinguish as characters things that are alone by themselves?

Yes indeed.

b   Rest assured, he said, that you hardly even have yet begun to grasp how great the perplexity is, if you are going to assume that each character of things that are is one, ever marking it off as something.

How so? he said.

c   There are many other difficulties, he said, but the greatest is this. If someone said that it does not even pertain to the characters to be known if they are such as we say they must be, one could not show him that he was mistaken unless the disputant happened to be a man of wide experience and natural ability, willing to follow many a remote and laborious demonstration. Otherwise, the man who compels them to be unknowable would be left unconvinced.

Why is that, Parmenides? said Socrates.

Because, Socrates, I suppose that you and anyone else who assumes that the nature and reality of each thing exists as something alone by itself would agree, first of all, that none of them is in us.

No, for how would it still be alone by itself? said Socrates.

d   You are right, he said. And further, as many of the characteristics as are what they are relative to each other have their nature and reality relative to themselves, but not relative to things among us—likenesses, or whatever one assumes they are—of which we have a share and in each case are called by their names.[12] But things among us, in turn, though they are of the same name as those, are relative to themselves but not to the characters, and it is to themselves but not to those that as many as are so named refer.

How do you mean? said Socrates.

Take an example, said Parmenides. If one of us is master or slave *of* someone, he is surely not a slave of master itself, what it is to be master, nor is a master the master of slave itself, what it is to be slave. Being a man, we are

e   either of the two of another man. But mastership itself is what it is *of* slavery itself, and slavery in like manner slavery *of* mastership. Things in us do not have their power and significance relative to things there, nor things there relative to us. Rather, as I say, things there are themselves of and relative to themselves, and in like manner things among us are relative to them-

134a   selves. Or don't you see what I mean?

Of course I do, said Socrates.

And furthermore, he said, knowledge itself, what it is to be knowledge, would be knowledge of what is there, namely, what it is to be real and true?

Of course.

And each of the branches of knowledge in turn would be knowledge of what it is to be each of the things that are. Not so?

Yes.

But knowledge among us would be knowledge of the truth and reality among us? And does it not in turn follow that each branch of knowledge among us is knowledge of each of the things that are among us?

b

Necessarily.

Moreover, as you agree, we surely do not have the characters themselves, nor can they be among us.

No.

But the kinds themselves, what it is to be each thing, are known, I take it, by the character of knowledge?

Yes.

Which we do not have.

No.

Then none of the characters is known by us, since we have no share of knowledge itself.

It seems not.

Therefore, what it is to be beautiful itself, and the good, and everything we at this point accept as characteristics themselves, is for us unknowable.

c

Very likely.

Consider then whether the following is not still more remarkable.

What is it?

You would say, I take it, that if there is a certain kind of knowledge itself, it is much more exact than knowledge among us. So too of beauty, and all the rest.

Yes.

Now, if anything has a share of knowledge itself, would you say that no one but god has the most exact knowledge?

Necessarily.

d

Then will it be possible for the god, having knowledge itself, to know things among us?

Why shouldn't it be?

Because, Socrates, said Parmenides, we agreed that those characters do not have the power they have relative to things among us, nor things among us relative to those, but each relative to themselves.

Yes, we agreed to that.

Now, if the most exact mastership and most exact knowledge is in the god's realm, mastership there would never master us here, nor knowledge e there know us or anything where we are. In like manner, we do not rule there by our authority here, and know nothing divine by our knowledge. By the same account again, those there are not our masters, and have no knowledge of human things, being gods.

But surely, said Socrates, it would be too strange an account, if one were to deprive the gods of knowing.

Conclusion (134e-135d)

And yet, Socrates, said Parmenides, these difficulties and many more in
135a addition necessarily hold of the characters, if these characteristics of things that are exist, and one is to distinguish each character as something by itself. The result is that the hearer is perplexed, and contends that they do not exist, and that even if their existence is conceded, they are necessarily unknowable by human nature. In saying this, he thinks he is saying something significant, and as we just remarked, it is astonishingly hard to convince him to the contrary. Only a man of considerable natural gifts will be able to understand that there is a certain kind of each thing, a nature and
b reality alone by itself, and it will take a man more remarkable still to discover it and be able to instruct someone else who has examined all these difficulties with sufficient care.

I agree with you, Parmenides, said Socrates. You are saying very much what I think too.

Nevertheless, said Parmenides, if, in light of all the present difficulties and others like them, one will not allow that there are characters of things that are, and refuses to distinguish as something a character of each single thing, he will not even have anything to which to turn his mind, since he will not allow that there is a characteristic, ever the same, of each of the
c things that are; and so he will utterly destroy the power and significance of thought and discourse. I think you are even more aware of that sort of consequence.

True, he replied.

What will you do about philosophy, then? Which way will you turn while these things are unknown?

For the moment, at least, I am not really sure I see.

No, because you undertake to mark off as something beauty and jus-
d tice and goodness, and each of the characters, too soon, before being properly trained. I realized that yesterday when I heard you discussing with Aristoteles here. Believe me, your impulse toward argument is noble, and indeed divine. But train yourself more thoroughly while you are still young; drag yourself through what is generally regarded as useless, and condemned by the multitude as idle talk. Otherwise, the truth will escape you.

Part III.
The Hypotheses
about Unity (135d-166c)

Introduction (135d-137c)

What is the manner of training, Parmenides? he asked.

The one you heard Zeno use, he replied. Except for this: I admired you when you said, and said to him, that you would not allow inquiry to wander e among the things we see, nor even within their domain, but rather in the field of those things there, which one would most especially grasp by rational account and believe to be characters.

Yes, he said, for it seems to me easy enough, the other way, to show that things which are are both like and unlike, and affected in any other way at all.

And you were right, Parmenides replied. But it is also necessary to do this in addition: to examine the consequences that follow from the hypothesis, not only if each thing is hypothesized to be, but also if that same thing 136a is hypothesized not to be, if you wish to be more thoroughly trained.

How do you mean? he said.

Take, if you like, Zeno's hypothesis, if many is. What must follow for the many themselves relative to themselves and relative to the one, and for the one relative to itself and relative to the many? If, on the other hand, many is not, consider again what will follow both for the one and for the many, relative to themselves and relative to each other. Still again, should b you hypothesize if likeness is, or if it is not, what will follow on each hypothesis both for the very things hypothesized and for the others, relative to themselves and relative to each other. The same account holds about unlikeness, and about motion, and about rest, and about coming to be and ceasing to be, and about being itself and not being. In short, about whatever may be hypothesized as being and as not being and as undergoing any other affection whatever, it is necessary to examine the consequences c relative to itself and relative to each one of the others, whichever you may choose, and relative to more than one and relative to all in like manner. And the others, in turn, must be examined both relative to themselves and relative to any other you may choose, whether you hypothesize what you hypothesize as being or as not being, if you are to be finally trained accurately to discern the truth.

An extraordinary procedure, Parmenides! I don't quite understand. Why not explain it to me by hypothesizing something yourself, in order that I may better come to understand.

d You impose a difficult task, Socrates, Parmenides said, for a man of my age.

Then you, Zeno, said Socrates, why don't you explain it to us?

And he[13] said that Zeno laughed and said, Let us ask Parmenides himself, Socrates, for I fear it is no light thing he has in mind. Or don't you see how great a task you impose? If there were more of us, it would not even be right to ask it, for it would be unfitting, especially in a man of his age, to discuss[14] things such as this before a large company: for most people do not realize that without this kind of detailed answering and ranging through everything, it is impossible to meet with truth and gain intelligence. So Parmenides, I join in Socrates' request, in order that I too may learn from you after all this time.

e

After Zeno said this, Antiphon said that Pythodorus said that he and Aristoteles and the others begged Parmenides to illustrate what he meant, and not refuse. Parmenides said, I must do as you ask. Yet really, I feel like the old racehorse in Ibycus, who trembles with fear at the start of the race because he knows from long experience what lies in store. Ibycus compares himself, forced as an old man to enter the lists of love against his will.[15] When I remember how, at my age, I must traverse such and so great a sea of arguments, I am afraid. Still, I must oblige you, especially since, as Zeno says, we are alone among ourselves. Where then shall we begin? What shall we hypothesize first? Since it seems I must play this laborious game, shall I begin with myself and take my own hypothesis? Shall I hypothesize about the one itself, what must follow if one is or one is not?

137a

b

By all means, said Zeno.

Then who will answer me? he asked. Perhaps the youngest? For he would give least trouble, and be most likely to say what he thinks. At the same time, his answering would give me a chance to rest.

c I am ready, Parmenides, said Aristoteles. You mean me: I am the youngest. Ask your questions, and I will answer them.

Very well, he said.

I.1. First Hypothesis, First Deduction (137c-142a)

i. Part and Whole (137c-d)

c   If unity is, is unity many?

No.

Then it has no parts, nor is itself a whole.

Why?

Part, I take it, is part of a whole.

Yes.

What about whole? Is not a whole that from which no part is absent?

Of course.

Then if unity were a whole and had parts, on both grounds it would be composed of parts.

Necessarily.

Then on both grounds unity would be many, not one.

d   True.

But it must be, not many, but *just* one.

Yes.

Then if unity is to be one, it neither is a whole nor has parts.

ii. Limit and Unlimited (137d)

Now, if unity has no part, it has neither beginning, middle nor end; for such things would forthwith be parts of it.

Correct.

Moreover, beginning and end are limits of each thing.

Of course.

Therefore, unity is unlimited, if it has neither beginning nor end.

Yes.

iii. Shape (137d-138a)

Then unity also is without shape: for it has a share neither of straight nor round.

e   How so?

A thing is round, I take it, whose extremes are everywhere equally distant from its middle.

Yes.

But straight if its middle is in front of both extremes.

True.

So unity would have parts and be many, if it had a share of straight shape or round.

Of course.

138a   Then it is neither round nor straight, since it has no parts.

Correct.

iv. In Itself, In Another (138a-b)

And if it is of this sort, moreover, it is nowhere: for it is neither in itself nor in another.

How so?

If it were in another, it would be contained in a circle by what it was in, and touch it in many places with many parts of itself; but since it is one and without parts, and has no share of circularity, it cannot touch in many places in a circle.

No.

Furthermore, if it were in itself, it would contain nothing other than it-
b   self by itself, as in itself: for a thing cannot be in something that does not contain it.

No, it cannot.

Now, what contains is one thing and what is contained is another; for the same thing will not at once do and suffer both. So unity would no longer then be one, but two.

Of course.

Then unity is nowhere, if it is neither in itself nor in another.

True.

v. Motion and Rest (138b-139b)

Consider then whether if it is thus it can be at rest or moved.

Why could it not be?

Because if it were moved, it would either change place or alter character; for those are the only motions.

c   Yes.

But unity cannot alter its own character, I take it, and still be one.

No.

Then it does not move by altering character.

It appears not.

But by changing place?

Perhaps.

But surely, if unity changed place, either it would revolve in the same place in a circle or pass from one place to another.

Necessarily.

Now, if it revolves in a circle it must rest on a center, and have what revolves around the center as other parts of itself. But how can that to which
d   neither middle nor parts pertain ever be moved in a circle around its center?

There is no way.

Then does it come to be in different places at different times by changing place, and move in that way?

Yes, if at all.

Now, it appeared that it cannot be somewhere in something?

Yes.

So it is still more impossible for it to come to be somewhere in something.

I don't see why.

If a thing is coming to be in something, it necessarily is *not yet* in it since it is still coming to be in it; and no longer completely outside it since it is *already* coming to be in it.

Yes.

e   Then only that which has parts is affected in this way — part of it in the thing already and part at the same time outside. It is impossible for what has no parts, I take it, to be at the same time and as a whole either within or outside of something.

True.

But it is still more impossible for what neither has parts nor is a whole to come to be somewhere in something, since it can come to be in it neither part by part nor as a whole.

It appears so.

Then unity does not change by going somewhere or coming to be in

139a   something, nor does it revolve in the same place, nor alter character.

It seems not.

Then unity is unchanging with respect to every sort of change.

It is.

But further, we say that it cannot be in something.

Yes.

Then it is never in the same place.

Why?

Because then it would be in that in which same place it is.

Of course.

But it was possible for it to be neither in itself nor in another.

No.

Then unity is never in the same place.

It seems not.

b   Furthermore, what is never in the same place is not still or at rest.

Not possibly.

Then unity, it seems, is neither at rest nor moved.

No, so it certainly appears.

vi. Same and Different (139b-c)

Nor will unity be the same as itself or something different, nor again different from itself or something different.

How so?

If it were different from itself, it would be different from unity, I take it, and would not be one.

True.

Moreover, if it were the same as something different, it would be that thing, but not itself, so it would not then be what it is, unity, but different

c   from unity.

Of course.

Then it is not the same as something different, or different from itself.

No.

Nor will it be different from something different, so long as it is one. For it does not pertain to a thing *as one* to be different from something, but only to a thing *as different* from something different, and to nothing else.

Correct.

Then by virtue of being one it will not be different. Agreed?

Yes.

And further, if not by virtue of that, then not by virtue of itself; and if not by virtue of itself, then not *as* itself. And if *as* itself it is in no way different, it will not be different from anything.

d   Correct.

Nor will it be the same as itself.

Why?

The nature of unity is surely not also that of sameness.

How so?

Because when something comes to be the same as something, it does not thereby come to be one.

But what does it become, then?

If something comes to be the same as many, it necessarily becomes many, not one.

True.

But if unity and sameness in no way differ, then whenever something became the same, it would become one, and whenever one, the same.

e   Of course.

Therefore, if unity were the same as itself it would not be one with itself, and so, being one, it would not be one. But this is quite impossible. Therefore it is also impossible for unity to be different from another or the same as itself.

Yes.

So unity is neither different from nor the same as itself or another.

vii. Like and Unlike (139e-140b)

Nor will unity be like or unlike anything, either another or itself.

Why?

Because to be like is to be affected in the same way.

Yes.

140a   But it appeared that sameness is a nature separate from unity.

Yes, it did.

And, furthermore, that if unity had any affection separate from being one, it would be affected so as to be more than one, and that is impossible.

Yes.

Therefore, unity is not affected in the same way as another or itself.

It appears not.

Then it cannot be like another or itself.

It seems not.

But since to be like is to be affected in the same way, what is affected in a different way from itself or another is unlike itself or another.

b   Correct.

But it seems that unity, since it is not affected in a different way, is neither unlike itself nor something different.

No, it is not.

Therefore, unity is neither like nor unlike another or itself.

It appears not.

viii. Equal and Unequal (140b-d)

Moreover, if it is of this sort, it is neither equal nor unequal to itself or to another.

Why?

If equal, it has the same measures as that to which it is equal.

Yes.

And if greater or less than things commensurable with it, it has more

c   measures than what is less and fewer measures than what is greater.

Yes.

And in respect of what is incommensurable with it, it has smaller or larger measures.

Of course.

Now, can what does not have a share of sameness have the same measures, or the same of anything else?

It cannot.

Then since it does not have the same measures, it is equal neither to itself nor to another.

So it appears.

Furthermore, if it is of more or fewer measures, it has as many parts as mea-

d   sures, and so once again it will no longer be one, but as many as its measures.

Correct.

But if it were of one measure, it would become equal to its measure, and it appeared impossible for it to be equal to anything.

Yes, it did.

Then since it neither has a share of one measure nor of many nor of few, and has no share of sameness, it is never, it seems, equal to itself or to another; nor again is it greater or less than itself or than another.

ix. Older, Younger, Same Age (140e-141d)

e   What about this? Does it seem that unity can be older or younger or have the same age as anything?

Why couldn't it?

Because what has the same age as itself or another surely has a share of equality of time and likeness to itself or another, and we said that unity does not have a share of likeness or equality.

Yes, we did.

Moreover we also said that it does not have a share of unlikeness and inequality.

Of course.

141a   Then if it is of this sort, how will it be possible for it to be older or younger or to have the same age as anything?

In no way.

Then unity is neither older nor younger nor has the same age as itself or another.

It appears not.

If it is of this sort, can unity be in time at all? Or isn't it necessary that if something is in time, it is always becoming older than itself.

It is.

The older is ever older than a younger?

Certainly.

b   Then what is becoming older than itself is at once becoming younger than itself, if it is to have something than which it becomes older.

What do you mean?

I mean this. There is no need for one thing to be becoming different from another that is different already; what is different already is already different; what has become different has become different; what is going to be different is going to be different. But what is becoming different has not become and will not be becoming and is not yet different; it is becoming different, and nothing else.

c   Necessarily.

Furthermore, older is difference from younger and from nothing else.

Yes.

Then what is becoming older than itself is at once necessarily also be-coming younger than itself.

It seems so.

Furthermore, it does not become for a longer or shorter time than it-self: it comes to be, and is, and has come to be, and is going to be, for a time equal to itself.

That also is necessary.

d   Then it is also necessary, it seems, that for as many things as are in time and have a share of such a thing as that, each has the same age as itself and becomes at once older and younger than itself.

Very likely.

Furthermore, unity has no share of qualifications of this sort.

Of course not.

Then it has no share of time, nor is it in any time.

No, so the argument at any rate has it.

x. Conclusion (141d-142a)

What about this? Do not 'was' and 'has become' and 'was becoming' seem to signify sharing of time before?

Of course.

e   And 'will be' and 'will become' and 'will have become' of time after?

Yes.

And 'is' and 'is becoming' of time now?

Certainly.

Then if unity in no way has a share of time, it never has become or was becoming or was *before;* it has not become nor is becoming nor is *now;* and it will not become nor will have become nor will be *after.*

Very true.

Now, can anything have a share of being except in some one of those ways?

It cannot.

Then unity has no share of being.

It appears not.

Then it is not even such as to be one; for then it would already be a thing which is, and have a share of being. But as it seems, unity neither is one nor is, if such an account as this is to be trusted.

142a   Very likely.

But would anything be *to* or *of* that which is not?

How could it?

Then neither name nor account belongs *to* it, nor is there any knowledge or perception or opinion *of* it.

It appears not.

Then it cannot be named or spoken of, nor is it an object of opinion or knowledge, nor does anything among things which are perceive it.

It seems not.

Now, can these things be true of unity?

I do not think so.

I.2. First Hypothesis, Second Deduction (142b-155e)

Introduction (142b-c)

b   Shall we return to the hypothesis and go over it again from the beginning, to see if some other result may appear?

By all means.

Now, if unity is, the consequences that follow for it must be accepted, whatever they happen to be?

Yes.

Then examine from the beginning. If unity is, can it be, but not have a share of being?

It cannot.

Now, the being of unity is not the same as unity; otherwise, it would not be the being *of* it, nor would unity have a share of being; rather, to say that unity is would be like saying that unity is unity. But as it is, the hypothesis

c   is not what must follow if unity is unity,[16] but what must follow if unity is. Not so?

Certainly.

So 'is' signifies something other than 'one'?

Necessarily.

So when someone says in short that unity (one) is, that would mean that unity has a share of being?

Of course.

i. Part and Whole (142c-d)

Then let us again state what will follow if unity is. Consider: must not this hypothesis signify that unity, if it is of this sort, has parts?

d   How so?

For the following reason: if being is said of unity, since it is, and if unity is said of being, since it is one, and if being and unity are not the same, but belong to that same thing we have hypothesized, namely, the unity which is, must it not, since it is one, be a whole of which its unity and being become parts?

Necessarily.

Then shall we call each of those parts only a part, or must part be called

part of whole?
>Part of whole.
>Therefore, what is one is a whole and has a part.
>Of course.

(iia) Limit and Unlimited: First Argument (142d-143a)

What about each of those parts of the unity which is, namely, its unity
e   and its being? Would unity be lacking to the part which is, or being to the
part which is one?
>No.
>Then once again, each of the parts contains unity and being, and the least
part again turns out to consist of two parts, and the same account is always
true: whatever becomes a part contains those two parts. For unity always
contains being, and being unity, so that they are always necessarily becoming two and are never one.
143a   Quite so.
>Now, the unity which is would thus be unlimited in multitude?
>It seems so.

(iib) Limit and Unlimited: Second Argument (143a-145a)

Consider the matter still further.
>In what way?
>We say that unity has a share of being, because it is.
>Yes.
>And for that reason unity, since it is, appeared many.
>True.
>Then what about this? If by reflection we take unity itself, which we say
has a share of being, just alone by itself, without that of which we say it has
a share, will it appear to be only one, or will that very thing appear many as
well?
>One, I should think.
b   Let us see. Since unity is not being, but, as one, gets a share of being, the
being of it must be one thing, and it must be another.
>Necessarily.
>Now if its being is one thing and unity is another, unity is not different
from its being by virtue of being one, nor is its being other than unity by
virtue of being; they are different from each other by virtue of the different
and other.
>Of course.
>Then difference is not the same as unity or being.
>Certainly.

c   Well then, if we were to pick out, say, being and difference, or being and unity, or unity and difference, would we not in each selection pick out some pair that is rightly called 'both'?

What do you mean?

This. One can mention being?

Yes.

And unity?

Yes.

Then each of two has been mentioned?

Yes.

But when I mention being and unity, do I not mention both?

Yes, certainly.

Again, if I mention being and difference, or difference and unity, and so on, I in each case mean both?

Yes.

d   But for whatever is rightly called both, is it possible that they should be both but not two?

It is not.

But for whatever is two, is there any way in which each of two is not one?

No.

Therefore, since together they are pairs, each is one?

It appears so.

But if each of them is one, then when any one whatever is added to any couple whatever, does not the sum become three?

Yes.

Three is odd, and two even?

Certainly.

What about this? If there are two things, must there not also be twice,
e   and if three things, thrice, since it pertains to two to be twice one, and three thrice one?

Necessarily.

But if there are two things and twice, must there not be twice two, and if three things and thrice, thrice three?

Of course.

What about this? If there are three things and twice, and two things and thrice, must there not also be twice three and thrice two?

Yes, necessarily.

Therefore, there will be even-times even numbers, odd-times odd num-
144a   bers, even-times odd numbers, and odd-times even numbers.

True.

Now, if this is so, do you think there is any number left which must not necessarily be?

None whatever.

Therefore, if unity is, number must also be.

Necessarily.

But further, if number is, plurality is, and an unlimited multitude of things which are: or does not number become unlimited in multitude, and have a share of being?

Of course it does.

Now, if all number has a share of being, each part of number also has a share of it?

Yes.

b   Therefore, being is distributed to all of the many things which are, and is lacking to none of them, neither the smallest nor the greatest? Or is it absurd even to ask that, for how would being be lacking to anything among things which are?

There is no way.

Therefore, being is divided up among things of every sort, from the smallest to the greatest, and in all ways; it is of all things most divided, and there are limitless parts of being.

c   True.

So the parts of it are most multitudinous.

They are indeed.

What about this: is there any among them which is part of being, and yet not one part?

How could there be?

Rather, I suppose, since it is, it must always so long as it is, be one thing; it cannot be no thing.

Necessarily.

Therefore, unity must be present to every part of being, lacking neither to the smallest nor the largest part nor to anything else.

True.

d   Now, since it is one, is it in many places at the same time as a whole? Consider this carefully.

I have, and I see that it is impossible.

Then since not as a whole, divided; for it will not, I take it, be present to all the parts of being at the same time except as divided.

No.

Moreover, what is divisible must be as many as its parts.[17]

Necessarily.

Then what we said just now, namely, that being has been distributed to parts *most* multitudinous, is not true. For it has not been distributed to
e   more parts than unity, but to equally many; for what is does not lack unity, and what is one does not lack being; the two are always equal through everything.

So it certainly appears.

Therefore, unity itself has been divided by being, and is many and unlimited in multitude.

It appears so.

Then not only unity, as a thing which is, is many, but also unity itself must be many, having been distributed by being.

Certainly.

Moreover, because parts are parts of a whole, unity is limited in respect of its wholeness; or are parts not contained by the whole?

145a They must be.

And further, what contains is a limit.

Of course.

Therefore unity, if it is, is one and many, whole and parts, limited and unlimited in multitude.

It appears so.

iii. Shape (145a-b)

Now since it is limited, it also has extremes?

Necessarily.

Then what about this: if it is a whole, does it not also have beginning, middle, and end? Or is it possible for something to be a whole without those three? If any of them are lacking to a thing, will it still consent to be a whole?

It will not.

b Then unity, it seems, has beginning, middle and end.

Yes.

And further the middle holds off equally from the extremes; otherwise, it would not be a middle.

No.

Then it seems that unity, if it is of this sort, has a share of some shape, either straight or round or a mixture of both.

Yes.

iv. In Itself, In Another (145b-e)

Now if this is so, unity will be in itself and in another.

Why?

I take it that each of its parts is in the whole, and none are outside it?

True.

All of the parts are contained by the whole?

c Yes.

Moreover, unity is all the parts of itself, and neither more nor fewer than all.

Of course.

Now, unity is also the whole?

Certainly.

Then if all the parts are in the whole, and unity is both all the parts and the whole itself, and all the parts are contained by the whole, unity is contained by unity. So unity itself is forthwith in itself.

It appears so.

Nevertheless, the whole is not in the parts, neither in all nor any. For if
d   in all, then necessarily also in one; if it were not in some one, it surely could not be in all. But if that one is one among all, and the whole is not in it, how will the whole still be in all?

There is no way.

Nor will it be in some of the parts; for if the whole were in some, the more would be in the less, which is impossible.

Clearly.

But if the whole is not in one or more than one or all the parts, must it not be in something different, or be nowhere at all?
e   Necessarily.

Now if it were nowhere, it would be no thing; but if it is a whole, then since it is not in itself, it must be in another.

Of course.

Then insofar as it is a whole, unity is in another; insofar as it is all the parts, it is in itself; and so unity must be in itself and in something different.

Necessarily.

v. Motion and Rest (145e-146a)

Then if unity is of this nature, must it not both be moved and at rest?

How so?

It is at rest, I take it, if it is in itself: for if it is in one thing and does
146a   not pass from it, it would be in the same thing, namely, in itself.

That follows.

But what is always in the same thing must surely always be at rest.

Of course.

What about this? In an opposite way, must not what is always in something different never be in the same thing, and if never in the same thing, not at rest, and if not at rest, then moved?

True.

Then unity, which is always both in itself and in something different, must always be both moved and at rest.

It appears so.

vi. Same and Different (146a-147b)

Moreover, if unity has the foregoing qualifications, it must be the same as
b   and different from itself, and in like manner the same as and different from
the others.

How so?

Everything, I take it, is relative to every thing in the following way:
either it is the same, or different, or, if it is neither the same nor different, it
is part relative to whole or whole relative to part.

It appears so.

Now, is unity itself part of itself?

No.

Then it would not, by being a part relative to itself, be a whole relative
to itself as part of itself.

It could not be.

But is unity different from unity?

Of course not.

c   Then unity is not different from itself.

No.

Then if it is not different from itself nor relative to itself as whole or
part, must it not forthwith be the same as itself?

Necessarily.

What about this? Must not what is in something different from itself
while also in the same thing, namely in itself, necessarily be different from
itself, since it is in something different?[18]

So I should think.

But unity appeared to be that way —at once in itself and in something
different.

Yes, it did.

So in this respect, it seems, unity would be different from itself.

Yes, so it seems.

d   Then what about this? If something is different from something else, is
it not different from what is different from it?

Necessarily.

Then as many things as are not one are all different from unity, and
unity from things not one?

Of course.

So unity is different from the others.

Yes.

Then consider. Sameness and difference are opposites?

Of course.

Now, does sameness ever consent to be in what is different, or difference in what is the same?

No.

Then if difference will never be in what is the same, there is nothing
e   among things which are in which difference is for any time; for if it were in something for any time whatever, during that time difference would be in what is the same. Not so?

Quite so.

But since it is never in what is the same, difference is never in anything among things which are.

True.

Therefore, difference is neither in unity nor in things not one.

Of course not.

Then it is not by virtue of difference that unity is different from things not one and vice versa.

No.

Nor are they different from each other by virtue of themselves, if they do not have a share of difference.

147a   Of course not.

But if they are different neither by virtue of themselves nor by virtue of difference, the possibility of their being in any way different from each other forthwith escapes.

Yes.

But further, things not one do not have a share of unity; for then they would not be not one, but somehow one.

True.

Therefore, things not one would not be a number; for if they had a number, they would not then be completely not one.

Of course.

What about this? Are things not one parts of unity? Or would they thus have got a share of unity?

They would have got a share.

Then if unity is in every way one, and they on the other hand are not
b   one, unity would neither be part of things not one nor a whole of them as parts; nor, again, would things not one be parts of unity nor wholes of which unity is part.

Of course not.

But we further said that things that are neither parts nor wholes, nor different from each other, are the same as each other.

Yes.

So we may also say that unity, if it is in this way relative to things not one, is the same as they.

Yes.

Therefore unity, it seems, is different from the others and itself, and the same as the others and itself.

Yes, so it appears from this account.

vii. Like and Unlike (147c-148d)

c Now, is unity both like and unlike itself and the others?

Perhaps.

Well, at any rate, since it appeared different from the others, the others are different from it.

Of course.

Now, it is different from the others just as the others are different from it, that is, neither more nor less.

Certainly.

And if neither more nor less, then similarly?

Yes.

Then insofar as it is affected in a different way from the others and the others in like manner in a different way from it, in this respect unity would be affected in the same way as the others and the others in the same way as unity.

d What do you mean?

This. Do you not give each name *to* something?

Yes.

And you can say the same name once or many times?

Yes.

Then do you apply it to that of which it is the name if you say it once, but not if you say it many times? Or isn't it quite necessary that whether you utter the same name once or many times, you always mean the same thing?

Of course.

Now, 'different' is a name for something?

Certainly.

e Then when you utter it, whether once or many times, you are using a name for something, and naming that of which it is the name and nothing else.

Necessarily.

So when we say that the others are different from unity and unity different from the others, we are saying 'different' twice, but not for that reason applying it to something other. We always mean only that nature of which it is the name.

Quite so.

Then insofar as unity is different from the others and the others different

148a   from unity, unity, just in respect of being affected in a different way, is affected not in another but in the same way as the others. But to have been affected in the same way, I take it, is to be like.

Yes.

So just insofar as unity is affected in a different way from the others, it is entirely like them all; for they are all entirely different.

It seems so.

But further, likeness is opposite to unlikeness.

Yes.

And difference to sameness.

That also.

Furthermore, this also appeared, namely,[19] that unity is actually the same as the others.

b   Yes.

But being the same as the others is the opposite affection from being different from the others.

Certainly.

And further, in so far as unity was different, it appeared like them.

Yes.

Then insofar as it is the same, it will be unlike in respect to the affection opposite the affection that made it like. But difference, I take it, made it like?

Yes.

Then sameness will make it unlike, or it is not the opposite of difference.

c   It seems so.

Therefore, unity will be both like and unlike the others—like insofar as it is different, unlike in so far as it is the same.

Yes, some such account is correct, it seems.

And so is this one: insofar as a thing has been affected in the same way, it has not been affected in another way, and what has not been affected in another way is not unlike, and if not unlike, then like. But insofar as a thing has been affected as other, it has been affected in another way, and if in another way, it is unlike.

You are right.

Then since unity is the same as the others, and also since it is different, on both grounds or on either it is both like and unlike the others.

d   Of course.

So, too, with regard to itself; since it appeared different from itself and the same as itself, on both grounds or on either it will appear like and unlike itself.

Necessarily.

viii. In Contact, Not in Contact (148d-149d)

Really? Then what about this: consider whether unity both touches and does not touch itself and the others.

Very well.

Unity itself appeared, I take it, to be in itself as a whole?

Correct.

Now, unity is also in the others?

Yes.

Then insofar as it is in the others it would touch the others; but insofar as it is in itself it would be kept back from touching the others; it would touch itself, since it is in itself.

It appears so.

So unity touches both itself and the others.

Yes.

What about this: must not everything that touches lie in succession to what it is to touch, occupying *this* seat, which is next after *that*, in which seat what it touches lies?[20]

Necessarily.

Then unity, if it is to touch itself, must lie in succession immediately next to itself, occupying the place continuous[21] to that in which it is.

Of course it must.

Now, if unity were two it could do this, and come to be in two places at once. But as long as it is one, it will not.

Of course not.

Then the same necessity that prevents unity from being two prevents it from touching itself.

Yes.

Nor will it touch the others.

How so?

Because, we say, what touches must be separate from and in succession to what it is to touch, with no third thing between them.

True.

So there must be at least two things if there is to be contact.

Yes.

But if a third is added to two terms, they will themselves be three and the contacts will be two.

Yes.

So it is always true that to add one is to add a contact, and it follows that the contacts are fewer by one than the multitude of numbers.[22] For by the amount that the first two terms exceeded the contacts, as being greater

in number than the contacts, in that equal amount every number after will exceed all the contacts: for at every step that follows, adding one to the num-
c   ber at once adds one contact to the contacts.[23]

Correct.

Therefore, as many as is the number of things which are, their contacts are always fewer than they by one.

True.

But if unity alone is, and two[24] is not, then contact would not be.

Of course.

Now, we say that things other than unity neither are one nor have a share of unity, since they are others.

Of course.

So number is not in the others, since there is no unity in them.

Agreed.

Then the others are neither one nor two nor have the name of any other number.[25]
d   No.

So unity is only one, and there is no two.

It appears not.

Then since there are not two things, there is no contact.

None at all.

So according to this, unity both touches and does not touch the others and itself.

It seems so.

ix. Equal and Unequal (149e-151e)

Now, is unity equal and unequal both to itself and to the others?

How do you mean?

If unity were larger or smaller than the others, or the others larger or
e   smaller than unity, would unity, by virtue of being one, and the others, by virtue of being other than unity, be larger or smaller than each other by virtue of their own being? If, in addition to being what they are, each were to have equality, they would be equal to each other; and if the others had largeness and unity smallness, or if unity had largeness and the others smallness, then whichever character[26] to which largeness was added would be larger, and that to which smallness was added would be smaller.

Necessarily.

Now, largeness and smallness are really two characters? For if they were not two, I take it, they would not be opposite to each other and come to be in things which are.
150a   How could they?

So if smallness comes to be present in unity, it is present either in part or the whole of it.

Necessarily.

What if it came to be present in the whole? Would it not either be stretched out evenly with unity through the whole of it, or contain it?

Clearly.

Now, if smallness were even with unity, it would be equal to it; and larger if it contained it.

Of course.

Then is it possible for smallness to be equal to or larger than something, and so do the work of equality and largeness but not its own?

b   It is impossible.

So smallness is not in the whole of unity; if in it, it is in part of it.

Yes.

But again, not in all that part. Otherwise it will act as it does relative to the whole: it will be equal to or greater than any part in which it is.

Necessarily.

So smallness will never be in anything which is, since it comes to be neither in part nor whole; nor will anything be small except smallness itself.

It seems not.

Then largeness will not be in it. For if so, there would be something larger than largeness itself, namely, that in which largeness is present, even

c   though it has nothing small that it must exceed if it is to be large; that is impossible, since smallness is in nothing whatever.

True.

Furthermore, largeness itself is not larger than anything other than smallness itself, and smallness is not smaller than anything other than largeness itself.

Of course not.

So the others are neither larger nor smaller than unity, since they have neither largeness nor smallness; nor do those two things[27] have their power

d   of exceeding and being exceeded relative to each other, nor is unity, again, larger or smaller than they or than the others, since it has neither largeness nor smallness.

No, it appears not.

Now, if unity is neither larger nor smaller than the others, it can neither exceed nor be exceeded by them.

No.

Now, what neither exceeds nor is exceeded must be even, and if even, equal.

Certainly.

e   Moreover, this would also be so of unity itself relative to itself: having neither largeness nor smallness in itself, it neither exceeds nor is exceeded by itself, but, if even with itself, it is equal to itself.

Of course.

So unity is equal to itself and to the others.

It appears so.

Moreover, since it is in itself, it surrounds itself from without; as containing itself, it is larger than itself; as contained by itself, it is smaller;
151a   and so unity is larger and smaller than itself.

Yes.

Now, is it not also necessary that outside unity and the others there is
nothing?

Of course.

And further, that whatever is must be somewhere?[28]

Yes.

Now, what is in something is in something larger, since it is smaller?
Otherwise, one thing would not be in another.

No.

But since there is nothing separate from unity and the others, and they
must be in something, must they not forthwith be in each other — the others
in unity, unity in the others — or be nowhere at all?

b   It appears so.

Then because unity is in the others, the others are larger than unity, as
containing it, and unity is smaller than the others, as contained; but because the others are in unity, unity by the same account is larger than the
others and the others smaller than unity.

It seems so.

So unity is equal to, larger than and smaller than both itself and the
others.

It appears so.

Moreover, since it is larger and smaller and equal, it is of more and fewer
and equal measures as itself and as the others, and since of measures, also of
c   parts.

Of course.

So being of more, fewer, and equal measures, it is more and fewer in
number than itself and the others, and equal to itself and to the others in
the same way.

How so?

If it is larger than something else, it is, I take it, of more measures than it,
and of as many parts as measures; and if smaller, then in like manner fewer;
and if equal, then in the same way equal.

True.

Now, since it is larger and smaller and equal to itself, it is of more and
d   fewer and equal measures to itself, and since of measures, also of parts.

Of course.

Then being of equal parts to itself, it is equal to itself in multitude; as of more parts it is more than, and as of fewer, less than itself in number.

It appears so.

Now, is unity relative in like manner to the others? Because it appears larger than they, its number must be more than theirs. Because it appears smaller, the number must be fewer. Because it appears equal in magnitude, its multitude must be equal to the others.

Necessarily.

e   So then again, it seems, unity will be equal, more and fewer in number than itself and the others.

It will.

x. Older, Younger, Same Age (151e-155c)

Now, does unity also have a share of time? Is it, and does it become, older and younger than itself and the others, and neither older nor younger than itself or the others, as having a share of time?

How do you mean?

Since unity is, I take it, it pertains to it to be?

Yes.

But is to *be* anything other than to have a share of being in present time,
152a   *was* and *will be* are communion with time past and time to come?

No, it is not.

Then unity has a share of time if it has a share of being.

Of course.

Of time as it passes?

Yes.

So unity is always becoming older than itself, since it advances according to time.

Necessarily.

Now, we recall[29] that older becomes older than what is becoming younger.

Yes.

Then since unity becomes older than itself, it becomes older than itself as becoming younger.

b   Necessarily.

So it becomes both older and younger than itself.

Yes.

But it is older, is it not, when in becoming it is in time now, which is between was and will be? For I take it that in passing from before to after, it will not overstep the now.

No.

Then does it not stop becoming older when it reaches the now? It is then
c   not *becoming* older but forthwith *is* older. For if it were moving ahead it

would never be seized by the now: to move ahead is to touch both now and after, to let go of the now and grasp the after in the process of coming to be between the two, namely the after and the now.

True.

d   But if everything that comes to be must necessarily pass through the now, then when things are at it, they always leave off becoming and then are what they happened to be becoming.

It appears so.

So unity, when in becoming older it reaches the now, leaves off becoming and then is older.

Of course.

Now, what it was becoming older than is just that than which it is older. And it was becoming older than itself.

Yes.

But older is older than a younger.

It is.

So unity, when in becoming older it reaches the now, is then younger than itself.

Necessarily.

e   Yet surely the now is present to unity throughout the whole of its being; for whenever it is, it always is now.

Of course.

So unity always both is and is becoming older and younger than itself.

It seems so.

But is it, and does it become, for more time than itself, or equal time?

Equal time.

Furthermore, whatever is or becomes for equal time has the same age.

Of course.

But what has the same age is neither older nor younger.

No.

Then since unity both is and becomes for a time equal to itself, it neither is nor becomes younger or older than itself.

No, I think not.

Then what about the others?

Here I do not know what to say.

153a   But surely you can say this: things other than unity, since they are different things, but not *a* different thing, are more than one; for *a* different thing would be one, but different things are more than one and have multitude.

Yes.

And being a multitude, they have a share of a number greater than one.

Of course.

Well then, shall we say that of a number, the more or the fewer come to be and have come to be earlier?

The fewer.

So the fewest first. And that is one?

b Yes.

So unity has come to be first among all things that have number. And all the others have number, since they are others and not an other.

Yes.

And I suppose that since unity has come to be first, it has come to be before, and the others after; and that what has come to be after is younger than what has come to be before. And so the others are younger than unity, and unity older than the others.

Agreed.

But what about this: can unity have come to be contrary to it own nature, or is that impossible?

c It is impossible.

And further, unity appeared to have parts, and if parts, beginning, middle, and end.

Yes.

Now, of all things, a beginning comes to be first, whether of unity itself or of each of the others; and after the beginning all the others up to the end.

Certainly.

Moreover, we also say that all those others are parts of what is whole or one, and this itself comes to be, as one and whole, together with the end.

Yes.

But I suppose an end comes to be last, and that unity by nature comes
d to be together with it; so that if unity itself cannot come to be contrary to its own nature, it comes to be last, along with the end, and so by nature comes to be last among the others.[30]

It appears so.

Then unity is younger than the others, and the others older than unity.

That again appears to me to be so.

Really! Is not a beginning or any other part of unity, or anything else, if it is really *a* part but not parts—is it not necessarily one, since *a* part?

Yes.

Then unity would come to be with the coming to be of the first part, and the second, and is lacking to no one of the others which comes to be
e —whichever becomes added to whatever others—until it has passed through to the end and becomes one whole,[31] having not been absent from first, middle, last, or any other part in its generation.

True.

So unity holds the same age as all the others. The result is that unless unity itself is by nature contrary to its own nature, it has come to be
154a neither before nor after the others, but at the same time. And by this account, unity is neither older nor younger than the others, nor the others

than unity; but by the former account it is both older and younger than the others, and in like manner the others than it.

Of course.

This then is the way it is and has become. But next, what about unity becoming older and younger than the others and the others than unity, and also becoming neither older nor younger? Does it stand with becoming as it did with being, or differently?

b   I cannot say.

But I at least can say this: if one thing is in fact older than another, it would be impossible for it to become older still by an amount greater than its original difference in age; and again, what is younger cannot become still younger. For adding equals to unequals, in time or anything else, always makes the difference equal in the amount by which the unequals originally differed.

Of course.

Then what is would never be becoming older or younger than the unity which is,[32] since the difference in age is always equal: it is and has become older, and the other younger, but is not becoming so.

True.

So unity, since it is, is never becoming older or younger than things which are.

No.

Consider then whether it is becoming older and younger in this way, namely, insofar as unity appeared older than the others and the others older than unity.

Well?

When unity is older than the others, it has come to be, I take it, for a time greater than the others.

d   Yes.

Consider then again: if we add equal time to a greater and less time, will the greater differ from the less by an equal (proportional) part, or a smaller one?

By a smaller one.

Then whatever difference in age there was to begin with between unity and the others will not continue into the future, for since unity takes time equal to the others it will always differ from them in age less than before. Agreed?

Yes.

Now, what has less difference in age relative to something than before would become younger than it was, relative to those things than which it before was older.

Yes.

But if unity becomes younger, the others would become older relative to it.

Of course.

So what had been younger is becoming older relative to what earlier had been and is older; it never is, but always is becoming, older than that, for that is always advancing toward the younger, and the younger toward the **155a** older. Again, the older in like manner is becoming younger than the younger. For since the two move in opposite directions, they are becoming the opposite of each other, the younger older than the older, the older younger than the younger; but the two cannot be become so, for if they should, they would no longer be becoming but would be so. But as it is, they are becoming older and younger than each other: unity becoming younger than the others because it appeared to be older and to have come to be **b** after. And by the same account, the others are related this way to unity, since they appeared older than it and have come to be before it.

Yes, so it appears.

Now insofar as one thing is becoming older or younger than another by reason of their always differing from each other by an equal number, unity would become neither older nor younger than the others, nor the others than unity; but insofar as what became before must differ from **c** what became after, and vice versa, by a (proportional) part that is always different, in that respect the others must become older and younger than unity, and unity than the others.

Of course.

Then according to all this, unity itself both is and becomes older and younger than itself and the others, and neither is nor becomes older or younger than itself and the others.

Agreed.

xi. Conclusion (155c-e)

But since unity has a share of time and of becoming older and younger, **d** must it not also have a share of before and after and now, since it has a share of time?

Necessarily.

So unity is and was and will be, and has become and is becoming and will become.

Certainly.

And things belong to it and are *of* it, alike when it was and is and will be.

Of course.

There would be knowledge and opinion and perception *of* it, since we in fact now have all those things with respect to it.

Right.

Then it also has a name and an account; it is named and spoken of, **e** and as many things as pertain to the others also pertain to unity.

That is completely true.

I.3. First Hypothesis, Third Deduction (155e-157b)

Being and Not Being in Time (155e)

Let us take the matter up still a third time. If unity is as we have described it, then since it is both one and many and neither one nor many and has a share of time, must it not sometimes have a share of being, because it is, and sometimes not have a share of being, because it is not?

Necessarily.

Then when it has a share, will it be possible for it not to have a share; or when it does not have a share to have a share?

No.

So it has a share at one time and not at another; only in that way could it both have and not have a share of the same thing.

Correct.

Becoming and Perishing (156a)

156a   Then is there a time when it gets a share of being and when it gets rid of it? Or is it possible for it now to have and then not to have the same thing, without sometimes taking it and letting it go?

It is not.

Then do you call getting a share of being becoming?

I do.

And getting rid of being perishing?

Of course.

Then it seems that since unity both takes and lets go of being, it both
b   becomes and perishes.

Necessarily.

Qualified Becoming and Perishing (156b)

Since it is one and many and comes to be and ceases to be, does it, when it becomes one, cease to be many, and when it becomes many, cease to be one?

Of course.

And since it comes to be one and many, must it not combine and separate?

Certainly.

Moreover, when it comes to be like and unlike, must it not be made like and unlike?

Yes.

And when larger and smaller and equal, it must grow and diminish and be equalized.

c   True.

The Instant (156c-e)

But when it comes to rest after moving, and changes to being moved after resting, it is surely impossible for it to be in one time at all.

How so?

It is not possible for it to be at rest before and moved afterward, or to be moved before and at rest afterward, without changing.

Of course not.

Yes, but there is no time in which it is possible for it to be neither moved nor at rest.

No, there is not.

Furthermore, it does not change without being in the process of changing.

Hardly.

Then when does it change? Not while at rest, nor while moved, nor while in time.

d   No.

So there is this strange thing in which it is when it is changing.

What sort of thing?

The instant. For the instant seems to signify something such that change proceeds from it into either state. There is no change from rest while resting, nor from motion while moving; but this instant, a strange nature, is some-
e   thing inserted between motion and rest, and it is in no time at all; but into it and from it what is moved changes to being at rest, and what is at rest to being moved.

Very likely.

Then since unity is both at rest and in motion, it changes to each state; only so could it do both. But in changing it changes at an instant, and when it changes it is in no time at all, is neither moved nor at rest.

That follows.

Neither Because Both (156e-157b)

Is this also true relative to other changes? When unity changes from being to ceasing to be, or from not being to coming to be, is it then between certain
157a   motions and stations, such that it neither is nor is not, neither comes to be nor ceases to be?

It seems so, at any rate.

Then by the same account, unity, in passing from one to many and many to one, is not one or many, is not combined or separated; and in passing b   from like to unlike and unlike to like, it is neither like nor unlike, and neither becomes like nor unlike; and in passing from small to large and to equal, and vice versa, it is neither large nor small nor equal, neither grows nor diminishes nor becomes equal.

It seems not.

Then unity undergoes all these affections, if it is.

Of course.

II.1. Second Hypothesis, First Deduction (157b-159b)

Part and Whole (157b-158a)

If Unity is, should the qualifications that pertain to the others be examined?

They should.

Then we are to state how the others than unity must be affected, if unity is?

Yes.

Now, since they are other than unity, unity is not the others; for otherwise they would not be other than unity.

c   Correct.

Nevertheless, the others are surely not completely deprived of unity, but have a share of it in some way.

In what way?

As follows. The others than unity are others, I take it, by reason of having parts; for if they did not have parts, they would be completely one.

Correct.

Yes, but parts, we say, are of that which is whole.

We do.

And further, the whole of which the parts are parts must be one thing composed of many; for each part must be part, not of a plurality, but of a whole.

How so?

d   If something were part of a plurality, in which it is, then it would be part of itself, which is impossible, and also part of the others, since it is part of all. For if not part of one, it will be part of the others except for that one; thus it will not be part of each one, and if not part of each, then part of no one of the plurality. But being part of no one of all of them, it is impossible for it to be part or anything else of those things of none of which it is a part.

So it appears.

Therefore, part is part, not of plurality or of all, but of some one character and some one thing we call whole, since it has become one complete thing composed of all. That is what the part is part of.

e   Quite so.

Therefore, if the others have parts, they have a share of wholeness and unity.

Of course.

Therefore, the others than unity must be one complete whole which has parts.

Necessarily.

Furthermore, the same account holds for each part; for that part too must have a share of unity. For if each of these is a part, 'each' surely signifies that it is one, marked off from the others as a being by itself, since each is.

Correct.

But clearly, it has a share of unity, since it is other than unity; otherwise, it would not have a share, but be unity itself. But as it is, it is impossible, I take it, for anything except unity itself to be unity.

Yes, it is.

But both whole and part necessarily have a share of unity: for it is one whole of which the parts are parts, and again, what is part of a whole is one given part of that whole.

Limit and Unlimited (158b-d)

b   Now, things that have a share of unity will have a share of difference from it?

Of course.

But things different from unity are, I take it, many; for if the others than unity were neither one nor more than one, they would be nothing.

Agreed.

And since things that have a share of the unity of a part and things that have a share of the unity of a whole are more than one, is it not forthwith necessary that those things that get a share of unity are, just in themselves, unlimited in multitude?

How so?

We may observe that when things are getting a share of unity, they neither are nor have a share of unity.

Clearly.

c   Then they are multitudes, and unity is not in them?

Yes.

Well then, if we, by reflection, should subtract from such things the fewest we possibly can, must not what is subtracted be a multitude and not one, since it does not have a share of unity?

Necessarily.

Now, whenever we examine alone by itself the nature different from the characteristic (of being one), as much of it as we shall ever see will be unlimited in multitude?

It will indeed.

Moreover, when each part becomes one part, they forthwith have a limit
d   relative to each other and to the whole, and the whole a limit relative to its
parts.

Exactly so.

Then it follows for the others than unity that from the communion of
unity and themselves, something different, as it seems, comes to be in them,
which provides a limit for them relative to each other. Their own nature
provides, in themselves, unlimitedness.

It appears so.

So things other than unity, both as wholes and part by part, are unlimited
and have a share of limit.

Of course.

Likeness and Unlikeness (158e-159a)

e   Now, they are also like and unlike each other and themselves.

In what way?

I take it that insofar as they are all unlimited in respect to their own
nature, they are affected the same.

Of course.

And the same is also true insofar as they all have a share of limit.

Certainly.

But insofar as they are so qualified as to be both limited and unlimited,
they are qualified by affections that are opposite to each other.

159a   Yes.

But opposites are as unlike as possible.

Of course.

Therefore, in respect of either qualification taken singly they are, in
themselves, both like themselves and each other, but in respect to both
together they are quite opposite and unlike.

Very probably.

So the others, in themselves, are both like and unlike themselves and
each other.

True.

Other Characters (159a-b)

And since they have actually appeared to be so qualified, we shall find
no further difficulty in showing that the others than unity are the same as
and different from each other, are both moved and at rest, and are qualified
by all opposite affections.

b   You are right.

II.2. Second Hypothesis, Second Deduction (159b-160b)

Then if we may now dismiss these consequences as obvious, we ought to consider again whether, if unity is, the others than unity are only thus, or also not thus.

Of course.

Then let us state from the beginning how the others than unity must be qualified, if unity is.

Very well.

Now, unity must be separate from the others, and the others separate from unity.

Why?

c   Because, I take it, there is nothing besides them, nothing other than unity and the others. When unity and the others are once mentioned, everything has been mentioned.

Yes, it has.

So there is not still something different from them in which same thing unity and the others would be.

No.

So unity and the others are never in the same.

It seems not.

Then separate?

Yes.

And surely we say that what is truly one does not have parts.

Of course.

So neither unity as a whole nor parts of it are in the others, if it is both separate from the others and lacks parts.

Of course.

d   Then there is no way in which the others have a share of unity, if they have a share neither of part nor the whole of it.

It seems not.

So the others are in no way one, nor have any unity in themselves.

No.

Then the others are not many; for each of them would be *one* part of the whole if they were many. But as it is, the others than unity are neither one nor many, whole nor parts, since they in no way have a share of it.

Correct.

Then the others are not themselves two or three either, nor is two or three in them, since they are in every way deprived of unity.

e   True.

Then the others themselves are neither like nor unlike unity, nor is likeness and unlikeness in them; for if they were themselves like and unlike, or had likeness and unlikeness in them, the others than unity would, I take it, have two characteristics in themselves opposite to each other.

It appears so.

But it is impossible for what does not have a share of even one thing to have a share of two things.

It is.

160a   Therefore, the others are neither like nor unlike, nor both. For if they were either like or unlike, they would have a share of one among different characteristics;[33] if both, then of the two opposites. But that appeared to be impossible.

True.

Therefore, they are neither the same or different, moved or at rest, becoming or ceasing to be, greater, less, or equal, nor qualified as anything else of that sort. For if the others submit to being qualified as something of that sort, they would have a share of one and two and three and odd and even; but it appeared impossible for them to have a share of those things,
b   since they are in every way utterly deprived of unity.

True.

Conclusion of the First and Second Hypotheses (160b)

So then, if unity is, unity is both all things and not even one (or, nothing), both relative to itself and in like manner relative to the others.

Completely so.

III.1. Third Hypothesis, First Deduction (160b-163b)

Very well. But isn't it necessary to examine next what must follow if unity is not?

It is.

Now, just what is this hypothesis, 'if unity is not'? Doesn't it differ from, 'if not unity is not'?

Of course.

Does it only differ, or is it in fact completely opposite to say 'unity is
c   not' and 'not unity is not'?

Completely opposite.

Suppose someone says that largeness is not, or smallness is not, or something else of that sort. It is in each case clear that he means that something different from the other is not.

Of course.

So it is also now clear that when he says unity is not, he means that what is not is different from the others. And we know what he means?

We do.

First of all, therefore, he means something knowable, and next, something different from the others when he says "unity," whether he adds "is" or "is not" to it. For what is said not to be is none the less known, and known to be different from the others. Isn't that so?

Necessarily.

So we must state from the beginning what must be if unity is not. First of all, it seems, this must pertain to it, namely, that there is knowledge of it. Otherwise, when someone said that unity is not, it would not even be known what he meant.

True.

Again, the others must be different from it, or it could not be said to be different from the others.

Of course.

Therefore, difference belongs to it in addition to knowledge. For when one says that unity is different from the others, he does not mean the differentness of the others, but of that.

It appears so.

Furthermore, unity, if it is not, has a share of *that* and *something* and *this*, and of being *relative to* this and *of* or *than* those, and so on; for neither unity nor things different from unity could be spoken of, nor could anything be relative to it, nor would it be called something, if it did not have a share of something and the rest.

Correct.

Then although it is not possible for unity to be, since it is not, nothing prevents it from having a share of many things. On the contrary, this is necessary, since it is unity rather than something else which is not. If, however, it is neither unity nor *that* which is not, and the account is about something else, we cannot so much as utter it. But if it is that one thing and not another that is hypothesized not to be, then it must have a share of *that*, and many other things as well.

Of course.

Then unity has unlikeness relative to the others: for things other than unity, since they are different, are also different in kind.

Yes.

And things different in kind are of another kind.

Of course.

But things of another kind are unlike.

They are.

Now, if they are unlike unity, things unlike clearly are unlike what is unlike them.

Yes.

So unity has unlikeness, relative to which the others are unlike it.

It seems so.

But if it has unlikeness to the others, must it not have likeness to itself?

Why?

If unity has unlikeness to unity, the account is not about a thing of the same sort as Unity, nor would the hypothesis be about unity, but about something other than unity.

Of course.

c   But that can't be.

No, of course not.

So unity must have likeness to itself.

Yes.

Furthermore, unity is not equal to the others; for if it were equal, it would forthwith be, and be like them with respect to equality. But those are both impossible, since unity is not.

Yes.

But since it is not equal to the others, are not the others necessarily also not equal to that?

Yes.

But things not equal are unequal?

Yes.

And things unequal are unequal to what is unequal?

Of course.

Then unity has a share of inequality, relative to which the others are unequal to it.

d   It does.

But largeness and smallness belong to inequality?

Yes.

So a unity of this sort has largeness and smallness?

Very likely.

But surely largeness and smallness are ever farthest apart from each other.

Of course.

So there is ever something between the two.

Yes.

Now, can you say there is anything between them except equality?

No, only that.

So equality belongs to whatever largeness and smallness belong to, since it is between the two of them.

e   It appears so.

Then it seems that unity, if it is not, would share in equality and largeness and smallness.

Yes.

Moreover, it must also have a share of being in a way.

How so?

It must be as we say it is, for if it were not, we would not speak truly in saying that unity is not. For if we speak truly we clearly say things which are. Isn't that so?

Certainly.

And since we claim to speak truly, we must claim to say things which are.

162a   Necessarily.

So it seems that unity is, if it is not; for if it is not to be a thing which is not, but in some way is to let go of being for not-being,[34] it will straightway be a thing which is.

Certainly.

So if it is not to be, it must have being a thing which is not as a bond of its not-being, and in the same way, again, what is must have not being a thing which is not in order completely to be. For it is in this way and only in this way that what is can be, and what is not can not be, namely, by what

b   is, if it is completely to be, having a share of being in order to be a thing which is and a share of not-being in order to be a thing which is not; and by what is not having a share of not-being in order not to be a thing which is and of being in order to be a thing which is not, if again what is not is completely not to be.[35]

Very true.

Now, since what is shares in not-being and what is not shares in being, unity, since it is not, must share in being in order not to be.

Necessarily.

It appears then that unity, if it is not, has being.

Yes.

And not-being also, since it is not.

Of course.

Now, is it possible for what is in a certain condition not to be so, if it does not change from that condition?

It is not.

c   Then everything that is such that it is both so and not so implies change.

Of course.

But change implies motion. Do we not agree?

Yes.

Now, it appeared that unity both is and is not?

Yes.

Then it also appears that it is both so and not so.

Apparently.

Then unity, if it is not, has been shown to be in motion, since it has been shown to change from being to not being.

Very likely.

But further, if it is nowhere among things which are—as it is, since it is not—it does not shift from this place to that.

Of course not.

Then it does not move by changing places.

d   No.

Nor does it revolve in the same, for it nowhere touches the same. For what is the same is a thing which is, and it is impossible for what is not to be in any of the things which are.

It is indeed.

So unity, if it is not, cannot revolve in that in which it is not.

No.

Nor, I take it, does unity alter character, whether it is or is not. For the account would then not still be about unity, but about something else, if it really altered character.

Correct.

But if unity neither alters character nor changes place nor revolves in the same, can it still in any way change?

No, how could it?

e   But surely, what is motionless is necessarily still, and what is still is at rest.

Yes.

So it seems that unity, if it is not, is both at rest and moved.

Yes.

163a   Moreover, since it is moved, unity must necessarily alter character; for the degree that something is moved, it is by so much no longer the same as it was, but different.

True.

So unity, since it is moved, also alters character.

Yes.

Moreover, since it is in no way moved, it in no way alters character.

No.

Then insofar as unity, if it is not, is moved, it alters character; and insofar as it is not moved, it does not alter character.

It appears so.

But must not what alters character come to be different from before

b   and cease being in its previous condition, while what does not alter character neither comes to be nor ceases to be?

Necessarily.

Then unity, if it is not, both comes to be and ceases to be, because it alters character, and neither comes to be nor ceases to be, because it does not alter character. And so unity, if it is not, both comes to be and ceases to be, and neither comes to be nor ceases to be.

Quite so.

III.2. Third Hypothesis, Second Deduction (163b-164b)

Let us return again to the beginning to see if the same results appear for us as did just now, or different ones.

Let us do so.

c   Now, we ask what must follow about unity, if unity is not?

Yes.

When we say it is not, does that signify anything except absence of being from what we say is not?

Nothing else.

Now, when we say that something is not, are we saying it somehow is not and somehow is? Or does the expression 'is not' signify without qualification that what is not in no sense is, in no way has a share of being.

The latter, surely.

Then what is not cannot be or have a share of being in any way at all.

d   No.

Are coming to be and ceasing to be anything except getting a share of being and utterly losing it?

No.

But surely, what has no share of that can neither get nor lose it.

How could it?

So, since unity in no way is, it can in no way have or lose or come to have being.

Likely enough.

So unity, if it is not, neither comes to be nor ceases to be, since it nowhere has a share of being.

It appears not.

e   Then it does not alter character in any way; if it did, it would forthwith come to be and cease to be.

True.

But if it does not alter character, it cannot move.

Necessarily true.

Shall we say that what is nowhere is at rest? For what is at rest must ever be in something the same.

Of course it must be in the same.

So again, we may say that what is not is never at rest or moved.

Quite so.

Furthermore, nothing among things which are belongs to it, for if it had a share of them, it would forthwith have a share of being.

164a   Clearly.

So unity has neither largeness, smallness, nor equality.

No.

Nor likeness or unlikeness, relative either to itself or to the others.

It appears not.

What about this: can it have others, if it must have nothing?

Surely not.

So the others are neither like nor unlike it, neither the same as nor different from it.

No.

What about this: will *of* that, or *to* that, or *something* or *this*, or of
this or of another or to another, or before or after or now, or knowledge
b   or opinion or perception, or account or name, or anything else among
things which are, pertain to what is not?

No.

So unity, if it is not, has no character at all.

No, it certainly seems it doesn't.

IV.1. Fourth Hypothesis, First Deduction (164b-165e)

Let us go on to state how the others must be qualified, if unity is not.

By all means.

I take it they must be. For if there were no others, we could not speak
of them.

True.

But if our account is about the others, the others are different. Or don't
you call the same things other and different?

I do.

c   But we surely say, I take it, that what is different is different from what
is different, and the other other than another.

Yes.

So to be others, the others have something than which they are other.

Necessarily.

What would that be? They are not other than unity, since it is not.

No.

Then they are other than each other—for either that is still left, or they
are other than nothing.

Correct.

Then each is other than each other as multitudes; they cannot be other
than each other as one, since unity is not. But each of them, as it seems, is
a mass unlimited in multitude, and should someone take what seems small-
d   est, then, in an instant, as in a dream, in place of what seemed one there
appears many, and in place of what seemed smallest something enormous
appears relative to the little pieces into which it is split up.

Quite correct.

Then the others are other than each other as masses of this sort, if the
others are, and unity is not.

Completely true.

Now, there will be many masses, each appearing one but not being so,
since unity is not.

True.

And since they are many, there will seem to be a number of them, if
each seems to be one.

e   Of course.

And some among them will appear odd, and some even, but without truly being so, since unity is not.

Of course.

Moreover, there will seem to be a smallest among them; but it appears many and large relative to each of the multitude taken to be smaller.

165a   Of course.

And each mass will have been conceived to be equal to what is many and small; for it would not pass from larger to smaller in appearance without seeming to come to an intermediate stage, and that would be an appearance of equality.

Likely enough.

So, relative to another, a mass has a limit, even though relative to itself it has neither beginning nor limit nor middle.

How so?

Because always when someone by reflection takes any of them as if it were something which is, another beginning ever appears before the begin-

b   ning, a different end is left over after the end, and in its middle a more centrally located but smaller middle. The reason for this is the impossibility of taking each of them as one, because unity is not.

Very true.

So I suppose everything that someone may take by reflection is necessarily broken up into bits and pieces; for it is always taken as a mass without unity.

Certainly.

So, looked at from afar and seen with a dull eye, such a thing as this will

c   necessarily appear one; but seen near at hand and with sharp intelligence, each one appears unlimited in multitude, since it is deprived of unity, which is not.

Necessarily.

Then if unity is not, but things other than unity are, each of the others must appear both limited and unlimited, both one and many.

Yes.

Then they will also seem both like and unlike.

Why?

It is like standing at a distance from scene-paintings, where everything appears to be one, qualified so as to be the same and like.

Yes.

d   But if you come close, they appear many and different, other in character and unlike each other, because of their appearance of difference.

True.

So the masses must appear like and unlike themselves and each other.

Of course.

Now, they must also appear the same as and different from each other, and in contact with and separate from themselves, and moved in all motions and at rest in all respects, and appear to come to be and cease to be and neither come to be nor cease to be, and everything else of the sort, I take it—it would be easy enough to forthwith go through it in detail—if unity is not and plurality is.

e   Very true.

IV.2. Fourth Hypothesis, Second Deduction (165e-166c)

Let us go back still again to the beginning, and state what must be if unity is not, but the others than unity are.

By all means.

Now, the others will not be one.

How could they?

Nor for that matter many. For if many, then unity would be in them. But if none of them is one thing, all of them are no thing, so there is no many.

True.

But since unity is not in the others, the others are neither many nor one.

No.

166a   Nor do they appear one or many.

Why?

Because the others can have no communion of any sort at all with things which are not, nor is anything among things which are not present to them: for what is not has no parts.

True.

Therefore, there is no seeming present to the others of what is not, nor any appearance, nor is what is not in any way conceived by other things.[36]

Of course not.

So if unity is not, none of the others is conceived to be one or many;

b   for without unity, it is impossible to conceive of many.

Yes.

So if unity is not, the others neither are nor are conceived to be one or many.

It seems not.

Nor, therefore, like or unlike.

No.

Nor same or different, in contact or separate, nor as many other things as we went through before. If Unity is not, the others neither are nor appear to be any of those things.

True.

c   Now, would it be right to summarize by saying that if unity is not, nothing is?

It certainly would.

Conclusion (166c)

Then let this be said, and also that, as it seems, whether unity is or is not, both unity and the others are and are not, and appear and do not appear to be, all things in all ways, relative both to themselves and to each other.

Quite true.

Plato's *Parmenides*
Analysis

I have come to believe more firmly, and I hope to follow more consistently, as a principle of criticism, the idea that in a great work of art, whether a play, a picture, or a piece of music, the connexion between the form and the content is so vital that the two may be said to be ultimately identical.

If this is true, it follows that it is quite meaningless to consider one of them without constant reference to the other. It seems that when a critic approaches a play in the grand manner, as a philosopher, a historian of ideas, or of literature, he can say almost anything about it, according to his own sympathies and prepossessions. But there is a simple control: we can look to the structure of the play, in all its details. If the interpretation that we advance implies that the play is imperfectly designed, then either the dramatist has not done his job very well, or the critic has failed in his. The presumption with Aeschylus, Sophocles and Shakespeare when he wrote Hamlet, is that the dramatist was competent. If the dramatist had something to say, and if he was a competent artist, the presumption is that he has said it, and that we, by looking at the form which he created, can find out what it is.

H. D. F. Kitto, *Form and Meaning in Drama*

Introductory Conversation (126a-127a)

The *Parmenides* is narrated by Cephalus of Clazomenae, who has heard it from Plato's half-brother, Antiphon, who heard it in turn from Pythodorus, a student of Zeno (*Alcibiades* I 119a, cf. *DK* I 248, 33), who was present at the original conversation. This narrative scheme is complex and unusual: the *Parmenides* is Plato's only dialogue in which the narrator is three stages removed from the conversation he narrates. It is, indeed, the only dialogue, with the single exception of the *Symposium*, in which the narrator was not present at the original conversation; the details of the *Symposium*, narrated to Apollodorus by Aristodemus, were verified by Socrates (173b), who could not himself have been narrator if the remarkable scene with Alcibiades was to be included.

This complex narrative scheme is not accidental, and the reader is constantly reminded of it. The dialogue is cast throughout in indirect discourse, with direct discourse occurring within it; this is specifically true of the whole of the concluding part of the dialogue, which is in direct discourse governed by indirect discourse (137c 4). This peculiarity cannot usually be preserved in translation, except in such passages as 130a and 136e, where the narrative scheme is explicitly recalled. The structure might be likened to a set of Chinese boxes, which Plato can fit together at will; thus at 130a Antiphon reports what Pythodorus said, whereas at 136e, Cephalus reports what Antiphon reported that Pythodorus said that he and Aristoteles said to Parmenides.

This structure is designed to produce a sense of remoteness from the conversation, an impression heightened by the prose style of the dialogue itself.

That style is extremely bare and plain, devoid of poetry; as Cornford remarked (*PP* 64), "Even Parmenides' reference to the veteran charioteer in Ibycus' poem (137e) stands out like a single patch of colour on a grey background." It is as though the conversation had been worn away by being passed from hand to hand, so that finally only the hard structure of dialectic is left, without adventitious covering. This plainness reinforces the effect of distance, just as the lyric vividness of the *Phaedrus*, the *Parmenides'* near neighbor in date of composition, produces a sense of presence.

Complexity of narrative scheme is connected with remoteness in time. The dramatic date of the conversation is probably 450 B.C. It is natural to suppose that Cephalus is reporting the conversation to interested friends in Clazomenae, or some other Ionian city, shortly after his return from Athens. If so, the lapse of time to be imagined between Antiphon's account and Cephalus' recital of it is brief—or at least need not be long. The date of Antiphon's narration to Cephalus must be fixed after the death of Socrates in 399; as Proclus remarks, if Socrates were not dead, Cephalus would have gone to him, not to Antiphon, for the conversation. The date of the conversation, indeed, may perhaps be considerably later than 399. Antiphon was Plato's half-brother by his mother's second marriage. His birth-date is unknown, but he was of course younger than Plato, who was born in 428/7. He is here portrayed as no longer young (126c), which suggests that Socrates has been dead for some time; and this conjecture is supported by the consideration that if Socrates were to be imagined as having died recently, we should expect some mention of the fact. There is, then, a period of at least fifty years, and perhaps considerably more, between the original conversation and Cephalus' report of it, a lapse of time unparalleled in Plato's dialogues. For Antiphon and Cephalus, as for the reader, the conversation is a thing that happened long ago, a memory out of the distant past. The persons who held that conversation are dead, part of a generation itself now only a memory.

The introduction to the *Parmenides* is designed to produce dramatic suspense, to arouse the reader's curiosity about the conversation by emphasizing its importance. Well over fifty years after the event, Cephalus, an infrequent visitor, leads a delegation of fellow citizens "much interested in philosophy" across the Aegean from Asia Minor to Athens for the express purpose of hearing a conversation handed down to a man unborn when it occurred, but who found it so important as to work to get it by heart. The conversation is treated as one of the important intellectual events of the fifth century, as indeed it would have been had it ever occurred. Socrates, in later dialogues, is made to refer to the noble depth that Parmenides, "a reverend and awful figure," displayed on this occasion (*Theaetetus* 183e) and to the magnificence of the arguments he employed (*Sophist* 217d). These references are to the *Parmenides*, not to any historical meeting between Socrates and Parmenides, and they provide an index of the seriousness with which Plato himself regarded it. We are led to expect in the conversation that follows a serious discussion of serious issues, a discussion of great moment to philosophy. Given that Plato was a competent philosopher and a competent artist, the very introduction to the *Parmenides*, by itself, forbids treating the dialogue as some sort of odd joke, or trivializing it as mere gymnastic or an exercise in the detection of simple ambiguities. No doubt there are simple ambiguities, and there is gymnastic, and some of the reasoning is downright funny. But the reader is cautioned, from the beginning, that he must be prepared to think hard about philosophy. That warning will often be repeated.

Of Cephalus of Clazomenae, the final narrator, we know only what we are here told: he is an old man, now grown a bit forgetful, but distinguished in his city and respected and well-liked in Athens; Plato's elder brothers, Glaucon and Adeimantus, greet him warmly, and Antiphon, who met him last when only a child, seems to remember him with affection. There is of course no connection, beyond the accident of a name, between Cephalus of Clazomenae and the Cephalus of the *Republic*, a metic of the Piraeus, and by 399, dead to boot.

That we know no more than that this is the narrator of the *Parmenides* may be a historical accident; it may be something more. The conversation that follows is fiction: it could not have occurred, and it is important to its interpretation to realize that it could not have occurred. It is difficult to see why Plato should have taken such pains to emphasize its remoteness, unless he intended thereby to mark this fact. He may well have chosen to mark it in another way as well, by making the narrator, contrary to his usual custom, fictional; if that were true, it would further explain the presence of a third stage in the narrative scheme.

It has been asked why Plato should have chosen a narrator from Clazomenae. Presumably this requires no explanation beyond the fact that relations between Athens and Clazomenae were historically close, and communication between them at the narrative date of the dialogue open and free. In absence of further evidence, it must be regarded as accidental to the interpretation of the *Parmenides* that Clazomenae was also the birthplace of Anaxagoras. Proclus, indeed, suggested (660.30 ff.) that the geographical origins of the characters in the *Parmenides* symbolize a Platonic synthesis of schools. Parmenides and Zeno represent the Italian school, concerned with the contemplation of intelligible being. Cephalus is from Clazomenae in Ionia, and the Ionian school troubled less with the contemplation of intelligibles than it did with physics and the workings of nature. But Socrates and Plato, whose thought partook of both traditions, were Athenians, and Athens, where the dialogue is laid, represents the middle or mean between Ionia and Italy, and the middle or mean through which awakened souls obtain passage from Nature to Mind. This geographical distinction of schools, if not the symbolism attached to it, had by Proclus' time become conventional. It is found, for example, in Diogenes Laertius I, 13-15; Diogenes ends the Italian school with Democritus of Abdera, in Thrace, and Epicurus, in youth an Athenian cleruch in Samos. It is not Platonic, for Plato's distinction was rather between Gods and Giants (*Sophist* 246a-d, cf. 242d-e), whose warfare still continues. The geographical distinction is a mere product of the Hellenistic succession-writers, and as so often with inventive pedantry, obscures more than it clarifies. Nor will venturesome appeal to symbolism, which has not grown more chaste since Proclus died, enable the reader to distinguish bestween essential and accidental in the understanding of the *Parmenides*.

Characters and Setting (127a-d)

There are seven people present (129d 1): Zeno and Parmenides from Elea, and Pythodorus, Socrates, and Aristoteles, all Athenians. The sixth and seventh members of the group are unnamed, and play no part in the discussion — another mark of its remoteness. Presumably they are Athenians too.

With great economy of means, Plato establishes the character of his speakers and dates the conversation. Socrates is presumably between eighteen and twenty-one years old, an ephebe: he is addressed and treated as a man, but still "quite young" 127c, cf. 130e, 135d. His youth and relative inexperience will stand in sharp contrast to the age and wisdom of Parmenides throughout the dialogue. Since Socrates died at seventy in 399, the dramatic date of the conversation probably falls between 452 and 449 B.C. Granting those limits, it is possible to be more precise. The occasion of the meeting is the Great Panathenaea, the chief civic festival of Athens, which was celebrated, like the Olympic Games, at intervals of four years. That festival fell in 450. The Greek world at that time was at peace, and Italians like Zeno and Parmenides would have found it easy to visit Athens.

The relative ages Plato here assigns to Socrates, Zeno, and Parmenides may or may not be correct. If they are, Parmenides was born about 515 B.C. and Zeno about 490; these dates are now generally accepted, on the evidence of the *Parmenides*. Still, they are something less than certain. Diogenes Laertius (IX, 23), relying on the chronologist Apollodorus, gives Parmenides' ἀκμή or *floruit*, the time when he was forty, as the 69th Olympiad (504-501 B.C.), and makes Zeno (IX. 29) forty years younger. Burnet has shown that this is far from compelling testimony (*Early Greek Philosophy*, 4th ed., London, 1930, pp. 169-170.) On the other hand, given two pieces of evidence, demonstration that one is weak does not strengthen the other unless their disjunction is exclusive. The *Parmenides* is fiction, meant to be read as such. If this does not preclude its accuracy in the matter of the relative ages of its speakers, it certainly does not imply it. Indeed inaccuracy in such a matter would be a further indication of the fiction that Plato is concerned to stress.

Nor do we know enough of the other named characters to gain further light. Pythodorus son of Isolochus is mentioned by Thucydides (III, 115) as superseding Laches as general commanding the Athenian fleet around Sicily in the winter of 426; the Athenians later exiled him (IV, 65). Of Aristoteles, later one of the Thirty Tyrants (127d), we know somewhat more. He is younger than Socrates (137c), but old enough to answer questions. He may be the Aristoteles son of Timocrates mentioned by Thucydides (III, 105) as an Athenian general in 426, who in turn may have been a treasurer of the Delian League in 421/20 (*Corpus Inscriptionum Atticorum* I, 260.) We learn more of him from Xenophon's *Hellenica*. He returned from exile to Athens in 405 (II. 2. 18), when, if the *Parmenides* is accurate, he must have been in his sixties; he joined the

Thirty (III. 3. 2), was sent by them as an envoy to Sparta (II. 3. 3), and later acted as a general, fortifying the peninsula commanding the Piraeus (II. 2. 46) during their last desperate days. All this may be proof that some Greek gray-beards were singularly venturesome (it may be observed that Nicias was fifty-five when sent to Sicily, and regarded as extremely old to be a general). But it may also suggest that Plato, in making Aristoteles a youth in 450 B.C., was engaging in conscious anachronism, a device he uses for other purposes in other dialogues.[37] But then, one would not have expected Socrates to have been father of a child in arms at the time of his death at seventy (*Phaedo* 60a), and it may be that not much weight should be given to such arguments.

In any event, if Plato's account of relative ages is correct—a thing we do not know—there is nothing intrinsically improbable in the meeting he describes. Zeno is known to have visited Athens (*Alcibiades* I 119a, Plutarch, *Pericles*, 4. 4), and Parmenides may well have done so too. The Way of Truth, after all, is one which "leads the man who knows through all the towns" (Fr. 1. 3), and the geographical reference of this phrase is assured by *Sophist* 216c, where Socrates refers to genuine, as distinct from sham, philosophers, as "going from town to town, surveying as from a height the life beneath them." Athens in 450 B. C. was the first city in Greece, both in culture and power, and the Great Pananthenaea, though a civic festival, provided a spectacle almost as pleasing to Greek eyes as the Olympic Games themselves; in normal times, if peace is normal, visitors came from all parts of Greece to attend. It would have been natural for Parmenides to have come on such an occasion, and to have made his visit in the company of Zeno, a fellow-countryman, a philosophical ally, and a friend. It would be equally natural for Pythodorus, Zeno's pupil, to entertain them. And it is not impossible that, in that small and close-knit society, they should meet the young Socrates, eager to have contact with the foremost philosophers of his day. Questions of chronology aside, such a meeting is not implausible. It has been suggested that the absence of reference to it in later or contemporary sources, had the meeting occurred, would in inexplicable. Perhaps this is true, though it is to be remembered that Socrates had not yet risen to prominence, and that the conversation could not possibly have followed the course which the *Parmenides* describes.

For whether or not a meeting between Parmenides, Zeno, and Socrates took place, the conversation Plato here reports is fiction. Cornford's agrument by itself is decisive: "To suppose that anything remotely resembling the conversation in this dialogue could have occurred . . . would make nonsense of the whole history of philosophy in the fifth and fourth centuries" (*PTK* 1). Neither the historical Parmenides nor the historical Socrates could have spoken as they will here be made to speak. Their chief topic of discussion is the Theory of Ideas, a theory which, if the historical Socrates held a version of it, he came to entertain in middle life (*Phaedo* 96a-100a). Parmenides himself is portrayed as a Platonist: he accepts the theory against which he states perplexities, and its attendant pluralism (135b-c), and his method of argument is itself Platonic, using a respondent and making use of the things the respondent agrees that he knows (cf. 137b, *Meno* 75d). The *Parmenides* presents historical figures in a fictional conversation. It is itself a work of fiction.

So much, indeed, might be said of any of the middle dialogues. But whereas in, say, the *Phaedo* or the *Republic*, the commanding resources of a master style are used to disguise the fact, here, in the *Parmenides*, they are used to emphasize it. We have already seen that this must have been Plato's motive in stressing the remoteness of the conversation, and perhaps also in introducing Cephalus as narrator. It must also have been his purpose in drawing his characters as he has drawn them. Those who were to read the *Parmenides* were students in the Academy, who would have read and remembered the *Phaedo*. They could hardly have supposed, what is in any case patently absurd, that Socrates held as a lad of twenty the theory he there defends on the day of his death. The *Phaedo* itself forbids this view: it tells us that Socrates, when young, devoted himself to the study of the physical philosophers (96a ff.), and that it was not until he had abandoned their sort of speculation that he developed the Theory of Ideas (99d-100b). As with Socrates, so too with Parmenides. To draw a Parmenides converted to the pluralism of the Theory of Ideas is, according to the testimony of the *Parmenides* itself, to contradict one of the most striking features of his known thought. The *Parmenides* is not only a work of fiction: it is a work of fiction meant to be understood as such. It must first be interpreted if its relevance to the Eleatic tradition is to be made clear.

This result has a consequence. Just as the purpose of the *Parmenides* is not trivial, so Plato is not writing the history of philosophy. He is rather pursuing philosophy, specifically with reference to metaphysical and physical issues raised by the Eleatic tradition, which he inherited, and which his Theory of Ideas had transformed. The fictional character of the conversation is a clear warning to the reader that the *Parmenides* is not to be interpreted as though the Eleatics who speak are historical figures. The primary question is not what the historical Parmenides and Zeno meant, or could or would have said, but of the use to which Plato puts them as fictional characters in order to express an issue of philosophical importance.

The dialogue that follows is divided into three main parts, of uneven length, distinguished from each other both by their subject-matter and their speakers. In the first and briefest part (127d-130a), Socrates offers the Theory of Ideas in solution to a problem raised by Zeno. In the second part (130a-135d), Parmenides states a series of perplexities, *aporiai*, concerning Socrates' theory. Then, after an interlude to explain an unfamiliar method of inquiry by hypothesis (135d-137c), that method is applied in the third part by Parmenides, with the help of the young Aristoteles (137c-166c). This final part forms more than two-thirds of the whole; as Diès remarked (*Parménide*, p. 3), the movement of the whole dialogue is directed toward emphasizing and enhancing its importance.

Part I.
Zeno's Paradox
and the Theory of Forms (127d-130a)

Zeno's Paradox (127d-128e)

The *dramatis personae* of the first act of the *Parmenides* are Zeno and Socrates. Zeno has been reading aloud from a book that he has brought to Athens for the first time. When he is finished, Socrates fastens on one of his 'hypotheses,' and uses the theory of Ideas to refute it.

Zeno's hypothesis is a paradox. If things which are are many, it follows that the same things must be both like and unlike. This is impossible; like things cannot be unlike, nor unlike things like. Therefore, there cannot be many things: plurality is impossible.

In structure, this paradox is valid; the logical form is *modus tollens*. Its sense, however, is extremely unclear. It is not explained why plurality must imply that the same things are both like and unlike; nor is it explained why, granted that this is true, such qualification is to be regarded as absurd. The argument is elliptical, and appears to be a mere sophism. Many critics, overlooking its connection with what follows, have discounted its significance. It is to be remembered, however, that Socrates will reply to it with the theory of Ideas, and no man trundles in artillery to shoot fleas. The paradox that initiates the dialectic of the *Parmenides* is of considerable importance to its interpretation.

Socrates accuses Zeno of intellectual pretentiousness, of attempting to convince his audience that he is saying something new, when in fact he is only agreeing with Parmenides. The charge is more important for the light it throws on Socrates than on Zeno. One of the characteristic features of Plato's dialogues is the tact and urbanity with which disputants customarily deal with each other. Yet Socrates' remarks are rude, and quite unprovoked; they stand in sharp contrast to the politeness with which Zeno corrects them. Such rudeness is the mark of a young man, impetuous in argument;[38] it is a feature of characterization, meant to remind the reader of Socrates' youth and inexperience—a reminder that will recur in later passages.

This point bears on a common misunderstanding. It has been supposed that Plato's attitude toward the historical Zeno was one of disdain, that he saw him, not as a philosopher, but as an eristic, arguing for fame or love of victory.[39] Apart from this passage of the *Parmenides*, which does not support it, the main evidence for the view has been drawn from the *Phaedrus* and the *Sophist*.

At *Phaedrus* 261d, the arguments of the "Eleatic Palamedes," Zeno, are classed, along with political and forensic oratory, as representative of *anti-logikē*, the art of disputation. Cornford roundly declared that, "the whole is condemned as an art of deception" (*PTK* 177). But that is not so. The art of disputation is said to require ability to represent, or misrepresent, one thing as like another (261e), which requires in turn, if the art is to be properly practiced, knowledge of the truth about how things resemble and differ from each other (262a-b). This foreshadows one of the main conclusions of the *Phaedrus*, that there is need for a reformed rhetoric put to the service of philosophy; it implies neither commendation nor condemnation of Zeno, who, unlike the other representatives of disputation, is conspicuous by his absence in the satire on oratory at 266c ff. Nor is 'Palamedes' a contemptuous epithet. Palamedes was the Inventor, a culture-hero like Prometheus, who gave to Greek the adjective παλαμήδεως, 'ingenious.' He is one of the people Socrates hoped to meet in the after-life (*Apology* 41b), and a symbol of wisdom, as opposed to political power, in *?Epistle* II (311b).

At *Sophist* 225b ff., the Eleatic Stranger, using the method of Division, classifies the Sophist as an eristic; it has long been supposed that Zeno is here markedly in view. That may be true. But it is also true, as Campbell saw, that the Stranger's description of the eristic applies not only to Zeno but to Socrates, whom no one doubts to be a philosopher, and that in the next division in the dialogue (226a-231b), the Sophist is defined as a purifier of the soul from deceit, a description that can apply only to the philosopher. Indeed it is an odd but certain fact that, throughout the *Sophist*, we seem continually to stumble on the Philosopher in our pursuit of the Sophist (see especially 267b-268c; cf. *Meta.* IV 1004b 17 ff.), and the reason is not far to seek. It is that the Sophist is assumed, on the basis of a single collection (219a-221c), using the method of Example (218b-e, cf. 226c, 233d, *Politicus* 277d-278e, *Pr. Anal.* 69a 14 ff.), to be a species of artist. If that were true, Sophist and Philosopher would be coordinate species of a common genus, as possessing knowledge. But in fact it is false: art requires knowledge, which the Sophist has not got; he has only a τριβή, a 'knack,' which allows him to feel his way in the darkness of not-being, and therefore he is not an artist at all (254a, cf. 253d, *Politicus* 285b, *Phaedrus* 260e ff., 272d ff., *Gorgias* 463b, 501a). The divisions in the *Sophist* are meant to serve a dialectical, not a demonstrative, purpose; they do not succeed in defining the Sophist, as the mathematical joke that begins the *Statesman* (257a-b) shows; and if there is implicit reference to Zeno in them this in no way implies that Plato thought him anything but an acute philosopher — as indeed he was.

In the *Parmenides*, at any rate, Zeno is not treated unsympathetically, nor is his paradox discounted. He is made to remark that the book in which it appeared was stolen and published without his permission, and that it was written in a spirit of youthful contentiousness which he would now disown. That is, he apologizes for the polemical tone of his work; but he nowhere questions the validity of its arguments. Had he done so, he would not have brought it to

Athens to read. Nor does Socrates doubt for a moment the seriousness of the paradox of likeness. On the contrary, he directly sets out to solve it, though with the false optimism of youth, he thinks the solution will be easy.

Zeno's Treatise

The paradox itself is in the style of the historical Zeno, two of whose arguments against plurality have been preserved by Simplicius;[40] their structure is strictly analogous to this. Each begins with the assumption that things are many (εἰ πολλά ἐστίν), and deduces from it that the same things must then be qualified by opposites—in one case, that they must be both large and small, in the other, limited and unlimited. These conclusions are taken to be absurd. Since Zeno also used 'like' and 'unlike' in his arguments (*Phaedrus* 261d), there is good reason to suppose that the paradox presented in the *Parmenides* is not merely in the style of Zeno, but in skeletal outline, Zeno's own. If that is so, the story that the treatise which contained it was stolen and published without Zeno's permission is likely to have had a basis in fact; certainly its presence here is otherwise difficult to explain.

If the paradox is Zeno's, then Plato's account of the treatise to which it belonged is likely to be correct; indeed, the fragments preserved by Simplicius may well have belonged to it. That treatise was divided into 'arguments,' λόγοι, which contained 'hypotheses,' ὑποθέσεις,[41] of which this paradox is one (127d). Each argument was directed against plurality. The distinction between arguments, then, presumably lay in the fact that each took up in turn the implications for plurality of a different set of opposites—like/unlike, one/many, rest/motion, limited/unlimited, large/small, and so on—in a set of related hypotheses. Rhetorically, such a structure would be compelling, producing the effect of cumulative absurdity, and Proclus claimed that the paradox of likeness was one of a set of forty (*in Parm.* 694.23 [Cousin]). If the book dealt with motion and rest, as the *Phaedrus* seems to suggest (261d), it may be that it also contained Zeno's more celebrated arguments against motion—the Flying Arrow, the Achilles, the Dichotomy, and the Stadium—which Aristotle reviews in the *Physics* (VI. ix), and solves by the distinction, forged by mathematicians such as Theaetetus and Eudoxus, between the potential and actual infinity of continua. (*Phys.* VIII 263a 4 - b 5, cf. *de Gen. et Corr.* I 316a 15 - 317a 14). Note, however, that the abstract style of the book does not fit the vivid imagery of the arguments presented by Aristotle: Zeno lectured. The structure of the arguments given by Aristotle does not involve qualification by opposites; but if these arguments derived from the present treatise, they must have been meant to prove that the same thing is both in motion and at rest, and that this is absurd. The assumption that plurality implies motion would have been dialectical, not demonstrative; the critics Zeno opposed were defending the reality of the sensible world, and must have agreed that things are both many and moving, as they must also have agreed, and insisted, that the same things are both like and unlike.

Purpose of Zeno's Paradox

Parmenides had argued that the All is one, and some critics made light of this as ridiculous. Zeno's treatise was meant to pay them back in kind, with interest, by demonstrating that their own pluralism was itself multiply absurd. His defense of Parmenides, then, is by *reductio ad absurdum*; it is also dialectical, as proceeding from premises that pluralists concerned to defend the reality of the sensible world would be compelled to grant.

As a pattern of argument, *reductio ad absurdum* did not originate with Zeno. It is used by Parmenides, and it is a characteristic and pervasive method of Greek mathematics, one which may well antedate not only Zeno but Parmenides.[42] In the *Phaedo*, it is made an essential element in inquiry by hypothesis,[43] whereas in earlier dialogues it is used informally as the basis of *elenchus*, Socratic refutation. In Zeno's hands, the *reductio ad absurdum* is used not only to destroy a position, but to establish one. Given that something exists—a claim Gorgias of Leontini, in reaction to Eleaticism, later thought it good to deny—Zeno's proof that many things do not exist entails Parmenides' result that only one thing exists. In form, Zeno's work differed from the didactic and deductive poetry of Parmenides. As Socrates remarks (128b), in impulse its object was much the same.

Zeno and Parmenides

Zeno's arguments are obviously and explicitly reductions to absurdity. It has less often been remarked that the same pattern of argument is fundamental to Parmenides' *Way of Truth*, the first attempt in the history of philosophy to establish metaphysical propositions by proving them.

Parmenides' argument rests on a disjunction between two ways of inquiry, the way that is and the way that is not (Fr. 2). The disjunction is one of strict alternation, and Parmenides, by refuting the possibility of the second disjunct on grounds of self-referential inconsistency, proves the necessity of the first: there are not two ways, but only one, the way that is. The principle of his argument, on which everything depends, is that the same thing exists for thinking and for being. It follows that the way that is not is not a way of inquiry at all; for what is not does not exist for thinking, cannot be known, cannot be uttered. The true way of inquiry is the way that is, and it is the only way.

Parmenides goes on to suggest a third way, a way that both is and is not (Fr. 6). This is the way of the sensible world, which mortals—hordes devoid of judgment, two-headed because, as Simplicius remarks, they combine opposites—take to be real. Since this way implies that to be and not to be are the same and not the same, a *reductio* again applies. Given that the way that is not is unknowable and unutterable, the way that is and is not will also be unknowable and unutterable. The way that is and is not, in short, reduces to the way that is not (Fr. 7), and Parmenides' original disjunction is repeated in Fragment 8.16 in lowest terms: "It is, or it is not." The reduction is complete.

In Fragment 8, Parmenides deduces a variety of properties of what is: it can neither come to be nor perish, and does not admit change of place or quality; it is entire, immovable, without end; it exists neither in past nor future, but in a now; it is all alike, continuous, and one. The way of truth, then, involves a straightforward rejection of the reality of the sensible world and all that is in it, and Parmenides—or to be accurate, the Goddess whose *logos* he reports—proceeds to offer a cosmology for that world, a cosmology that rests on the dual contrariety of the physical principles of light and darkness. That cosmology represents reduction: analysis of the sensible world shows that it combines contraries, and therefore reduces to the way that is and is not, and therefore to the way that is not.

The primary thesis of Parmenides' thought is that what is absolutely excludes what is not, and therefore generation and destruction. No doubt he also held, as the *Parmenides* puts it, that the All is one, in that Being is one and indivisible (Frr. 4, 8.6, 8.22-25, 8.42-49; cf. *Sophist* 244e). But that claim is derivative, not primary, in his thought. Plato and Aristotle, however, both treat Parmenides primarily as a monist—treat him as assuming as his fundamental hypothesis that the All is one—and the historical Zeno, defending Parmenides, leveled his awesome powers of argument against pluralism, the hypothesis that things which are are many. As an interpretation of Parmenides, this would seem to involve misplaced emphasis.

The propositions that generation and destruction are impossible, and that plurality is impossible, are independent, in that there might be a plurality of things that do not admit generation and destruction. The great Pluralist systems of the fifth century all rest on this point. Empedocles, Anaxagoras, and the Atomists, Leucippus and Democritus, each in their several ways, follow Parmenides in rejecting generation and destruction, and seek to reconcile that rejection with the fact of change and the existence of a sensible world by accepting plurality. Anaxagoras put the nub of their enterprise with admirable brevity (Fr. 17): "Nothing comes to be or passes away, but is mixed or separated from things which are." The solution is to distinguish between elements and compounds: the elements of the world satisfy the primary Parmenidean criterion, in that they are neither generated nor destroyed; change is change in compounds of elements. As often in the history of philosophy, subsequent development is here diagnostic; there is no tight connection between Parmenides' monism and his denial of generation and destruction. Plato himself illustrates the point. His theory of Ideas satisfies the primary Parmenidean criterion; but there are many Ideas, and they are shared in by many sensibles. What the fifth century pluralists undertook to accomplish by mixture of elements, Plato accomplished by participation.

It follows that Zeno, if he was saying very much the same thing as Parmenides, was not saying exactly the same thing. He was primarily attacking, not generation and destruction, but pluralism; he was not defending Parmenides' main thesis, but developing a dependent theme in Parmenides' thought, and doing so, it would appear, on grounds independent of those which Parmenides had offered.

Yet the result confirms the Parmenidean conclusion: to deny plurality is to deny the existence of the sensible world, and thus to support the most striking and paradoxical feature of Parmenides' thought. The vividness of sense-perception must yield to the putative requirements of logic. So it was that, if Parmenides' result seemed absurd, Zeno undertook to reduce its critics to greater absurdity.

This very accurately describes the historical relationship between Zeno and Parmenides. But in the *Parmenides*, they interchange their roles. It is Zeno who, relative to the dialogue, presents an independent thesis, the denial of plurality. It is Zeno who is attacked by a pluralist, the young Socrates. And it is Parmenides who, by internal criticism of the theory of Ideas, will indirectly support Zeno's original claim. Socrates will reply to Zeno by drawing a sharp distinction between opposites and the things they qualify, distinguishing what Zeno had presumed identical. Parmenides will aim to show that this distinction, as Socrates expounds it, is absurd, and in the concluding section of the dialogue, in the hypotheses concerning Unity, will found a fresh set of antinomies, Zenonian in character, on that absurdity.

Who were the critics Zeno attacked? Tannery suggested that they were Pythagoreans, reacting against Parmenides' criticism of their school (*Pour l'histoire de la science hellène*, Paris, 1930 ch. x; cf. *PP* ch. iii). If this view has found wide favor, it has also been sharply contested, but the merits of the dispute are not the issue here. Socrates in the *Parmenides* treats Zeno as attacking, not merely the position of some distinct philosophical school, Pythagorean or otherwise, but the ordinary common-sense belief in the reality of the physical world, and its attendant pluralism (see 129c, d, 130a). So far as the *Parmenides* is concerned, even this is too narrow. Zeno's paradox of likeness is stated with absolute generality. It is directed, not against this sort of plurality, or that, but against any sort of plurality at all. If it were valid, it would refute not only common sense, but fifth century pluralism, though we have no firm knowledge of the relative dates of Zeno's treatise and those of Empedocles and Anaxagoras. More broadly still, if the paradox were valid, it would condemn not only the plurality of the sensible world, but also the plurality of the world of Ideas by which Socrates will undertake to vindicate the plurality of the sensible world.

The Sense of the Paradox of Likeness

If it is true that the paradox of likeness is the work of the historical Zeno, its exact sense has been irretrievably lost. The arguments by which Zeno must have defended its premises are left unstated, and even the meanings of ὅμοιον and ἀνόμοιον, the terms here translated like and unlike, are in some degree uncertain. The primary sense of ὅμοιον is 'like,' but it can also mean 'same,' 'equal,' or 'proportional,' and Parmenides held that Being was indivisible because 'all alike,' homogeneous. Cornford fastened on this last sense, which is specifically Eleatic, to explain the paradox (*PP* 68): "If things are many, they must be both homogeneous and heterogeneous. For (1) each of them must be one, and what is one is homogeneous. But (2) if they are many, they must be distinguishable, and therefore unlike one another; therefore they are heterogeneous." But this account is unsatisfactory. To begin with, it does not generate a paradox; there is no absurdity in a plurality being (collectively) heterogeneous and (distributively) homogeneous. Nor could Zeno have used ὅμοιον in so specific an Eleatic sense. He had undertaken to refute pluralism by *reductio ad absurdum*. But to ply such criticism, one must attack on the ground one's opponents have chosen, not on the ground one would choose for one's self.

It would be good to know more of the historical Zeno than we do. Yet so far as the *Parmenides* is concerned, the question is not what the historical Zeno meant by his paradox, but what is meant by the paradox here. That question, if it is to be answered at all, must be answered by examining the use to which the paradox is put, the role it plays in the dialectic of the dialogue. If the paradox is elliptical, it is by Plato's own design. It is that design which is here to be understood.

In the absence of evidence to the contrary—there is none—we ought surely take ὅμοιον in its primary and normal sense, to mean 'like' or 'similar.' Indeed, so far as the *Parmenides* is concerned, there is no alternative: ὅμοιον will later be defined as τὸ ταὐτόν ... πεπονθός, "qualified by the same characteristic" (139e, 148a), a definition repeated by Aristotle,[44] and at 132d-e it is agreed that things are ὅμοιον if they participate in the same thing, that is, have the same characteristic. There is no reason to suppose that the term as used in Zeno's paradox should be understood to have a meaning different from what it does later in the *Parmenides*. Zeno's paradox, then, is a paradox of likeness, and it may fairly be claimed that this is what Plato, in the *Phaedrus*, supposed the historical Zeno to have meant: "Do we not realize that the Eleatic Palamedes could, by his art, so speak that the same things seemed to his hearers to be both like and unlike, one and many, in motion and at rest?"[45]

The major premise of the paradox is conditional: if there is plurality, the same things must be like and unlike. The quantity of the apodosis is unspecified, but may be supplied from context. Socrates, in his reply to Zeno, will be at pains to stress that there is one thing, namely Likeness, which cannot be unlike, and another thing, Unlikeness, which cannot be like. He would hardly find it necessary to insist on this had Zeno not supposed that all members of a plurality must be both like and unlike. The apodosis of the conditional, then, is to be understood as universal. No justification is offered for its truth, but it is a premise that any defender of sensible plurality would grant.

The minor premise of the paradox is that nothing can be both like and unlike, and this premise, combined with the major, implies that there is no plurality. Yet the minor seems patently absurd. If we are to understand Zeno's reasons for thinking it true, we must look to Socrates' reasons for thinking it false. The paradox, so far as the *Parmenides* is concerned, must be understood in and through its solution.

The Dialectical Relation between Zeno's Paradox and Socrates' Solution

In his reply to Zeno, Socrates will connect the denial that things can be both like and unlike to a kindred denial, that things can be both one and many. The denial that the same things can be both one and many recurs in later dialogues. It is implicit in Socrates' "dream" in the *Theaetetus* (201e ff.) that the world consists in ultimately simple constituents that can only be given a name. It is found in the *Sophist* (251b-c, cf. 259c-d), where the Eleatic Stranger treats with ironical contempt certain youths and their elders, "old men come to learning late in life,"[46] who refuse to call one thing by many names—make a variety of assertions of a single subject—on the ground that "many things cannot be one, nor one thing many." It is mentioned again in the *Philebus* (14d ff.), where it is dismissed as "childishly easy, a mere hindrance to discussion."

But it is not dismissed in the *Parmenides*. It is solved. Socrates, in his reply to Zeno, will claim that the same things can be like and unlike, one and many. But he will claim this only on a condition, and the condition is metaphysical: *if* Ideas of Likeness and Unlikeness, Unity and Plurality, Rest and Motion, exist, *then* the same things may be both like and unlike, one and many, in motion and at rest.[47] This reply can hardly be a mere denial of the minor premise of the paradox. It must be a solution; that is, it must correct Zeno's reason for supposing that premise true.

This is related to a further point. To deny that the same things cannot be like and unlike, one and many, there is no need to adduce a theory in metaphysics: one need only appeal to the facts of daily life. Had Plato supposed that common-sense examples could refute the paradox, he would surely have used them. Instead, Socrates is made to counter with the theory of Ideas. This implies that the paradox rests on an assumption which, since it is to be contradicted by metaphysics, is itself metaphysical.

Zeno's Paradox not a Confusion over Relations

The foregoing consideration forbids a common interpretation of Zeno's paradox of likeness. The paradox is often dismissed as a mere sophism, because it is supposed that Zeno was confused on the subject of relations; he passes from the truth that no two things can be like and unlike in the same respect to the falsehood that they cannot be like and unlike in any respect, and he finds this transition easy because he confuses contrary relations with contrary properties, confuses terms such as 'like' and 'unlike' with terms such as 'square' and 'round.' Given the confusion, it would be no less absurd for the same thing to be like and unlike than for the same figure to be round and square, or the same number odd and even.

There is no trace of this confusion in the remaining fragments of the historical Zeno on plurality, which use the relatives large and small, and limited and unlimited. If it were indeed the root of Zeno's difficulty with likeness, Plato might easily have dealt with it; he had analyzed relatives with considerable precision in the *Republic* (IV 438b ff.). Instead, Socrates, replying to Zeno with the theory of Ideas, provides an answer of considerably greater metaphysical generality than the analysis of relatives. The supposition, therefore, that Zeno's paradox turns on the confusion of contrary relatives and contrary properties is inconsistent with the dialectical structure of this portion of the *Parmenides*: it makes Socrates' solution irrelevant to the problem he has undertaken to solve.

It has been suggested, however, that Plato was himself confused about relations, and unable to identify the root of Zeno's difficulty. The claim may be backed by appeal to Greek syntax. In English, we say that *a* is like *b*. The Greek says that *a* is like to (dative) or toward (πρὸς) *b*; that *b* is therefore like *a* represents a separate inference. So relations are grammatically exhibited as relative predicates, distinguished from other predicates by the fact that they are *to* or *toward* or *of* or *than* or *from* something. An example of this is found at *Parmenides* 160e 1-2: "When one says that Unity is different from (genitive) the others, one does not assert the difference of the others, but the difference of Unity." If *a* is like *b* and unlike *c*, it will follow that *a* is like and *a* is unlike, *toward* different things.

Cornford found in this the root of deep-seated confusion. In the *Theaetetus* (154b-155d), Socrates, undertaking to establish a connection between the hypothesis that knowledge is perception and the doctrine that all things are in flux, adduces a series of puzzles concerning size and number to help his cause. If six dice are compared with four, they must be said to be more than four and half again as many as four; if they are compared with twelve, they are fewer and half as many. So the four dice are more and fewer, both half as many and half again as many. Yet, though qualified by opposites, the six dice have neither increased nor diminished in number. This should be connected with the mathematical puzzles of *Phaedo* 96d-97b. Instead, Cornford connected it with a failure in analysis of relations (*PTK* 43-44):

> It is clear that the difficulty here exists only for one who thinks of 'large' as a quality residing in the thing which is larger than something else, with 'small' as the answering quality residing in the smaller thing. If that is so, then, when the large thing is compared with something larger instead of something smaller, he will suppose it has lost its quality 'large' and gained instead the quality 'small.' By suffering this internal change it will have 'become small.' He will then be puzzled when we point out that the thing has not altered in size.

This unfortunate piece of analysis has been the source of much superstition. "Plato thinks of tallness as an internal property on the same footing as 'hot' or 'white.' "[48] In fact, the confusion is not Plato's: for Plato knew that relative terms must be asserted *toward* something (*Republic* IV 438b ff., *Charmides* 168b ff., *Sophist* 255c-d).

There is in fact nothing inherently vicious in treating relations as relative properties, as Leibniz remarked (as quoted by Bertrand Russell, *The Philosophy of Leibniz*, pp. 12-13):

The ratio or proportion between two lines L and M may be conceived three several ways: as a ratio of the greater L to the lesser M; as a ratio of the lesser M to the greater L; and lastly as something abstracted from both, that is, the ratio between L and M, without considering which is the antecedent, or which the consequent; which the subject, and which the object.

Modern logic, when it follows Russell, treats relations as n-place predicates, capable of applying to multiple subjects. "L is greater than M" is a statement about both L and M, and perhaps even, if one is a 'logical platonist,' about 'greater than.' Relations, if they are not sets of ordered couples, triples, and so on, are construed as holding 'between' things, as Cornford insisted; and leaving aside Russell's assimilation of one-place predicates to relations, assertions in which relations are introduced are assertions about a plurality of subjects. But the truth-value of the assertion of a relation between two terms is also the truth-value of the assertion of a relative predicate of a single subject toward the other, and the fact that Greek is an inflected language makes that not only a natural but a necessary way of speaking. Nor is this merely a symptom of the putative tyranny of language over ontology. Nothing in this form of expression requires fallacy, and the *Republic* provides an analysis of relatives that would have resolved Zeno's paradox without difficulty, had the nub of that paradox been confusion over relatives.

Cornford, in his treatment of relatives, was influenced by Russell's arguments against assimilating relations to the logical form of subject-predicate statements. More recent ordinary language-analysis has glossed Cornford with the claim that Plato's treatment of relations is infected with a more general confusion over 'incomplete predicates.' Statements such as '*a* is like *b*' or '*a* is equal to *b*' are incomplete in that, taken apart from context, they do not specify the respect in which likeness or equality obtains, and without that specification, the truth-value of statements in which 'like' or 'equal' occur is undetermined. Perhaps 'one' is also incomplete: if Socrates is one man with many parts (129c-d), the use of 'one' requires implicit reference to kinds of things counted. This has led Professor Owen to a generalization (G. E. L. Owen, "A Proof in the *Peri Ideon*," SPM 310):

> The incompleteness which so embarrassingly characterizes 'equal' in its ordinary application cannot, it seems, characterize it when it designates the Forms. This is the natural sense of Socrates' warning that the 'equal' he is discussing is not "stick equal to stick or stone equal to stone but just equal" (*Phd.* 74a). . . . One main aim of the second part of the *Parmenides*, I take it, is to find absurdity in a similar treatment of 'one.' It is the extreme case of Greek mistreatment of 'relative' terms in the attempt to assimilate them to simple adjectives.

But the attempts at linguistic therapy are misplaced. Plato did not in fact assimilate relatives to simple adjectives. On the contrary, he distinguished them, on the ground that relatives are applied *toward* something. And it is a simple logical blunder to suppose that, since some adjectives are relative in their application, the corresponding abstract nouns must be conceived to be implicitly relative as well: it is false that the adjective 'equal,' as applied to sticks and stones, characterizes the Idea of Equality; it is equally false that the adjective 'equal' varies in meaning according as given sticks and stones are equal in length or equal in weight. The theory of Ideas implies that things equal in length and equal in weight share the common character of equality, and that character is an objectively existing essence or Idea. This is a metaphysical claim, which may or may not be true. But it will not be proved false and will not be even properly understood by appeal to the fact that words in ordinary use are often used elliptically, or, it may be added, by assimilating Ideas to 'predicates,' properties of subjects. Only if we falsely assume that the Idea has what it is, that Equality, say, is equal to something, does 'incompleteness' become a ground for suggesting confusion over relatives.

The point extends beyond relatives. When Meno is asked what virtue is, he answers by offering definitions of the virtue of a man, a woman, an old man, a child, a slave; and Socrates responds by requesting an account of the Idea common to them by which they are all virtues (*Meno* 71e-72c). Meno, in short, gives multiple uses of the word 'virtue,' treating it as 'incomplete,' whereas Socrates asks for the common essence. Socrates' request, no doubt, is open to criticism. If we suppose that the meaning of a word is its use in the language, and that instead of seeking sameness of meaning we ought rather to look for a family resemblance of uses, we will be inclined to favor Meno's reply over any search for essence, and reject any single defining formula. The Platonic response is direct. Either there is sameness of meaning in diverse contexts, or there is not. If there is, linguistic universals exist after all. If there is not, we equivocate every time we speak: meaning must depend not only on use, but on occasions of use, and if we ever step into the same river twice, we cannot say so. Given then that there are linguistic universals, those universals answer to the structure of the world, or they do not. If they do, it is a legitimate aim of reflection to penetrate beyond language to universality of world-structure. If they do not, language must distort the world, which in itself is unsayable and hence unknowable. In either case, the issue of incompleteness raises questions about universality; relatives and comparatives offer interesting and important examples of universality, but they by no means exhaust the field. And it is surely mistaken to project a modern form of linguistic nominalism into an ancient text concerned to state a realistic theory of universals.

The claim that Plato was confused about relatives, so that he fell into elementary blunders of reasoning, or that Zeno's paradox rests on such a blunder, is untrue. Socrates replies to Zeno's paradox with the theory of Ideas, and this answer implies that the root of the difficulty lies elsewhere. It lies, not in confusing relations with properties, but in failure to distinguish characteristics from the things they characterize.

I.ii. Socrates' Solution to Zeno's Paradox (128e-130a)

Socrates' reply to Zeno begins with a solution, and ends with a challenge. There exists, alone by itself, an Idea or Form of Likeness, and also an Idea of its opposite, what it is to be unlike, that is, Unlikeness. The things we call 'many' are both like and unlike; but in this they differ from the Ideas of which they partake, since things that are *just* like[49] cannot be unlike, nor things just unlike like. Still, it is no more surprising that the same things should come to partake of both Likeness and Unlikeness than that a thing should be both one and many by partaking in Plurality. But Unity itself is not many, or Plurality one. And so with other Ideas. Socrates would be filled with wonder if someone should show that Likeness and Unlikeness, Unity and Plurality, Rest and Motion (cf. *Phaedrus* 261d), can be combined and separated. Ideas cannot be qualified by their own opposites.

These remarks determine the structure of the remainder of the dialogue. In the next part, Parmenides will urge upon Socrates a series of objections to his solution, objections putatively meant as refutative. In the third and final part, he will take up Socrates' challenge at a level of utmost generality, and provide him with matter for surprise.

The theory Socrates has outlined is substantially that of the *Phaedo* and the *Republic*. In the *Phaedo* (74a-c), equal things are distinguished from Equality on the ground that they are equal to one thing but not to another, whereas Equality cannot be Inequality, nor things just equal unequal (cf. *Symposium* 211a, *Epistle* VII 343a-b). At *Republic* V 479a-c, the chief ground for positing the existence of Ideas is that sensible objects are qualified by opposites; the argument is clarified at *Republic* VII 523b ff., where it is held that unless things qualified by opposites are distinguished from the opposites that qualify them, the result is absurdity. The structure of the *Parmenides*, then, suggests that difficulties in explaining qualification by opposites, difficulties of the sort that Zeno's paradox raises, were an important motive of origin for the theory of Ideas. This is confirmed by the *Phaedo* and *Republic*.

The essence of Socrates' reply to Zeno is that a distinction obtains between things qualified by opposites, and the opposites that qualify them. There would have been no point in drawing that distinction unless Socrates thought that Zeno had assumed its denial.

That denial generates the paradox. Assume, as the defenders of plurality must have done, that the existence of a plurality implies that each of its members must be both like and unlike the others; for example, each of its members is like every other in that they all are, or have being (cf. *Sophist* 243d-e, *Parmenides* 142a-b), while each of its members, since it is different from every other, must be different in some identifiable respect and so be unlike the things from which it differs. Let *a* then be a member of that plurality, and both like and unlike toward *b*. Likeness and unlikeness are no doubt here asserted in different respects;

but it is true to say of *a* that it is both like and unlike. If then there is no distinction between things qualified by opposites and the opposites that qualify them, and likeness and unlikeness are opposites, it must follow that there is no distinction between being *a* and being like, and being *a* and being unlike. But if there is no distinction, then by transitivity of identity, to be like and to be unlike are the same. Do the relatives trouble? Very well: there is no distinction between being *a* and being unlike *b* or being *a* and being like *b*. Does 'incompleteness' trouble? Very well: there is no distinction between being *a* and being unlike *b* in respect to C, and being *a* and being like *b* in respect to D.

Opposites have been identified — as Heraclitus had done. Put otherwise, Zeno's paradox follows from a primitive nominalism that identifies meaning and naming in such a way that the *meaning* of a term is identified with the subject it is *true of*. Plurality implies that the same things must be both like and unlike; if the same things are both like and unlike, the opposites likeness and unlikeness are identical; this is impossible; therefore, there is no plurality. Nothing in this argument, it may be observed, is restricted to relatives or opposites, though opposites are logically dramatic. If this horse is white, the argument identifies being white and being a horse.

So the result, once reached, can be generalized. Many things cannot be one nor one thing many, for if many things have one character, there will be no difference between them: things the same as the same thing are the same as each other. In like manner, if one thing has many characters, there will be no distinction between those characters, whence it will follow that one thing cannot have many characters. This is the basis of the Dream of Socrates in the *Theaetetus* (201d-202c), of the paradox of the Late Learners in the *Sophist* (251a-c), and of the Childish Hindrance in the *Philebus* (14c-e).

Socrates, with the theory of Ideas, corrects the guilty assumption by distinguishing characteristics from things characterized. That distinction, once drawn, cannot be limited to relatives or opposites: it implies Ideas answering to every distinction of character — though the young Socrates will prove unaware of the implication (130b-e), and Ideas of opposites produce an especially vivid incompatibility.

Zeno's paradox, then, is a special case applied to opposites of a more general failure to distinguish characters from things characterized. Zeno and Parmenides were indeed saying the same thing in different ways, since Parmenides' hypothesis that the All is one follows directly from this failure: if there is no distinction between being and being *a*, then any second thing, *b*, must either be the same as *a* or not be. So there can be no plurality. This argument is put as one horn of a dilemma directed against pluralism in the *Sophist* (243d-244b): pluralists must either admit that Being is distinct from the physical principles they claim to have being, or abandon their pluralism. In altered terms, this also represents Aristotle's diagnosis of Parmenidean monism: Parmenides claimed that Being is one and plurality impossible because of his failure to distinguish predicates from that of which they are predicated (*Physics* I 186a 24-34, cf. *Soph. Elench.* 182b 26 ff.):

(Parmenides') conclusion does not follow, because if we take only white things, and if 'white' has a single meaning, none the less what is white will be many and not one. For what is white will not be one either in the sense that it is continuous or in the sense that it must be defined in one way. 'Whiteness' will be different from 'what has whiteness.' Nor does this mean that there is anything that can exist separately, over and above what is white. For 'whiteness' and 'that which is white' differ in definition, not in the sense that they are things which can exist apart from each other. But Parmenides had not come in sight of this distinction. It is necessary for him, then, to assume not only that 'being' has the same meaning, of whatever it is predicated, but further that it means (1) what *just is* and (2) what is *just one.*

Aristotle supposes that Parmenides' monism arose from failure to distinguish characters from the things they characterize, so that if 'being' has a unitary meaning, all that is or is characterized as being will be identical with being, and so be one. The solution lies in distinguishing characters from things characterized, whiteness from white things, being from things which are. In keeping with a fundamental tenet of his philosophy, Aristotle, in contrast to Socrates in the *Parmenides*, warns against supposing that this distinction implies that characters are capable of existing separately from things characterized. But Aristotle's and Plato's diagnosis of Eleatic monism is the same: that monism rested on an implicit and unstated nominalism, a nominalism necessarily inarticulate, in that a theory of universals had yet to be formulated — "Parmenides had not come in sight of this distinction." Socrates, with the theory of Ideas, corrects the guilty assumption, and thereby sterilizes Zeno's paradox. By implication, he has removed Parmenides' ground for supposing that the All is one, a result that followed from a nominalism that identified unity and being because it identified being with what is, and thereby identified things that are.

Zeno Revisited

Socrates' reply to Zeno makes no sense, as a simple matter of dialectical structure, unless Zeno assumed a tacit nominalism, assumed that no distinction obtains between the meaning of 'like' and 'unlike' and the things to which those terms truly apply. But to say that this assumption is tacit is precisely to say that it did not occur as an explicit premise in his arguments. The historical Zeno must have defended his paradox of likeness, and specifically the claim that it is absurd that the same things should be both like and unlike, on other grounds.

That Zeno in fact had other grounds is confirmed by all that we know of him. The remaining paradoxes against plurality, and the paradoxes against motion summarized by Aristotle in *Physics* VI. 9, show that the paradox of likeness is skeletal, that the propositions presented as premises are in fact conclusions for which Zeno argued, and that his argument turned, not on assumptions about characteristics and things characterized, but on assumptions about continuity, discreteness, and infinity.

It would appear, then, that the reader of the *Parmenides* in the Academy — the audience to whom the dialogue was primarily addressed — was entitled to be puzzled by Plato's account. Why solve a paradox by attributing to its author a premise that he did not and could not consciously hold? More particularly, why attribute that premise to him in lieu of premises he *did* consciously hold? The point becomes more pressing in that we have good reason to suppose that there existed in the mathematics of Plato's time, and familiar to his readers, a general and valid solution to Zeno's paradoxes, resting on a potentialist analysis of infinity. If that is so, then the *Parmenides*, in suggesting the theory of Ideas, not only does not take account of the historical Zeno's actual premises, but also does not take account of their known mathematical solution.

Zeno's arguments against plurality, as preserved by Simplicius, assume that plurality implies plurality of magnitudes, and that every magnitude is infinitely divisible, a thing Zeno could not have known unless he was familiar with the proof of incommensurability (*DK* B 1 and 2, trans. Kirk and Raven):

> If there is a plurality, things will be both great and small; so great as to be infinite in size, so small as to have no size at all.
>
> If what is had no size, it would not even be. For if it were added to something else that is, it would make it no larger; for being no size at all, it could not, on being added, cause any increase in size. And so what was added would clearly be nothing. Again if, when it is taken away, the other thing is no smaller, just as when it is added it is not increased, obviously what was added or taken away was nothing.
>
> But if it is, each thing must have a certain size and bulk, and one part of it must be a certain distance from another; and the same argument holds about the part in front of it — it too will have some size and there will be something in front of it. And it is the same thing to say this once and to go on saying it indefinitely; for no such part of it will be the last, nor will one part ever be unrelated to another.
>
> So, if there is a plurality, things must be both small and great; so small as to have no size at all, so great as to be infinite.

If every magnitude consists of infinitely many parts, then one of two things is true; either each of those parts has magnitude, or it does not. If it does not, then no collection of parts without magnitude will yield a magnitude. If it does, then a collection of infinitely many parts that have magnitude is not a finite magnitude, but must be infinitely large. We thus reach the conclusion that if there is plurality, things must be so small as to have no size at all, and so large as to be infinite. It will be observed that this presents a logical structure truly paradoxical: since it is false that all magnitudes are infinite, the pluralist is forced to agree that there is no magnitude; since it is false that there is no magnitude, the pluralist is forced to agree that all magnitudes are infinite.

On the assumption that there are finite magnitudes, either horn compels the other, and the pluralist is whipsawed.

Since numbers are pluralities of units, and units are assumed to have magnitude, the paradox may be extended from magnitude to multitude (*DK* B 3, trans. Kirk and Raven):

> If there is a plurality, things must be just as many as they are, no more and no less. And if they are just as many as they are, they must be limited.
>
> If there is a plurality, the things that are are infinite; for there will always be other things between those others. And so the things that are are infinite.

Plurality implies that things must be as many as they are, and therefore limited; but since there are always other things between things that are, they must also be unlimited; so they are limited if they are unlimited and unlimited if they are limited. The extension to likeness and unlikeness is conjectural, but direct. Of any two magnitudes, it is true that they are infinitely large and have no magnitude; so they are alike. Of any two magnitudes, it is true that one is infinitely large, and the other has no magnitude; so they are unlike. They are like in the respect in which they differ, and unlike in the respect in which they are the same. And this, truly, is absurd.

The Greek mathematicians dealt with the paradoxes of infinite divisibility by offering a finitist or potentialist solution. Zeno had supposed that infinite divisibility implies the possibility of infinite division, that is, that infinite division may be conceived to have been carried through; proceeding backwards, this supposition raises the unanswerable question of how finite magnitude may be derived from combination of the putatively resulting parts. But there is no such combination, for there are no such parts. To say that a magnitude is infinitely divisible is to say that it is divisible into parts, and that every part is a magnitude divisible into parts. Magnitude is not infinitely divided, but infinitely divisible; that is, the products of any division of a magnitude admit of further division. Zeno's argument derives contradictions because it rests on a contradiction: it assumes that the infinite can be gone through, whereas in fact the infinite is precisely what can not be gone through.

Presumably, this analysis was thoroughly familiar to Plato and his readers in the Academy, though owing to our exiguous knowledge of the development of mathematics, this cannot be independently confirmed. But it is typical of everything we know of later Greek mathematics, and Zeno's paradoxes of plurality, which attack the very possibility of mathematics, surely did not wait a century or more for their solution. Plato betrays no sense of intellectual discomfort in dealing with them—consider, for example, his confident treatment of Zeno in the *Phaedrus*. One could scarcely classify the paradoxes as *antilogike* unless one were aware they had been solved.

If then the first part of the *Parmenides* is to make sense, Plato must have supposed a direct and intimate connection between a foundational analysis of plurality and the theory of Ideas; the mathematical solution to Zeno's paradoxes is to be understood as essentially incomplete, and as requiring the theory of Ideas for its completion. Otherwise, the theory of Ideas would be otiose.

This a far-reaching but familiar claim. Mathematicians attain to nothing clearer than (*Republic* VII 533b-c, cf. VI 510c-d, 511d. trans. Cornford):

> a dream-like vision of the real so long as they leave the assumptions they employ unquestioned and can give no account of them. If your premise is something you do not really know and your conclusion and the intermediate steps are a tissue of things you do not really know, your reasoning may be consistent with itself, but how can it ever amount to knowledge?

Knowledge is found only through dialectic, which treats the hypotheses of the mathematical sciences as stepping stones, and undertakes to grasp the nature of each thing as it is in itself, proceeding from Ideas through Ideas, and ending in Ideas (*Republic* VII 533b-c, cf. VI 510b-c, 511b). So it is that Plato will say of geometry (*Republic* VII 527a-b) that:

> No one who has even a slight acquaintance with geometry will deny that the nature of this science is in flat contradiction with the absurd language used by mathematicians, for want of better terms. They constantly talk of 'operations' like 'squaring,' 'applying,' 'adding,' and so on, as if the object were to *do* something, whereas the true purpose of the whole subject is knowledge—knowledge, moreover, of what eternally exists, not of anything that comes to be this or that at some time and ceases to be. . . . Geometry is knowledge of the eternally existent.

The point is put with considerable force in the *Phaedo*, where Socrates offers a set of mathematical paradoxes, which are to be resolved by the theory of Ideas. The paradoxes are in effect restated in the *Theaetetus* (154c-155c) as puzzles of size and number. The paradoxes are these (*Phaedo* 96d-97b):

> I used to think it sufficient when a large man standing next to a small one appeared larger by a head; so too with horses. Still more clearly, I thought that ten is more than eight by reason of the addition of two, and two cubits larger than one because it exceeds its half. But now I am far from thinking I know the cause of these things. I cannot convince myself that when one is added to one, either the one added or the one added to becomes two, or that they become two by reason of their addition. It is surprising if when separate they are therefore one and not two, but they become two when put together, and their collocation is the cause of it. Nor can I persuade myself that when one is divided, the cause of becoming two is the division: for that is opposite to the cause of two before—before, they were brought together and added, and now they are being taken apart and separated. Indeed, I no

longer persuade myself that I know why anything that exists even becomes one or becomes or perishes or exists, according to this way of proceeding.

The difficulty is this. Suppose that operations such as addition and division are to be analyzed in terms of combination and separation of units. Then the state of affairs before addition takes place may be represented as follows:

(1)   A̲   B̲

The state of affairs after addition will then be:

(2)   A̲   B̲

Now, to divide is to separate. Therefore, the state of affairs before division takes place may be represented as follows:

(3)   A̲   B̲

And the state of affairs after division takes place will be:

(4)   A̲   B̲

The configuration in 1) is the same as the configuration in 4), and the configuration in 2) is the same as the configuration in 3). But 4) represents two, and 1) does not represent two; 2) represents two whereas 3) represents one. This is absurd. Therefore, if addition and division involve combination and separation of units, addition cannot explain why anything should be numbered as two.

This, of course, is not to deny the arithmetical truths that $2 = 1 + 1$, $2 - 1 = 1$. It is rather to deny that the addition of one is the reason why $1 + 1 = 2$, for if that were so, one and two must be analyzed as one and two units, respectively, and this destroys the distinction between what *has* unity or duality and what *is* unity or duality, and thereby reintroduces the absurdity. Number cannot be understood as a mere plurality of units (*Phaedo* 101b-c):

> You would shrink from saying that addition of one and one, or division, is the cause of two. You would loudly proclaim that you know no other way of becoming each than by partaking in the peculiar nature and reality of each. You can have no other cause of becoming two than participating in the Dyad: whatever is to be two must partake of that, and whatever is to be one of Monad. But as for these divisions and additions and other refinements, you would dismiss them, leaving them for wiser men to deal with.

The wiser men are experts in *logistike*, the art of computation; Socrates is here concerned with *arithmetike*, the science of number independent of quantity (*Gorgias* 451b-c, *Republic* VII 525b-c, *Theaetetus* 145a, 198a, cf. *Philebus* 56d-57a; see also *HGM* i 13-16). That science implies the existence of Ideas. Unity is something that A, B, and AB share. Any unit may be taken as two, and any pair as one, depending on the reference of the numeral to what is numerated. One and Two are therefore not units or pairs, but Ideas, which the same things partake of in different respects. There is, then, no difference between the number One and the Idea of Unity, the number Two and the Idea of Duality: they are respectively what is common to all units considered as units, and all pairs considered as pairs. This point was settled by Cook Wilson in 1904. (See "On the Platonist Doctrine of the ἀσύμβλητοι ἀριθμοί," *Classical Review* xviii (1904): 247-260. See also *REA*, 33 ff.)

As with multitude, so *mutatis mutandis* with magnitude. The line AB and the half-lines A and B are each one, and one in such a way as to be also many, as divisible. The mathematical solution to Zeno's paradoxes makes no sense unless Unity and Plurality are Ideas, common to and therefore distinct from things that are one and many. That solution requires distinction between what is one and potentially divisible and what is many and actually divided; the former is infinite in the precise sense that, for any division, further division is possible, whereas any actual division is finite. If, then, the mathematical solution to the paradoxes presupposes the existence of Ideas, it is essentially incomplete, and requires the form of inquiry that Plato in the *Republic* calls Dialectic, and that we, by a historical accident, call metaphysics. To deny the existence of Ideas is to leave Zeno's paradoxes unresolved.

The *Parmenides* and the *Republic*

The connection between the nonidentity of opposites and the theory of Ideas is important to the argument of the *Republic*. There, when asked to state the difference between genuine philosophers and those lovers of beautiful sights and sounds who resemble philosophers, and are not what they resemble, Socrates claims to be able to do so only on a premise, and the premise is this (*Republic* V 475e-476a, trans. Cornford):

> That since beauty and ugliness are opposite, they are two things; and consequently each of them is one. The same holds of justice and injustice, good and bad, and all the essential Forms: each in itself is one; but they manifest themselves in a great variety of combinations, with actions, with material things, and with one another, and so each seems to be many.

Opposites, though they combine in the things they qualify, are not to be identified with what they qualify, or with each other.

This premise is used to establish a division between the world of opinion, contemplated by lovers of sights and sounds, and the world of knowledge, contemplated by the philosopher (*Republic* V 479a-d, condensed from Cornford's translation):

> I shall call for an answer from our friend who denies the existence of Beauty itself or of anything that can be called an essential Form of Beauty remaining unchangeably in the same state forever, though he does recognize the existence of beautiful things as a plurality — that lover of things seen who will not listen to anyone who says that Beauty is one, Justice is one, and so on. I shall say to him, be so good as to tell

us: of all these many just and righteous actions, is there one which will
not appear unjust and unrighteous? . . . And again the many things
which are doubles are just as much halves as they are doubles. And the
things we call large or heavy have just as much right to be called small
or light. . . . Any such thing will always have a claim to both opposite designations. . . . These things have (an) ambiguous character,
and one cannot form any stable conception of them either as being
or as both being and not being, or as neither. . . . The many conventional notions of the mass of mankind about what is beautiful or hon-
ourable or just and so on are adrift in a sort of twilight between pure
reality and pure unreality.

Not only are things qualified by opposites distinct from the opposites that qualify them; their distinction is a distinction in degree of reality.

An important part of the force of this is brought out later in the *Republic*,
when Socrates turns to discuss the nature of the advanced education that the
guardians of the just state shall receive: The aim of that education is to lead
men upward to the light, to the vision of the Good—and the intellectual discipline most suited to do this, at the outset, is mathematics. The reason has to
do with the identity of opposites.

There are, Socrates argues, two kinds of perception: those which provoke
reflection and those which do not (VII 523b-c):

Reflection is provoked when perception yields a contradictory impression, presenting two opposite qualities with equal clearness, no matter
whether the object be distant or close at hand. When there is no such
contradiction, we are not encouraged to reflect.

Consider the fingers of a hand. One is larger, the other smaller, a third between
them in length. They are all equally fingers, and the mind is not therefore
compelled to reflect on what it means to be a finger. But with the size of the
fingers it is different, for sight presents two opposite qualities with equal clearness, declaring that the third finger is both large and small. This discussion must
be distinguished from the treatment of sense-error at 602c ff., as Plato himself suggests (523b 5-7). Sense-error is to be dispelled by counting, weighing,
and measuring; but measurement will only confirm the appearance that the
third finger is both large and small—smaller than the middle finger, larger than
the little finger. When this occurs, the mind is driven to question what the
senses mean, and so comes to regard largeness and smallness as distinct things,
confusingly mingled in the thing seen (VII 524b-c):

It is natural in these circumstances for the mind to invoke the help of
reason with its power of calculation, to consider whether any given
message it receives refers to a single thing or two. If there appear to be
two things, each of them will appear as one thing, distinct from the
other; and accordingly, each being one and both together making two,

the mind will conceive them as separate; otherwise, it would think of them not as two, but as one.

Unless Largeness is distinguished from Smallness, their coincidence in sensibles implies that they are not two but one. By recognizing them as distinct, the mind is led to distinguish objects of intelligence from objects of sight.

This is the basis of the educational importance of mathematics, a science that hinges on Unity (VII 524d-525a):

> If unity can be satisfactorily apprehended, just by itself, by sight or any other sense, as we said of the finger, then it will not have the quality of drawing the mind toward reality. But if it is always seen in some contradictory combination, so as to appear no more one than the opposite of one, then a judge will be needed to decide: the mind will be forced to seek a way out of the difficulty, setting thought in motion and asking what unity means. In this way the study of unity would be one of those which convert the soul and lead it to the contemplation of reality.

And sight does present such a contradiction: we see the same things both as one and as indefinitely many. Since this is true, reflection on unity, and thereby its distinction from plurality and number, must have the power of leading the mind toward reality.

The point of this argument is precisely the point of Socrates' reply to Zeno in the *Parmenides*. The coincidence of opposites in sensibles requires us to conceive of opposites as two, and each of them as one; if opposites were not distinct, the mind, in thinking them, would be thinking that two opposite things are one. The crucial premise of Zeno's paradox is that the same things cannot be both like and unlike. The Platonic Socrates understands this to mean that if the same things were like and unlike, then, without more, to be like would be the same as to be unlike. This result is impossible, but fortunately it is also unnecessary. Once the separate existence of Likeness and Unlikeness, Unity and Plurality, Largeness and Smallness, is acknowledged, once opposite characteristics are distinguished from what they qualify, the crucial premise of the paradox is seen to be false. Without the theory of Ideas, the coincidence of opposites implies the identity of opposites—the identity, indeed, of every characteristic and what it characterizes. The theory of Ideas prevents this. The combination of opposites in sensibles leads us to recognize the existence of purely intelligible objects, characteristics that exist apart from combination. That is, it leads us to recognize the existence of Ideas. Once recognized, their existence may be generalized: we may assume an Idea answering to every common term of discourse (*Republic* X 596a, cf. 435a-b).

Socrates' Challenge

Socrates' solution to Zeno's paradox is combined with a challenge. The same things may be both like and unlike, and Socrates one man of many parts. But though sticks and stones and things of that sort may be both one and many, Unity cannot be many, nor Plurality one, any more than things just like can be unlike or things just unlike alike. Socrates would be surprised if someone should distinguish Ideas alone by themselves — Likeness and Unlikeness, Unity and Plurality, Rest and Motion, for example — and then prove that those Ideas can be combined and separated among themselves. He would be surprised if, as Zeno and Parmenides have shown it to be with the things we see, so it is also with what we apprehend by reflection.

This passage offers a conditional denial: *if* Ideas are distinguished apart, *then* those Ideas cannot both be combined and separated. The condition on which the denial rests is that Ideas be distinguished from their participants. But the precise force of the denial is unclear. What does it mean to be combined and separated?

In the discussion of the Communion of Kinds in the *Sophist* (251d ff.), the Eleatic Stranger raises the question whether Ideas combined with one another, and answers with a qualified affirmative: some Ideas combine, and some do not. Motion and Rest, for example, combine with Being, since both are. Neither of them, however, combine with the other, for Motion is not at rest, nor Rest in motion. Two Ideas are said to combine, then, when they are such that one characterizes the other, and this meaning is plainly required of combination in the *Parmenides*. The word used for combination in the *Parmenides* is συγκεράννυσθαι; in the *Sophist*, a variety of synonyms are used, of which this (253b 2) is one. διακρίνεσθαί τε καί συγκρίνεσθαι occur in the *Parmenides* in the sense of physical or quasi-physical mixture. See 156b 5, 157a 6, and compare *Meta.* I 984a 10. Socrates supposes that if Ideas are distinct and combine, the same problem Zeno and Parmenides had found among the things we see will also be found among Ideas (129e-130a). This suggests that Likeness combines with Unlikeness if Likeness is unlike something, and Unity with Plurality if Unity is many.

The *Sophist* also sheds light on what it means to be separated. Knowing how to separate according to Kinds is equivalent to distinguishing according to Kinds and both are equivalent to not believing that the same Idea is different or a different Idea the same (253d). The condition, then, on which Ideas are to be separated is that they are different, other than each other.

These meanings plainly fit the *Parmenides*, and as a result, it has often been supposed that Socrates, in denying combination, means to deny the Communion of Kinds maintained in the *Sophist*. But this makes 129d-e, where Socrates' challenge is issued, irrelevant to anything that has gone before or will come after; the interpretation does not fit its context. Denial of combination can scarcely be reconciled with dialectic and definition in the early and middle dialogues, and communion is assumed in the *Republic* (V 476a) and the *Phaedo* (103c-105b). It is essential to the theory of Ideas, which Socrates means to defend.

To understand the force of Socrates' denial, it is important to be clear on a point of construction. If the antecedent of ταῦτα, 'they,' in 129e 2, were the list

of opposites mentioned in d8-e1 taken *singly*, then Socrates would indeed by implication deny the Communion of Kinds; for he would be denying that any Idea
can combine with any other. But the antecedent of ταῦτα may also be the list of
opposites taken as *pairs*, an interpretation grammatically supported by the brack-
eting effect of the conjunctions in d8 - e 1. The sense of the passage is then that
one cannot suppose that these opposites *are* pairs, and therefore distinct, and yet
also suppose that they combine with each other, characterize one another.

Socrates has already said, with considerable emphasis, that though things that
partake of Ideas may be qualified by the Idea and its opposite, Ideas cannot be
qualified by their own opposite (129b-c). His challenge restates the point, denying that the qualification by opposites found among the things we see is interwoven in Ideas among themselves, the objects we apprehend by reflection. Thus,
the problems under direct discussion in the *Sophist* and *Parmenides* are different:
the *Sophist* is concerned with the question whether any Ideas combine; the *Parmenides*, with the question whether Ideas of opposites combine.

Socrates' challenge has an analogue in the *Phaedo*, where Socrates undertakes to prove the immortality of the soul by the doctrine of Recollection. The
argument assumes the existence of Ideas (74a):

> We say, I suppose that there is something equal—I do not mean as stick
> is equal to stick or stone to stone or anything of that sort, but some-
> thing different, beside these things—the Equal itself.

The difference between Equality and particular equal things is that sensible
equals sometimes appear (φαίνεται) equal to one thing but not to another,[50]
whereas things that are *just* equal never appear unequal, nor Equality to be
Inequality (74c 1-2). Therefore, Equality is not the same as sensible equals.

It will be observed that Socrates does not take the distinction between Equality and sensible equals as self-evident; he argues for it, on the grounds of contrast. That contrast would not hold unless Equality were understood to be a
thing just equal and never unequal, as in the *Parmenides* Likeness is understood
to be *just* like and never unlike. For otherwise, the fact that sensible equals
also appear unequal would not imply their difference from Equality. The argument therefore assumes, if indeed 74c 1-2 is not intended explicitly to state,
that Ideas cannot be qualified by their own opposite. In the *Phaedo*, then, as in
the *Parmenides* and *Republic*, Ideas of opposites cannot combine.

Why should this be so? One reason lies in the deficiency of sensibles. After
Socrates has distinguished Equality from sensible equals, he goes on to discuss
their relation. He asks whether sensible equals are equal in the same way that
Equality is equal, or whether they fall short of being of such sort as Equality.
The answer is that they fall short: the things we see 'wish' (βούλεται, 74d 9)
to be of such sort as another sort of thing (οἷον ἄλλο τι τῶν ὄντων), namely
Equality, but fall short and are unable to be of such sort as that; they resemble
(προσεοικέναι, 74e 3) it, but are very deficient. It is for this reason that we refer
sensible equals to Equality, as to a standard, because all of them desire (ὀρέγεται,

75a 2, b 1) and strive (προθυμεῖται, 75b 7) to be of such sort as Equality, but are very inferior to it (74c-75b). This account holds (75c-d),

> not only of Equality and Largeness and Smallness, but also of all other such things as well. For our present account is no more concerned with Equality than with Beauty and Goodness, Justice and Holiness, and, in a word, with all those things which, in our dialectic, we ratify with the seal of reality.

The claim that sensible equals are deficient with respect to Equality minimally implies that sensible equals can also be unequal. No Idea can be qualified by its own opposite, since it can scarcely be true that any Idea is deficient with respect to itself. To put the matter in another way, Socrates means to establish a distinction between Ideas and sensibles: Ideas are ἕτερα ὄντα. But that distinction would collapse if Equality were unequal, or Beauty ugly, or Justice unjust. If Equality were unequal, it would be deficient with respect to itself; that is, it would no longer *be* what it is, but only something that *has* what it is, and also unequal. The parallel inference is drawn at *Parmenides* 158a-b (cf. *Sophist* 255a-b).

This result is required by the premises on which the *Parmenides* proceeds. Likeness is what it is to be like (cf. 129a 2), as Unity is what it is to be one (129b 7). Assume then that what it is to be like is unlike. Then Likeness has or participates in Unlikeness. Given that whatever is like is unlike and whatever unlike is like—Zeno's major premise—then if Likeness is unlike, Likeness participates in Likeness. Now, Likeness is the same as itself. But a participant is not the same as what it participates in (cf. 130b 2-3, 129b 1-4, *Phaedo* 74a-c). So Likeness is not the same as Likeness. But this is absurd. Furthermore, by addition, either Likeness is the same as itself or Likeness is the same as Unlikeness, or any other Idea. So if Likeness is not the same as itself, Likeness is the same as Unlikeness. But it is not possible that Likeness should be Unlikeness, and Socrates introduced the theory of Ideas in answer to Zeno's paradox precisely to prevent that result (cf. *Phaedo* 74c 1-2). We must therefore deny that Likeness partakes of itself, since it must surely be the same as itself. But Likeness partakes of itself if Likeness partakes of Unlikeness. Therefore, Likeness does not partake of Unlikeness. There is a gulf between being and having. What it is to be like can have neither Likeness nor Unlikeness. And this will be true of all other Ideas that satisfy the conditions of the argument; in general, Ideas cannot be qualified by their opposite, because they cannot be their opposite, or fail to be themselves.

If follows that though Likeness and the things that partake of it may both be said to be like, they are so in different senses. Likeness is like because it is *just* like; that is, it is what it is to be like, and therefore by its very nature excludes participation in Unlikeness, and in Likeness. No such implication attaches to its participants, which may be both like and unlike. So Likeness and like things are like in different senses, answering to the distinction between ' . . . *is* what it is to be like' and ' . . . *has* what it is to be like' (cf. 158a 4-5). It follows that Likeness cannot be part of the plurality of like things, or Unity one thing among many things that are one. The distinction between participants and Ideas is a distinction in kind—even as the *Phaedo* had said. If things that are *just* equal were unequal, Equality would be Inequality.

To sum up: Socrates' solution to Zeno's paradox, and his challenge, are directly and intimately connected. He had solved the paradox by distinguishing Ideas of opposites from the things those opposites qualify. He then challenged Zeno and Parmenides to show that Ideas, thus distinguished, can combine. The challenge is a direct consequence of the solution: the distinction of Ideas from the things that partake of them implies that Ideas of opposites do not combine, that Likeness cannot be unlike, or Unity many. Therefore, a proof that Ideas of opposites do combine would imply that the condition on which the challenge depends, that Ideas be distinguished from the things that partake of them, cannot be satisfied. The theory of Ideas would then be false, and Zeno's paradox left unanswered.

Part II.
Parmenides' Criticisms
of the Theory of Forms (130a-135d)

II.i. Parmenides' Criticisms

When Socrates has finished his outline of the theory of Ideas, Parmenides, who has been listening quietly to the conversation with Zeno, turns to Socrates and raises a series of criticisms.

Those criticisms are internal, meant to show that the theory of Ideas has inconsistent or impossible consequences. In outline, their structure is this. Parmenides begins by asking the extent of the realm of Ideas, and Socrates confesses that he cannot tell. Parmenides then presses the Dilemma of Participation, the Paradox of Divisibility, and the Largeness Regress, a series of connected objections to the possibility of participation in the Ideas. Socrates cannot provide an answer. Instead, he attempts to shift ground, first by suggesting that Forms are thoughts, and then that they are paradigms. His attempt ends in failure. Parmenides then concludes his examination with a flourish, using Socrates' own admissions to prove that participation is impossible and that the Ideas are unknowable. In conclusion he suggests—what has become clear—that Socrates needs more training in dialectic.

The internal structure of this scheme of argument is neat to the point of elegance. Perhaps no theory in the history of philosophy has been exposed to a more tight-knit and subtle series of objections.

Still, the precise force of these objections is far from clear. As arguments, they are brief and elliptical, couched in almost deceptively simple language, often depending on unstated premises, often containing ambiguity or vagueness in stated premises. It is by no means easy to determine what stated premises should be taken to mean, or what additional premises should be supplied. Nor is it surprising that, given the difficulty in understanding the arguments, there should have been long-standing debate over whether Plato thought them valid or invalid. If Plato thought them valid, he must have abandoned or radically altered the theory of Ideas after writing the *Parmenides*; yet it is surprising, had this occurred, that he should nowhere have explicitly marked the fact, and that he should continue to accept the theory of Ideas in dialogues written after the *Parmenides*. On the other hand, if he did not think them valid, why does he make Parmenides elaborate them so forcefully and with such obvious care, and allow Socrates to leave them unanswered?

The Validity Theory

If the criticisms are valid, they are decisive: they show that the theory of Ideas is prey to absurdity, and must therefore be false. Given that the theory criticized is essentially that of the *Phaedo* and *Republic*, given further that Plato was competent to know whether criticisms he had devised were valid against a theory he had invented, the *Parmenides* must then be taken to herald a radical change in Plato's later metaphysics. It marks a sharp discontinuity between the middle and the later dialogues—a kind of revolution in philosophy.

The nature of that revolution, however, has been very variously interpreted. Henry Jackson, writing in 1882, supposed that the *Phaedo* and *Republic* had treated Ideas as 'immanent' in particulars, and that the criticisms in the *Parmenides* refute that view and announce that Ideas are transcendent paradigms ("Plato's Later Theory of Ideas: ii. The *Parmenides*," *Journal of Philology* xi (1882): 299). As an incongruous counterpart, many contemporary scholars suppose that the *Phaedo* and *Republic* hold a theory of Ideas as paradigms, which the *Parmenides* is intended to refute, and which is therefore rejected in later dialogues.

In fact, it may be said with certainty that the claim of revolution is false, and this on the basis of Parmenides' own stated view of his criticisms. At 133b, Parmenides says that a man of wide experience and natural endowment could show (or be shown) that the concluding criticism is mistaken. The comment is directed to only one argument; but that argument, as we shall see, is structurally so related to those preceding it that it applies to them as well. The generality of the remark is confirmed by 135c, where Parmenides holds that to reject the theory of Ideas is to destroy the power of discourse. Thus, assuming that texts ought not to be understood to mean the opposite of what they say, the *Parmenides* itself forbids the view that the criticisms are valid.

This by itself is dispositive; but external evidence also bears. The first criticism Parmenides will offer is the Dilemma of Participation (131a-c), and that dilemma is restated at *Philebus* 15b-c, where it is explicitly said that it can be solved. This shows that at least one of the criticisms is not to be regarded as valid. Since the Dilemma of Participation is implicated with the other criticisms that follow it, including the last, it also shows more. It would be a strange procedure to mix valid arguments with a reticulated set of arguments known not to be valid, if one were undertaking to announce and justify a revolution in philosophy (see *PED* 233).

Nor can the claim of revolution be sustained in the face of clear texts: for Ideas are paradigms in the *Phaedo* and *Republic*, and Ideas are also paradigms in dialogues written after the *Parmenides*. The former is proved by *Phaedo* 74b-75d: we refer sensible equals to the Idea of Equality on the ground that they are striving to be like it, but are inferior to it; the same account holds for everything that, in our discourse, we ratify with the seal of reality (*PEF* 148-51). The latter is proved by *Politicus* 285d-286a, where the Eleatic Stranger remarks that, "Most people have failed to notice that, while some of the real entities naturally have certain likenesses . . . , of the greatest and most precious entities no image has been made clearly perceptible to men."[51] The *Timaeus*, in which the sensible world is held to be a unique copy of an intelligible model, is further and massive confirmation. So is the *Seventh Epistle* (342b-c), which, even if not genuine, shows the Academy's understanding of Plato's later views.

To this evidence it may be added — the argument is merely dialectical — that putative revolution in Plato's thought finds no support in Aristotle. Aristotle contrasts the views of Plato and Socrates. But his account of Plato is that Ideas were separate; that they were both individual and universal; and that they were eternal sensibles. Nothing indicates that he thought Plato ever changed these views.

Perhaps no more persistent thesis in the literature of Platonism, and anti-Platonism, has been advanced than that the criticisms in the *Parmenides* are meant to herald a rejection of the theory of Ideas or Forms found in the *Phaedo* and *Republic*. Few claims are more demonstrably false.

The Invalidity Theory

The best argument for supposing Parmenides' criticisms valid is the difficulties that arise if it is supposed they are meant as invalid. In the same way, the best argument for supposing them invalid is the difficulties that arise if it is supposed they are meant as valid.

If Parmenides' criticisms are invalid, why choose so respected a figure to present them? Why elsewhere praise him for the noble depth he displayed on this occasion, and for the magnificence of the arguments he employed (*Theaetetus* 183e, *Sophist* 217d)? In short, if the *Parmenides* offers bad criticisms of a good theory, why are the criticisms put?

When that question is squarely faced, as it often is not, one of two answers suggests itself. The first is that the criticisms are invalid against Plato's own theory, but are meant to be understood as valid against some other theory, perhaps that of Eudoxus (cf. *PP* 86-87). The second is that the criticisms present difficulties urged against Plato's own theory, in the Academy or perhaps by Megarian or Eleatic critics, which Plato means to clear up (cf. *PP* 101). These two answers are sometimes combined with a third: the criticisms, or some of them, present problems Plato did not or could not solve; this suggestion, it will be observed, implies that certain of the criticisms must be valid after all.

These three answers are mutually incompatible, and to maintain any combination of them requires an assumption, usually unstated, about the structure of this part of the dialogue. That assumption is that the structure is merely serial, that the criticisms are strung together like so many beads on a string, and may be treated independently of each other. They are randomly ordered like the epitaph of Midas the Phrygian (cf. *Phaedrus* 264c-d). This must be so, since they mix incompatible purposes and effects.

This is a pastiche theory of structure, and the pastiche theory is false. It is false because a competent writer would not without explanation mix arguments with incompatible purposes into a single sequence (cf. *PED* 233). More important, it is false because Parmenides' criticisms are not strung like beads on a string, but neatly reticulated. The concluding proof that the Ideas are separate and unknowable (133c-134d) assumes the initial Dilemma of Participation (131a-c); so does the Paradox of Divisibility (131c-e); so does the Largeness Regress (131e-132b). The refutation of the claim that Ideas are thoughts (132b-c) assumes a premise of the Dilemma; the Likeness Regress (132c-133a) assumes the separation of sensibles on which the Dilemma depends. Thus the question of why the criticisms are put requires a unitary answer; for the criticisms themselves exhibit a unitary structure, of which the Dilemma of Participation is the focus.

Rejecting the pastiche theory, we may examine its ingredients. The claim that Parmenides' criticisms represent misunderstandings that Plato means to clear up may be dismissed. One does not answer criticisms by stating them. Perhaps then Plato intended that the criticisms, when properly stated, should be seen to be blatant and obvious fallacies. But this is refuted by the fact that Socrates — young, but bright enough to invent the theory of Ideas — cannot answer them. It is also refuted by *Philebus* 15b-c, which restates the Dilemma of Participation and maintains that though it is answerable, the answer is neither easy nor obvious. So the criticisms do not represent an attempt to clear away more or less transparent misunderstandings by stating them. It may further be observed that analytical reticulation is not characteristic of a mere set of fallacies.

Then there is the view that Parmenides' criticisms are not valid against Plato's own theory of Ideas, but are valid against some other theory, which is the real object of criticism. Those critics who suppose that Plato did not believe that Forms are thoughts, but that the refutation of that claim at 132b-c is valid and profound, are committed to this proposition in the case of at least one criticism. There is also external evidence, deriving from Aristotle's lost treatise *On Ideas,* that the proposition may be taken more generally; for arguments derived from the *Parmenides,* including the Dilemma of Participation, are there applied to Eudoxus, who is taken to have sponsored the view that the Ideas are in their participants (*Meta.* I 991a 8-19 = XIII 1079b 12-23; Alexander, *in Metaph.* 97.27-98.24). This assumption is found at *Parmenides* 131a-b, in the Dilemma of Participation. It is also found in *Philebus* 15b-c.

But the suggestion that Parmenides' criticisms are directed against a theory other than Plato's would make those criticisms a mere *ignoratio elenchi* in relation to what has gone before. It is Socrates' *own* distinction between Ideas and participants that is under discussion (130b); the theory he outlines is essentially that of the *Phaedo* and the *Republic* (see above and *PED* 229-230); and the account of participation at 130e-131a exactly reproduces the thought of the *Phaedo,* and in part quotes the *Phaedo* (102b). There can be no doubt that the criticisms are to be understood as directed against Plato's own theory. Once again, this is supported by *Philebus* 15b-c, where the theory toward which the Dilemma of Participation is directed is Plato's own.

Given that Parmenides' criticisms are directed against the theory they criticize, the question of why the criticisms are put remains unanswered. The answer is direct. The criticisms are put as *aporiai*, perplexities, which must be faced and thought through if philosophy is to be pursued.

Aporetic Inquiry

The disjunction 'valid or invalid' seems logically required, and yet unsatisfactory in its consequences. The way out is between the horns. Parmenides' criticisms are peculiarly porous in their texture; brief, elliptical, ambiguous, vague. A single form of words has been chosen to cover a variety of possible admissions, and in attempting to understand any given argument, we are compelled to ask what must be accepted if the conclusion is to follow, and what must be denied if it is not to follow. The question, then, is not whether the criticisms are valid or invalid, but what must be assumed if they are to be valid or invalid.

This is confirmed by the *Philebus.* Socrates there dismisses as childish and a mere hindrance to reflection the 'portent' that arises when a man distinguishes the limbs and parts of a single thing and is then mockingly compelled to agree that one thing is many and many things one (14d-e). This sort of portent is taken as a treasure of wisdom by young men on their first introduction to the One and the Many (15d-16a)—and by some of their elders who have come to learning late in life (*Sophist* 251a-c). A similar portent gave rise to Zeno's paradox of likeness in the *Parmenides* (127e), and was robbed of its portentousness by Socrates' distinction between Ideas and the things that partake of them (129b-d). But when Ideas, or as the *Philebus* calls them, Monads, have once been distinguished, when a unity is posited that is not the unity of things that come to be and perish, when it is supposed that Man, or Ox, or Beauty, or Goodness, is one, then problems *do* arise about the One and the Many. These are two in number (*Philebus* 15b-c, construed after Cherniss, *AJP* LXVIII (1947): 230, nn. 61, 62):

> First of all, whether we are to suppose that such units exist; next, how we are in turn to suppose that those units, each being one and the same and admitting neither generation nor destruction, is most steadfastly this one thing, and nevertheless in turn thereafter in things which come

to be and are unlimited (whether each unit is held to be dispersed and become many, or a whole separate from itself—which would appear most impossible of all), how it gets to be one and the same thing both in one thing and many things at once. It is these issues, Protarchus, issues about this sort of one and many, and not those others, which cause perplexity (*aporia*) if you make the wrong agreements and easy passage (*euporia*) if you make the right ones.

The second problem, consequent on the assumption that Ideas exist, is the Dilemma of Participation. The *Philebus* restates the leading criticism of the theory of Ideas in the *Parmenides*, presenting it as a problem of the One and the Many. The basis of the problem had been laid down long before (*Republic* V 475e-476a, trans. Cornford):

> Since beauty and ugliness are opposite, they are two things; and consequently each of them is one. The same holds of justice and injustice, good and bad, and all the essential Forms: each in itself is one; but they manifest themselves in a great variety of combinations (*koinonia*), with actions, with material things, and with one another, and so each seems to be many.

The Dilemma of Participation is founded on the fact that Forms or Ideas are one, and yet universal, shared by many things. The *Philebus* implies that the Dilemma is solvable, and thus not destructive of the theory of Ideas; that it is directed toward Plato's own theory; and that it is not a blatant fallacy. The *Philebus* further implies that the question raised by the Dilemma is not whether it is valid or invalid, but what admissions will make it so; the Dilemma will be a source of *aporia*, perplexity, lack of passage, if you make the wrong admissions, but of *euporia*, easy passage, if you make the right ones. This, then, is reason to suppose that the Dilemma of Participation, and the criticisms of the Ideas in the *Parmenides* generally, constitute a collection of arguments, putatively refutative, which in fact are a set of problems to be solved.

The suggestion is indirectly supported by Aristotle, who treats the statement and use of *aporiai* as central to philosophical method. (*Meta.* III 995a 27-33. The aporia stated at 999a 24 - b 21 offers several variations on the Dilemma of Participation, and is more influenced by the *Parmenides* than the *Philebus*.)

> For those who wish to get clear of difficulties, it is advantageous to discuss the difficulties well; for the subsequent free play of thought implies the solution of the previous difficulties, and it is not possible to untie a knot of which one does not know. But the difficulty of our thinking points to a 'knot' in the object; for in so far as our thought is in difficulties, it is in like case with those who are bound; for in either case it is impossible to go forward. Hence one should have surveyed all the difficulties beforehand, both for the purposes we have stated and because people who inquire without first stating the difficulties are like

those who do not know where they have to go; besides, a man does not otherwise know even whether he has at any given time found what he is looking for or not; for the end is not clear to such a man, while to him who has first discussed the difficulties it is clear.

This sets the task to which the third book of the *Metaphysics* is devoted. In a Platonic mood, one might suppose that Aristotle's last sentence suggests that the proper statement of aporiai, difficulties, will lead to that learning which is Recollection. For it restates the *Meno* paradox (80e) to which the theory of Recollection is the solution.

All of this fits the *Parmenides*. Parmenides does not suppose that his criticisms of the theory of Ideas cannot be answered. On the contrary, he thinks that Socrates gives mistaken answers because of his youth (130e), that a man of natural ability can know that there are Ideas and what Ideas there are (133b), and that to deny that there are Ideas is to deny the power of thought and discourse (135a). Parmenides consistently refers to his criticisms, in fact, as aporiai, perplexities, rather than as refutations (e.g. at 129e, 130b, c, 135a). Socrates cannot solve them, and Parmenides offers a diagnosis of his inability: it is that he has undertaken to mark off things as Ideas too soon, before being properly trained (135c-d). This remark looks both forward and backward: forward, to the hypothetical exercise on Unity that is to follow; backward, to Parmenides' remark that Socrates is perplexed about what things have Ideas because, owing to his youth, he still pays attention to what people will think (130e). Socrates, in short, has failed to make the right admissions. He is compelled to find a means of passage by learning that the way is blocked; a better way can be found only by further training.

The perplexities Socrates has failed to solve suggest a kind of inquiry that is in essence dialectical: the respondent, and the reader, are required to pass from what cannot be admitted to recognition of what must be denied. The statement of aporiai, perplexities, answers at the level of metaphysics to the moral inquiry forced by Socratic elenchus. By convicting men of ignorance, it teaches them to inquire.

Given that the criticisms in the *Parmenides* are aporetic, it is reasonable to suppose that the hypothetical exercise with which the dialogue concludes may also be aporetic, meant to exhibit in greater detail the consequences of wrong admissions, and perhaps further to direct attention to which admissions are wrong. If that were so, the aporetic character of the *Parmenides* would be the key to its structural unity.

Aporetic Structure and Characterization

The aporetic structure of the *Parmenides* is also the key to its peculiarities of characterization. Thus, for example, Parmenides accepts the theory he so diligently attacks, and does not accept the identity he indirectly defends. The fact is remarkable, but certain. After concluding a series of criticisms that would, if valid, overthrow the theory of Ideas, Parmenides remarks that to reject that theory is to destroy the significance of thought and discourse (135b-c). No man could say this who did not accept the theory, and least of all Parmenides, for whom, historically, the intelligibility of Being was the motive principle of thought. Nor could anyone who thought the criticisms valid remark, as Parmenides remarks, that a man of outstanding gifts could answer them (135a-b, cf. 135c-d, 133b, 130e). It is curious but true: Parmenides in this dialogue implicitly rejects his own hypothesis that the sum of things is one, accepts in its place the theory of Ideas, and levels against that theory a series of objections he knows to be unsound. If Plato ever abandoned the theory of Ideas, he did not announce his intention in this part of the *Parmenides*, and it is a remarkable testimony to the vagaries of scholarship that anyone ever thought he did.

It is surely one of the most peculiar features of dramatic characterization in the *Parmenides* that Parmenides should be made to attack what he accepts and defend what he denies. It is so peculiar, indeed, that many critics have shut their eyes to the palpable fact. What accounts for it? And why, if the objections are unsound, does Socrates have such difficulty in seeing through them?

Parmenides answers the second question directly: he says that Socrates, though he has a noble passion for argument, is young and in need of training in dialectic (135c-d, cf. 130e). This fits precisely with Plato's characterization of Socrates throughout the dialogue: his youthful impetuousness with Zeno, his inability to withstand the onslaught of Parmenides' criticisms. He is brilliant, so brilliant as to invent a theory that a much older man, a great philosopher himself, will accept in place of his own. But he is young in philosophy; his mind leaps to conclusions before it has thought problems through, and despite its imaginative power, it lacks the essential patient discipline that philosophy requires. And therefore, when put to the question, Socrates is able only feebly to defend himself.

In light of this, we can see why Parmenides should criticize what he accepts. The motive is not doctrine, but education. Parmenides is a man of sixty-five, old in philosophy and a teacher, teaching a youth of twenty that he must think better before he thinks well. His aim is itself Socratic: it is to remove the false conceit of knowledge, to force Socrates to inquire further into questions he has answered correctly, and too soon. His method is the statement of perplexities, that Socrates, young and inexperienced in dialectic, cannot resolve.

If this is true, it leads to another striking feature of Plato's dramatic characterization. Parmenides is Socratic in his purpose, Socratic in the underlying irony of his approach, and Socratic in his method. Socratic dialectic has an Eleatic root. It is Zenonian dialectic freed of its geometrical rigor, the *reductio ad absurdum* adapted to the flexible needs of conversation, depending less on the formal implication of propositions than on the admissions of a respondent in discussion. Parmenides criticizes as a man steeped in this new method of conversation, which Socrates was to invent long after his death. Furthermore, Parmenides has a grasp of the language and tenets of the theory of Ideas which strongly suggests that he has read and remembered the *Phaedo*, a dialogue recording the views of a Socrates who is fifty years older than the Socrates of the *Parmenides*, and about to die. Parmenides, in a word, speaks as a man who has lived on after his own death, who has glimpsed a new philosophy and a new pattern of discussion, and embraced them in the ashes of his tomb. He is a ghost holding converse with the living, instructing Socrates in a technique of dialectic that Socrates himself will one day invent, instructing a Socrates who is young and undisciplined and not yet the Socrates who speaks for the *Phaedo*. It is nothing strange that artistically, dramatically, the *Parmenides* leaves one with a curious impression of timelessness, the impression that the conversation, even though it occurs in Athens in the middle of the fifth century, has occurred in the nowhere and the nowhen. The color of place and time, the bustle of human activity, which Plato could so easily capture when he wishes, are absent from it. It is a dialogue of the living and the dead, and the dead, agelessly contemporary, live on in the tenseless vitality of their thought.

II.ii. Separation and the Extent of Ideas (130a-e)

Parmenides begins his examination of Socrates by recalling a crucial distinction. Socrates had supposed that the characters he has mentioned must be distinguished separately, alone by themselves (129d). Ideas are separate from the things that partake of them, from "you and I and the other things we call many" (129a). Parmenides now takes this up, and raises two questions: 1) Is it Socrates' own distinction to set certain Ideas apart (χωρίς) on one side, and the things that partake of them apart (χωρίς) on the other? 2) Does he think that there is likeness separate (χωρίς) from the likeness that we possess, and so on with unity and plurality and the other terms Zeno just mentioned? Socrates accepts both claims.

The Symmetry Assumption

Parmenides' first question assumes that, if Ideas are separate, separation is a symmetrical relation: if *a* is separate from *b*, then *b* is separate from *a*. The symmetry of separation is also assumed in the Second Deduction of the Second Hypothesis (159a), in the course of a proof that other things cannot participate in Unity, and therefore cannot be one.

The assumption appears straightforward enough. To be separate implies, minimally, not to be the same, and the denial of sameness is symmetrical. If the assumption is merely that if *a* participates in *F*, then *a* is not the same as *F* and *F* is not the same as *a*, it is surely required by Socrates' theory.

But separation, if it does not imply, certainly suggests something more: things are separate when they are capable of existing apart. Socrates, in maintaining that Ideas must be distinguished separately, alone by themselves, presumably assumed that Ideas are capable of existing apart from their participants, which merely get or come to have a share of them. If Parmenides' first question assumes not only that Ideas can exist apart from participants, but also that participants can exist apart from Ideas, this is more than a simple implication of the proposition that Ideas are not the same: it is an independent ontological claim, and a substantial one. It is tantamount to the assumption that the things we see can exist apart from the things we apprehend by reflection (cf. 130a), that the sensible world, or some element of it, can exist apart from Ideas.

This inference is not required; it is merely open. It is supported, however, by the fact that the parts of the soul are separate in the *Republic* (X 595b); this implies that they are not the same, but hardly that each is capable of existing apart from the other. Death, in the *Phaedo* (64c), is the state in which the body is alone by itself, separate from the soul, and the soul is alone by itself, separate from the body; this does not imply, but surely suggests, that soul and body can exist apart. In the *Republic* (V 476a-b), philosophers are separate from men of action and amateurs of the arts; here what is separate can and does exist apart. In the *Timaeus* (51e), intelligence and true opinion "must be said to be two, because they have come to be separately and are unlike"; here again, what is separate can and does exist apart.

The inference that to be separate is to be capable of existing apart is not only open; it is supported by Aristotle. Aristotle holds that Plato separated the Ideas from sensibles, and by this he meant that Plato understood Ideas to be individual and capable of existing apart (*Meta.* XIII 1086a 30 - b11, trans. Ross. Cf. V 1017b 25, VII 1040a 9, 28, XIII 1078b 30):

> As regards those who believe in the Ideas one might survey at the same time their way of thinking and the difficulty into which they fall. For they at the same time make the Ideas universal and again treat them as separable and as individuals. That this is not possible has been argued before. The reason why those who described their substance as universal combined these two characteristics in one thing, is that they did not make substances identical with sensible things. They thought that the particulars in the sensible world were in a state of flux and none of them remained, but that the universal was apart from these and something different. And Socrates gave the impulse to this theory . . . by reason of his definitions, but he did not separate universals from individuals; and in this he thought rightly, in not separating them. This is plain from the results: for without the universal it is not possible to get knowledge, but the separation is the cause of the objections that arise with regard to the Ideas. His successors, however, treating it as necessary, if there are to be any substances besides the sensible and transient substances, that they must be separable, had no others, but gave independent existence to those universally predicated substances, so that it followed that the universals and individuals were almost the same sort of thing.

Aristotle supposes that it is precisely the notion that universals are individual and capable of existing apart which is, "the cause of the objections that arise with regard to the Ideas." Separation in this sense is attested in many of Plato's dialogues: in the proof of immortality from Recollection in the *Phaedo* (74a ff.), in the doctrine of Two Worlds in the *Republic* (V 475e ff.) and the *Timaeus* (17d-28a-c). For himself, Aristotle had no doubt that sensibles are individual and exist apart, and that forms or universals are neither individual nor separate.

Socrates in the *Parmenides* agrees both that Ideas are separate from their participants, and their participants separate from Ideas. What has he agreed to? That participants can exist apart from Ideas? Or merely that they are not the same as Ideas?

Substance and Separation

This is not a minor question, but an important issue in metaphysics. In the *Categories* (2a 34 - b 6, trans. Ackrill), Aristotle holds that:

> All other things are either said of the primary substances as subjects, or in them as subjects. This is clear from an examination of cases. For example, animal is predicated of man and therefore also of the individual man; for if it were predicated of none of the individual men it would not be predicated of man at all. Again, colour is in body and therefore also in an individual body; for if it were not in some individual body it would not be in body at all. Thus all the other things are either said of the primary substances as subjects or in them as subjects. So if the primary substances did not exist, it would be impossible for any of the other things to exist.

Aristotle had said earlier that, "By in a subject I mean what is in something, not as pertains to a part, and cannot exist separately (χωρίς) from the thing in which it is" (1a 24-25). So particular items in categories other than substance cannot exist apart from the subject they are in, and secondary substances, the species and genera of primary substance, cannot exist apart from primary substances.

For Aristotle, sensible substances are prior to their characteristics. In the *Timaeus*, Plato precisely reverses this. Sensibles are perpetually becoming, so that they cannot so much as properly be called 'this' or 'that,' or by any phrase that indicates they have permanent being (*Timaeus* 49d-e). Their whole nature is such as to be *in* space and *of* the Ideas (52c), and such things, plainly, are separate from Ideas in that they are not the same as Ideas, but not separate from Ideas in that they have no existence independently of Ideas. It will be observed that on one point, Aristotle and Plato in the *Timaeus* are in complete accord: it cannot be that characteristics exist independently of sensibles and that sensibles *also* exist independently of characteristics.

Yet is is precisely the possibility of mutual separation, in the sense of ontological independence, that Parmenides' first question suggests. The suggestion is natural enough. I come to you and convince you that Ideas exist apart from sensibles, and that were it not so, knowledge, thought, and discourse would be rendered impossible by Zenonian paradoxes. You come away convinced that, whereas you had once believed that only the things you see are real, there is in fact a second set of real things. Besides the things you see, the objects of your familiar common world, other things also exist, which you can apprehend only by reflection. So there are two sets of things, the members of each set having their own nature and reality. Having come so far, you may find yourself puzzled as to how the two sets are related. But your naive conviction, in which you, and Dr. Johnson, recapitulate the long phylogeny of common sense, that sticks and stones and things of that sort are independent realities, is left firm and unshaken — so you think.

Immanent Characters

The *Parmenides* connects the issue of separation and the issue of the extent of Ideas so closely that they may only artificially be divided. Parmenides' second question is stated as though it were a mere corollary of the first: if Ideas are separate from their participants and their participants from Ideas, is there then Likeness separate from the likeness we possess, and Unity and Plurality, and the other terms Zeno just mentioned? Socrates agrees that there is.

This suggests a distinction, not only between Ideas and the things that partake of them, but between Ideas and the characters possessed by the things that partake of them. If this given stick or stone is like that one, the theory requires that we distinguish (1) the Idea, Likeness, (2) given sticks and stones that are like each other, (3) the likeness in the given sticks and stones.

This distinction is found in the *Phaedo* (102a-e). When Socrates has elicited Cebes' agreement that Forms exist, and that other things get a share of them and are named after them, he goes on to ask whether, since Simmias is larger than Socrates and smaller than Phaedo, there is not largeness and smallness *in* Simmias. Simmias agrees that there is, and Socrates marks the consequence. The statement that Simmias is larger than Socrates is true; but it is not true precisely in the terms in which it is stated. Simmias is not larger than Socrates by nature, that is, larger because he is Simmias; he is larger by reason of the largeness he happens to have. Nor is he larger than Socrates because Socrates is Socrates, but because Socrates has smallness relative to his largeness. Similarly, Simmias is smaller than Phaedo, not because Phaedo is Phaedo, but because Phaedo has largeness in relation to Simmias' smallness. Therefore (102c-d, after Burnet),

> Simmias has the name of being both small and large, when he is in the middle of both, submitting his smallness to the largeness of Phaedo to be surpassed by it, and presenting his own largeness to Socrates as something surpassing his smallness.

In short, "Simmias is larger than Socrates" might mistakenly be understood to obtain because of what Simmias and Socrates by nature *are*, but in fact it obtains because of the largeness and smallness they happen to *possess*. And that largeness and smallness is *in* them.

At this point Socrates apologizes, quite properly, for talking like a book; but he goes on to draw a conclusion. Largeness itself will never be both large and small. But neither will the largeness in us (τὸ ἐν ἡμῖν μέγεθος, 102d,7, cf. 103b 5); it will not admit the small or allow itself to be exceeded and when smallness advances on it, it will either give ground or be destroyed. But it will not receive smallness and become other than what it is (102d-e). This is true generally of opposites, both those in us and those in nature; so Ideas and immanent characters such as the largeness in us differ in this respect from participants, which admit qualification by opposites.

This distinction between Largeness itself and the largeness we possess, or, more generally, between Forms and, to use Cornford's excellent phrase, immanent characters, is forced by the treatment of relations as relational properties—relatives. Largeness is universal, the single Idea in which all large things partake. But large things are large only toward other things. Therefore, relational properties in participants must be distinguished from Ideas of relations. Otherwise, the following paradox would result. Simmias and Phaedo are both large, and therefore in this respect the same, as partaking in the same Idea; but Phaedo is larger than Simmias; therefore, Phaedo and Simmias differ in precisely the respect in which they are the same. One way to avoid this result is to distinguish Largeness itself from the largeness in things. Simmias and Phaedo are the same in that they partake of the same Idea, Largeness itself. They differ in that Phaedo possesses his own largeness, an immanent character of Largeness itself, in relation to the smallness in Simmias, whereas Simmias does not possess largeness in relation to the smallness in Phaedo; he does, however, possess largeness in relation to the smallness of Socrates. Thus the largeness in Phaedo differs from the largeness in Simmias, though both Phaedo and Simmias partake of the same Form or Idea, Largeness itself. Thus also, the largeness in Simmias cannot be said to be small, since it cannot be surpassed in that respect in which it surpasses. This is merely a specimen case of the general rule of the *Republic* (IV 436b, trans. Shorey), that "It is obvious that the same thing will never do or suffer opposites in the same respect in relation to the same thing and at the same time." In the *Phaedo*, that Simmias cannot be small relative to that in relation to which he is large is taken as equivalent to the claim that his largeness can never be small.

Likeness and unity and plurality differ from largeness. Simmias may be larger than Socrates, but hardly "liker" than Socrates, let alone more "one or many" than Socrates. But once immanent characters have been distinguished from Ideas, the extension from comparative relatives to all Ideas may perhaps be supposed to follow by analogy. There may also be a more general reason for distinguishing Ideas from immanent characters. Suppose that the immanent character is what things are or become by virtue of participating in an Idea (cf. *Phaedo* 100c). If that were so, the distinction between Ideas and immanent character would appear to be a direct corollary of the distinction between Ideas and the things that partake of them.

But this raises the issue of separation once again. If the Idea is separate from the immanent character, and if the immanent character is what the participant gets by reason of participation, there must be some further element in participants over and above what they are or get by virtue of their participation. There is more to us than the likeness we possess, more to Simmias than the largeness in him. Immanent characters presumably cannot exist apart from their Ideas. But presumably also, they cannot exist apart from the participants they are in. So the question recurs. To what has Socrates assented in agreeing that Ideas are separate from their participants, and their participants from Ideas, and that Likeness itself is separate from the likeness we possess? Specifically, has he thereby granted an independent reality to participants, as subjects in which immanent characters inhere? If Simmias is large, and not the same as Largeness or the largeness which is in him, is Simmias then a substrate, a bearer of characters distinct from the characters he bears? Is the sensible world, or some element in it, capable of existing apart from Ideas? The answers Socrates gives concerning the extent of Ideas imply that this indeed is true.

It will be observed that, though Parmenides' question is phrased generally, it does not directly deal with the possibility of participation of Ideas among themselves. That possibility has been raised only in so far as participation of opposites in each other has been denied. The context requires that participants be understood to be sensible participants, sticks and stones and things such as that (129d), things we see in contrast to things we apprehend by reflection (130a). At least some sensibles are separate from Ideas, and one reason for this is that it would be absurd to dignify them by supposing that there are Ideas of such things.

Extent

Socrates is certain of the existence of two kinds of Ideas: first, such highly general Ideas as Likeness, Unity, and Plurality, and second, moral or evaluative Ideas such as Justice, Beauty, and Goodness. He is in aporia, perplexity, as to whether there are Ideas of animals, such as Man, or of the elements, such as Fire and Water. But he is not in perplexity about such things as hair, mud, and dirt, parts of animals and combinations of elements. These things have no separate Idea; they are just what we see them to be, and he refuses to dignify them with Ideas lest he tumble into nonsense. Yet he is troubled by a scruple that what is true in one case may be true in all. Parmenides tells him that his neglect of these things is the result of his age and too much respect for common opinion. He will neglect none of them when philosophy has taken greater hold on him.

This passage is not a report on Plato's own views of the extent of Ideas in earlier dialogues. The purpose of the exchange is dialectical, and it is not adventitiously placed. On the contrary, it is the foundation of the criticisms to follow.

Unrestricted Terms

It has often been supposed that the first set of Ideas Socrates accepts is purely mathematical. This is a mistake. The list includes not only Likeness, Unity, and Plurality, which have application beyond mathematics as well as in it, but also "all the other terms you just heard Zeno mention." It includes, that is, Unlikeness, Motion, and Rest (129d-e), and presumably also Generation and Destruction, Being and Not-Being, mentioned in 136b. None of these Ideas is purely mathematical; many are not primarily mathematical; and some are not mathematical at all.

The distinguishing feature of these Ideas is not that they are mathematical, but that they are general. Motion and Rest, Generation and Destruction, are Ideas that apply to all sensibles. Unity and Plurality, Likeness and Unlikeness, Being and Not-Being, would seem to apply to everything that is—not only the things we see, but those we apprehend by reflection. Of these Ideas, Unity is mentioned in the middle dialogues, where it is the basis of arithmetic (see *Republic* VII 524d-525a, cf. *Phaedo* 101c, 105c. πλῆθος is mentioned as an Ideas in *Phaedo* 101b 4-6.) But they become important in other dialogues to which the *Parmenides* is closely related. In the *Sophist*, Sameness and Difference, Being, and Motion and Rest, are among the very great or most important Kinds. Being, Sameness, and Difference combine with everything, including each other, and the Eleatic Stranger suggests that because they pervade all kinds, they connect kinds so that they can blend (253c). The same three kinds play an important role in the cosmology of the *Timaeus* (35a), and are among the Common Terms of the *Theaetetus* (184b-186d). It is there argued that some things are proper and peculiar to a given sense, in that what is perceived through one sense cannot be perceived through another; there is no hearing of colors or seeing of sounds. But sound and color *exist*; each is *different* from the other and the *same* as itself; each is *one,* and both together make *two*; and it may be asked whether they are *like* or *unlike* each other. So being and nonbeing, likeness and unlikeness, sameness and difference, and further, unity and numbers in general, and odd and even, are common to all objects of sense (185c-d). Indeed, they apply not only to all objects of sense, but to everything that is: they are, in short, common by reason of their generality,[52] as is perhaps also true of evaluative terms. As common, they are not themselves the objects of any sense; the mind contemplates them through itself, not through any bodily faculty. Because this is so, knowledge cannot be reduced to perception; for these terms are the foundation of knowledge.

It will be observed that the *Theaetetus* lists numbers, along with odd and even, that define the science of arithmetic, among the Common Terms that the mind apprehends through itself. The reason is given in the *Sophist* (238a-b): number must exist if anything exists, and proof will be offered later in the *Parmenides* (143a-144a). Not all general terms are mathematical; but the existence of mathematics is a function of generality.

Mathematical ideas are prominent in the early and middle dialogues. The *Euthyphro* makes Number a genus, of which Odd and Even are species (12d). The *Euthydemus* claims that mathematicians are hunters, who discover or capture realities, but must turn their catch over to the dialectician for proper use (290b-c). The *Phaedo* mentions Ideas of Equality and Inequality (74b-c, cf. 76d), Odd and Even (104a-c, e) and of numbers themselves (101b-c, cf. 96d-97b, 104a-b). One and Two are mentioned, apparently as Ideas, in the *Hippias Major* (300d-302b). Geometrical Ideas such as Round, Straight, and Figure occur in the *Meno* (74b, 74d-e). The *Republic* mentions Double and Half (V 479a-b), Unity and the numbers (VII 524e-525a, 525e-526a), the three species of Triangle, and other similar things (VI 510c, cf. 511a-d and VII 527a-b).

Moral Terms

The second class of Ideas Socrates accepts are moral or evaluative Ideas such as Goodness, Beauty, and Justice. Such Ideas are among the most prominent in the early and middle dialogues (See, for example, *Phaedo* 65d, 70d-71e, 76d, 100c-d, *Symposium* 210e-211d, *Hippias Major* 286d, 288d, 298d, 300a-b, *Republic* V 479a-b.) The argument that led Socrates to accept an Idea of Unlikeness in addition to Likeness, Plurality in addition to Unity, also requires Ideas of Evil, Ugliness, and Injustice. Such Ideas are mentioned in other dialogues (*Republic* V 475e-476a, 479a-b, cf. *Theaetetus* 176e-177a, 186a; depending on a textual variant, perhaps also Unholiness at *Euthyphro* 5d), but the difficulties they suggest are here left undiscussed.

Moral Ideas are closely linked in the middle dialogues to mathematics. Thus in the *Gorgias* (508a, cf. 504a-d), heaven and earth and gods and men are bound together by communion and friendship, orderliness, and justice; the reason Callicles preaches the life of excess, is that he has "failed to observe that geometrical proportion (ἰσότης) exercises great power among gods and men." As moral Ideas are linked to mathematics, and especially proportion theory, so are they also highly general. In the *Republic*, the Good is the first principle of reality and explanation, responsible for the existence and intelligibility of other Ideas. Yet though goodness cannot be responsible for evils (*Republic* II 379a-c, cf. X 617e and I 335b-d), Evil, Injustice, and Ugliness are Ideas.

Elements and Natural Kinds

Socrates is in *aporia* over whether Man, Fire, and Water exist, Ideas of animals, or natural kinds generally, and of the elements. Such Ideas are substantival; their distinctive feature is that, unlike those Socrates has just accepted, they have no opposite (*Phaedo* 104a-b, 105a, *Republic* VII 524d-525a). Since Socrates introduced the theory of Ideas to explain why qualification by opposites does not imply the identity of opposites, it may seem an open question, so far as the *Parmenides* is concerned, whether Ideas are required where opposition is not involved (as is also true of *Republic* VII 523c ff.). But his argument is in fact more powerful than its immediate result, which is the refutation of Zeno's paradox of likeness, and implies an Idea of Man no less than of Largeness, if this man is large. The *Meno* (72b-c) mentions an Idea of Bee, the *Cratylus* (389d) the Shuttle, the *Phaedo* (103c-105d) apparently assumes Two, Three, Snow, and Fire, and the *Republic* (X 596b) Ideas of Bed and Table. Aristotle, indeed, testifies that Plato did not recognize Ideas of artifacts (*Meta.* XII 1070a 19-21; cf. Alexander, *in Metaph.* 79.21 - 80.6), and dismisses the notion that there might be a separate Idea of House as an obvious absurdity. But in the very passage in which he denies Ideas of artifacts, he testifies to Ideas of natural kinds: "Plato was not far wrong when he said that there are as many Ideas as there are kinds of natural objects (if there are forms distinct from the things of this earth)."[53] The *Republic*, of course, suggests that the accustomed method of inquiry is to assume an Idea answering to every common term of discourse (*Republic*, X 596a, cf. 435 a-b), and the extent of Ideas in dialogues later than the *Parmenides* is very broad. The *Timaeus* recognizes Ideas of the four elements, Earth, Air, Fire, and Water (51b), and of the species of living creatures contained within the Animal itself (30c). The *Philebus* (15a) recognizes Man and Ox along with Beauty and Unity. And if the *Seventh Epistle* is genuine, Plato at the end of his life recognized Ideas of all shapes and surfaces, of the moral terms, of all bodies natural or artificial, of the elements, of every animal, of every quality or character, and of all states active and passive (342d).

Parts of Animals and Combinations of Elements

Socrates is not in aporia over whether there are Ideas of hair, mud, and dirt. He rejects them with confidence, on the ground that they are worthless and trivial; it would be absurd to suppose that there is a separate Idea for such things.

Socrates' confident rejection here is odd, in view of his preceding doubt. If he were to accept Ideas of animals and elements, it would at least seem an open question whether he should not also accept Ideas of parts of animals and combinations of elements. Parmenides' remark that Socrates will neglect none of these things when he is older is reflected in later dialogues. In the *Politicus* (266d), the Eleatic Stranger suggests that dialectic is, "No more concerned with the noble than the base, pays no more honor to the great than to the small." In the *Sophist* (227a-b), the Stranger remarks that the true dialectician would take under consideration the louse-catcher, if it helped him in his inquiry.

The Question of Extent

Why does Parmenides preface his criticisms of the theory of Ideas with a question about their extent?

The reason is not that the *Parmenides* presents Plato's own earlier doubts, for the pattern of question and response does not fit the middle dialogues. In the first place, kinds of Ideas that Plato there recognizes are here unmentioned: for example, Light and Heavy, Large and Small (*Republic* V 479b), Hot and Cold (*Phaedo* 103c-e), Life (*Phaedo* 106d), Health, Size, and Strength (*Phaedo* 65d-e, cf. *Meno* 72c-73c). In the second place, substantival Ideas such as Man, which here fill Socrates with aporia, are accepted in the middle dialogues—the Bee of the *Meno*, Snow and Fire in the *Phaedo*, not to mention the Divine Bedstead of the *Republic*. And unrestricted Ideas, such as Likeness and Unity, of which Socrates is here most sure, are given a prominence in the *Parmenides* they have scarcely had before. Finally, Socrates' rejection of separate Ideas of hair, mud, and dirt is philosophically clumsy. Grant that these things are worthless and trivial; still, he has adopted a pattern of argument that ought to lead him to accept Ideas of Evil and Injustice, recognized in the *Republic*. If one must countenance Ideal Evil, why stick at Ideal Trivia? And, if he did but know it, Socrates has a further reason for accepting Ideal Trivia; for though he is in perplexity about animals and elements, his own solution to Zeno's paradox should have led him to see that such Ideas as Man and Fire must be distinguished no less than Ideas of opposites, and if animals and elements are once admitted, their parts and compounds are not obviously beyond the pale (see *Timaeus* 51b-e, and Cornford, *PC*, 189-191). There is much reason in Socrates' concern that what is true in one case may yet prove true in all.

The discussion of the extent of Ideas is not a report of Plato's own views in other dialogues. It is meant to serve a dialectical purpose within the body of the *Parmenides* itself. To begin with, it reminds us forcibly of Socrates' youth and inexperience. Parmenides, indeed, calls attention to this in so many words (130e); he will later remark that it takes a man of natural gifts and wide experience to deal with the objections to Ideas he offers (133a, 135a), implying what is then stated (135c-d), that Socrates is still insufficiently experienced. The discussion of the extent of Ideas, then, serves to emphasize a recurring feature of characterization in the dialogue. But it does more. Socrates, having invented the theory of Ideas, may reasonably be expected to know what sorts of things have them. Yet he is doubtful, objecting to examples, offering no principle. His perplexity, in short, is connected with his youth; he has not thought through the requirements of his own theory. At 135c-d, this is explicitly remarked.

Socrates' perplexity is important. Parmenides had begun the discussion by raising the issue of separation; but to ask the extent of Ideas is simply to ask in what cases separation is to be found. The possible answers were afterwards listed, in altered vocabulary, by Aristotle (*Meta.* III 999a 32 - b 1, cf. 999b 17-20, 995b 31-37, XI 1060a 10-17, b 23-28):

> If we admit in the fullest sense that something exists apart from the concrete things, whenever something is predicated of the matter, must there, if there is something apart, be something apart from each set of individuals, or from some and not from others, or from none?

Socrates has chosen the second disjunct: there is an idea apart from some things, but not others. Thus there is a separate Idea corresponding to Likeness and Unity; there is no separate Idea corresponding to mud, hair, and dirt, and perhaps not to animals such as man and elements such as fire and water. It is significant that Parmenides should tell Socrates in so many words that his denial of separate Ideas of hair, mud, and dirt is mistaken: philosophy has not yet taken hold of him as one day it will; he will despise none of these things then. The generality of this remark is confirmed by 135b-c. If a man refuses to distinguish as something an Idea of each single thing, he will have nothing toward which to turn his mind, and to deny an Idea for each of the things that are is to destroy the significance of discourse.

So Socrates has made a wrong admission. Specifically, because hair, mud, and dirt are worthless and trivial, he has implicitly endowed them with independent reality.

The Issue of Separation

If Simmias is large, and Largeness is an Idea, Simmias is other than Largeness, and partakes of Largeness, and there is largeness in Simmias.

So far we are merely on the ground of the *Phaedo.* But the admissions that Socrates has already made about separation in the *Parmenides* introduce further complexity in a matter on which the *Phaedo* was silent. Socrates has agreed to the following propositions:

1) That Ideas are separate from their participants.
2) That participants are separate from Ideas.
3) That Ideas are separate from their immanent characters in participants.
4) That there is no separate Idea for some kinds of sensibles.

Ideas are separate from their participants, and from their immanent characters in participants, as capable of existing apart. But the claim that no separate Idea exists for some kinds of sensibles implies that participants are in some sense capable of existing apart from Ideas.

Suppose that Simmias is larger than Socrates. Then by the *Phaedo's* account (102a-e), Simmias is not larger by nature, by virtue of the fact that he is Simmias, but by virtue of the largeness he happens to have; and this implies that he participates in the Idea of Largeness. This pattern of argument is of considerable importance in the hypothetical examination of Unity with which the *Parmenides* concludes, where it is applied to the relations of Ideas among themselves (see for example, 139c, 143b, 147c-148a, 160d-e).

But Simmias is not only large. He is a man. And by Socrates' account in the *Parmenides*, though not in the *Phaedo*, where the question is not directly raised, that Simmias is a man does not, or need not, imply a separate Idea of Man. If there is no Idea of Man, and there are men, then some things in our world do not derive their nature from Ideas.

That Simmias is large implies that he participates in Largeness; no such consequence attaches to the fact that he is a man, since no separate Idea of Man exists. Thus, Simmias *qua* large is not capable of existing apart from an Idea; Simmias *qua* man exists apart from any Idea at all. Given that Simmias is by nature a man, it follows that Simmias by nature exists apart from everything of which Simmias partakes. Participants, in short, are separate from Ideas not only because they are not the same as Ideas, but because they have a nature of their own. And in so far as they have a nature of their own, they exist apart from Ideas.

To say that participants have a nature of their own is to imply that they have reality in their own right, apart from participation. Given that this is so, it might further be supposed that it is only by virtue of that reality that participation is possible. Largeness itself is separate from the largeness in Simmias. But the largeness in Simmias must be in Simmias as incapable of existing apart from him, since that largeness is precisely *his* largeness, and not the largeness of Phaedo or Socrates or anyone else. It would seem that Simmias must have a core of substantiality distinct from the Ideas, if Simmias is to be the bearer of the immanent characters that are in him.

It is irrelevant in this context that Simmias, as a man, has a soul, a fact that elsewhere would introduce additional ontological complexity. The argument carries through, not only for men, but for sticks and stones, and for hair, mud, and dirt—for whatever should be classed as a distinct kind of sensible. There is a double edge to Parmenides' remark that Socrates has denied such Ideas because, owing to his youth, he still pays attention to what people will think. Common sense would suppose it absurd to assume a separate Mud laid up in Heaven; it would equally suppose it absurd to deny the reality of mud. Socrates, in assuming that hair, mud, and dirt are "just what we see them to be," has committed himself to the common sense assumption that things in the sensible world have a reality of their own, independent of the world of Ideas.

The *Phaedo* has provided a universe in which Ideas are separate from participants, and in Aristotle's terms, prior to participants (*Meta.* V 1019a 1 ff.):

> Some things then are called prior and posterior . . . in respect of nature and substance, i.e., those which can be without other things, while the others cannot be without them—a distinction which Plato first used.

Thus in the *Phaedo* Largeness is prior to large things, in that given things can exist as large only because Largeness exists, whereas Largeness exists whether or not those given things are large. But Socrates' admissions about separation in the *Parmenides* imply a kind of ontological parity over and above the ontological priority of Ideas. The sensible world, though it depends on Ideas in certain crucial respects, also has a nature and reality of its own. This assumption will prove to be the source of much further perplexity.

Participation and Substantialization

In solving Zeno's paradox, Socrates had claimed that Ideas must be distinguished as separate, and Parmenides begins his examination by asking whether Ideas are separate from their participants and participants separate from Ideas. Socrates answers with an unqualified affirmative, and the force of his affirmation is indicated by the fact that mud, hair, and dirt answer to no Idea, but are just as we see them to be. So some of the things we see have an existence independent of the things we apprehend by reflection.

It will be observed that, though Parmenides' question is put generally, it does not directly deal with the issue of participation of Ideas among themselves. That issue has been raised only in so far as participation of opposites in their own opposite has been denied. The context suggests that participants are to be understood as sensible participants, sticks and stones and things such as that (129d), things we see in contrast to things we apprehend by reflection (130a). At least some sensibles are separate from Ideas, and one reason for this is that it would be absurd to dignify them with Ideas. There is a dialectical twist or, if you will, a piece of dramatic irony in this: precisely because hair, mud, and dirt are worthless and trivial, Socrates had endowed them with independent and substantial reality.

Parmenides concludes his inquiry concerning extent with a summary in which the theory of Ideas is reduced to three connected propositions: 1) that certain Ideas exist; 2) that other things participate in those Ideas; 3) that because they participate in them they are named after them. The summary is put in language drawn directly from the *Phaedo*,[54] and from the same passage in which immanent characters are distinguished from Ideas and from participants. The linguistic corollary that participants are named after Ideas by reason of their participation in them was anticipated in the *Phaedo* by the claim that participants are called by the same name as their Ideas (*Phaedo* 78e; cf. *Parmenides* 133d, *Timaeus* 52a; see also A. E. Taylor, *Commentary on Plato's Timaeus*, 342, on *Timaeus* 52a 5). Aristotle, in his first summary of Plato's doctrines in the *Metaphysics* (I 987b 3 ff.), remarked precisely this feature: "Sensible things, (Plato) said, were all named after (Ideas), and in virtue of a relation to them; for the many existed by participation in the Ideas that have the same name as they."

The linguistic corollary implies that if Simmias is large, and Largeness is an Idea, Simmias is other than Largeness, and partakes of Largeness, and is named large by reason of his participation. The theory of Ideas is primarily a theory of the structure of the world; but it is also, and importantly, a theory of meaning (cf. *Cratylus* 439a-440d). Thus at 147d-e, when we say that the others are different from Unity, and Unity different from the others, we say 'different' twice, but we always mean the nature of which it is the name; that is, we mean Difference. Similarly, when we name Simmias large, the meaning of 'large' is not Simmias, but Largeness. This, of course, is the Platonic response to Eleatic nominalism. It rests on the possibility of participation.

We must inquire, then, as to the structure of fact by virtue of which 'participation' may be asserted to obtain. How can sensibles be named after Ideas?

By Socrates' account in the *Parmenides*, though not in the *Phaedo*, Simmias probably, and this mud-pie certainly, exist apart from any and every Idea. This has a direct consequence. Let it be supposed that a given participant, Simmias, is the bearer of a set of immanent characters by reason of participation. Now Simmias, by reason of his existence apart from Ideas, must have a core of substantiality independent of Ideas. In what does that substantiality consist? It cannot consist in the collection of immanent characters in him, but in his own distinctive nature. He is both substance and substrate.

That Simmias is large implies the existence of two ontologically distinct things, Simmias and Largeness, as well as an ontologically dependent thing, the largeness in Simmias. We may ask now how Simmias and Largeness are related or connected. They cannot be the same. Nor can they merely be different; for although Simmias is substantially independent of and therefore different from Largeness, he would be different from Largeness even if he were not large. How then can two distinct things, Simmias and Largeness, be so related that Simmias is large?

Parmenides has suggested, and Socrates agreed, that Simmias has a share of Largeness, and is named large by reason of his sharing. This pushes the question back a stage. We are dealing with things that are not merely different, but intimately different, in that they are so related that one may be said to share in the other though it is not the same as the other (see 157e-158b). Given that we are dealing with two distinct things, how is sharing to be understood?

Socrates' answer to Parmenides' question of the extent of Ideas has committed him to a world order in which the relation of characters to things characterized must be construed as a relation obtaining between items substantially distinct in nature and reality, and further, a world order in which sensibles, or some of them, are substrates, bearers that exist separately from the properties derived from Ideas they bear. If participation is to be possible, that derivation must be explained.

II.iii. The Dilemma of Participation (131a-c)

Parmenides' first objection to the theory of Ideas is the Dilemma of Participation. It is not too much to say that this dilemma is fundamental to everything in the *Parmenides* that follows, and it is the only criticism that Plato will afterwards, in the *Philebus* (15b-c), repeat. The *Philebus* suggests that the dilemma is aporetic, a source of perplexity if the wrong admissions are made, and of easy passage, given the right ones. This statement is a reason to suppose that the Dilemma of Participation, and the criticisms of Ideas in the *Parmenides* that depend on it, are put neither as trivial fallacies nor fatal objections, but as problems to be solved.

The dilemma is in structure a reductio. If there is participation, there is participation either in the whole of an Idea or in part of it; there can be participation neither in the whole Idea nor in part of it; therefore, there is no participation. The reductio is important to Parmenides' later argument that since Ideas exist alone by themselves, they can have no connection with things in our world since they cannot be in them (133a-e), and are hence unknowable (134a-e). But though the dilemma is in structure a reductio, an implication derives from difference in the modality of its disjuncts: if there is participation neither in whole or part of an Idea, there is no participation; but if there is participation, it must be of part and cannot be of whole.

The major premise of the dilemma is a hypothetical disjunction. Instantiated, it is that if *a* participates in *F*, then either *a* participates in the whole of *F* or *a* participates in part of *F*. The transposition of this proposition is also stated: the claim that there can be no participation apart from these alternatives (131a 7) implies that if *a* participates neither in the whole of *F* nor in part of *F*, *a* does not participate in *F*. Protasis and apodosis are coimplicatory, since either disjunct of the apodosis implies the protasis.

The Dilemma is characteristically aporetic, as resting on two undefended and unanalyzed assumptions. The first is that participation is either of the whole or part of an Idea (131a 4-6). The second is that the whole or part of the Idea is then *in* the participant (131a 8-9, b 1, c 6). The first assumption answers to Socrates' claim that the things we see have a share of Ideas: if this is so, it is natural to inquire whether they have a share of the whole Idea or part of it; (131a 4-5). The genitive is the regular genitive with verbs of sharing, already used at 129a 2, 4, 6, 7, 8, b 2, 5, 6, c 8, d 1, 130e 5, 131a 1-2, cf. *Phaedo* 101c 3-4. The genitive of the share is to be distinguished from the accusative of the share taken; the latter requires a genitive of sharing, expressed or understood (Smyth, *Greek Grammar*, 2nd ed., para. 1343-1344). If you have a share, you have a share *of* something, and the question raised here is whether you, having a share of an Idea, have a share of part or the whole of it (cf. 131c 6). The shift in focus from what you have a share of to what is taken or received as a share is expressed in the second assumption, that the Idea, in whole or in part, will be *in* the participant, if the participant has a share of the Idea. The use of 'in' here is consistent with Aristotle's remark that the senses of 'in' correspond to the senses of 'have' (*Meta.* V 1023a 23-25), and may be taken to do duty for the accusative of the share taken. Compare "the likeness which we have" (130b 4, genitive of possession) and "the largeness in us" (*Phaedo* 102d 7, cf. 103b 5).

The second assumption may be read as closely connected with the first: if a thing has a share of an Idea, a share of the Idea is taken or received by the thing, and that share is in the thing that receives it. At the level of language, the difference between the two assumptions may be taken as a mere shift in perspective from active to passive.

First Disjunct: Participation in Whole Idea

Parmenides offers a proof of the falsity of the first disjunct. Instantiated, it is that if *a* and *b* participate in the whole of *F*, then the whole of *F* is in *a* and the whole of *F* is in *b*; that is, each receives the whole of *F* as its share (131a 8-9).

But if the whole of F is in a and the whole of F is in b, and if a and b are separate (χωρίς), then F will be separate from itself. Since the claim that a and b are separate minimally implies that they are not the same (131b, cf. 129d), the claim that F is separate from itself implies that F is not the same as F, which is absurd.

It will be observed that the first disjunct assumes multiple participation. No absurdity would follow if it were held that no Idea can have more than one participant, that is, that if a participates in the whole of F, there is no x such that x participates in F and x is not identical with a. This, of course, would be tantamount to denying the universality of Ideas. But given multiple participation, it must follow that if a participates in F, the whole of F is not in a, and thus that a does not participate in the whole of F. There are echoes of the requirement of multiple participation in Aristotle: see *Meta.* VII 1040a 22-27, 1038b 10-14. That Plato did not believe that *all* participation implies multiple participation is suggested by the argument for the uniqueness of the universe in *Timaeus* (31a-b). See *de Caelo* I 278a 17-21. Given that the disjunction of whole and part is both exclusive and exhaustive, this would imply that if a participates in F, a participates in part of F.

The argument may be compared with Aristotle's proof that a universal, being common to many things, cannot be the substance of that to which it is common (*Meta.* VII 1038b 7-14, cf. 16-33):

> The universal also is thought by some to be in the fullest sense a cause, and a principle; therefore let us attack the discussion at this point also. For it seems impossible that any universal term should be the name of a substance. For firstly the substance of each thing is that which is peculiar to it, which does not belong to anything else; but the universal is common, since that is called universal which is such as to belong to more than one thing. Of which individual then will this be the substance? Either of all or of one; but it cannot be the substance of all. And if it is to be the substance of one, this one will be the others also; for things whose substance is one and whose essence is one are themselves also one.

That is, if a universal were the substance of a and the substance of b, then a and b would be the same, whence it would follow that the universal is not common after all and thus not universal. This argument is an inverted image of Parmenides' argument here: if a and b are not identical, and if both partake of the whole of an Idea, then the Idea cannot be the same as itself. Aristotle found in this, the first disjunct of the Dilemma of Participation, succinct proof that no universal can exist apart (*Meta.* VII 1040b 25-28):

> That which is one cannot be in many places at the same time, but that which is common is present in many places at the same time; so that clearly no universal exists apart from its individuals.

Parmenides' argument was to become a structural basis for Aristotle's treatment of universality, and thereby of substance.

Second Disjunct: Participation in Parts of Ideas

Socrates attempts to evade the conclusion that the Idea will not be the same as itself with an analogy: the Idea would not be separate from itself if it were like one and the same day, which can be in many places at once and still not separate from itself (131b 3-6). Parmenides replies by altering the metaphor: "You might as well spread a sail over many men and then claim that one thing, as a whole, is over many" (131b 8-10). In fact, only part of the sail is over each man, and Parmenides thus leads the reluctant Socrates to agree to the alternate disjunct, already logically required by his previous admissions: if *a* and *b* participate in *F*, part of *F* is in *a* and part of *F* is in *b* (131c 5-7). This must be understood to mean that each thing that participates in an Idea has *its own* part of the Idea, since if the part of *F* in *a* were identical with the part of *F* in *b*, the argument of the first disjunct would apply (cf. 131c 6-7). Thus it is that at 142b-c, Unity, if it partakes of Being, partakes of *its own* being, whence it is inferred that its own being is part of it, though also a part of Being.

If each participant must have its own part of the Idea, that part is unique to the participant that has it. It is but a short step to infer that that part cannot exist separately from its participant, that it depends for its existence on what it is in (cf. *Meta.* VII 1031b 15-18); for it can be *this* part, as distinct from other parts, only by reason of its connections with *this* participant rather than other participants. Given that Ideas are wholes composed of parts depending for their existence on participants, this implies the ontological priority of participants to Ideas, and denies the ontological priority of Ideas to participants. Applied to sensibles, this collapses the distinction between Ideas and phenomena Socrates had earlier drawn at 129c-130a, and contradicts the ontological priority of Ideas implied by Parmenides in his own summary of the theory of Ideas at 130e-131a. Indeed, the core of Aristotle's doctrine of the priority of primary substance both to secondary substance and to items in categories other than substance (*Categories* 3a 7 ff.) is latent in the second disjunct.

The Day and the Sail

Socrates' analogy of the Day has often been praised for its spirituality: it shows the immaterial nature of Ideas. In fact, it is a mere blunder in argument. Parmenides has offered a deductive proof of inconsistency in the proposition that participation is participation in Ideas as wholes. Socrates attempts to evade the conclusion with an analogy. But clearly, if the analogy is consistent, it is not analogous; and if it is inconsistent, it is not a reply. To overthrow an argument of the sort that Parmenides here offers, it is necessary either to establish invalidity, or falsity, of some premise. Socrates does neither. His appeal to the Day is not an answer, but an evasion.

It is also an absurd evasion. Assume that Day (ἡμέρα) means, not the light of day, but a period of time. Then Socrates has suggested that a period of time may be one and the same and yet in many places at once. If 'at once' (ἅμα, *simul*) is given its normal temporal sense, this implies that a period of time can be in many places at the same time. Since a time cannot be in a place at a time, this is absurd. Aristotle, in what may be an echo of this passage, gives a spatial sense: "Things are said to be together (ἅμα) in place when they are in one place (in the strictest sense of the word 'place') and to be apart (χωρίς) when they are in different places" (*Phys.* V 226b 21-23). But the suggestion that a period of time may be in many places in one place hardly helps the argument. And as Proclus points out, the day as a period of time is divisible, since noon differs from place to place.

'Day' must mean the light of day, as opposed to night, and Parmenides so treats it. As Plato must have intended, Socrates' metaphor calls to mind the *Republic*, and the great image there given for the Good and the intelligibility it produces: the Sun, and the light it sheds. But the Idea is now likened, not to the Sun, the source and cause of light, but to the light itself, and nothing could better illustrate the inexperience of the young Socrates. Had he compared the Idea to the source of the Day, to the one cause that exists apart, his metaphor might have served to illumine that connection of Ideas and participants he has now been called on to explain. Instead, he compares the Idea to what is, in the *Republic*, product of the Idea, and in so doing, implicitly abandons the claim he means to defend. Light, for the Greeks as for us, is physical; one and the same light cannot as a whole be in many places at once. By this metaphor, then, things do not participate in the whole Idea, and when Parmenides suggests another metaphor, the Sail, it is not to change the force of Socrates' own metaphor, but only to make it more explicit. For the Day is like the Sail, one thing spread over many part by part.

Parmenides has often been accused of sophistry in making this transition: days are delicate and immaterial, whereas sails are gross and physical. In fact, Parmenides acts as a good teacher, skilled in argument and wise in the ways of words. The logic of his metaphor serves to make that of Socrates' more precise, but also precisely matches the logic of the argument. 'Day' cannot without absurdity mean a period of time; but even if it could, and even if time itself did not depend on the physical motion of the heavens, the logical issue would remain. Socrates has accepted an exclusive disjunction; either the whole Idea is in many things, or part is in each thing. He has been met with an argument to show that the first disjunct is absurd. If he cannot refute that argument, he is logically committed to the second disjunct, and as it happens, the Sail is an admirable analogue of that disjunct: participation is participation in parts. Socrates' appeal to the Day exhibits, not the immateriality of Ideas, but his own need for further training in dialectic (see 127c, 130e, 133b, 135a-b, c-d). Parmenides in leading him from the Day to the Sail, has thereby led him to face the consequences of his own admissions.

Those consequences are uncomfortable. For Socrates is not willing to say that Ideas can be divided into parts, and still be one.

The Hinge

Socrates rejects both disjuncts of the Dilemma of Participation; but the modality of those disjuncts is very different. The first disjunct, given plurality of participants, involves logical absurdity; the Idea is not the same as itself, and this applies universally, to every Idea. The second disjunct, whether true or, as Socrates believes, false, does not involve logical absurdity, at least so far as anything in the argument has shown. However odd it may be to construe the relation of Ideas to participants in terms of the relation of part and whole, it is not thereby logically absurd, and Socrates' own use of the language of sharing or participating makes it a natural assumption.

The Dilemma of Participation, therefore, though a reductio, issues in an implication by reason of the difference in modality of its disjuncts: if there is participation neither of whole nor part of an Idea, there is no participation; but if there is participation, it cannot be of whole but must be of part of an Idea. This difference in modality is explicitly marked at 144d 2, and at *Philebus* 15b 6-7, where the Dilemma is restated. The hinge effect of the Dilemma—no participation, or participation in parts—is important for arguments that follow.

Taken as a reductio, the Dilemma functions not as a hinge but as a wedge, splitting the propositions that (1) certain Ideas exist, and (2) that other things participate in those Ideas. If there is no participation, (2) is false even if (1) is true. And given a wedge between (1) and (2), there is also a wedge between (1) and (3), that participants are named after Ideas; for the ground for naming things after Ideas is precisely that they participate in them. Thus it is that (1) is assumed and (2) and (3) are denied in the argument that Ideas are unknowable (133a-134e). The assumption that Ideas exist, but that they are not in us or in things in our world is equivalent, so far as the sensible world is concerned, to the denial of participation (131a-b); it implies that things in our world, though they have the same name as Ideas, are named for themselves and not for Ideas, which have no power or significance for things in our world. The Dilemma of Participation, then, if construed as a valid reductio, does not of itself show that (1) is false. It shows that, even if (1) is true, (2) and (3) are false.

But the Dilemma, due to difference in the modality of its disjuncts, may be construed not only as a reductio but as an implication: the Dilemma is a Hinge. The implication is used in Deduction 2 of Hypothesis I, which assumes that Unity participates in Being (142b). Given participation, it follows that Unity, even conceived apart from its own being, must have parts; for whatever is is one, and Being has infinitely many parts, since the numbers are and are unlimited in multitude; because Unity must be present to every part of Being, and one thing cannot be in many places at once as a whole, it follows that Unity is divisible, and has many parts (144c-d).

One over Many

Parmenides has offered the Sail as a device for explicating the claim that the Idea is a 'One over Many' (131b 9), and Socrates will shortly be led to agree that his reason for thinking that Largeness is one is that something is the same over all large things (132a 2-4). Aristotle refers to the 'one over Many' argument in a way that suggests it is so well known it does not need stating, and objects to it on the ground that it implies Ideas even of negations. Alexander of Aphrodisias explains (*In Metaph.* 80.8 - 80.15, on *Meta.* I 990b 13. Cf. 990b 7, 991a 2, 1040b 29. Alexander also offers a second version, from the meaningfulness of negative predication, 81.10 - 81.18. Cf. *Cratylus* 439b-c, *Sophist* 218b-c. Hayduck's L offers a variant to the same effect. See further *ACPA* 228-229.):

> They also use the following argument to establish the existence of Ideas. If each of the many men is a man, and each of the many animals an animal, and so too in all other cases, and these are not instances of a thing being predicated of itself, but there is something predicated of all men, etc., but identical with none of them, there must be something belonging to all of them which is separate from the particular things and eternal; for in every case it is predicated alike of all the numerically different examples. But that which is one over many, separated and eternal, is an Idea; therefore there are Ideas.

If we substitute the notion of participation for that of predication and ignore the question of extent, this is faithful to the account of the *Parmenides*. But given that there is participation at all, the Hinge implies that only part of each Idea is in each participant. As we have seen, this notion requires that each participant must have its own part of the Idea, since if any two participants shared one part, the argument of the first disjunct would immediately apply. The diversity of parts, therefore, is as great as the diversity of participants, and parts no more than wholes can be one thing over many. Given that parts must be part of a whole (137c), it follows that Ideas can be universal only in the sense that they are one whole of parts, which parts are distributed to the many participants. Thus at 144b, Being is distributed to all of the many things that are, and is divided up among things of every sort, and has parts without limit, since there are numbers without limit and the numbers are. In respect to Ideas as divisible wholes, the appropriate analogy is, of course, the Sail.

To turn the Hinge in either direction is to exclude the universality of Ideas; for either Ideas cannot be participated in, or they can be participated in only part by part. No Idea is in the strict sense One over Many; for either it is not over many, or it is not one. It is not over many if there is no participation; it is not one if each participant partakes of a different part of it. The unity of an Idea can therefore be only the unity of a whole of parts, if it is participated in.

Presence

In Greek as in English, one way of saying that Simmias is large is to say that there is largeness in Simmias. Another way of saying the same thing — highfalutin', perhaps, but not technical — is to say that he has a share of largeness (see, for example, *Protagoras* 323c 1, and H. C. Baldry, *CQ* xxxi (1937): 145-146). But this, without more, would hardly imply absurdity of the first disjunct of the Dilemma, and it is often suggested that Parmenides is here taking these locutions, which are metaphorical, in the most literal and material sense. He is assuming that the Form is in the thing as the Jack is in the box. Getting a share of an Idea is like getting a share of a pie, and the absurdity involved in getting a share of a whole Idea is like the absurdity of many people getting a share of a whole pie. One and the same pie cannot be in many at once.

On this view, then, Parmenides gives a materialist interpretation to terms, which, when applied to the relation of participants to Ideas, must be understood in an immaterial way. The argument confuses a physical relation with a metaphysical (or logical) relation, as the analogy of the Sail clearly shows. Socrates, had he known what he was about, would have said that participation is a unique and indefinable relation, but one quite compatible with participation in the whole of an Idea. Once that is admitted, the first disjunct of the Dilemma stands, and the Hinge collapses. As it is, the Dilemma rests on nothing more than abuse of a metaphor, or if you will, a pun.

This is a widely accepted view, and given the aporetic character of Parmenides' objections, it is not false: perplexities may be read at many levels. But is is reasonable to expect that an objection on which so much that follows in the *Parmenides* depends, and which the *Philebus* (15b-c) explicitly restates as serious, and which Aristotle most certainly took seriously, has a foundation that is more than verbal. This conclusion is confirmed by dialectical structure. If this simple reading went to the root of the matter, we should expect Socrates to offer the obvious reply. He has already distinguished between the things we see and what we apprehend by reflection (130a); physical objects fall on one side of that division, and Ideas on the other, and nothing can prevent restatement of that distinction here. To portray Socrates as at a loss for an answer to the Dilemma is to imply that the Dilemma does not turn on confusing a distinction he has himself already drawn.

The notion that participation is a unique and indefinable relation is conveniently *ad hoc*. It offers a verbal solution that neatly avoids the issue of how distinct things can be so related that one may be said to characterize the other. The conviction that characteristics are somehow immanent in the things that have them, tied as it is to the conviction that this our world of sensibles is primarily real, is an enduring element in the history of metaphysical reflection. It is as old as Aristotle and Anaxagoras, and as an unconscious assumption it is as old as mankind; no one questioned it before Plato and the historical Parmenides, and very few people have questioned it since. Yet it presents a problem. If characters are to be in sensibles, and sensibles in place or space, how is it that characters are not in place or space? And if they are, how can they be universal, any more than sensibles are universal? If they are not, how can they be said to be in sensibles after all?

The Dilemma of Participation presents this issue directly, and it was with the

Dilemma in mind that Aristotle in the *Categories* formulated his own account of predication (*Categories,* cc. i-v; for further discussion, see *Phronesis* XIV (1969), 37-38). The Dilemma led Aristotle to distinguish what is said of a subject, its genus or species, from what is in a subject as incapable of existing apart from it, such as its color or its place, and to maintain that what is in a subject may be individual or indivisible and one in number, whereas what is said of a subject, as universal, can be neither. Thus, what is in a subject is not universal if the subject is individual, and what is said of a subject is neither one nor many in number —no question now of the one Idea or Form being divisible. Aristotle further made place a category, the individual instances of which depend for their existence on the substance they are in, so that substance *qua* substance is not located, because it is the ontological condition for the existence of locations (cf. *Phys.* IV 210b 24-26). Those who think the Dilemma of Participation, in its physical or locative reading, trivial may be asked to inspect the shifts to which Aristotle was put to solve it.

Part and Whole

The example of Aristotle is in fact diagnostic of deeper perplexity. The root ontological assumption of the *Categories* is that sensibles—Simmias, or these given sticks and stones—have an independent and substantial existence. This is precisely the assumption Socrates has made in the *Parmenides*, in discussing the extent of Ideas. But Socrates has also assumed that Ideas as well as sensibles are capable of independent and substantial existence: they exist apart. This introduces further complexity in aporetic structure.

Suppose that, if Simmias is large, that fact implies the existence of two ontologically distinct things, Simmias and Largeness. Then, if Simmias is large, this also implies that those two things are somehow related or connected. They cannot be the same: to say that Simmias is large is not like saying that Simmias is Simmias. They cannot merely be different: for although Simmias is different from Largeness, he would be different from Largeness even if he were not large. How then can two distinct things, Simmias and Largeness, be so related that Simmias is large?

This question, it may be observed, is not restricted to the relation of sensibles to Ideas. It arises if Justice and Unity are distinct Ideas, and Justice is one; or if Justice and Likeness are distinct Ideas, and Justice is like Temperance.

The answer Socrates has given to this question is that Simmias has a share of Largeness, and is named large by reason of his participation. This pushes the question back a stage. We are dealing with things that are not merely different, but intimately different, related in such a way that one may be said to have a share of the other though it cannot be said to be the same as the other (see 157e-158b). Given that we are dealing with two distinct things, how is sharing to be understood?

The answer assumed by the *Parmenides* is direct. At 146b, it is stated with

Eleatic generality that everything is related to everything else in one of the following ways: either it is the same, or different, or if it is neither the same nor different, then it is related either as part to whole or whole to part. That is, given any two things, *a* and *b*, either *a* is the same as *b* or *a* is different from *b*, or if *a* is neither the same as nor different from *b*, then *a* is part of *b* or *b* is part of *a*. Given that participation—sharing—is not a simple relation of sameness or difference,[55] this proposition reduces sharing—participation—to the relation of part and whole. If this mudpie is large, then either the mudpie is part of Largeness or Largness is part of the mudpie. Since by Socrates' account the mudpie has a share of Largeness but Largeness does not have a share of the mudpie, it remains only to inquire whether the mudpie has a share of the whole of Largeness or part of Largeness. If then sharing is to be understood in terms of part and whole—the mudpie is not the same as Largeness nor, since it is large, simply different—this reduces to the question of whether the whole of Largeness or part of Largeness is *in* the mudpie, and 'in' here must mean in as part of. So it is that at 142b-c, Unity, since it has a share of Being, has being as a part of itself.

This reduction follows, not from the mere language of sharing, but from analysis of the corresponding fact. We are given distinct things that are so related that one is of the same sort as the other though it is not the same as the other. They are, that is, not the same, and not different, but distantly the same, or intimately different. What relation, then, will satisfy the requirement of intimate difference? That relation must be, if you will, a real or proper relation; for it obtains between ontologically distinct things.

An obvious example of such a relation is the relation of part and whole. As Aristotle remarks (*Phys.* IV 210a 28-30, b 1-2; cf. VI 240a 19-25, IV 210a 15):

> A thing is described in terms of its parts, as well as in terms of the thing as a whole, e.g., a man is said to be white because the visible surface of him is white, or to be scientific because his thinking faculty has been trained. . . . It is from these, which are 'parts' (in the sense at least of being 'in' the man), that the man is called white.

The *Parmenides* offers no proof that the part/whole relation is the only possible candidate for explaining the fact of intimate difference in the ontologically distinct. Indeed, another such relation, that of resemblance, is later suggested and shown to be inadequate. But failure to explain participation in terms of the part/whole relation will raise the question of whether participation can be understood as a relation between independent existents.

Part, Whole, and Hinge

The Dilemma of Participation assumes that the relation of participant to Ideas is to be construed in terms of the relation of whole and part. Given that the part/whole relation may be understood in terms of mixture, this is indirectly attested by Aristotle (*Meta.* I 991a 8-19 = XIII 1079b 12-23, with Alexander, *in Metaph.* 97.27-98.24), and it is basic to the Hypotheses that conclude the *Parmenides*. I.1. proves that if Unity is not a whole of parts, no characteristic belongs to it (137 c-d, cf. 159c-d). I.2. proves that if even one characteristic belongs to it—the bare characteristic of being—Unity is a whole of parts (142b-d), and goes on to derive precisely the characteristics denied of it in I.1. The propositions that if Unity is not a whole of parts no characteristic belongs to it, and that if a character belongs to it it is a whole of parts, are transpositionally equivalent, and assume that the assertion of a characteristic of a subject is to be understood in terms of the relation of part and whole. The generality of this result is implied by Parmenides' treatment of the Others, that is, things other than Unity. II.1. argues that if the others are not Unity but have a share of Unity, they must have parts; if they did not, they would be *just* one (157b-c). II.2. argues that if Unity is separate (χωρίς) from the others and has no parts, the others cannot have a share of Unity, since they can have a share neither of part nor the whole of it, and thus the others can be neither one nor many, whole nor parts (159b-d).

This structure, it will be observed, assumes not only that if *a* participates in *F*, it participates either in the whole of *F* or part of *F*; it further assumes that if *a* participates in *F*, *F* in whole or in part is in *a*. That is, Ideas are parts of the participants that partake of them. This assumption grounds the impossibility of the first disjunct of the Dilemma. If two participants, *a* and *b*, each have the whole of *F* in them as part of them, then, since parts are parts of a whole, this implies that two distinct wholes, *Wa* and *Wb*, may be so related as to have a common part, *p*. But surely, if two distinct wholes have a common part, they are not distinct wholes: If *Wap* and *Wbp*, then *Wabp*, through common part *p*. If one Idea is common to many things by reason of their participation in it, then either it is separate from itself, or its participants, contrary to hypothesis (131b 1) are not separate from each other, in that they are parts of the same whole. The problem becomes the more obvious if we consider common participation in Unity and Plurality, or in another Idea yet to be mentioned, Being (136b). If the unity of *a* is the same as the unity of *b*; if the plurality of *a* is the same as the plurality of *b*; if the being of *a* is the same as the being of *b*; then *a* and *b* are the same. This is a precise anticipation of Aristotle's proof that a universal cannot be the substance of that to which it is common. We are thus led to the second disjunct of the Dilemma: participation is participation in parts of Ideas, and it is parts of Ideas that are parts of participants. The pivot of the Hinge has been forged.

Univocity and Divisibility

The Hinge bears directly on the linguistic corollary of the theory of Ideas, that things are named after Ideas by reason of their participation in them. This implies that the ground or reason for applying the same name to different things is that they partake of the same Idea. But the Hinge introduces unlooked-for complexity: participation is participation in parts of Ideas, and those parts are not common to a plurality of participants. The Idea, as Parmenides remarks (131b 9) is one over many as a sail is one over many. It is this sort of unity, and only this sort, that Socrates is entitled, in view of the second disjunct, to ascribe to Ideas (cf. 131c 9-10).

The consequence is that if Simmias and Phaedo are both large, the name 'large' is not applied to them on the same ground; for the largeness in Simmias is not the same as the largeness in Phaedo. If we are to deny that the name 'large' applies to them equivocally, we must do so on the ground that the largeness in Simmias and the largeness in Phaedo are both parts of the same whole, Largeness. So things are named after Ideas, not by reason of their participation in them, but by reason of their participation in parts of them. It follows that the meaning of an expression must be distinguished from the foundation in things by which it applies. In a similar way, Aristotle, in *Metaphysics* VII distinguishes the universal, which is predicated, from substantial form, which makes predication possible and is not predicated. If it were denied that sameness of meaning may be accompanied by difference in ground, it would follow from the second disjunct that all assertion is inherently and radically equivocal: Vortex reigns.

The Locative Reading

Analysis of participation in terms of wholes and parts provides a foundation for a locative reading of the Dilemma of Participation which rests on something more substantial than a metaphor. Given that participants, "sticks and stones and such things as that" (129d) are in place or space, and that Ideas are in them as part of them,[56] it is but a short step to infer that Ideas are in place or space (cf. 149e-150b). A thing cannot be *in* something that does not contain it (138a), and as Aristotle remarks, in the strictest sense of all a thing is 'in' a vessel or more generally 'in' a place (*Phys.* IV 210a 24). If Simmias is located in place, and Largeness in whole or in part is part of Simmias, there is added reason to suppose that Largeness is located in place or space. For Largeness either is or has parts that are part of a located whole. The Dilemma of Participation then follows in stated terms, and with it comes the Hinge. If the whole Idea were part of each thing as a located part of a located whole, the Idea would be separate from itself, not merely on the abstractly logical ground of nonidentity, but on the more intuitively obvious ground that the same thing cannot be located in two places at once (πολλαχοῦ ἅμα, 131b 4, 7, cf. 144d 1; see also 148e 149a, and 146c 4-6). If there is multiple participation in Ideas, Ideas must be wholes of parts, and part of each Idea is in each participant.

The Dilemma Applied to Ideas

If the Dilemma of Participation is applied to the relation of sensibles to Ideas, it admits a locative reading; and if the Dilemma is construed in terms of sensible participants as wholes that contain Ideas as parts, the locative reading is strengthened. But is is important to see that the Dilemma is stated quite generally. The context in which it is put makes it natural, and indeed inevitable, to apply it to sensibles. But nothing in its logical structure binds it to sensibles, and it is so stated as to apply to any relation of participation. If Ideas participate in other Ideas, the Dilemma applies to the relation of Ideas among themselves. If Justice and Temperance participate in Unity, the question arises whether the whole of Unity is in Justice, or only part. Thus at 142c, Unity is said to participate in Being; at 144c-d, Being is said to have parts without limit, since there are numbers without limit, and Unity is present to all the parts of Being as divided.

Aristotle supposed that the Dilemma applied to the relation of Ideas among themselves, in respect of species and genera (*Meta*. VII c. 14):

> It is clear from these very facts what consequence confronts those who say the Ideas are substances capable of separate existence, and at the same time make the Form consist of genus and differentiae. For if the Forms exist and 'animal' is present in 'man' and 'horse' it is either one and the same in number, or different. . . . Now (1) if the 'animal' in 'the horse' and in 'man' is one and the same, as you are with yourself, how will the one in things that exist apart be one, and how will this 'animal' escape being divided even from itself? . . . But (2) suppose the Form to be different in each species. Then there will be practically an infinite number of things whose *substance* is 'animal'; for it is not by accident that 'man' has 'animal' for one of its elements. Further, many things will be 'animal-itself.' For the 'animal' in each species will be the substance of the species; for it is after nothing else that the species is called; if it were, that other would be an element in 'man', i.e. would be the genus of man. . . . Further, (3) in the case of sensible things both these consequences and others still more absurd follow.

If Animal is in Man and Horse, it is in them either as one and the same, or as different. If one and the same, while yet existing apart, as separate and individual, how does Animal escape being divided from itself? If different in each of its species, there will be many things of which Animal is substance, and many things will be Animal-itself. This and other difficulties apply, not only to the relation of Ideas among themselves, but to the relation of Ideas to sensibles. That is, Aristotle supposes that, for Plato, Animal must be a constituent element, not only of Man and Horse, but perhaps also of individual men and horses.

The problem is the problem of the unity of definition: how can one thing, a species, be two things, a genus and a difference? (See *Meta*. V 1015b 16-1017a 6, VII 1037b 8ff., 1040a 7 ff., *PEF* 89-90.) But the issue in general. It is as broad as participation, and arises quite independently of sensibles, or of the genus/species relation. It arises, for example, if Unity participates in Being.

The Materialization of Ideas

To suggest that parts of Ideas are parts of sensible objects, located in them and incapable of existing apart from them, is to suggest that parts of Ideas are themselves material, as located in sensibles, which are themselves located both in place and time. That Ideas are wholes having material parts, and that a whole is that from which no part is absent, suggests that Ideas are themselves material.

This supposition is important to the Hypotheses. I.2. assumes that Unity is an extensive magnitude, a conclusion drawn directly from the fact that it is a whole of parts. More precisely, it is assumed without argument that any whole of parts must have beginning, middle, and end, and therefore shape (145a-b). In Deduction 1 of Hypothesis I, on the other hand, the denial of shape follows immediately on denial of beginning, middle, and end, which in turn follows on the denial that Unity is a whole of parts. So being a whole of parts and having shape are taken as equivalent.

This materialist assumption runs throughout the Hypotheses. Thus it is straightforwardly assumed that to be is to be *somewhere* (145e, 151a), and that to be is to be *in time* (141e, 131e). Aristotle was later to suggest that Plato's Ideas are eternal sensibles (*Meta*. III 997b 5-12, cf. VII 1040b 30-34, X 1059a 10-14), and to assimilate Plato's claim that the mode of being of the Ideas is timeless and eternal to the claim that Ideas have endless duration in time (*E.N.* I 1096b 1-5). He also maintained that if the participant is in place, the Ideas must be in place (*Phys*. IV 109b 33-35). The connection between Aristotle's account of Plato's doctrines and the *Parmenides* is prettily brought out in the *Topics* (II 113a 24-32; see also Alexander, *in Topicorum* 188.10-19):

> Or again, look and see if anything has been said about something, of such a kind that if it be true, contrary predicates must necessarily belong to the same thing: e.g. if he has said that the 'Ideas' exist in us. For then the result will be that they are both in motion and at rest, and moreover that they are objects both of sensation and of thought. For according to the views of those who posit the existence of Ideas, those Ideas are at rest and are objects of thought; while if they exist in us, it is impossible that they should be unmoved: for when we move, it follows necessarily that all that is in us moves with us as well. Clearly also they are objects of sensation, if they exist in us: for it is through the sensation of sight that we recognize the Form present in each individual.

If the Ideas are in us, they must be objects both of sensation and of thought, both in motion and at rest, "for when we move, it follows necessarily that all that is in us moves with us as well." In similar vein, Deduction 2 of Hypothesis I assumes that Unity partakes of Being, and infers that Unity is both in motion and at rest (145e-146a), and that it is an object both of knowledge and perception (155d). This inference depends on the materialization of Ideas suggested by the Dilemma of Participation.

Plato's own doctrine was otherwise. The *Timaeus* (52a-c) maintains that what truly is cannot be in space: it pertains to an image, and only to an image, to be in something other than itself. An Idea neither receives anything into itself from elsewhere, nor itself enters into anything anywhere. (See also *Symposium* 211a, and compare the distinction between characters in us and in nature, *Phaedo* 102d, 103b.) Ideas and space cannot be in each other, though images of the eternal Ideas are in the eternal receptacle (see Shorey, *AJP* X (1889), 68); therefore what truly is cannot be somewhere. Again, what truly is cannot be in time (37d-38c), any more than it can be in motion: Ideas are eternal, not as having endless duration in time, but as things divorced from time and separate from all that changes and is sensible and composite. (See, for example, *Timaeus* 37c, 38a-c, 52a.) The denial that Ideas are in space and time, that they are somewhere or somewhen, or for that matter everywhere and everywhen, is a consequence of their separation, of the fact that they are ontologically prior to phenomena in that their existence is a condition for the becoming of their sensible likenesses in space. (See for example, *Timaeus* 51b-c, 52a-c, *Symposium* 210e-211a.)

But the Dilemma of Participation, taken as a *reductio*, has forced separation to the denial of participation; taken as an implication, it has forced participation in parts of Ideas, with the corollary that those parts are dependent for their existence on the participant they are in. The Dilemma is Janus-faced, guardian of a door that swings outward to a transcendence of the irrelevant, and inward to an immanence of the indistinct.

So the Dilemma of Participation, if the wrong admissions are made, issues in perplexities, perplexities that either collapse the distinction between the ideal and the sensible world or destroy their connection. Both the *Philebus* (15b-c) and the *Parmenides* (135a-c) suggest that those perplexities can be resolved; they do not suggest that resolution will be easy. There is an echo of this notion in the *Timaeus*. We are dreamers who mistake images in space for realities, and, "Because of this dreaming state, we prove unable to rouse ourselves and to draw all these distinctions and others akin to them, even in the case of the waking and truly existent nature, and so to state the truth" (*Timaeus* 52b-c, trans. Cornford). The dreamer mistakes images for reality. It is worth recalling that the young Socrates of the *Parmenides* has already assumed that sensibles have independent and substantial reality; they exist apart from Ideas, in a way no image can. Aristotle was afterwards to make the same assumption, and it is not by accident that his criticisms of Ideas swing like a gate between the claim that Ideas, being separate, are unknowable and irrelevant to the sensible world, and the claim that they are themselves in sensibles and a kind of sensible. The gate turns on the Hinge of the Dilemma of Participation. Aristotle, assuming the independent and primary reality of the sensible world, found that, unless the theory of separate Ideas was abandoned, the perplexity could not be resolved. The alternate resolution, of course, is to deny the independent reality of sensibles. As Aristotle put it, with remarkable accuracy (*Meta.* VII 1031b 15-18):

> At the same time it is clear that if there are Ideas such as some people say there are, it will not be substratum which is substance; for there must be substances, but not predicable of a substratum; for if they were they would exist only by being participated in.

II.iv. The Paradox of Divisibility (131c-e)

The Paradox of Divisibility is a function of the Hinge. It is impossible that things should participate in the whole of an Idea: the Idea would then be separate from itself. No such impossibility has been adduced for the claim that things participate in parts of Ideas, and Parmenides now proceeds to offer a subordinate proof to show that for certain specified Ideas, participation in parts implies unacceptable consequences.

The three Ideas here considered, namely Largeness, Smallness, and Equality, figure prominently in the *Phaedo* (Equality at 74a ff., Largeness and Smallness at 100e ff.), and are related in a complex way. Largeness and Smallness are opposites; but together, as the argument shows, they constitute the conditions of the Unequal, the opposite of Equality (see below, 140b-d, 149d ff., and *Meta.* X 1055b 30 ff).

The Paradox of Divisibility follows from the second disjunct of the Dilemma of Participation, applied to these specific Ideas. If *a* is large, it will be large by a part of Largeness smaller than Largeness itself; this is ἄλογον, absurd or irrational. Again, if *a* is equal to something, it will be equal by a part of Equality smaller than Equality itself. If *a* is small, it will be small by a part of Smallness smaller than Smallness itself, whence it will follow that Smallness is larger than its part, and further that, in apparent violation of mathematics, a thing to which a part of Smallness is added will become smaller by reason of addition.

The argument assumes that if *a* is *f*, it is *f* by or in virtue of (instrumental dative) a part of F-ness. This assumption answers, with appropriate revisions, to the assumption found in earlier dialogues that if *a* is *f*, it is *f* by or in virtue of F-ness, that if, for example, Simmias is large, he is large by or in virtue of Largeness. Parmenides has altered this claim according to the requirements of his argument. Since *a* participates, not in the whole of F-ness but in a part of it, it is *f* by or in virtue of a part of F-ness rather than the whole of it.

Cornford remarked of the Paradox that it "assumes that the instance of Largeness which falls to the share of a large thing is a 'part' of the Form in the sense of a bit into which the Form is cut up and which is consequently smaller than the Form Largeness. This is to understand 'part' and 'whole' in the most gross and material sense" (*PP* 85).

This account is not mistaken; if participation is construed as a relation between distinct individuals, it lends itself to analysis in terms of wholes and parts, and given that participants are located, Ideas may be located as parts of located wholes. But if the account is not mistaken, it is also not necessary. The Paradox may be construed formally, without direct reference to materialism, given the axiom that the whole is greater than its part, an axiom of Greek mathematics,[57] and one which is not restricted to physical applications.[58] Since the assumption on which the Paradox rests is that things partake of parts of Ideas, and since a part is part of a whole (137c), the Idea is a whole, and by axiom greater than its part.

Because things participate, not in the whole of an Idea but part of it, things have their character by or in virtue of part of the Idea rather than the whole of it. If *a* is large, it will be large by a part of Largeness smaller than Largeness itself, and will therefore be large by what is small; and since Largeness is larger than any part of itself, Largeness is large.[59] If *a* is equal to something, it will be equal by a part of Equality smaller than Equality itself, and will therefore be equal by what is small. If *a* is small, it will be small by a part of Smallness smaller than Smallness itself, and therefore Smallness is large. The Paradox thus implies that Smallness is large and Equality unequal and the largeness in things small, in contradiction to Socrates' confident claim that Ideas cannot be qualified by their own opposite (129be), and in contradiction of the *Phaedo's* claim that neither Largeness itself nor the largeness in us can admit its own opposite (*Phaedo* 102d-e, 103b, cf. *Parmenides* 129b - 130a). So the Paradox of Divisibility issues in a result that the theory of Ideas was supposed to prevent.

The Absurdity

In the *Phaedo* (96e-97a), Socrates explains that he had once supposed that one man may be taller than another by a head; that ten was greater than eight by two; that a two-cubit rule was larger than a one-cubit rule by half. That is, he supposed that things may be greater by what is smaller. Similarly, people claim that the addition of two units and the division of one unit both account for two. That is, they think the same result may be obtained by opposite operations. These puzzles are closely similar to the puzzles concerning size and number in the *Theaetetus* (154c-155d), and are solved in the *Phaedo* by introducing the theory of Ideas. One man is not larger than another by a head, which is small, but by reason of Largeness; it would be a portent if something were large by what is small (101b). So too for the relation of ten and eight, and of the two-cubit and one-cubit rule. Again, things do not become two by addition or division, but by reason of participating in Two.

This pattern of reasoning is made general in the Hypotheses that follow in the *Parmenides*. If Unity and Being are different, they must be different, not by virtue of themselves, but by virtue of Difference (cf. 139b-c, 143b, 146e-147a, 147c-148c). If Unity is larger or smaller than the others, that is, than things other than Unity, it is so, not by virtue of its own nature or the nature of the others, but because it has Largeness or Smallness in it (149e).

The portent which in the *Phaedo* Socrates claims to find in the notion that something could be large by what is small is matched by the portent he claims to find in the *Parmenides* in the notion that Likeness can be unlike, or that in general any opposite can be qualified by its opposite (129b-e). It is also matched by the results of the Paradox of Divisibility. It is argued below (150a-b) that Smallness cannot be in Unity, on the ground that if it were, it would either be equal in extent to Unity or a part of Unity, or contain Unity or a part of Unity; in either case, Smallness would be equal to something or larger than something, and thus "do the work of" or "act the part of" Largeness or Equality, and not its own. This result is treated as a manifest impossibility: a participant cannot gain a character by reason of something that has the character opposite to the character it gains.

The impossibility derives from qualification by opposites. Assume that if Smallness is large, then Smallness does the work of Largeness. Then if whatever is small partakes of Smallness, whatever is small is large. Thus, if a is smaller than b by virtue of Smallness, a is larger than b by virtue of Smallness. Since a must in fact be larger than b by virtue of Largeness, this implies that Smallness is Largeness, or, since Smallness does not do its own work, that Smallness is not Smallness. The alternative is to deny that anything participates in Smallness, and that denial issues at 150b.

This result cannot be avoided by arguing that since participation must be analyzed in terms of the part/whole relation, a is not smaller than b by Smallness, which is large, but by a part of Smallness, which is small. For the difficulty then transposes into a difficulty concerning Largeness, the parts of which are small (cf. 150c).

Generalization

The Paradox of Divisibility, though it turns on qualification by opposites, cannot be generalized to all Ideas of opposites. From the fact that Beauty or Justice is a whole of parts because of multiple participation, it does not follow that Beauty is ugly or Justice unjust, but only that Beauty and Justice are larger than their parts and therefore large. The Paradox does not, therefore, establish as a universal conclusion that there can be no participation in parts of Forms. It shows rather that participation in parts of Ideas implies absurdity in the special case of Largeness, Smallness, and Equality.

Yet the conclusion of the Paradox suggests considerable generality: Parmenides asks, "How will the others get a share of Ideas, if they can get a share neither part by part nor whole by whole?" And Socrates grants that the thing seems difficult to determine. The implication of the question is that both disjuncts of the Dilemma of Participation are false, and more especially that the second disjunct has been shown to be false by the Paradox of Divisibility. That Paradox, then, stands as a reason for supposing that Ideas cannot be divided and still be one, and more generally, that participation cannot be participation in parts of Ideas. The Dilemma is then a reductio.

The basis for such an inference is clear. If participation is analyzed in terms of the part/whole relation, every Idea participated in is a whole and has parts. Every idea is therefore qualified by Largeness as a whole, and by Smallness with respect to its parts. Largeness and Smallness therefore become terms of unrestricted generality. If participation in them implies absurdity, there is good reason to suppose that that absurdity extends to every Idea that is participated in, and that therefore participates in them.

Homoeomereity and Mixture

If Ideas are participated in and have parts, it is reasonable to suppose that insofar as those parts are parts of the same Idea, they are like parts—analogous to the parts of gold, not the parts of the face (cf. *Protagoras* 329d). It is further reasonable to suppose that the whole differs from given parts only in respect to largeness and smallness: Largeness is like the largeness in Simmias. To use a word Aristotle was later to apply both to Plato and Anaxagoras, Ideas would then be homoeomerous (cf. *Meta.* I 984a 14, 992a 6-7, *ACPA* 531). The Paradox of Divisibility, dealing with Largeness, Equality, and Smallness, proves that some wholes of like parts are unlike their parts. Smallness is unlike the parts of Smallness, in that Smallness in relation to any part of itself is large. Largeness is unlike the parts of Largeness in that the parts of Largeness in relation to Largeness are small.

In the *Metaphysics*, Aristotle connects Plato with Anaxagoras and Eudoxus, contrasting their views in respect of separation and mixture (*Meta.* I 991a 8-19 = XIII 1079b 12-23, trans. Ross):

> Above all one might discuss the question what on earth the Forms contribute to sensible things, either to those that are eternal or to those that come into being and cease to be. For they cause neither movement nor any change in them. But again they help in no wise either toward the knowledge of the other things (for they are not even the substance of these, else they would have been in them), or toward their being, if they are not *in* the particulars which share in them; though if they were, they might be thought to be causes, as white causes whiteness in a white object by entering into its composition. But this argument, which first Anaxagoras and later Eudoxus and certain others used, is very easily upset; for it is not difficult to collect many insuperable objections to such a view.

This paragraph coheres neatly with the pattern of Parmenides' criticisms. It begins with the objection that Forms or Ideas contribute nothing to the being or knowledge of 'the others,' and cannot serve as causes of sensibles. This recapitulates the results of Parmenides' final argument that Ideas, if separate, are unknowable (133a-134e), an argument that follows from supposing that the Dilemma of Participation is a valid destructive dilemma; and that since Ideas cannot be in their participants either in whole or in part, there is no participation. The premise that Forms or Ideas are *in* the things that have a share of them is drawn from the Dilemma of Participation (131a-b), but Aristotle ascribes it to Anaxagoras, "and later Eudoxus and certain others." Aristotle's example of white causing whiteness in a thing by being mixed with it is an echo of *Lysis* where Plato rejects mixture as an account of participation.

The latter account is "very easily upset." Alexander of Aphrodisias, in his commentary on the *Metaphysics*, explains (*In Metaph.* 97.27 -98.24 (Hayduck), trans. Ross. Ross' numbering of the objections is here followed for convenience. Note that (4), for example, is simply the conclusion of the dilemma put in (3):

> To prove that it is not, as Eudoxus and some others thought, by the in-termixture of Ideas that other things exist, Aristotle says it is easy to collect many impossible conclusions that follow from this opinion. These would be as follows: If the Ideas are mixed with other things, (1) they will be bodies; for it is to bodies that mixture appertains. (2) Ideas will be contrary to one another; for it is to contraries that mix-ture occurs. (3) Mixture will take place in such a way that either an Idea will be present whole in each of the things with which it is mixed, or only a part of it will be present. But if it is present whole, something that is numerically one will be present in several things (for the Idea is numerically one); but if mixture be by way of parts, it will be that which shares in a part of man-himself . . . that will be a man. (4) The Ideas would then be divisible and partible, though they are not subject to change. (5) The Forms must consist of like parts, if all the things that contain a part of a certain Form are like one another. But how can Forms consist of like parts? A piece of a man cannot be a man, as a piece of gold is gold. (6) As Aristotle himself says a little later, in each thing there will be an admixture not of one Idea but of many; for if there is one Idea of animal and another of man, and a man is both an animal and a man, he will partake of both Ideas. And the Idea man-himself, inasmuch as it is also animal, will no longer be simple, but composed of many com-ponents, and some Ideas will be primary and others secondary. If on the other hand man-himself is not animal—it is surely absurd to say that a man is not an animal. (7) If the Forms are mingled with the things that exist by reference to them, how can they still be patterns, as these think-ers maintain? It is not thus, by mixture, that patterns cause the likeness of the copies of them to them. (8) On this showing, the Ideas would be destroyed along with the things in which they are. Nor would they have a separate existence, but only existence in the things which share in them. (9) On this showing, the Ideas will no longer be exempt from change; and there are all the other absurd implications which Aristotle in the second book of his work *On Ideas* showed this theory to involve. This is why he said, "It would be easy to collect many insuperable objections to this view"; they have been collected in that work.

It is probable that all of these arguments are derived from Aristotle's lost trea-tise *On Ideas* (cf. *ACPA* 531, and Appendix VII generally), from which it follows that *On Ideas* reproduced many of the criticisms of the theory of Ideas put in the *Parmenides*. This may be verified by inspection. Alexander's third objection applies the Dilemma of Participation to Man, a Form of which Socrates in the *Parmenides* expressed explicit doubt; the fourth objection is the conclusion of the second disjunct of the Dilemma; the fifth is a consequence of the Dilemma, namely, homeomereity, and explains Aristotle's application of the "insuperable objections" to Anaxagoras; the sixth is a consequence of the Dilemma applied to the problem of the unity of definition (as is shown by *Meta.* VII 1039a 24 - b 19, cf. 1038b 8 -15, III 999b 20 ff); the seventh is connected with the Likeness Regress (132c-133a). Furthermore, given that the *Parmenides* assumes that to be is to be somewhere, and to be in time, there are grounds for the first, second, eighth, and ninth objections in the *Parmenides* as well.

The proposition under attack is that Ideas are in their participants. Aristotle associates Anaxagoras with that proposition, and Eudoxus with Anaxagoras. Alexander, missing the connection with homeomereity, took the main subject of criticism to be Eudoxus himself. Of this we know too little to judge, but for present purposes, names are unimportant; it is the proposition that counts. The consequences Aristotle drew from that proposition in *On Ideas* are directly connected with the criticisms of Ideas in the *Parmenides*. They are also directly connected with Aristotle's own treatment of universality, and thereby of substance.

The Paradox of Divisibility and the Hinge

The Dilemma of Participation assumes that if there is participation, there is participation either in the whole Idea or in part of it, and that the Idea, in whole or in part, is in many participants. Because the latter assumption presupposes that the Idea, in whole or in part, is part of many participants, and because participants with common parts are not, contrary to hypothesis, separate from each other, there can be no participation in the whole of an Idea; for the Idea would then be separate from itself. Since the minimal meaning of separation is nonidentity, this is equivalent to the claim that F ≠ F. The modality is that of impossibility.

So if there is participation, there is participation in parts of Ideas, a consequence Socrates is loath to accept, but to which he is driven. The Paradox of Divisibility provides a reason that it should seem unacceptable: if there is participation in parts of Ideas, then at least some Ideas, namely Largeness, Equality, and Smallness, are qualified by their opposite either in respect to themselves or, as with Largeness, distributively, in respect to their parts.

This is incompatible with Socrates' earlier claim that no Idea can be qualified by its own opposite (129b-e), a claim insisted on in dialogues earlier than the *Parmenides*; Parmenides has shown that for at least some Ideas, it is with the things we apprehend by reflection as it is with the things we see (cf. 130a). Given that this consequence of the Paradox is incompatible with the denial that Ideas can be qualified by their own opposite, this shows that the two claims cannot stand together, but it does not show which of the two claims we are to reject. The result, that is, is dialectical, not demonstrative. No surface contradiction is involved in holding that at least some Ideas are qualified by their opposites, and if we reflect on the very general character of certain Ideas that Socrates admits, the claim seems intuitively true: it is, for example, reasonable to suppose that the Idea of Unlikeness is like other Ideas, and the Idea of Plurality one. The *Sophist* implies that, because the nature of Difference pervades all the Ideas (255e), Sameness is different from other Ideas, and in II.2., denial that Sameness and Difference qualify each other because they are opposite is used to construct a proof that nothing can be different from anything, and specifically that Unity and the Others are not different from each other (146d-147a).

The result, therefore, is that the modality on which the Hinge depends continues to obtain; so far as anything that has yet been shown, the claim that participants partake of parts of Ideas, if false, has not been shown to be impossible. The implication that if there is participation, there is participation in parts of Ideas, is assumed as necessary at 144c-d. On the other hand, if there is no participation in parts of Ideas—if, that is to say, the Dilemma of Participation is taken as destructive, as it must be if the claim that no Idea can be qualified by its opposite is to be maintained—there is no participation.

II.v. The Largeness Regress (131e-132b)

The Paradox of Divisibility assumes the second disjunct of the Dilemma of Participation: if there is participation, there is participation in parts of Ideas. It further assumes the axiom that the whole is greater than its parts, that is, large relative to any part. Given these premises, it follows that Largeness is a whole of parts if it is participated in, and that it is participated in if any Ideas are participated in. It also follows that Largeness is large (cf. 149e, 150b-c, and *Phaedo* 100e-101b, 102a-d, especially 102b 4-6). Parmenides now uses this result to construct an infinite regress. That regress has often been treated as an independent argument, a jewel in its own setting. In fact, it is a direct consequence of the Dilemma and the Paradox of Divisibility, and depends for its cogency on the cogency of those arguments.

Parmenides begins with the assumption that each Idea is one (132a 1), and specifically that Largeness is one (132a 3); he concludes that each of the Ideas is not one, but infinite in multitude (132b 1-2). If this conclusion is meant to contradict the premise, as it seems to do, then the schematic form of the argument is, if P then not-P, whence it follows that not-P. Since a proposition can imply its own denial only if it is itself contradictory or if the premises by which the implication is derived are incompatible, it follows that the Largeness Regress, if consequent contradicts antecedent, is vicious, as following from incompatible premises; we must therefore expect to find a contradiction latent in the argument. On the other hand, an Idea may be many in one sense and one in another;

it will be so, for example, if it is one whole of many parts, and this sort of unity is required for Largeness by the second disjunct of the Dilemma. But if Ideas are one as being wholes of parts, there is no *prima facie* ground for supposing incompatible premises; for one whole may have infinitely many parts (142b, 144e).

If the One over Many premise with which the argument begins is construed as requiring merely the unity of a whole of parts, the Largeness Regress supplies a simple addendum, a further implausibility, derived directly from the Paradox of Divisibility.[60] But if it is so construed as to imply a contradiction, it shows that the second disjunct of the Dilemma is not only false but logically impossible, and thus that the alternate turn of the Hinge is inevitable: there is no participation. The way is then cleared for the final proof that Ideas, because separate, are unknowable. They are separate in a way that precludes participation (cf. 159b-c, 147a).

The One over Many Premise

The proposition that each Idea is one is not merely asserted. It is argued for by an application of the One over Many argument, which provides a key premise in the regress:

> I suppose you think that each character is one for some such reason as this: when some many seems to you to be large, there perhaps seems to be some one characteristic which is the same when you look over them all, whence you believe that the large is one.

Abstracting for the moment from the reference to Socrates' beliefs, and examining the content of what it is he is said to believe, the argument is that if a plurality of things is large, then there is some one Idea that is the same over all of them; if there is some one Idea that is the same over all of them, then Largeness is one.

The function of the One over Many premise, in its context, is not to provide an argument to show that Largeness exists; the existence of Ideas generally, and of Largeness specifically, has already been assumed. The premise is used not to provide a reason for supposing that Ideas *are*, but that they are *one* — a proposition that the second disjunct of the Dilemma has drawn into question. Socrates had earlier granted that if the whole of an Idea, being one, were in each of its participants, it would follow that one and the same thing would be in many things, and thus be separate from itself; whereas if the Idea were present in its participants part by part, the Idea, as divided, could not be one. The argument is directed, not to the existence of Ideas, but to their unity, and more generally, to the possibility of participation. Nowhere in his criticisms does Parmenides challenge the claim that Ideas exist. His criticisms rather reinforce the Hinge effect of the Dilemma of Participation: if Ideas are participated in, they cannot be one except as one whole of parts; if they are not one as one whole of parts, they cannot be participated in. The One over Many premise, then, and the implication in which it issues, is not precisely the same as the One over Many argument that Alexander, following Aristotle, offers for Ideas (*in Metaph.* 89.8 ff., *Meta.* 990b 13); for Alexander's argument is directed to the existence of Ideas, whereas Parmenides' premise is directed to their unity. The relation, however, is very close, since what is is one. If many things are large, Largeness is, and is one.

The conditional that expresses this implication is present general: the protasis refers to any plurality thought to be large, and the apodosis, introducing one single Idea that is the same over all, indicates what is customarily or repeatedly done, or a general truth (W. W. Goodwin, *Greek Moods and Tenses*, Boston, 1900, para. 462). Since the argument is generalized to all Ideas—it offers a reason for holding that *each* of the Ideas is one[61] —and the apodosis, if read as expressing what is customarily or repeatedly done, answers to the remark of the *Republic* that, "We have been accustomed, I suppose, to posit each Form as a single thing, in the case of each plurality to which we apply the same name" (*Republic* X 596a, cf. 597a 7-9, 435a-b, *Parmenides* 157d-e). In the *Parmenides*, this claim must be understood under a restriction: Socrates has expressed doubt about the existence of Man, Fire, and Water, and has definitely rejected Ideas of Mud, Hair, and Dirt. But allowing that the conditional requires a qualification on its protasis in respect to the extent of Ideas, the argument implies that Ideas, which are, are one.

But one in what sense? Socrates is dialectically committed to the second disjunct of the Dilemma of Participation: if Ideas are participated in, they can be one only as being one whole of many parts, which parts are in their participants (see 142d *et passim*, and *Sophist* 245a). As Parmenides has already pointed out (131b), the Idea is then One over Many in a way neatly analogous to a Sail. It is this sort of unity, and only this sort, that Socrates, in view of the second disjunct of the Dilemma, is entitled to ascribe to Ideas.

But what a man is entitled to say and what he wishes to believe may be quite different things, and the One over Many premise is here phrased with explicit reference to Socrates' beliefs—what seems true to him. One thing that has seemed true to him is that Ideas cannot be divided or divisible, that is, have parts, and still be one (131c). If this belief obtains, then the One over Many premise cannot be construed in terms of the second disjunct; on the contrary, it must be understood to deny the second disjunct. That there is reason so to understand it is shown by the conclusion of the Largeness Regress, which suggests that if Ideas are unlimited in multitude, they cannot be one. It may be that the One over Many premise should then be understood as implying the first disjunct of the Dilemma, that participation is participation in the whole of an Idea. But since as a dialectical matter it has been shown that the first disjunct is not only false but absurd, the One over Many premise may then be taken merely to state Socrates' reason—an insufficient reason, unless he can refute the absurdity, which he does not do—for having thought the first disjunct true. In this connection it may be well to observe that as parts are parts of a whole, so a whole is, and is by definition, that from which no part is absent (137c). The very application of the part/whole distinction to Ideas is indicative of the root ontological difficulty of combining separate entities in such a way that assertion is possible.

Reiteration

The next premise in the argument is presented as a reiterative application of the first:

> What about the large itself and the other larges? If with your mind you should look over them all in like manner (ὡσαύτως) will not some one single large in turn appear, by which all these things appear to be large?

The conditional is future vivid. The truth of the protasis is left open, but it is distinctly supposed, and the apodosis expresses what will be the case if the condition should be fulfilled (Goodwin, *Greek Moods and Tenses*, para. 392.1).

The force of the protasis is that Socrates may look over large things and Largeness 'in the same way.' This must mean that both the many large things and Largeness are to be viewed as large, that, in short,

1) Largeness is large (i.e., is a large thing).

If this were not so, a further Largeness would not appear. There is thus good reason that the protasis should be distinctly supposed, for the Paradox of Divisibility, because it assumes that Largeness is a whole of parts, implies that Largeness is large relative to any part of itself, and therefore large. So Largeness is a member of the plurality of large things. We may indeed look at Largeness and large things 'in like manner': the protasis of the second premise is true, and the condition satisfied.

The assumption that Largeness is large is not, by itself, sufficient to require a further Largeness. It must also be true, as perhaps Alexander[62] and presumably Aristotle saw, that

2) Largeness does not partake of itself.

If this were not so, if other large things were large by partaking of Largeness and Largeness were large by partaking of itself, a further Largeness would not be required, since the One over Many would be part of the Many it is over. But this can hardly be so. Socrates has already agreed (130b 2-3) that things that partake of Ideas are separate from Ideas: Largeness cannot be what it has. And if many things partook of Largeness and Largeness partook of itself, it would follow by the Paradox of Divisibility that Largeness is large by a part of Largeness smaller than Largeness and therefore large by virtue of Smallness. This result has already been rejected as unacceptable (131d 2, cf. 150c-d, 146b), and the unacceptability is confirmed by 158a, where it is argued that anything that partakes of Unity must be other than Unity, since if it were not, it would not partake of Unity but be Unity; it follows from this that if Unity partakes of Unity, Unity is other than itself. So if Largeness partook of itself, it would be other than itself. If *a* is larger than *b*, then *a* is not the same as *b* and *b* is not the same as *a*.

It will be observed that, without more, the assumptions that,

1) Largeness is large,

and that,

2) Largeness does not partake of itself,

are not incompatible, any more than it is incompatible to assert of a given stick or stone that it is large but does not partake of itself. It has been suggested that the protases of the two conditionals on which the regress is based are inconsistent, in that the first makes a plurality of things large in virtue of Largeness₁, whereas the second makes a plurality large in virtue of Largeness₂, and so on. (See G. Vlastos, "The Third Man Argument in the *Parmenides,*" *Philosophical Review* LXIII (1954): 319-349; *SPM* ch. xii.) But the pluralities, of course, are different, in that the first does not contain Largeness₁ and the second does. Inconsistency will indeed arise if we identify the predicate " . . . is large" with a unique Idea of Largeness, in which case every stage of the regress yields a different predicate, which is yet assumed to be the same. But there is no incompatibility—without a further semantical premise—in claiming that the ground or reason for naming the first plurality large is its participation in Largeness₁, and the ground or reason for naming the second plurality large is its participation in Largeness₂. The regress arises precisely from the assumption that the predicate remains the same at every stage, but that the ground or reason for applying it differs at every stage. As Aristotle saw, the solution must be that each thing and its essence are one: "Largeness is large" can only be an identity statement (*Meta.* VII 1032a 5).

The Regress

If Largeness and other large things are large, there is some further Idea of Largeness by reason of which they are large. So a second Largeness has appeared, and the apodosis is continuative; by reiteration, a third Largeness (note γεγονός in 132a 11) will make its appearance alongside the Largeness that has been generated and the things that come to partake of it; and again, another one over and beyond all those—that is, a fourth—by which all of them will be large. So each of the Ideas will not be one, but infinite in multitude. The regress has been established.

The propositions (1) that Largeness is large, and that (2) Largeness does not partake of itself, follow directly from the Dilemma of Participation and the Paradox of Divisibility. If Largeness is a whole of parts, Largeness is large in just the same way that any whole of parts is large. Thus (1). But if Largeness partook of itself, it would be large by a part of Largeness smaller than Largeness itself, which is absurd (131d 2). Thus (2). But (1) and (2) taken in conjunction with the One over Many premise generate the Regress. By (1), we may put Largeness as a member of a plurality of things that are large. The One over Many premise requires that there be a Largeness that is the same over all that plurality. By (2) the Largeness that is the same over all that plurality is not the Largeness originally put, but another one. The difference here implied is explicitly stated at 158b: things participating in Unity must be different from Unity. Given that the members of the new plurality participate in the new Largeness thus produced, and that that Largeness is therefore a whole of parts, the argument reiterates indefinitely.

Generalization

The resulting regress may be generalized to every Idea, insofar as it is participated in. Beauty, Justice, Likeness, and so on, are also wholes of parts, and therefore large. They thus partake of Largeness. But as members of an infinitely expanding plurality of large things, they must, by the One over Many premise, partake of infinitely many Largenesses. But this is to say that each has in it a part of infinitely many Largenesses, which parts are parts of itself. So each of the Ideas, not only of Largeness but of everything else, has infinitely many parts in so far as it is participated in. The generalization involved may be compared with the generalization of the Paradox of Divisibility at 131e 3-5.

This construction of the argument implies that the Idea of Beauty, say, has infinitely many parts, and not that there are infinitely many Ideas of Beauty. The construction is not only implied by the argument, but confirmed by the language. The conclusion of the argument is that each of the Ideas will no longer be one, but infinite in multitude, or that their multitude is infinite (ἄπειρα τὸ πλῆθος 131b 2). Analogous reasoning will show that Unity is infinite in multitude (ἄπειρον . . . τὸ πλῆθος 143a 2)—infinite, that is, as a whole of infinitely many parts. Again, because Unity is distributed by Being, its multitude is many and infinite (πολλά τε καὶ ἄπειρα τὸ πλῆθός ἐστιν 144e 4-5): Unity is a whole of infinitely many parts even when considered apart from its own being. When Parmenides wishes to say that there are infinitely many numbers, he uses a different locution: ἄπειρος ἀριθμὸς πλήθει (144a 6). The difference in use is significant; number is not treated as a whole of parts. The conclusion of the Largeness Regress uses the language appropriate to the infinity of a whole of parts. The consequence is that the conclusion of the Largeness Regress does not generalize the regress; it generalizes an implication of the regress, in exactly the way Parmenides generalized an implication of the Paradox of Divisibility at 131e 3-5.

The Virtuous Regress

So far, the argument has issued in a virtuous regress. It establishes that Ideas, as wholes of parts, are not only many as having parts corresponding to their participants, but are also many, and infinitely many, as being themselves participants in infinitely many Largenesses. No more contradiction inheres in this than in recognizing that if you accept the existence of one, two, and three, you are committed to the existence of infinitely many numbers (143a-144e). The infinity of Largenesses established is successive, and the premises by which it is established are compatible.

On this reading, the conclusion of the regress, that each of the Ideas will no longer be one but unlimited in multitude, only apparently contradicts the premise that each of the Ideas is one. For each Idea may be one as being one whole, but without logical absurdity participate in infinitely many largenesses and thus have infinitely many parts. The contingency attaching to the second disjunct of the Dilemma of Participation, which allowed the Hinge to turn toward the implication that if there is participation, it is participation in parts of Ideas, still stands.

To say that the regress is virtuous is not to say, if we may look outside the *Parmenides* for the moment, that Plato would have found such a regress acceptable. In the *Republic* (X 597c-d), God could not have made two Ideas of Bed, for if he had, there would appear a single Bed of which they both would have the Form, and that would be the truly existent bed, rather than the other two. The principle of the argument is that if two things *have* a common character, they cannot *be* that character (cf. *ACPA* 196, *SPM* 370-372). The same type of argument is put in the *Timaeus* (31a-b). There cannot be two Intelligible Living Creatures, since if there were, there would have to be a third embracing those two, which would be parts of it, so that our world would not be an image of them but of that other, which would embrace them. Again, in the *Cratylus* (421e-422b), the analysis of names cannot go on indefinitely, but must arrive at names that are the elements of other names and words but are not themselves composed of other names. A very similar claim is the basis of the Dream of Socrates in the *Theaetetus* (201d-205e; cf. *Republic* III 402a-c, *Politicus* 277d-278d, *Timaeus* 48b-c, *Philebus* 18b-e). In the *Lysis* (219c-220b), not everything valuable can be valuable for the sake of something else; the process must terminate in a Primary Valuable (ὅ ἐστι πρῶτον φίλον), for the sake of which all other things are valuable. The argument anticipates Aristotle's proof (*E.N.* I 1094a 18-22) that there must be one primary good, since if everything were desired for the sake of something else, the process would go on to infinity, and all desire would be empty and vain. With the optimistic assumption that all desire is not empty and vain, Aristotle begins his account of ethics.

If infinite regresses, however virtuous, raise problems in ethics, they become vicious in epistemology. The early and middle dialogues assume that it is necessary to know Ideas in order to know what things have them, that Ideas are standards or criteria of judgment. So, for example, in the *Euthyphro*, it is important to learn what Holiness is in order to determine whether Euthyphro's action in prosecuting his father is holy. But if this assumption is introduced, the Largeness Regress becomes epistemologically vicious, for we should have to traverse the infinite to judge whether anything is large. The infinite, according to Aristotle, is untraversable: it is impossible to arrive at the final term of a sequence that by definition has no final term. It follows either that to know that anything is large we must accomplish the impossible, or that we cannot know that anything is large, since no ultimate standard exists by which to judge that large things are large. And since the second disjunct of the Dilemma of Participation implies that all Ideas that are participated in are large, we cannot know that there are Ideas.

But these consequences depend on premises drawn from outside the *Parmenides*. It may be that if the Dilemma of Participation is accepted, and with it the Paradox of Divisibility and the Largeness Regress, the notion that Ideas function as standards in epistemology must be abandoned, along with whatever consequences that assumption may have for ethics. But this does not, of itself, prove that the Largeness Regress is vicious. It only proves that one cannot accept that Regress, and the matrix of arguments on which it depends, and still accept certain prominent theses connected with the theory of Ideas.

Univocity

The Largeness Regress, even if taken as virtuous, yields an uncomfortable result in respect of univocity. The Dilemma of Participation implies that each thing is named after the Idea in virtue of the part of the Idea that is in it. A plurality of largenesses in things is produced, as it were, by division. The Largeness Regress has produced a plurality of Largenesses by addition.

The change from division to addition is not without consequence. In division, sameness of meaning might still be fixed by reference to a single whole. By addition, it cannot be so fixed, since every step of the regress generates a different Idea, and, because the regress is infinite, there is no last Idea by which fixity can be obtained; nor does this change if we suppose that each Idea in the sequence is a whole of parts, for there can then be no last whole. Yet it cannot be that 'large' is used equivocally at each step in the sequence; for the regress would not arise without the assumption that the whole is larger than its parts, and that Largeness—each Largeness—is a whole of parts. So 'large' must be univocal at every step.

The Largeness Regress presupposes univocity. How, then, in view of the result of the argument, is univocity to be explained? One answer that suggests itself is that the meaning of 'large,' as one and the same, is a mental concept, and has the unity appropriate thereto: a thought that cannot come to be present anywhere but in minds. This hypothesis, if it could be sustained, would relieve us of the necessity of supposing that Largeness is a whole of parts, and so cut the root of the Regress. It is in fact the hypothesis that Socrates, with some doubt, will next suggest (132b-c).

The Contradiction

We are entitled, after all, to expect a contradiction in the Largeness Regress. The Regress begins with the assumption that each of the Ideas is one, and specifically, that Largeness is one. It concludes that each of the Ideas is not one, but unlimited in multitude. The Regress can be so construed as to make the contradiction only apparent. But as stated, surely, it appears to be real.

The propositions that (1) Largeness is large, and that (2) Largeness does not partake of itself, are not inconsistent in content. Nor are they inconsistent with the One over Many premise, if the unity is supposed to be that of a whole. But inconsistency ensues if we examine these propositions, not in terms of their content, but in terms of their justification.

The ground for asserting (1) is Socrates' agreement that Ideas are divisible, which implies that they are wholes of parts. The ground for asserting (2) is Socrates' agreement that it is absurd to claim that anything, specifically Largeness, can be large by what is small. So the reason for asserting (2) is a reason for denying that Ideas are wholes of parts, and therefore that they are divisible. In short, the Largeness Regress rests on agreements that suggest that Largeness is and is not a whole of parts.[63]

If Largeness is not a whole of parts, then, given the implication attaching to the Dilemma of Participation, Largeness is not participated in; since Largeness must be participated in if any Idea is participated in, the way is then clear for Parmenides' concluding argument that Ideas have no relation to things in our world, and are unknowable (133a-134e). On the other hand, if Largeness is a whole of parts, participation in Ideas is possible, but it is false that a thing cannot be large by what is small, and more generally, that no Idea can be qualified by its own opposite: Largeness, taken distributively, and Smallness are examples to the contrary. In short, given the Dilemma of Participation, some Ideas are qualified by their opposite if there is participation, and to deny this implies denial of participation. Thus for example, we shall find that Unity, if it excludes plurality, can neither participate nor be participated in; otherwise, it is not only many but unlimited in multitude. The Largeness Regress exhibits in miniature a dialectical pivot that determines the structure of the *Parmenides* at large: the Hinge turns outward to the transcendence of the irrelevant, or inward to the immanence of the indistinct. The Largeness Regress rests on a latent contradiction, of which the young Socrates is unaware. Contradiction will be made explicit in the Hypotheses with which the *Parmenides* will conclude.

Being and Having

The Largeness Regress assumes that to say that Largeness is large is exactly like saying that Simmias is large, except for the difference in subjects: Both are large things, large 'in like manner.' Were it not so, no regress of Largeness would follow.

But a very simple argument, drawn from premises already stated in the *Parmenides*, shows that Simmias and Largeness cannot be large 'in like manner.' Things that partake of Likeness may also be unlike, but Likeness cannot be unlike (129a-b); things that partake of Unity are also many, but Unity is not many nor Plurality one (129b-d); Smallness cannot be large, nor Equality unequal, nor that by which large things are large, small (131d). It follows that Largeness cannot in principle be small: for as Unlikeness is what it is to be unlike (129a 2), and Unity what it is to be one (129b 7), so Largeness is what it is to be large. It cannot be large as Simmias is large, since Simmias may also be small.

The inference is confirmed by other dialogues. Thus for example in the *Protagoras* (330c-d), Justice is just and Holiness holy, for it is impossible that Holiness should be unholy. Socrates also asserts that Justice is holy and Holiness just, on the ground that they are either the same or very like each other. He is trying to show that the virtues are one; see 349b. In the *Phaedo*, things that are just equal cannot be unequal, nor Equality Inequality (74b-c), and Beauty is beautiful (100c). In the *Symposium* (210e-211a), Beauty is beautiful and in no way ugly. In the *Cratylus* (439d), Beauty itself is always such as it is. In the *Republic* (V 475e-476a), since Beauty and Ugliness are opposite, they are two things, and each of them is one. So too for large and small and other such opposites (VII 524b-c).

The force of these assertions is direct. It is that Largeness, or any opposite, essentially excludes qualification by its own opposite. If this were not so, it would have been useless to distinguish between Likeness and like things to begin with, since the distinction would not have solved Zeno's Paradox but would have been prey to it.

This supposition admits indirect proof. Assume that what it is to be large is small. Now, large and small are opposite and correlative terms; anything that has smallness relative to one thing may have largeness relative to something else. Therefore, if what it is to be large is small, what it is to be large may have largeness. But this implies that something that has Largeness may be Largeness, and that is impossible. For anything that has largeness may also have smallness, and if something that has largeness may also be Largeness, then something that has smallness may also be Smallness. Since, by hypothesis, largeness has both largeness and smallness, it is possible that Largeness and Smallness should be the same. But it is precisely not possible that Largeness and Smallness should be the same, and the theory of Ideas was introduced in answer to Zeno's Paradox to prevent that absurdity. Largeness cannot be a large thing precisely because it cannot in principle be small, since it cannot in principle be Smallness. There is a gulf between being and having—or if you will, a separation.

This further implies the unity of Ideas. If there were two Ideas of Bed, there would be a single Bed of which they both would have the form, and that would be the truly existent bed, not the other two (*Republic* X 597c-d); so similarly for Intelligible Living Creatures (*Timaeus* 31a-b). This rests on mere transitivity of identity. If *a* is what it is to be *F* and *b* is what it is to be *F*, then *a* and *b* are one and the same; if both of two things are *F* in the same way, they must have what it is to be *F*; they cannot be what it is to be *F*.

Apply this to the expression ' . . . is large.' Asserted of Largeness, it is shorthand for the fact, founded on analysis and argument, that Largeness is what it is to be large, and therefore by its very nature excludes participation in Smallness. No such implication attaches to ' . . . is large' when applied to Simmias, who may be large and small and equal. So the expression ' . . . is large' is systematically ambiguous, differing in meaning according to the kind of subject to which it is applied: differing, that is, between ' . . . *has* what it is to be large' and ' . . . *is* what it is to be large.' It is, then, simply false that large things and Largeness may be viewed 'in like manner.'

This shows that the premise that Largeness is large, in the sense of having largeness, cannot be generalized to any Idea you please on the mere ground that Ideas are 'self-predicative.' 'Largeness is large,' as premise in the Regress, is not a mere substitution instance of 'F-ness is F.' The fact that Beauty is beautiful, as excluding any tincture of ugliness, will not produce an infinite regress of Beauties; on the contrary, it will render such a regress impossible. The Largeness Regress assumes that Largeness is a large thing, and this is a function of the Hinge of the Dilemma of Participation. If Largeness is participated in, Largeness is a whole of parts; if Largeness is a whole of parts, then Largeness is large in precisely the sense that any whole of parts is large — in the sense that Simmias, for example, is large relative to the head of Simmias, which is part of him.

So the statement that Largeness is large is amphibolous. One of its senses is grounded in the fact that Largeness cannot be what it has, a fact that implies the exclusion of opposites. The other is grounded in the second disjunct of the Dilemma of Participation. It is the second sense that makes the Regress run.

The Semantical Premise: Unique Reference

If the Largeness Regress is to generate contradiction, it requires more than that the predicate 'large' be univocal at each stage. It requires that when the predicate is applied univocally, it applies to things that participate in the same Idea.

This assumption is implied by the claim that other things are named after Ideas by reason of their participation in them (130e-131a). If this is so, then the ground or reason for applying the same name to different things in the same sense is that they participate in the same Idea; the univocity of the name implies the uniqueness of the Idea. The point is put with considerable explicitness at 147d-e. Each name is given to something, and whether it is uttered once or many times, it always means the same thing: specifically, it always means the nature of which it is the name. To mean is to name; to mean the same thing is to name the same thing, and that thing is a unique Idea.

This, of course, is the normal and natural import of the One over Many premise: if many things are called by the same name, they partake of the same Idea. It requires a further inference to conclude that the Idea of which they partake has the mere unity of a whole of parts. That inference implies the Largeness Regress, which turns on the requirement that Largeness should partake of a further Largeness, because it is a whole of parts. But this raises a searching problem about participation. At 158a (cf. *Republic* X 597c), things that have or partake of Unity, and by extension of any Idea, are other than Unity; for if they were not, they would not *have* Unity but *be* Unity, whereas only Unity itself can be Unity. The Idea cannot participate in itself, since if it did, it would be other than itself; it cannot *have* X because it *is* X. The reason for this has already been given: if Unity participated in Unity, it would no longer, as a participant, essentially exclude its opposite, but might also participate in Plurality, in which case it would do the work of Plurality, and not its own. This goes to the very root of the Largeness Regress. Because the Dilemma of Participation implies that Largeness is a whole of parts, Largeness is large; thus it is that Largeness and large things can be conceived 'in like manner.' But the one over many premise, if it is construed in terms of 158a, construed, that is, in terms of the principle that Ideas of opposites must essentially exclude their opposites, implies precisely that Largeness and large things cannot be conceived in like manner, because Largeness is what it is to be large and therefore cannot partake of what it is to be large. The One over Many premise, given essential exclusion, implies that the One cannot be in the Many it is over: Largeness and large things cannot be conceived 'in like manner.' It is easy to say that 'Largeness is large' is amphibolous. One must immediately add, however, that the two senses of the amphiboly are incompatible. The semantical premise, that univocity implies unique reference, rests on the assumption that Ideas are what they are, and as such, essentially exclude the opposite of what they are, and participation in what they are. Given that this is so, the incompatible amphiboly of "largeness is large" implies that the Largeness regress is vicious.

The Vicious Regress

The virtuous regress assumes that the word 'large' has the same meaning as applied to each plurality that arises in the regress, but that the ground or reason for applying it differs for every plurality, in that the term is always applied in virtue of participation in a further Idea. But if whenever the term 'large' is applied with the same meaning, it applies to things that participate in the same Idea, the result is not virtuous but vicious. By (1), Largeness is large, in the sense that it is a member of the plurality of large things. But the unique meaning of 'large' is Largeness, and if x is a large thing, x participates in Largeness. Therefore,

2*) Largeness partakes of itself.

But by (2), Largeness does not partake of itself. Therefore, Largeness does not partake of Largeness. Therefore,

1*) Largeness is not large.

(1) and (1*) are contradictory, and (2) and (2*) are contradictory. The regress now implies both that Largeness is a large thing and that it is not a large thing; that Largeness participates in itself and that it does not participate in itself. These contradictions entail contradiction between the One over Many premise and the conclusion of the Regress. Given the radical distinction between being and having, the One over Many premise must be understood to imply that there is one and only one Idea of Largeness corresponding to unambiguous uses of the word 'large'; the Regress proves that there are infinitely many Ideas of Largeness corresponding to unambiguous uses of the word 'large.' So the Regress issues in a conclusion inconsistent with its premise.

Vicious Generalization

This has implications for other Ideas, such as Beauty, Justice, and the rest. Because they are participated in, they are wholes of parts and therefore large. They thus participate in an Idea that must, and cannot, be one. Indefinite in multitude, the condition of their multitude now implies a contradiction. Furthermore, because the Largeness Regress implies a contradiction, or a nest of them, it may easily be transposed into a proof that nothing can be large. If that is done, it will follow that other Ideas cannot be large; if not large, then not wholes of parts; if not wholes of parts, then by the second disjunct of the Dilemma of Participation, not participated in. So the Largeness Regress, read in this way, implies denial of participation of any kind. It implies the turn of the Hinge.

Dialectical Consequences of the Largeness Regress

Parmenides has demonstrated the following. If participation is to be construed in terms of the part/whole relation, there is participation in parts of Ideas; Ideas, therefore, are wholes of parts; wholes of parts are larger than their parts; therefore, Largeness is large; therefore, there is an infinite regress of Largeness. Given further that Largeness is what it is to be large, and excludes its opposite, and is unique, this regress is vicious, as implying multiple contradiction.

If the incompatible grounds that generate that contradiction are accepted — and the aporetic structure of the dialogue does not require that Socrates accept them, though it does require that he face the consequences for the theory of Ideas of not accepting them — the Largeness Regress, though it assumes the second disjunct of the Dilemma of Participation for its working, implies that that disjunct is not only false, but absurd. If the first disjunct is also absurd, there is no participation.

So the Dilemma of Participation issues in a Hinge, and the Largeness Regress forces that Hinge in a single direction: toward the transcendence of the irrelevant. The young Socrates has been brought face to face with the consequences of his own admissions. He believes that each Idea is one because when many things are called by the same name, they partake of the same Idea. He also believes that if anything participates in an Idea, that Idea, in whole or in part, is in it. But how can one Idea be *over* the Many, and yet *in* the Many? If that question were squarely faced — the young Socrates never squarely faces it — it would prompt reconsideration of other admissions. Socrates believes that there are sensibles that exist apart from any corresponding Ideas: Mud, for example, and perhaps Man. If that is so, the universe contains two kinds of individuals, relatively independent of each other: intelligible Ideas such as Largeness, and sensible objects such as Simmias, or his hair. When both sensibles and intelligibles have been endowed with an independent and substantial reality, one must face the problem of their connection. How is it, Simmias and Largeness being distinct things, that Simmias can truly be called large? Socrates has tacitly assumed that this may be so if participants are wholes of which Ideas are parts; whence it follows that Ideas are in their participants, in whole or in part. The foundation of the Dilemma of Participation has been laid. If this complex set of admissions yields unsatisfactory results—and the Largeness Regress gives good reason to think that it does—then it may be that the assumption that sensibles and Ideas are separate individuals needs fresh examination. This would certainly appear to be Aristotle's diagnosis of the matter. For after stating an argument concerning the relation of universality and substance that is a mirror image of the first disjunct of the Dilemma of Participation (*Meta.* VII 1038b 1-14, cf. 16-33), and assuming the substantiality of sensibles, he concludes that the root of the difficulty lies in assuming the substantiality of Ideas (*Meta.* VII 1038b 34 - 1039a 3):

> If, then, we view the matter from these standpoints, it is plain that no universal attribute is a substance, and this is plain also from the fact that no common predicate indicates a 'this,' but rather a 'such.' If not, many difficulties follow and especially the 'third man.'

II.vi. Ideas as Thoughts (132b-c)

Socrates had earlier tried to save the self-identity of Ideas with an analogy, that of the Day, and had failed: attempting to save their identity, he was forced to abandon their unity, and so was led into the Paradox of Divisibility and the Largeness Regress. Caught in a dialectical morass, he did not retrace his path, but stepped sideways and got in deeper.

He now steps sideways again. Instead of turning back to examine the primary assumptions of the arguments that have produced his perplexity, he introduces a further assumption. He had earlier said that Ideas are apprehended by reflection. Now, in an attempt to save their unity, he suggests that Ideas perhaps are thoughts, which cannot come to be present anywhere but in minds or souls. In that way, they may still be one.

This suggestion, if it could be sustained, would avoid the Largeness Regress, as Socrates intends: There would be no ground for grouping the thought of large things with large things, nor for supposing that the Idea depends, by way of its parts, on the sensible things that partake of it. Proclus (891.22 -899.2) correctly says that Socrates intends by his suggestion not only to save the unity but also the immateriality of Ideas. The suggestion that Ideas are thoughts implies that if they depend for their existence on anything, they depend not on sensibles but on minds. But this admirable result would be bought at a price. Socrates has done nothing to overturn the implication on which the Dilemma of Participation depends, namely, that if (*if*) there is participation, either the whole or part of the Idea must be in the participants.

The suggestion that Ideas are thoughts, that the unity of the Many is a mental unity, is philosophically volatile. If the characters of things are mind-dependent, it would seem to follow that things in themselves, apart from thoughts, are un-knowable because uncharacterizable, and for aught we know, uncharacterized. The suggestion then anticipates Kant's transcendental idealism, with its com-mitment to the thing in itself. But this leads easily to Hegel's criticism that nothing is easier to know than the thing in itself, since it is the bare thought of an object without any content. If the characters of things are in minds as in-capable of existing apart from them, things in themselves will not long remain outside: transcendental idealism leads back to idealism proper, with its doc-trine that *esse* is *percipi* or *percipere*.

Parmenides might have criticized Socrates' suggestion in various ways. He might have inquired whether, since Ideas are present in minds—plural—the same Idea is present in different minds, with consequent problems about divisibility, or whether it is a different Idea which is present in different minds, with con-sequent problems about discourse and communication. Parmenides might indeed have simply restated the Dilemma of Participation, applying it now not to sen-sibles but to minds. Jones' thought of Largeness, which is in his head, is plainly different from the Acropolis, which Jones thinks is large, but which is not in his head. But if Largeness is present in Jones' head as a whole, there would seem to be none left over for Smith, who, poor fellow, will find it literally in-conceivable that anything should be large. If, on the other hand, the thought of Largeness in Jones' head is the same as the thought of Largeness in Smith's head, then either Jones and Smith are identical, or the thought is divided from itself, and thus not one. And so on.

Again, Parmenides might have asked whether thoughts may not be true or false, correct or mistaken, adequate or inadequate to their objects, with conse-quent problems about not-being. Or he might have asked what status the Idea, which comes to be present in minds, has if it is not present. Alexander (*in Metaph.* 92.18-23) offers an interesting variation on this theme. "But again, if they (the Ideas) are thoughts, as some say, and reality is in Ideas by being thought, how will he who thinks them think them at the same time? For it is impossible to think opposites or contraries at the same time, at least where not thought simply as plural. But if the Ideas are thought part by part, they are short-lived, not eternal: for when they are not thought, they will not be, if their being really is in being thought." In short, contraries can exist at the same time; they cannot be thought at the same time; there are Ideas of con-traries; therefore the being of Ideas cannot consist in being thought. But the argument would seem to make *reductio ad absurdum* impossible, and Parmenides fashions an argument from the content of thoughts.

The Word 'Thought'

The word here translated 'thought,' νόημα, is rare in Plato. Ast lists three other occurrences, none of them in contexts of philosophical importance: *Politicus* 260d, *Symposium* 197e (Agathon), and *Meno* 95e (Theognis). Brandwood adds

Sophist 237d and 258d, quoting Parmenides B 7.1-2. But it was frequently used by the historical Parmenides. In the *Way of Truth*, never shall this be proved, that things are not are; we must hold back our νόημα from this way of inquiry. [B 7.2, cf. B 8.34 and 8.50]. In the *Way of Seeming*, that which thinks is the same for each man, namely, the substance of their limbs; for that of which there is more is νόημα (B 16.4). In the latter use, the term plainly means perception or sense awareness, and Aristotle construed the passage to imply that knowledge is sensation [*Meta.* IV 1009b 12-1010a 1, cf. Empedocles B 105.3 and perhaps B 110. 10]. Socrates, in formulating his suggestion that Ideas are thoughts, has done so in a vocabulary that consciously echoes the historical Parmenides.

The argument that follows provides a further reason that the historical Parmenides cannot be identified with the Parmenides of the dialogue. Parmenides will criticize Socrates' suggestion that Ideas are thoughts, on the basis of the distinction between thought and its content. In the *Sophist*, a parallel argument is directed against the historical Parmenides. The argument is there put in terms of naming (*Sophist* 244c-d, Cornford's translation abbreviated):

> It is equally absurd to allow anyone to assert that a name can have any existence, when that would be inexplicable. If, on the one hand, he assumes that the name is different from the thing, he is surely speaking of *two* things. Whereas, if he assumes that the name is the same as the thing, either he will have to say that it is not the name of anything, or if he says it is the name of something, it will follow that the name is merely a name of a name and of nothing else whatsoever.

If 'thought' is substituted for 'name' throughout this passage, the argument is closely similar to that which Parmenides here offers against the suggestion that Ideas are thoughts. Plato supposes that the historical Parmenides may have refused a distinction that the Parmenides of the dialogue insists on as crucial.

The word νόημα, like the English words 'thought' and 'perception,' is implicitly equivocal. The neuter suffix -μα, added to a stem, has a passive sense. It etymologically indicates a result: a νόημα is a thing thought, the result of thinking, just as a πρᾶγμα is a thing done, a ῥῆμα a thing said, a ποίημα a thing made (Smyth, *Greek Grammar*, 841.12, 861.2; Buck and Petersen, *Reverse Index of Greek Nouns and Adjectives*, 221). But in classical Greek the suffix applies with equal ease not only to the result of an activity, but to the activity that brings about the result. So similarly, of course, with the English word 'thought.' Socrates, in suggesting that Ideas are thoughts, may be suggesting that Ideas are activities of thinking, or that they are results of thinking — concepts (s. v. *LSJ* 3). The ambiguity, of course, is consistent with aporetic structure. The refutation Parmenides offers turns in part on distinguishing these two senses.

Thought *of* Something

Parmenides begins his criticism of Socrates' suggestion by eliciting the premise that if each of the thoughts is to be one, it is of something; it cannot be of nothing.

With this single premise, Plato has often been supposed to have offered a refutation of conceptualism or Idealism, anticipating that given by Moore in this century (G. E. Moore, "The Refutation of Idealism," reprinted in Moore's *Philosophical Studies*, London, 1922). The genitive in 'thought *of* something' is objective, and forces the distinction between act of thinking and object thought. An objective genitive is passive in sense, as a subjective genitive is active (Smyth, *Greek Grammar*, 1330-1331). Thus, to take a neatly ambiguous example, "fear of the barbarians" may (subjectively) denote their fearing, or (objectively) their being feared. Parmenides has then provided the basis for a reductio of Socrates' suggestion that Ideas are thoughts. A thought is a thought of something; that is, thoughts have objects. But the thought of an object implies a distinction between the object and the thought of it; a thought cannot be identical with that of which it is the thought. If, as Parmenides goes on to argue, thoughts are thoughts of Ideas, Ideas cannot be thoughts. The argument at this point is complete, and Cornford, who accepts it, dismisses Parmenides' own conclusion to the passage, which reapplies premises drawn from the Dilemma of Participation, as merely *ad hominem* (*PP* 91-92).

Cornford and other commentators who have discovered in this passage a piece of profound modern epistemology have also dismissed the rest of Parmenides' criticisms as resting on more or less trivial misunderstandings, without explaining why we are to suppose that we have found here a nugget of refined epistemological gold in the midst of what is otherwise a dialectical slag heap. On the other hand, those interpreters who find Parmenides' criticisms to be cogent refutation of the metaphysics of Plato's middle dialogues may well be asked whether this argument refutes any thesis Plato ever held. There is no evidence in the early or middle dialogues that Ideas are thoughts in the human mind, as the plural 'in minds' suggests, and very little to show that they are thoughts in the divine mind, as later commentators sometimes supposed. Thus, for example, it has been claimed that the proposition that God made the Bed (*Republic* X 597b-d) is a metaphor for the claim that the Bed depends for its existence on the mind of God. But this is not said, and it can hardly be supposed to be implied by what is said (cf. Adam, *ad loc*). Parmenides' refutation, if sound, shows that making Ideas thoughts is unavailing, and this is true whether the thoughts are human or divine.

To read the genitive in 'thought of something' as objective is possible, but not necessary. It must be taken as definitory or, as Smythe calls it, 'adnominal' (*Greek Grammar*, 1290-1291), marking off or limiting the meaning of the substantive on which it depends: thought of Largeness, light of day, hope of immortality, as distinct from thought of Smallness, light of a candle, hope of extinction. The genitive in 'Idea of Largeness' is of precisely this sort. There can no more be a thought that is not a thought *of* something, in this definitory sense, than there can be animals that are not some kind of animal—horses, cows, pigs, and so on. If thought is the activity of thinking, that activity must have a content, the result of the thought. If thoughts are to be one and yet distinct, this can be so only if they differ in content. The thought of apples is one thing, and the thought of oranges another, because, while both thoughts, they are thoughts of different things. So if Socrates is correct in supposing that each of the thoughts is one, it can be one only by virtue of the fact that it is of something, as the Idea of Largeness is an Idea of something. A thought of nothing (132b 9) is not a thought; it has no content.

This reading does not preclude an objective as well as a definitory reading of the genitive: it merely does not imply it. We may well wish to argue that apples and oranges must be if there is to be thought of them. But as a principle of scholarly economy, we do well not to assume what we do not yet need.

Indeed, even if we grant that thoughts must have objects, this still does not show that Plato accepted a rigid act/object distinction; it may be that at least some thoughts are reflexive, and have themselves as objects. If we may look outside the *Parmenides* for the moment, the question is raised as early as the *Charmides* of whether there is not a kind of knowledge that is knowledge of itself and other kinds of knowledge (167b-c); the question is left unanswered, though it would take a great man to determine that there is "nothing which by nature has its own power in relation to itself" (169a). That Plato believed that there is at least one such thing is proved by the fact that he later defined soul as self-moving motion (*Phaedrus* 245c, *Laws* X 895a-b, 896a); and thought is presumably a power of soul (cf. *Laws* X 987a, *Republic* I 353d). Aristotle indeed —surely no idealist—characterized his God as thought that thinks itself (*Meta.* XII 1072b 26-27, 1075a 2-5), and maintained that in the case of objects that have no matter, what thinks and what is thought are identical, that actual knowledge is identical with its object (*De Anima* III 403a 2, 431a 1, *Meta.* XII 1072b 20-21). Indeed, if the question raised in the *Charmides* is applied to philosophy, and if philosophy is the contemplation of all time and all existence (*Republic* VI 496a), it must follow that philosophy is essentially self-referential, as the reflection on dialectic and philosophical method throughout the dialogue shows; that which is directed toward all things contains itself an element in its object.

To sum up. The genitive in 'thought of something' must be definitory, and may be objective. If it is also objective, it need not be taken to imply that some thoughts are not thoughts of themselves, or that objects of thought do not depend on thinking for their existence.

Thought of Something Which Is

Parmenides next goes on to elicit Socrates' agreement that if each thought is a thought of something, not of nothing, it is of something which is, not of something which is not.

This, of course, is good Platonic and Parmenidean doctrine: the term 'not-being' cannot be applied to something (*Sophist* 237c), and that premise leads to the conclusion that, "One cannot legitimately utter the words, or speak or think of that which just simply is not; it is unthinkable, not to be spoken of or uttered or expressed" (*Sophist* 238c, trans. Cornford; cf. 262e-263c). This result is anticipated in the second deductions of Hypotheses III and IV (see also 143a, 147d-e), and contradicted by the first deductions of these same Hypotheses, a result showing that the Hypotheses cannot be regarded as a positive or dogmatic statement of doctrine.

Parmenides' contention that thought is of something which is, not of something which is not, easily transposes into an argument for the inconceivability of not-being, in anticipation of the *Sophist*. But it has a further function here. Socrates has identified Ideas with thoughts in order to evade the Paradox of Divisibility and the Largeness Regress, to allow Ideas both to be and to be one. He has now agreed that if a thought is to be one, it is one only by virtue of the fact that it is of something, has a given content, and that content must be if the thought is to be one. Put otherwise, if a thought depends for its unity on its content, that content must be if the thought is. It follows that if a thought is not of something which is, it is not one.

The One over Many Premise

Parmenides next infers that a thought that is of something which is, must be a thought of some one thing, namely a certain single Idea which that thought thinks as always the same over all. τὸ νόημα . . . νοεῖ in c 3 is pleonastic, a nominative construction analogous in this respect to a cognate accusative. As one thinks a thought of something, so here the thought thinks of something. A parallel construction appears below, 134e 1. The verbal analogy with Aristotle's description of God as 'thought of thought,' νόησις νοησέως may not, however, be accidental. But why, after all, should there not be one thought of many things—a single thought of a sensible plurality? Compare Alexander, *in Metaph.* 79.11-15, offering a varient of the 'Argument from the Sciences': If medicine is not knowledge of this given health but simply of health, something will be Health-itself; and if geometry is not knowledge of this given equal and that given diameter, but of what is strictly equal and strictly diameter, something will be Equal-itself and Diameter-itself; but those things are Ideas.

Put otherwise, the thought of apples differs from the thought of oranges. Why should not the content of those respective thoughts be apples and oranges, rather than Applehood and Orangeness? The question becomes more pointed if we consider that Socrates' original suggestion was amphibolous, in a way that cannot be preserved in translation. It may mean,

1) Each *of these* Ideas is a thought,

or

2) Each of the Ideas is a thought *of these things*.

The second reading raises the immediate question of what 'these things' are.

Since the purpose of Socrates' suggestion is to preserve the unity of Ideas, and since his reason for supposing that Ideas are one is that they are over many things, the reference must be to the many things that participate in Ideas (cf. 132a), for example, the many large things that participate in Largeness. The suggestion is confirmed by the conclusion of the argument, which assumes that if Ideas are thoughts, other things must have a share of thoughts (132c).

This is an important result. Socrates has suggested that the Idea of X = the thought of X. But the Idea of X = X. Therefore, the thought of X = X. If Ideas are thoughts, the analysis appropriate to Ideas attaches to the thoughts with which they are identified. Therefore, (1) and (2) are equivalent. Ideas were made thoughts in order to save their unity, and the need to save their unity arose precisely from the need to show that the Idea could be over many and still be one. Socrates accepts the One over Many premise because, as a dialectical matter, he must: he is therefore committed to participation in thoughts. Had he stood by his claim that thoughts can come to be present only in minds and drawn the conclusion that this prevents participation, he would have frustrated the very reason for which he offers his suggestion that Ideas are thoughts. He would have turned the Hinge outward.

The 'Refutation of Conceptualism'

Most commentators have assumed that the argument is here complete. Thoughts are Ideas. But thoughts are thoughts of Ideas. The thought of an Idea is not identical with the Idea of which it is the thought, because the Idea is the object of the thought. Therefore, thoughts are not Ideas. Parmenides has exposed the confusion between the act of thinking and the object thought latent in the word *noema*; when this is once pointed out, we are led to realize that Ideas must exist independently of thoughts.

This is received wisdom, almost universally accepted, and wrong. The conclusion does not follow from the premise, and the analysis distorts the argument.

Parmenides' argument is presented as one and continuous, with its refutative conclusion offered at the end, not as two separate arguments, one of which shows that the object of thought exists independently of the act of thinking. Nothing in the mere observation that thought is of something which is and is one over many requires the conclusion that what is thought exists independently of the thinking of it, and the assumption that there are two distinct arguments is unmarked in the text; and can be purchased only at the cost of strained translation. Cornford translates Socrates' final response at 132c 12 as, "that too is unreasonable"; the *too* is not found in the text, which merely says that it is not *even* reasonable. The surprised interrogatory τί δὲ δή in c 9 Cornford translates as 'besides'; at 131e 8 it had been a mere 'but.' Cornford's account makes the putative first argument inconsistent with the conclusion, in that the conclusion assumes that thoughts are *in* participants, as minds. It may be added that had

Socrates' suggestion merely rested on the ambiguity of νόημα, on confusion of the act of thinking with the object thought, Parmenides' natural refutation would have been a Third Thought Argument. If every Idea is a thought, and if thoughts are not identical with their objects, and if the object of every thought is an Idea, then each thought is a thought of a thought, ad infinitum. The regress is vicious, in that epistemically we should have to think infinitely many things to think anything. Yet it is unoffered. Furthermore, if the conclusion that thoughts are of Ideas that are over the Many were meant as refutative or complete in itself, we should expect some indication of the fact, for such indication is forthcoming in all previous cases (see, for example, 131b 3, c 11, d 2-7, 132b 1-2, c 12, 133a 5-6, 134e 7-8). Nothing, in fact, except interpreters' conviction of epistemological profundity — the interpretation happens to coincide with the Realistic criticism of Idealism offered during the first third of this century — serves to mark this as the conclusion of an independent argument.

Conceptualism

Parmenides infers that that which is thought is an Idea, one and always the same over all. The inference tenuously allows three interpretations, only one of which will do.

The inference might mean that what is thought, the Idea, exists independently of the thinking of it. Nothing in the argument requires this result, and it may be excluded on the ground that it not only does not imply the refutation that Parmenides in fact offers of Socrates' suggestion, but makes that refutation impossible.

The inference might mean that what is thought, the Idea, simply is the activity of thinking, whose object is the sensible things thought. The Idea of Applehood is simply the activity of thinking of apples. But what is thought of is taken to be Applehood, not apples, so that this gives a strained sense, if indeed it gives any sense, and the result may be excluded on the ground that it implies that what is thought of may be many, not one, and the thought of apples is not thought of itself.

The inference must mean that what is thought, the Idea, is a result of the act of thinking. The Idea, that is to say, is a concept or universal that the act of thinking thinks as one over all of the sensible objects of its thought. This explains what may otherwise appear to be a curious reduplication of premises in an argument that does not waste a word. Thought (νόημα) thinks one Idea as being over all (132c 3-4); here νόημα has an active sense, thinking. What is thought (τὸ νοούμενον) is one Idea always the same over all (132c 6-7); here the passive corresponds to the passive or resultive sense of νόημα. The two premises, extensionally equivalent, stress the distinction between the active and passive senses of 'thought.' Ideas are thoughts in that they are what is thought, the result of thinking: they are concepts of universals, the content of thought. The thought of apples implies the thought of Applehood, a result that is dialectically

justified on the ground that Ideas are *ex hypothesi* thoughts, and one that may
be defended on the ground that the content of thinking must be and be one if
the act of thinking is to be and be one; the unity of the content is a condition
for the unity of the thought, for the fact that this act of thinking is one, as distinct from that act of thinking. The transition from apples to Applehood might
also have been justified on the basis of an Academic argument, known to Aristotle, that something is known when particular things have perished (*Meta.* I
990b 14-15, XIII 1079a 10-11). Alexander (*in Metaph.* 81.25-82.1) gives it as
follows: The argument fashioned from thinking for the existence of Ideas is
of this sort. If when we think man or foot or animal, we both think something among things that are and nothing among things that are particular (for
the same thought remains when those things have perished), it is clear that
there is something besides the particulars and sensibles, which we think when
those things both are and are not; for we do not then think something that is
not; but that is the Form and Idea. Asclepius (*in Metaph.* 75.2-7, Hayduck)
follows Alexander closely, but is less full. If the content of thought were sensibles, thoughts would be always changing. Cf. *Cratylus* 439c-440c. The argument does indeed provide a distinction between the act of thinking and the
content of thought, but in no way suggests or implies that the content of thought
exists independently of minds. Socrates' suggestion has provided the basis for
an abstractionist theory of universals. It also makes Parmenides' refutation
possible. The *act* of thinking taken in itself, on this view, would seem to resemble
Aristotle's account of mind as *passive* intellect, which can have no nature of its
own apart from a certain capacity (*de Anima* III 429a 21-31). In the same
passage (a 27), Aristotle commends those who say that the soul is the place of
forms, and Philoponus (*in de Anim.* 524.6-16) suggests that Aristotle is referring
to Plato. But see *ACPA* 565.

To step outside the *Parmenides* for the moment, the theory that Ideas are the
product of mental abstraction is rejected in the *Phaedo* (96b), and for very good
reason. It had earlier been explained that although sense perception performs the
office of stimulating our recollection of Ideas (74c), the mind must use Ideas in
order to recognize the character of perceptions (75b, 76d-e). To recognize that
these given sticks and stones are equal, we must first have knowledge of Equality, which sensible equals only deficiently exhibit. The argument, formulated in
terms of Equality, applies generally (75c-d). The abstractionist theory implies
that it is by grasping the many equals as a unity that we arrive at our concept
of equality; the Platonic response is that without knowledge of Equality, it
would be impossible to recognize that any given things are equal. There is, indeed, some evidence of an Academic argument from the unity of thoughts to
the existence of the corresponding Ideas (see *Meta.* 1 990b 25, XIII 1079a 21).
But such an argument would have been possible, in Plato's view, only because
the unity and existence of the Idea is a condition of the unity and existence
of the thought. Thus in the *Phaedrus*, men understand by means of Ideas, and
the process of passing from many perceptions to one thing comprehended by

reasoning is Recollection. (*Phaedrus* 249b-c, cf. *Parmenides* 130a, 135b-c. Recollection is thus the basis of collection and division, that is, dialectic. Cf. *Phaedrus* 265d-266b, 277b-c.) Plato was not a conceptualist. But this in no way implies that Socrates' suggestion that Ideas are thoughts in the *Parmenides* does not attempt to evade the consequences of the Paradox of Divisibility and the Largeness Regress by an appeal to conceptualism. It only remains for Parmenides to show how and why that appeal must fail.

Parmenides' Refutation

Parmenides at this point has forced the distiction between the activity of thinking and the content of thought. The content of thought is an Idea, One over Many. It follows that since sensibles partake of Ideas, and Ideas are thoughts, sensibles partake of thoughts, that is, the contents of acts of thinking.

Now, Socrates had earlier agreed that if there is participation, the Idea, in whole or in part, is in the participant. He did not go back to reexamine the agreement in light of the uncomfortable consequences to which it led; instead, he suggested that Ideas are thoughts, which can come to be present only in minds. But the One over Many premise implies participation, and therefore produces an unfortunate result.

If a given stick is large, it partakes of Largeness. If it partakes of Largeness, Largeness is in it in whole or in part, and the stick is composed of what is in it, since what is in it is part of it. Therefore, since Largeness is a thought, a thought is in the stick in whole or in part, and part of the stick. Since a thought cannot be in anything but a mind, the stick is a mind, whence it is reasonable to conclude that the stick thinks. This result is absurd on the face of it, as implying that sticks and stones think because they have qualities or characters in them.

Given that the result is absurd, suppose we deny it. We then get the punning result νοήματα ὄντα ἀνόητα εἶναι (132c 11). ἀνόητα has an active meaning: if thoughts are present only in minds, and thoughts are present in things that do not think, those things must be stupid or unconscious. Aristotle quotes Homer as describing a warrior knocked unconscious as "thinking other thoughts" (*Meta.* IV 1009b 30-31, cf. *de Anima* I 404a 30). The context suggests a connection with the present passage. Aristotle is examining the views of those who identify knowledge and perception, and argues that this implies identification of reality with the sensible world. It follows that, "In general, if only the sensible exists, there would be nothing if animate things were not; for there would be no faculty of sense" (*Meta.* IV 1010b 3-32).

On the other hand, ἀνόητα also has a passive meaning: thoughts in things that do not think are unthought or unthinkable —much too deep for tears. There is an additional overtone. The suggestion that thoughts are ἀνόητα recalls the injunction of the historical Parmenides to leave aside the Way that Is Not as unthinkable and nameless (ἀνόητον ἀνώνυμον, B 8.17). Thoughts in things that do not think are unthought, and thus not thoughts, and thus not thoughts *of* anything. So if things are composed of such thoughts, those things are themselves ἀνόητα in Parmenides' sense: we deal here with a way that is not. Socrates' response that the suggestion is hardly reasonable (οὐδὲ . . . ἔχει λόγον) has the further overtone that it is not to be expressed in discourse.[64]

This refutation would be impossible if Ideas had already been proved to exist separately from minds; the argument, so far from requiring the act/object distinction of twentieth-century epistemology, precludes it. For Parmenides' refutation turns on the assumption that Ideas are in their participants, and that therefore thoughts are in their participants if Ideas are thoughts.

Parmenides' refutation is not a piece of sophistry, but a penetrating argument of considerable philosophical weight. Aristotle, in order to avoid the consequences of making universals mind-dependent, as the products of abstraction, distinguished in *Metaphysics* VII between the universal—"the composite *taken universally*"—and substantial form, the foundation in things on which universality rests and in terms of which predication of universals is possible. The distinction is subtle, but unsuccessful. If the universal is different in nature from the form, and knowledge is of the universal, then knowledge implies systematic distortion of reality; we never know things as they are in themselves. Alternately, if the universal is the same in nature as the form which is the substance of each thing, the universal is the substance of each thing, and there is nothing for minds to know but their own products. To push further, if we insist on the plurality of substances, the result is nominalism, so that there is no universal after all, and thus no knowledge; whereas if we insist on the reality of universals, the result is monism, so that there is no universal because there is no plurality, and so no knowledge. Avicenna, much later, undertook to cure this weird dialectic with his doctrine of neutral essence or common nature; the same nature is one in the mind and many in things. This proposition, however, is sufficiently refuted by mere considerations of transitivity of identity. In general, if the characters of things are mind-dependent, and if things in themselves exist independently of minds, then those things are unknowable because uncharacterizable. But skepticism easily transposes into idealism: if the characters of things are in minds as incapable of existing apart from them, things in themselves will not long remain outside, and the stuff of reality becomes mental. Parmenides' conclusion, that if Ideas are thoughts, other things that partake of characters either all think, or do not think and are unthought or unthinkable, foreshadows the course of much future speculation.

Conclusion

Socrates, young and insufficiently experienced in dialectic, suggests that Ideas are thoughts in order to evade perplexities arising from the Dilemma of Participation. He has been refuted by use of a premise on which the Dilemma itself depends, that if there is participation, the Idea is in the participant. The function of Socrates' suggestion, so far as the reader is concerned, is not only to suggest that the perplexities Socrates has encountered cannot be evaded by making Ideas concepts, but also to direct attention to a crucial assumption. If Ideas were indeed thoughts, the thought of Mud would differ from the thought of Man no less surely than the thought of Justice differs from the thought of Unity. The reader is led once again to ask whether Socrates' restriction on the extent of Ideas is not a further token of youth and inexperience, and to ask in what ways it is related to the perplexities that have followed.

II.vii. Ideas as Paradigms (132d-133a)

Socrates had suggested that Ideas are thoughts with a certain hesitation: *perhaps* they are thoughts. This has now been refuted. But Socrates is quite confident that Ideas are paradigms fixed in the nature of things, and that the other things that participate in Ideas are likenesses of them. To participate in an Idea is nothing other than to resemble that Idea; to say that *a* has a share of *F* is merely a way of saying that *a* is a resemblance of *F*.

This suggestion, if it could be sustained, would solve the Dilemma of Participation by implicitly denying a crucial premise on which it depends. The Dilemma assumes that if there is participation, either the whole Idea or part of the Idea must be *in* the participant. But if participation is resemblance, there is no more reason to suppose that Ideas are in their participants than there is to suppose that the face reflected in the mirror is itself in its reflection. The question of whether the whole Idea or part of it is in the participant becomes otiose, and the Dilemma fails.

So Socrates' suggestion, this time, is not wholly an evasion. He has side-stepped by offering further premises instead of going back to examine the primary assumptions that have produced his perplexity. But those further premises, that Ideas are paradigms and that participation is resemblance, if followed up, would imply that Ideas are not in their participants, and solve the Dilemma of Participation.

Parmenides offers in reply an argument that is diagnostic of the deeper assumptions on which the Dilemma of Participation depends. The young Socrates had assumed that the extent of Ideas is limited, in that some kinds of sensible have a character that does not answer to any Idea. This assumption implies that things that partake of Ideas have or may have an independent nature and reality of their own; they are capable of existing apart, as separate individuals, which are yet somehow related to Ideas. Parmenides now offers an aporetic regress, which is valid on this assumption. The result is that the Dilemma of Participation is reinstated, since no satisfactory alteration of its premises has been achieved. The way is then open to deny that participation in Ideas is possible.

Socrates' confidence that Ideas are paradigms and participation resemblance is easily explicable. Ideas are called paradigms as early as the *Euthyphro* (6e). The suggestion that participants resemble Ideas but are deficient with respect to them is clearly put in the *Phaedo* (74-76), as the basis on which sensibles prompt recollection of Ideas. So it is that in the *Phaedrus* (249e-250b), a dialogue that may be close to the *Parmenides* in date of composition, recollection of things in the other world is prompted by perception of their likenesses in this, though only a few people, approaching images through the dull organs of sense, are able to behold, over them, the nature of what they imitate. The thesis that participants are images that depend upon and are resemblances of Ideas recurs throughout the middle dialogues. In the *Republic*, it is made the basis of the greatest of all metaphysical metaphors, in the connected symbols of Sun, Line, and Cave—connected because the Cave combines in a single and unified symbol the fundamental metaphor of dependence found in the Sun and the fundamental metaphor of resemblance found in the Line. As imitation is vital in metaphysics and epistemology, so it is also vital in education and ethics, which require ability to discern both Ideas and their images in anything in which they are. (See, for example, *Republic* III 401b-402c. But see also Adam, *Republic* i. 168.) Socrates' suggestion that participation is imitation is founded on the doctrine of the middle dialogues. It is a doctrine that Aristotle attests. (Cf. *Meta* I 987b 10-14, with *ACPA* n. 426. See also *Meta.* I 911a 20-31.)

The Symmetry Assumption

Parmenides attacks the doctrine with a deceptively simple inference. If to participate in an Idea is to be a resemblance of an Idea, then the participant must be like the Idea. But if *a* is like *F*, *F* is like *a*: likeness is a symmetrical relation. Therefore, if the participant is like the Idea, the Idea is like the participant (132d). In brief, if one thing is a resemblance of another, then there are two things that are like each other. As Parmenides himself points out, this proposition is the foundation of the regress that follows: "Continual generation of a new character will never stop, if the character should come to be like what has a share of it" (133a). Proclus (913.11-14), in analyzing the argument, explicitly denies that the symmetry assumption obtains in respect of paradigms and their images.

The One over Many Premise

Parmenides next provides a version of the One over Many premise with specific references to likeness. If one thing is like another, those two things must have a share of one and the same Idea.[65] Therefore, it is necessary that that of which like things have a share so as to be like should be the Idea itself.

The immediate question, of course, is *what* 'Idea itself'? The most economical answer, as well as one directly supplied by Socrates' own admissions (129a) and required by his limitation of the extent of Ideas, is that 'the Idea itself' is the Idea of Likeness. If *a* and *b* are like, they are like by sharing in one and the same Idea (132d 9 - 14), and that Idea is Likeness (132e 3-4). On this reading,

132 9 - 14 and 132e 3-4 are not simple equivalents, since the latter specifies the former.

But the One over Many premise plainly suggests, if it does not imply, another reading. No doubt if *a* and *b* are like, they are like by virtue of Likeness; but they are also like in respect of some further common character. Likeness, after all, is definable as an indirect relation: to be like is to be qualified by the same characteristic (139e, 148a). It is intuitively plausible, even obvious, that the One over Many premise should be so construed as to imply participation in a further Idea besides Likeness, in respect of which the relation of likeness obtains. Thus if *a* and *b* are like in respect of being just, they must not only partake of Likeness but of Justice.

Read in this way, the One over Many premise is implicitly incompatible with Socrates' earlier limitation of the extent of Ideas. Simmias is like Cebes in respect of being a man, and this mud-pie is like that mud-pie in respect of being mud; so the One over Many premise would seem to imply that there are Ideas of Man and Mud after all. In short, if the One over Many premise is construed in terms of Socrates' earlier limitation of the extent of Ideas, it must be read as requiring, not any Idea, but the Idea of Likeness. But if it is so read, the fact that Likeness is definable in terms of possession of further common characters immediately calls into question Socrates' limitation of extent. The aporetic structure of the argument, the ambiguity of reference of 'Idea' or 'character' in its context, neatly encapsulates the predicament. The reader is forced by the One over Many premise to inquire whether Socrates' limitation of extent was in fact well founded. If it is not, it is reasonable further to inquire whether the separate existence of sensibles implied by that limitation is true. The Likeness regress that follows provides independent reason for supposing that it is not true.

The Likeness Regress

Parmenides next infers that it is impossible for anything to be like the Idea, or the Idea like anything else; otherwise, another Idea will make its appearance beside the first, and so on *ad infinitum*, if the Idea is like what has a share of it. The argument is aporetic, and couched in purposefully ambiguous terms. It follows from the first construction of the One over Many premise that the Idea that recurs in the regress must be Likeness. On the second construction, the Idea that recurs in the regress may be any Idea. The first construction yields a more economical and penetrating argument than the second. But both constructions imply that the others do not get a share of Ideas by likeness to them (135a 5), and so refute the suggestion that Ideas are paradigms.

The Likeness regress is direct. If Simmias and Cebes are like each other, then, by the One over Many premise, they share in one and the same Idea, namely, Likeness. But to share is to resemble, to resemble is to be like, and likeness is symmetrical. Therefore, Simmias and Cebes are like Likeness, and Likeness like Simmias and Cebes. By reapplication of the One over Many premise, there must be some further Idea in which they share, and, since they are like, that Idea must be Likeness. The regress begins — an infinite regress of Likenesses. If that regress is virtuous, it provides good reason for denying that participation is likeness, simply by virtue of the regress. If the regress is vicious, the assumption that participation is likeness is absurd.

The regress runs on the basis of two propositions. The first is that,

i) Likeness is like (i.e., is a like thing).

For if this were not so, a further Likeness would not be generated. And it is so, since Socrates has granted that what is like is like what is like it, and that resemblance implies likeness. So i) follows from the symmetry assumption.

The second proposition is that,

ii) Likeness does not partake of itself.

For if other things are like by partaking of Likeness, and Likeness were like by partaking of itself, a further Likeness would not be generated. But if Likeness partook of itself, then, since to participate is to be like, Likeness would *ex hypothesi* stand to itself as image or resemblance to paradigm, and thus be different from itself (cf. 158a-b). Furthermore, it would be like the like things that partake of it, and by the One over Many premise, this new set of things must be like by partaking in some further Idea. So (ii) follows both from Socrates' original hypothesis and from the One over Many premise.

The result is a valid regress. Therefore, the claim that participation is resemblance implies the existence of infinitely many Likenesses, and if that result is unacceptable, the hypothesis that produced it must be rejected as false. The others do not get a share of Ideas by resembling them.

The Third Man

There is another reading of the One over Many premise; it leads to an argument that Aristotle and Alexander of Aphrodisias called 'the Third Man.' Suppose that Simmias and Cebes are like each other in that both are men. Given that Likeness is an indirect relation, one that obtains by virtue of participation in some further Idea, the One over Many premise may then be taken to imply that Man is an Idea, of which Simmias and Cebes partake. Since Simmias partakes of Man, he is by hypothesis a resemblance of Man; it follows that Simmias is like Man, and Man like Simmias. If like, then like in some respect, and by reapplication of the One over Many premise, that respect will answer to a further Idea. What is that Idea?

We might suppose that the One over Many premise continually yields a further Idea, without specifying what that Idea at each step in the sequence may be. If a and b are like in respect to C, then a is like C and C like a in respect to D, and so on. This regress requires *some* further Idea at every stage, but does not specify *what* further Idea at any stage. But it is reasonable to assume that the nature of the elements in the sequence may be specified by analysis of participation. If Simmias is like Man because he partakes of Man, he is like Man in such a way that he can properly be called a man, and not a horse or a house. By the symmetry assumption, it would appear to follow that Man is also to be called a man, and that Simmias and Man resemble each other in being men. By the One over Many premise, there is now a Third Man, and the regress begins. That regress depends, it will be observed, on the premise that

a) Simmias is like Man in that respect in which Simmias is a man.

Given that premise, it follows that the Third Man is homologous with the Likeness regress. For if (a) is true, it will follow by the symmetry assumption that,

ia) Man is a man.

And since no Idea is a resemblance of itself and thus other than itself, or among the Many it is over, it must also be true that,

iia) Man does not partake of itself.

This establishes a regress, which may be generalized to every Idea that is participated in, since the reason for accepting (a) lay in an analysis of participation.

It is the Likeness regress, not the Third Man, that is fundamental to Parmenides' argument, though the aporetic character of the argument admits the Third Man as a possible interpretation. The Likeness regress is fundamental because it derives directly from Socrates' admissions, assumes an Idea he has explicitly recognized, and does not assume Ideas he has refused to recognize; furthermore, all other readings of the regress imply a regress of Likeness. But to state the Likeness regress is immediately to open the way for an analysis of resemblance that will yield the Third Man. The Third Man requires the assumption that likeness is an indirect relation, and the further assumption of (a), which is not given in the premises of the argument and must be inferred *ab extra*. So the Third Man may be regarded as a dialectical variant of the Likeness regress.

The Likeness Regress and the Largeness Regress

The Likeness Regress and the Largeness Regress are homologous. Neither can be directly generalized to all Ideas; they imply an infinite regress of Largenesses and Likenesses, not of Justices or Men. Each turns on the assumption that Largeness and Likeness have what they are, that Largeness is a large thing and Likeness a like thing; and each further assumes that Largeness and Likeness cannot partake of themselves, so that their possession of what they are implies participation in a further Idea of the same sort. Each implies a regress whose elements are in succession, in that they are the same in kind and differ only by their position in the sequence. Each admits a virtuous, if unacceptable, regress, which becomes vicious if the semantical premise is assumed that the meaning of 'like' and 'large' is the unique Idea of Likeness or Largeness; the semantical premise, indeed, is explicitly stated in a sub-proof dealing with likeness and unlikeness in the Hypotheses that follow (147d-e).

The Likeness Regress and the Largeness regress are structural homologues, but their foundation and their function are very different. The Largeness regress is a direct product of the Dilemma of Participation; the crucial premise that Largeness is a Large thing derives from the premise that every Idea, in so far as it is participated in by many things, is a whole of parts, and that the whole is greater than its parts. Largeness, therefore, is large relative to its parts, which are small relative to it. The premise that Likeness is a like thing rests on a different basis. It assumes that Likeness is a symmetrical relation implied by resemblance, whence, if participation is resemblance, Likeness is like those things that are like it; a parallel argument generates the Third Man, given the additional assumption of (a). The suggestion that participation is resemblance, so far from deriving from the Dilemma of Participation, would, if it could be sustained, solve the Dilemma. It cannot be sustained.

Likeness and Separation

Parmenides' first question to Socrates had been whether Ideas are separate from their participants, and their participants separate from Ideas. That question, innocuous in itself, takes on new force from Socrates' limitation of the extent of Ideas: not only Ideas but sensibles are then endowed with an individuality and substantiality of their own. It is this assumption, never directly expressed, that is the foundation of the Dilemma of Participation. If sensibles and Ideas are separate individuals, and yet intimately different, in that sensibles are named after the Ideas of which they partake, it is plausible to suppose that the relation of participation may be analyzed in terms of the relation of part and whole.

The results are unacceptable, and Socrates has therefore suggested that Ideas are paradigms and that participation is resemblance; that is, he substitutes resemblance for part/whole as an account of participation. Given that resemblance implies likeness, and that likeness is symmetrical as separation is symmetrical, the suggestion fails. It is a lovely curiosity that analysis of participation in terms of such different relations as resemblance and part/whole should produce homologous regresses. As an aporetic matter, lovely curiosities excite inquiry about fundamental assumptions.

Certainly it seems clear that if sensibles, or participants generally, have an individual and substantial existence, and participation is resemblance, the Likeness regress is inescapable. (See further, "Participation and Predication in Plato's Middle Dialogues," *SPM* 43-60.) If *a* and *b* are substantially separate from each other, each having an independent reality of its own, it would seem surely to follow that if *a* is a resemblance of *b*, *a* is like *b*, and *b* therefore like *a*. So separation, if it is symmetrical, implies the symmetry assumption for likeness. By the One over Many premise, if two things are like, they partake of Likeness; therefore, they resemble Likeness, and the regress begins.

The result is that resemblance cannot explain how two distinct things such as Simmias and Justice can be so related that Simmias may truly be said to be just, or to partake of Justice. The dialectical structure directs the attention of the reader—if not the young Socrates—back to the separation assumption. How, after all, can two substantially separate things be so related that participation —or if you will, predication—is possible?

There is evidence enough elsewhere to indicate that Plato thought it was not possible. In the *Sophist* (240a-b), images are not real and true, but really and truly are images; they are a riddling mixture of Being and Not-Being, very like the objects of Opinion in *Republic* V. In the *Timaeus*, sensibles cannot so much as be said to be *this* (49d-e), and have no reality apart from what they are *in*, Space, and what they are *of*, the Ideas (52c). If this is so, separation is not a symmetrical relation: Ideas are separate from sensibles in that they are capable of existing apart from sensibles; sensibles are not separate from Ideas in that they are incapable of existing apart from Ideas. Sensibles, as wholly dependent images of Ideas, are neither individual nor substantial, and if this is once granted, the way is open to inquire whether the likeness of sensibles to Ideas is not asymmetrical as separation is asymmetrical. This is the basis for Proclus' claim that paradigms are not like their images, though their images are like them: the Likeness regress fails by reason of the failure of the symmetry assumption, and with it the One over Many premise as applied to the relation of participants and Ideas.

All of this, of course, lies outside the *Parmenides*, which is aporetic: the dialogue is meant to set problems, not offer solutions. But it may be remarked in passing that the issue raised by Proclus will not be settled by question-begging assumptions about 'the logic of our ordinary use' in respect to likeness and resemblance. Platonism asks us to think things, not words, and in so doing suggests the poverty of our ordinary conceptions in respect to reality. The 'logic of our language' is often a mask for the illogic of our thought.

The Third Man and the Extent of Ideas

As the Likeness regress directs attention back to the assumption that sensibles are substantially separate from Ideas, so the Third Man, as a variant, directs attention back to the limitation on the extent of Ideas that implies that assumption. Socrates, in his first response to Parmenides, had supposed that there are Ideas of Likeness and Unity and Justice; that there are no Ideas of hair, mud, and dirt; and that there are only doubtfully Ideas of man, fire, and water. Parmenides' argument calls that restriction into question. If things that are like each other must have a share of one and the same Idea, and if to assert participation in Likeness is to assert participation in further Ideas in respect of which relations of likeness obtain, Ideas of Man and Mud exist no less surely than Ideas of Likeness and Justice. So the examination of Socrates' suggestion that Ideas are paradigms suggests incongruity with his earlier pronouncements about extent. He had implicitly endowed sensibles with substantial reality because he refused to dignify mud, hair, and dirt with Ideas. But the premises of Parmenides' argument suggest that Ideas will be present wherever things may be said to be like in some respect, whether those things are just acts, or men, or mud-pies. To call into question Socrates' limitation on extent is immediately to call into question the separation of sensibles that limititation implies. This explains why Parmenides' criticism is ambiguous, issuing not only in the Likeness regress but in the Third

Man as a variant. The Third Man strikes at limitation of extent. The likeness regress strikes deeper: it calls into question the assumption of separate sensibles.

Aristotle and the Third Man

It is worth observing that the foregoing account coheres neatly with Aristotle's. In the *Metaphysics* (990b 15-17, cf. XIII$_2$ 1079a 12-13), Aristotle criticizes Plato on the ground that

> Of the more accurate arguments, some lead to Ideas of relations, of which we say there is no independent class, and others introduce the 'third man.'

Alexander of Aphrodisias, commenting on this passage, lists four arguments that went by the name of the 'third man' (*in Metaph*. 83.34 - 85.12). The first is ascribed to Eudemus in his book *On Diction*; the second and third are sophistical criticisms of the theory of Ideas, the third being ascribed to Polyxenus (for a summary of them, see *PP* 88-89; see also *ACPA*, App. IV); the fourth Alexander explicitly (85.11) ascribes to Aristotle in the fourth book of the *On Ideas*, remarking its close connection with the argument used by Eudemus and others (*in Metaph*. 84.20 - 85.5):

> The existence of the third man is also proved in this way. If that which is predicated truly of several things also exists in separation from these (this is what the believers in Ideas think they prove; the reason why, according to them, man-himself exists is that 'man' is predicated truly of the many particular men, and is other than they) — if this be so, there will be a third man. For if the 'man' which is predicated is different from those of whom it is predicated, and exists independently, and 'man' is predicated both of particular men and of the Idea of man, there will be a third man apart both from particular men and from the Idea. On this basis, too, there will be a fourth man, predicated both of the third man, of the Idea, and of the particulars; and similarly a fifth, and so *ad infinitum*. This argument is identical with the first [i.e., that of Eudemus], and follows from the assumptions that things that are like are like by participation in some identical thing, and that particular men and the Ideas are like.

This argument, it will be observed, is drawn directly from the Third Man variant in the *Parmenides*, and testifies to Aristotle's conviction that the claim that Ideas are paradigms of which their participants are images is not only useless (cf. *Meta*. I 991a 20-31), but prey to the regress Parmenides urges against it. Aristotle himself regarded the Third Man as a fallacy based on treating men and Man as separable individuals (*de Sophisticis Elenchis* 178b 37 - 179a 10, cf. 169a 31-36, *Post. Anal*. I 84a 7-28, 85a 31 ff.):

> Again, there is the proof that there is a 'third man' distinct from Man

and from individual men. But that is a fallacy, for 'man,' and indeed every general predicate, denotes not an individual substance, but a particular quality, or the being related to something in a particular manner, or something of that sort. . . . It is evident then that one must not grant that what is a common predicate applying to a class universally is an individual substance, but must say that it denotes either a quality, or a relation, or a quality, or something of that kind.

The Third Man, Aristotle believes, results from construing predication in terms of a relation between individual substances. This is precisely the root of the perplexities in the *Parmenides* concerning participation.

The outlines of Aristotle's own solution are stated with considerable economy in *Metaphysics* VII, in a passage already cited (1038b 34 - 1039a 3, cf. *ACPA* 288-89. See also 1031b 28 - 1032a 4, where Aristotle is compelled to claim that each thing and its essence are one, on pain of infinite regress):

It is plain that no universal attribute is a substance, and this is plain also from the fact that no common predicate indicates a 'this' but rather a 'such.' If not, many difficulties follow and especially the 'third man.'

You cannot treat Coriscus and Man both as substances, and since Coriscus is a substance, Man is not. Aristotle puts the point directly in the *Categories* (1a 20 ff.): sensible substances, such as this man or this horse, are individual and one in number, and can neither be in a subject nor said of a subject; what is said of a subject, such as Man or Horse, is neither individual nor one in number. In short, the universal that qualifies a this is not a this. Aristotle offers, later in *Metaphysics* VII, an argument that shows that he is aware of the Academic reply, and thinks it unavailing. After remarking that no universal can exist apart from its individuals, since what is common is in many places at the same time, and what is one cannot be in many places at the same time, he applies this directly to Ideas. (*Meta.* VII 1040b 27 - 1041a 5, cf. XIII 1079b 3 - 11. See Ross, *AM* ii, 220 on 1041a i):

But those who say the Forms exist, in one respect are right, in giving the Forms separate existence, *if* they are substances; but in another respect they are not right, since they say the one over many is a Form. The reason for their doing this is that they cannot declare what are the substances of this sort, the imperishable substances which exist apart from the individual and sensible substances. They make them, then, the same in kind as the perishable things (for this kind of substances we know) — 'man-itself' and 'horse-itself', adding to the sensible things the word 'itself.' . . . Clearly then, no universal term is the name of a substance, and no substance is composed of substances.

Imperishable substances are the same in kind as sensible substances, a claim that assumes the fundamental premise of the Third Man, that Man itself is a man (*E.N.* I 1096a 33 - b 5):

> And one might ask the question, what in the world they *mean* by 'a thing itself,' if (as in the case) in 'man himself' and in a particular man the account of man is one and the same. For in so far as they are man, they will in no respect differ; and if this is so, neither will 'good itself' and particular goods, in so far as they are good. But again it will not be good any the more for being eternal, since that which lasts long is not whiter than that which perishes in a day.

The Platonic reply, that Man is not *a* man, but Man itself, what it is to be man, would solve the duplication criticism and avoid the Third Man: for what it is to be man is not a man, in the sense of having manhood, any more than what it is to be large has largeness, or what it is to be like is like anything.

But if Aristotle's criticism is false to Plato's theory, it is hardly a mere blank fallacy or misunderstanding. The *Parmenides* assumes that sensibles have an independent and substantial existence apart from Ideas, and this assumption of the independent reality of sensibles is, of course, the core of Aristotle's account of substance. If then it is suggested that sensibles also resemble Ideas, themselves independent and substantial existents, it must be as two independent objects resemble each other. That sort of resemblance is indirect; it obtains by the joint possession of a common character. One need then only add the assumption that the resemblance between sensibles and Ideas obtains in virtue of the character that the Idea is in order to make Ideas eternal sensibles, the same in kind as perishable things, but long-lasting. Put otherwise, there are well-founded reasons for supposing that the proposition that Likeness is what it is to be like cannot be reconciled with the proposition that sensibles have an independent and substantial reality of their own, and yet gain their characteristics by participation in Ideas. The claim that sensibles are likenesses of Ideas, that participation is imitation, is characteristically Platonic; but if in our search for a real relation that will make participation of substantially independent sensibles in substantially independent Ideas intelligible, we should fall back on part and whole, the *Parmenides* contains much to suggest that we err. The 'thing itself' is then *in* sensibles, and this is a reason to think that it is in time, in place, and subject to change. Aristotle, assuming as a primary truth that sensibles have independent and substantial existence, found Plato's theory of Ideas incoherent. If Alexander's reports of *On Ideas* are correct, he reached that conclusion after long reflection on the *Parmenides*, which presents a fundamental and reticulated metaphysical perplexity which Aristotle believed that Plato could not satisfactorily solve.

Plato in fact solved it by other means. Aristotle's theory of substance is, as it were, a mirror image of Plato's account in the *Timaeus*. He supposes that since sensibles are thises, universals are neither individual nor one in number. Plato on the contrary supposed that since Ideas are individual and one in number, sensibles are not thises; they are only resemblances and images of thises, as insubstantial as a dream. The perplexities of the *Parmenides* derive from the assumption that both sensibles and Ideas have an independent and substantial reality. That assumption both Plato and Aristotle rejected, in opposite ways.

Conclusion

Socrates, young and inexperienced, attempted to evade the consequences of the Dilemma of Participation by suggesting as a further premise that Ideas are thoughts. The suggestion failed. He has now attempted to evade the consequences of the Dilemma once more, by suggesting that Ideas are paradigms and participation resemblance. Parmenides' examination of this suggestion directs the reader's attention back to two crucial assumptions: that Ideas are limited in extent, and that sensibles are separate from Ideas. The young Socrates does not see far enough to recognize the effect of this, and remains dialectically bound by his own admissions. The result is that his suggestion fails; he has achieved no satisfactory refutation of the premises of the Dilemma of Participation, and the Dilemma stands. "The answerer is bound either to accept the sense as taken by the questioner, or else himself to explain clearly whatever it is that his definition means" (*Topics* VI 151b 10).

The Likeness regress and the Third Man do not follow from the Dilemma of Participation, nor are they connected with the Largeness regress, except homologously. But they redirect attention to an assumption that is fundamental to the Dilemma of Participation, and thus of the Largeness regress: that as Ideas are separate from sensibles, so sensibles are separate from Ideas. That premise is the foundation of Parmenides' next, and concluding criticism.

II.viii. Separation and Unknowability (133a-134e)

Parmenides suggests that there are many perplexities, *aporiai*, in the theory that Ideas exist alone by themselves, but the greatest is this: if Ideas are such as we say they must be, we have grounds for claiming that they cannot so much as be known.

Parmenides' argument that Ideas are unknowable turns on the premise that knowledge is a relative, and that things in our world and Ideas are not relative to each other. The latter result is a function of the Hinge of the Dilemma of Participation: either participation is in parts of Ideas or there is no participation. Partitive participation issued in the Paradox of Divisibility and the Largeness Regress, and Socrates' attempt to evade those unfortunate consequences, by claiming that Ideas are thoughts, and that they are paradigms, has failed. He therefore remains bound by his original agreements, and the Hinge swings outward from the immanence of the indistinct to the transcendence of the irrelevant. The Dilemma of Participation becomes a reductio: there is no participation.

Taken as a reductio, the Dilemma of Participation functions as a wedge. It does not prove that Ideas do not exist. It rather splits the claim that Ideas exist from the claim that other things partake of them, and are named after them. The assumption that Ideas exist, but that they are not in us or in things in our world is equivalent, so far as the sensible world is concerned, to denial of participation; it implies that things in our world, though they may have the same name as Ideas (how can one say so?) are named for themselves and not for Ideas. Separation is radical.

The consequence that we cannot know things in the gods' realm, nor they in ours, is indeed 'too strange'; it implies denial of rational theology and divine providence (see *Philebus* 59a-c, 61d-62b, and *Laws* X generally, especially 901d-902b). It also severs connection between religion and conduct: as Adeimantus suggests in the *Republic* (II 365d-e), if there are no gods, or if they do not concern themselves with human affairs, we need not be concerned to escape their notice. In *Laws* X it is impiety, a punishable offense, to maintain that either of these claims is true.

Parmenides leads the young Socrates to admissions that seem very like a parody of the theory of Ideas. We deal with Two Worlds, and given that there is no participation, they are two independent worlds. Ideas have their nature and reality relative to each other, but not relative to the likenesses, or whatever they are, of which things in our world partake and from which they get their names. Things in our world are of the same name (133d 3) as Ideas, but whereas in the *Phaedo* (78e) and the *Timaeus* (52a) they had the same name as Ideas because they participate in them, and indeed, are named after them (*Phaedo* 102b 2, cf. c 10, 103b 7-8, *Parmenides* 130e 5; see also A. E. Taylor, *Commentary on Plato's Timaeus*, p. 342 on 52a 5)—are not only homonymous but eponymous—they are now, though homonymous, unrelated. They exist relative to themselves and not to Ideas, and get their names from themselves and not from Ideas. From the truth that a master is master of a slave, as a father is father of a child, (*Symposium* 199d-e, cf. *Republic* IV 438b-d, *Charmides* 168b-169a; see also *Sophist* 255c-d, *Theaetetus* 160b, and below, 160d-e, 164c), it is inferred that Mastership is Master of Slavery, and Slavery Slavery of Mastership, that the Idea of Knowledge is of the world of Ideas, and more generally, that Ideas of relatives are as such relative to Ideas. Mastership, after all, is what it is to be a master, and Knowledge is "most exact," that is, what it is to be knowledge. Parmenides infers that Ideas are related to each other as their instances are related to each other, but that Ideas are not related to their instances. The collapse of being and having is pretty to see, and occurs below at 146d-e with respect to Sameness and Difference, with important consequences for an important proof.

The Separation Premise

Socrates has earlier agreed that Ideas exist alone by themselves (128e 6, 129d 7), an assumption that Parmenides now recalls (133a 9). That proposition, thought through, implies that the Idea of *F* is what it is to be *F*, and that what it is to be *F* excludes its opposite and does not have what it is. Parmenides now leads Socrates to agree that if Ideas exist alone by themselves they are not in us or in things in our world (133c).

This result derives from the Dilemma of Participation. That Dilemma had assumed that if there is participation, Ideas are *in* the things that partake of them, either in whole or in part. The first disjunct proved impossible *ab initio*, and the second issued in the Paradox of Divisibility and the Largeness Regress, consequences that are unacceptable as destroying the unity of Ideas. Two attempts to avoid those consequences, by supposing that Ideas are thoughts, and that they are paradigms, have failed: there is no participation. The proposition that Ideas exist alone by themselves, then, implies that they do not have parts distributed to participants. Socrates sees the result: Ideas are not in us, an admission that implies denial of participation. So it is that separation and denial of participation are later to be taken as equivalent, for example at 159b-d.

The reference to participation in Likenesses in our world is aporetic and ambiguous.[66] It may mean that sensibles participate in each other and are likenesses of each other; for they get their names from each other, and not from Ideas—a claim that flatly contradicts the proposition that sensible participants get their names from Ideas by reason of sharing in them (130e). But Socrates had earlier agreed that Ideas are not only separate from their participants, but from the immanent characters their participants possess (130b): as Likeness itself is separate from us, so it is also separate from the likeness that we have. Perhaps then sensibles are now to be understood as participating in their own immanent characters, which are likenesses of immanent characters in other sensibles. It would presumably follow, on pain of the Dilemma of Participation, that the likeness we possess, and any other character in us, cannot be universal, One over Many, but must be unique to the thing in which it is and which is named 'like.' So construed, the denial of participation leads to a result very similar to that obtained by treating participation as participation in parts of Ideas: the difference is that the largeness in Simmias is no longer part of Largeness itself. This suggests that such knowledge as exists in our world must be the product of abstraction from sensibles. The coherence of this is left unexamined.

Relatives

The application to relatives is direct. To be relative is to be relative *of* or *than* or *to* something, and as Socrates had pointed out in the *Republic*, there is a sense in which relatives get their names from each other (*Republic* IV 438b-c, trans. Cornford, slightly altered):

> Surely, whenever you have two correlative terms, if one is qualified, the
> other must always be qualified too; whereas if one is unqualified, so

is the other. 'Greater' is a relative term; and the greater is greater than the less; if it is much greater, then the less is much less; if it is greater at some moment, past or future, then the less is less at that same moment. The same principle applies to all such correlatives, like 'more' and 'fewer,' 'Double' and 'Half'; and again to terms like 'heavier' and 'lighter,' 'quicker' and 'slower,' and to things like hot and cold.

It is further supposed in the *Republic* that relatives can be relatives only by participation in Ideas of relatives (V 479a-c, VII 523a-524d). But this cannot be true if there is no participation in Ideas, and Parmenides therefore assumes that sensibles get their names only by reference to each other. Simmias, if he is larger than Cebes, gets the name of 'large' from his relation to Cebes, not from participation in Largeness itself, and the largeness that Simmias has or of which he partakes is an immanent character in him. Parmenides brings out the point by example, in an argument so phrased as to show that Ideas and sensibles may have the same name, and yet have no connection. Ideas may be relative to each other, and sensibles relative to each other, but Ideas cannot be relative to sensibles, or sensibles to Ideas. Thus Mastership is what it is relative to Slavery;[67] but it has no relation to masters or slaves among us, which are what they are relative to each other, and not relative to Mastership or Slavery. Things in our world have no significance, or meaning, or power ($\delta\acute{\upsilon}\nu\alpha\mu\iota\varsigma$) relative to Ideas, nor Ideas relative to things in our world; for if either world were relative to the other, the other would be correlative to it. The symmetry assumption Parmenides had assumed for participation as likeness is simply a special case of this general point. Furthermore, given that relatives imply correlatives, and correlatives mutual and reciprocal qualification, Ideas, if they were relative to sensibles, would be qualified in a way corresponding to sensibles. Given that sensibles come to be and pass away, it would follow that Ideas must change character reciprocally with the sensibles to which they are relative, and thus would not exist 'alone by themselves' as independent entities. In short, correlation would come perilously close to collapse. This is a further, if unstated, reason for supposing that as Ideas are relative to Ideas, so sensibles must be relative to sensibles but not to Ideas, and named for each other.

Parmenides' argument does not by itself disprove the existence of Ideas. It rather assumes their existence, as it also assumes the independent existence of sensibles. Socrates had begun by assuming that Ideas are separate from their participants, and that sensibles have a reality separate from Ideas. He has now been led to two worlds that are radically separate as precluding any relation at all. This separation is, again, closely allied to collapse. Assume that difference is a relative. If so, then these two separate worlds cannot be different, and thus not separate, and thus not two. Radical separation, thought through, implies lack of distinction.

All of this, of course, turns on Parmenides' premise that if there is no participation of sensibles in Ideas, then there is no relation between sensibles and

Ideas or Ideas and sensibles. The proof of this is not demonstrative but dialectical. Ideas of relatives, specifically of Likeness, were introduced to solve a paradox involving qualification by opposites. To hold that sensibles are relative to Ideas, but do not participate in Ideas of relatives, would be to deny the principle on which Ideas were initially introduced: for their introduction required participation.

Knowledge

The *Republic*, in analyzing relatives, offered knowledge as a further example (*Republic* IV 438c-e, trans. Cornford, slightly altered):

> Take the various branches of knowledge. The object of knowledge pure and simple is the knowable — if that is the right word — without any qualification; whereas a particular kind of knowledge has an object of a particular kind. For example, as soon as men learnt how to build houses, their craft was distinguished from others under the name of architecture, because it had a unique character, which was itself due to the character of its objects; and all other branches of craft and knowledge were distinguished in the same way. This, then, if you understand me, is what I meant by saying that, where there are two correlatives, the one is qualified if, and only if, the other is so. I am not saying that the one must have the same quality as the other — that the science of health and disease is itself healthy and diseased, or that knowledge of good and evil is itself good and evil — but only that, as soon as you have a knowledge that is restricted to a particular kind of object, namely health and disease, the knowledge itself becomes a particular kind of knowledge. Hence we no longer call it merely knowledge, which would have for its object whatever can be known, but we add the qualification and call it medical science.

Parmenides now draws the appropriate inference. Since Knowledge is a relative, the example of Mastership applies *pari passu* to Knowledge. It is the nature of Knowledge itself to be of (or relative to) what is knowable in itself, and of the various kinds of knowledge to be marked off by specific kinds of knowables. The Ideas are known by the Idea of Knowledge itself.[68] But knowledge in our world must be relative to things in our world, and cannot be relative to Ideas. In short, we are in our own world, and can therefore have no knowledge of Beauty and Justice and other Ideas.

This result, it may be observed, cannot be avoided by the doctrine that learning is Recollection: for it is an essential part of that doctrine that sensibles remind us of Ideas by reason of their participation in or likeness to Ideas, and there is now no participation. Nor can souls be intermediate between sensibles and Ideas if there is no connection between Ideas and sensibles. Again, assuming that the god or gods have a share of Knowledge itself (*per impossible*), they could not know things in our world, since their knowledge cannot be relative to things among us. Notice that Parmenides passes from singular to plural in this passage (134c-e) without apparent sense of transition. Notice also that participation within the Ideal world is entertained as possible (134c 10), as it was within the sensible world (133d 2). What is denied is that the sensible world, the world here, participates in Ideas, the world there. But since Parmenides' criticisms, though directed against participation of sensibles in Ideas, apply to participation generally, then so long as this is conceived as a real relation between distinct things, both those claims are incoherent. Thus, if the most exact knowledge and the most exact mastership exist in the gods' realm, their mastership cannot master us nor their knowledge know us. It is left unremarked that their mastership could have nothing in common with ours but the name.

These consequences are not a mere tissue of fallacies. They result from taking the Dilemma of Participation as destructive, so that the possibility of participation is denied while the separate existence of Ideas and sensibles is assumed.

Aristotle and Irrelevance

It is part of the later history of this passage that Aristotle should have held that Plato was committed to so radical a separation between Ideas and sensibles as to render the hypothesis of Ideas useless for explanation. This, indeed, is the main criticism of Plato in *Metaphysics* I. ix. (990a 34 - b 8):

> But as for those who posit the Ideas as causes, firstly, in seeking to grasp the causes of the things around us, they introduced others equal in number to these, as if a man who wanted to count things thought he would not be able to do it while they were few, but tried to count them when he had added to their number. For the Forms are practically equal to — or not fewer than—the things, in trying to explain which these thinkers proceeded from them to the Forms. For to each thing there answers an entity which has the same name and exists apart from the substance, and so also in the case of all other groups there is a one over many, whether the many are in this world or are eternal.

Aristotle, it will be observed, takes it as evident that the One over Many applies, not only to the sensible world, but in the Ideal world as well, and proceeds to list a series of objections to Ideas that he takes to be well-known. He then proceeds, in the manner of the *Parmenides*, to argue that Ideas cannot explain because they are not in their participants, and cannot be known (*Meta.* I 991a 8-14):

> Above all one might discuss the question what on earth the Forms contribute to sensible things, either to those that are eternal or to those that come into being and cease to be. For they cause neither movement nor any change in them. But again they help in no wise either toward the knowledge of the other things (for they are not even the

substance of these, else they would have been in them), or toward their being, if they are not in the particulars which share in them; though if they were, they might be thought to be causes, as white causes whiteness in a white object by entering into its composition.

We are exactly on the ground of Parmenides' concluding criticism. Nor does it help to analyze participation in terms of imitation (*Meta.* I 991a 19-31):

But, further, all other things cannot come from the Forms in any of the usual senses of 'from.' And to say that they are patterns and the other things share in them is to use empty words and poetical metaphors. For what is it that works, looking to the Ideas? And anything can either be, or become, like another without being copied from it, so that whether Socrates exists or not a man like Socrates might come to be; and evidently this might be so even if Socrates were eternal. And there will be several patterns of the same thing, and therefore several Forms; e.g. 'animal' and 'two-footed' and also 'man himself' will be Forms of man. Again, the Forms are patterns not only of sensible things, but of Forms themselves also; i.e., the genus, as genus of various species, will be so; therefore the same thing will be pattern and copy.

Ideas are, in effect, mere eternal sensibles (cf. *Meta.* III 997b 3-12, VII 1040b 30-34, X 1059a 10-14, *E.N.* I 1096a 34 - b 5), and because they participate in other Ideas they are both paradigm and copy, $\pi \alpha \rho \acute{\alpha} \delta \epsilon \iota \gamma \mu \alpha \; \kappa \alpha \grave{\iota} \; \epsilon \grave{\iota} \kappa \acute{\omega} \nu$. It is, in fact, quite useless to speak of participation (*Meta.* I 992a 24-29):

In general, though philosophy seeks the cause of perceptible things, we have given this up (for we say nothing of the cause from which change takes its start), but while we fancy we are stating the substance of perceptible things, we assert the existence of a second class of substances, while our account of the way in which they are the substances of perceptible things is empty talk; for "sharing,' as we said before, means nothing.

In denying that participation is anything more than an empty metaphor, and that Ideas can be causes, that is, principles of explanation of anything in the sensible world, Aristotle accurately represents the content of Parmenides' concluding criticism. But there is also an important difference. Parmenides offers as examples of Ideas relatives such as Knowledge, Master, and Slave. But Aristotle testifies that, of the more exact arguments—'more exact' not because more logically cogent, but because more specific, as establishing that Ideas are not merely common but paradigms, and reproducing the vocabulary of Plato's Parmenides, who describes Ideas Mastership and Knowledge as 'most exact'[69] —"some lead to Ideas of relations, of which we say there is no independent class, and others introduce the 'third man'" (*Meta.* I 990b 15-17). Aristotle maintains, that is, that the Platonists either did not, or could not consistently, maintain Ideas of relatives (*Meta.* I 990b 22 - 991a 8, 991b 1-3); but he holds this only if there is participation, for, "If Forms can be shared in, there must be ideas of substance only" (*Meta.* I 990b 28-29; see further XII 1079b 3 - 11). He proceeds to confront the Platonists with a dilemma: if the Ideas and the particulars that share in them have the same form, there will be something common to them—the root of the Likeness Regress—and if they have not the same form they are merely homonymous, without any community (κοινωνία) between them (*Meta.* I 991a 2-8)—the root of the unknowability argument. Since Aristotle's claim that there are Ideas only of substance and not of relatives rests on the proposition that sensibles participate in Ideas, it is formally consistent with Parmenides' final criticism, which assumes that there is no participation, and that Ideas and sensibles are therefore merely homonymous. It may be added that if Ideas and sensibles are substantially distinct, the dilemma Aristotle poses is, it would seem, ineluctable: either Ideas and sensibles share common characters, and are therefore alike, or they have nothing in common but the name. This result was first put by Plato in the *Parmenides*.

Still, given the repeated evidence of Ideas of relatives, Aristotle's denial of such Ideas is jarring, and it is difficult to see how he could have reached this conclusion as an inference from Parmenides' final criticism. That criticism explicitly countenances Ideas of relatives: Mastership, Slavery, Knowledge. But Parmenides goes on to remark that the perplexities he has raised against Socrates' theory suggest that there are no Ideas at all, and that even if there are, they are unknowable (135a). The two propositions are intimately connected. If Ideas cannot be known by us, we know neither that they exist, nor that they have their οὐσία, their nature and reality, relative to each other. To make Ideas of relatives unknowable directly suggests, if it does not imply, that no Ideas of relatives exist. Aristotle uses this result as a step in a dialectical proof: there can be no Ideas of relatives, but only of substance; there are no Ideas of substance, for that would imply the Third Man; therefore, there are no Ideas. Clearly, Parmenides' final argument admits the same generalization.

It may be that there is also a further connection. Alexander (*in Metaph.* 82.11-83.17) offers as a 'more exact' argument a proof that Ideas of relatives must be homonymous with their instances, since the definition of relatives does not apply to instances. Relatives are contrasted to substantives on this ground, and the argument plainly reflects Aristotle's claim in the *Categories* that secondary substance is predicable of primary substance both in name and definition, and that this predication distinguishes substance from all categories other than substance, which therefore must have instances as incapable of existing apart from it. (See further, "Substance and Predication in Aristotle's Categories," *Exegesis and Argument* (ed. Lee, et al.), Assen, 1973 362 ff.) That the argument is Aristotle's own is indicated by its conclusion, that the Idea is παράδειγμα καὶ εἰκών of those things that have come to be in relation to it.[70] This is Aristotle's claim, not Plato's: the Idea must be both pattern and copy. (*Meta.* I 991a 31, cf. Alexander, *in Metaph.* 105.25-27). Allowing that this

implies that the Idea has what it is, it leads to the objection that the existence of
a paradigm, Equal-itself, implies an equal-itself to which it is equal, since what is
equal is equal to what is equal to it; therefore, there must be more than one
Idea of Equality (*in Metaph*. 83.26-28). This is a homologue of the Likeness Regress, and it is not by accident that Alexander proceeds to expound
the Third Man. But the primary objection Alexander offers, presumably drawing
upon *On Ideas*, is that, "The Platonists denied that there are Ideas answering to
relative terms, because for them Ideas exist in their own right (καθ' αὐτάs), being
substances, while relative terms (τὰ πρός τι) have their being in their relation to
one another" (*in Metaph*. 83.24-26, trans. Ross). As Cherniss very truly says
(*ACPA* n. 191), this turns on substituting πρός τι in the sense of 'dependent upon'
for πρός τι in the sense of 'relative.' It is an *ignoratio elenchi,* and one that precisely
matches Parmenides' treatment of relatives in his final argument (133c 8-9, e 6,
134d 5-7).

Aristotle's Debt to This Argument

It is not enough to remark the use to which Aristotle puts the *Parmenides* in
fashioning his own criticism of Plato's theory of Ideas. It is important to observe
to how great an extent the *Parmenides* enters into Aristotle's arguments for his
own positive doctrine. Thus for example it has already been observed that *Metaphysics* VII. 13, Aristotle's treatment of substance and universality derives
directly from the Dilemma of Participation in the *Parmenides*. The same is true
of *Metaphysics* VII. 6, Aristotle's analysis of the circumstances in which each
thing and its essence are one (1031a 28 - b 14):

> But in the case of so-called self-subsistent things is a thing necessarily the
> same as its essence? E.g., if there are some substances which have no other
> substances nor entities prior to them — substances such as some assert the
> Ideas to be? — if the essence of good is to be different from good-itself,
> and the essence of animal from animal-itself, and the essence of being
> from being-itself, there will, firstly, be other substances and entities and
> Ideas besides those which are asserted, and, secondly, these others will
> be prior substances, if essence is substance. And if the posterior sub-
> stances and the prior are severed from each other, (a) there will be no
> knowledge of the former, and (b) the latter will have no being. (By
> 'severed' I mean, if the good-itself has not the essence of good, and the
> latter has not the property of being good.) For (a) there is knowledge
> of each thing only when we know its essence. And (b) the case is the
> same for other things as for the good; so that if the essence of good is
> not good, neither is the essence of reality real, nor the essence of unity
> one. . . . The good, then must be one with the essence of good, and
> the beautiful with the essence of beauty, and so with all things which
> do not depend on something else but are self-subsistent and primary
> (καθ' αὐτά καὶ πρῶτα).

This account shows how seriously Aristotle took the argument of the *Parmenides* respecting separation and unknowability. It also shows that he understood that argument to be directly connected with a main variant of the Third Man. Aristotle took such statements as "Goodness is good," "Beauty is beautiful," "Unity is one," and "Being is," not as ordinary predications, but as statements of identity: each thing and its essence are one in no merely accidental way, and in the case of sulf-subsistent things such as Ideas, each is necessarily the same as its essence.

Conclusion

The proof that Ideas are unknowable, that there are Two Worlds, each mutually independent and unknowable by anything in the other, is a function of the Hinge. If there is participation, parts of Ideas are in participants; this destroys the unity of Ideas, and with it their claim to exist alone by themselves. If Ideas exist alone by themselves, as one, then they cannot be in participants. There is then no participation, whence it is inferred that there is no relation, and no knowledge. This result cannot be avoided by making participation resemblance, so long as the substantial distinction of participants and Ideas is assumed. If Ideas cannot be known by us, we know neither that Mastership or Knowledge exists, nor that, if they do exist, they are *of* anything. We have no ground for supposing either that things in the Ideal world are relative to anything, or that they are not relative to anything. Nor have we ground for supposing that Zeno's paradox of Likeness can be solved.

II.ix. Conclusion (134e-135d)

Parmenides now suggests that difficulties or ἀπορίαι such as these, and more in addition, are inevitable, if Ideas are to be distinguished as things by themselves, apart from sensibles — sensibles that, we recall, have also been distinguished as things by themselves, apart from Ideas. The hearer will be perplexed, and argue that Ideas do not exist, and that even if they do, they are unknowable by us.

It will be observed that Parmenides does not suppose that the arguments against participation cannot be solved. He rather supposes they can be solved, but that it will take a man of remarkable gifts to solve them.

It is evident from this single passage that Parmenides does not suppose that his criticisms of the theory of Ideas are a mera tissue of fallacies. On the contrary, they are deep and serious, and raise difficulties that must be thought through if the theory of Ideas is to be sustained. Socrates, young and inexperienced, has not yet thought them through with sufficient care.

If the criticisms are not trivial, neither are they fatal. Parmenides not only supposes that they *can* be solved, but that they *must* be solved, and he gives his reason: if the existence of Ideas is denied, thinking (διάνοια) will have no object, and the power and significance of discourse will be utterly destroyed. In short, the man who has criticized the theory of Ideas subscribes to the theory he has criticized. His arguments are not to be understood as a refutation of that theory, but as a set of perplexities that must be thought through if that theory is to be understood. The criticisms are answerable, and the answers must be found if philosophy is to be pursued.

Retrospect

The young Socrates has failed to answer Parmenides' criticisms, and Parmenides offers a diagnosis of his inability: he has undertaken to mark off Ideas too soon, before being properly exercised. This diagnosis looks both backward and forward: backward, to the question about the extent of Ideas with which Parmenides' examination of Socrates began; forward, to the hypothetical exercise on Unity that is to follow.

Looking backward, the diagnosis suggests—as Parmenides had suggested at the time (130e)—that Socrates has failed to give an adequate account of the extent of Ideas. It further suggests that the perplexities in which he has become entangled are the result of that failure.

Socrates' limitation on the extent of Ideas, thought through, implicitly endows sensibles with an independent and substantial reality. Because hair, mud, and dirt are worthless and trivial, they are assumed to have a nature, and therefore a reality, separate from that of any Ideas in which they partake. It may be that the same is also true of man, fire, and water, and perhaps more generally, of other substantival terms.

Suppose this is so. Suppose further that Simmias is a man, and that Simmias is like Cebes. By hypothesis, this implies that Simmias participates in the Idea of Likeness. We are now faced with the question in what this participation consists, remembering always that Simmias and Likeness are separate and distinct entities. How can separate entities be so connected that one can be said to participate in, and so be called by the name of, the other? How is it that Simmias can properly be called 'like'?

Parmenides suggested an answer to this question, and one that Socrates accepted without demur. If there is participation, then the Idea, in whole or in part, must be *in* the participant. This suggestion is not a logical consequence of the separation of sensibles from Ideas and the participation of sensibles in Ideas. It is rather meant to explain how separated participation is possible, and the explanation is dialectical: a real relation, not a formal or logical relation, is required to connect independently existing things; the part/whole relation is an obvious candidate, and the reader, presumably, is meant to ask himself whether any other real relation he may suggest will better serve; certainly likeness will not. But if the part/whole account of participation is accepted, it implies that if there is participation, it must be participation in parts of Ideas, not the whole of them, whence it follows that if there is no participation in parts of Ideas, there is no participation. This disjunction—either participation in parts, or no participation—is the hinge of the Dilemma of Participation, and neither turn of the hinge is acceptable. The assumption that participation is participation in parts of Ideas leads to the Paradox of Divisibility and the Largeness Regress—to the destruction of the unity of the Idea, its capacity to serve as a universal, One over Many. Indeed, if the assumption of universality, as a function of sameness of meaning, is applied to the Largeness Regress, it forthwith becomes vicious.

These consequences cannot be escaped by supposing that Ideas are thoughts, or that they are paradigms. The first suggestion is once again prey to the Dilemma of Participation. The second issues in a Likeness Regress homologous to the Largeness Regress, and redirects attention to the assumption that sensibles have an existence independent of Ideas.

So Socrates has failed to give an intelligible account of participation and the Hinge swings outward, to the transcendence of the irrelevant. If participation implies participation in Ideas, in whole or in part, and if both consequences lead to absurdity, there is no participation. Sensibles, having a substantial reality of their own, can have no relation to Ideas, nor can Ideas be known by us. If Ideas cannot be known by us, there is no reason for supposing that Ideas exist; which is a very good reason for supposing that they do not exist. An argument that began by questioning the existence of certain Ideas, such as hair, mud, and dirt, has been brought to a point where the existence of all Ideas has been called in question.

Prospect

Socrates has been brought to this impasse because he has not been properly exercised, and the concluding part of the *Parmenides* provides that exercise. The exercise will be performed on an Idea of utmost generality, namely Unity. It will assume, as Parmenides' criticisms have assumed, that sensibles and Ideas have separate existence, and that participation implies the Dilemma of Participation.

The result is a perfection of aporetic structure. In light of Parmenides' criticisms and Socrates' inability to answer them, it is tempting to assume, as Parmenides has already remarked (135a-b), that Ideas do not exist. The concluding part of the dialogue will prove that *whether or not* the existence of the Idea of Unity is asserted or denied, the results are absurd. And because Unity is an Idea of utmost generality, those results apply universally, to everything that is.

The exercise must not be construed as an a priori proof of the existence of Ideas. It is dialectical, proceeding from admissions Socrates has already made. It demonstrates that you cannot accept the criticisms that follow from those admissions as valid and deny the existence of Ideas without inconsistency; and that you cannot reject the criticisms that follow from those admissions as invalid and accept Ideas without inconsistency. The philosopher, deprived of every easy expedient, is forced to retrace his steps and to identify the ultimate assumptions on which the criticisms and the exercise depend.

So the exercise will teach the young Socrates that perplexities are not to be evaded, but traced to their source. And it will provide ample indication of where that source lies. But it will not teach the reader what must be put in their place. The *Parmenides* is not didactic: if it compels the reader to face metaphysical problems of considerable importance, it dictates no solution. Plato teaches here, as he had always done, by compelling his readers to inquire.

The ultimate problem arises from the assumption of the separate existence of sensibles and Ideas, a problem Aristotle was afterward to face and undertake to solve with his own doctrine of the priority of substance to universal. Plato's own solution, offered in the *Timaeus*, is the mirror image of Aristotle's: it is that sensibles have no independent reality of their own. Sensibles are relational entities, whose whole being is such as to be *in* something other than themselves, space, the Receptacle, and *of* something other than themselves, the eternal Ideas, which alone are truly existent. But these results lie outside the *Parmenides*.

The core of the problem is not the relation of sensibles and Ideas as such, but that of reconciling participation with separate existence. That issue extends to the relations of Ideas among themselves. Socrates is just, justice is a virtue, virtue is and is one. Are we then to say that Justice and Virtue, or Unity and Being, are relational entities—that they are in or of something other than themselves? Either to affirm or deny that Unity participates in Being is to generate the antinomies of the concluding part of the *Parmenides*, antinomies that extend Zeno's paradox to the uttermost level of metaphysical generality.

Part III.
The Hypotheses
about Unity (135d-166c)

Introduction (135d-137c)

Parmenides has criticized Socrates' theory of Ideas and has told him that the reason Socrates cannot answer the criticisms or successfully defend the theory of Ideas is that, owing to his youth, he has undertaken to distinguish Ideas before being properly trained. Socrates had earlier limited the extent of Ideas because he still paid attention to what people thought (130d). He is not called to undertake an exercise in what most people regard as useless, and would condemn as *adoleschia*, idle talk (135d).

The method of exercise is the one Zeno used, except for this: Socrates was right not to allow inquiry into the things we see; the inquiry should rather be directed toward things that may be grasped by an account, and believed to be Ideas. In addition, one must analyze the consequences that follow, not only if an Idea is assumed to be, but also if it is assumed not to be. The question of the extent of Ideas, it will be observed, is now raised again, with utmost generality, as an issue of philosophical method.

Take Zeno's hypothesis, if many is, as an example. The consequences of that hypothesis, and the consequences of its denial, must be traced relative both to Plurality and Unity; and the same is true if the hypothesis concerns Likeness, Unlikeness, Motion or Rest, Generation, Destruction, Being ($a\mathring{v}\tau\acute{o}\ \tau\acute{o}\ e\mathring{\iota}\nu a\iota$) or Not-Being ($\tau\grave{o}\ \mu\acute{\eta}\ e\mathring{\iota}\nu a\iota$). In general, it is necessary, for whatever is hypothesized, to examine the consequences relative to itself, to any one of the others, to more than one, and to all; and again, the others must be examined relative to themselves and to any other Socrates may choose, whether it is hypothesized to be or not to be. Parmenides reluctantly agrees to provide an example of the kind of exercise he has in mind by examining his own hypothesis. That examination constitutes the remainder of the *Parmenides*.

The Subject of Hypothesis

Parmenides' hypothesis is, περὶ τοῦ ἑνὸς αὐτοῦ ὑποθέμενος εἴτε ἓν ἔστιν εἴτε μὴ ἕν, τί χρὴ συμβαίνειν. The full ambiguity of this is quite untranslatable. The Greek is printed without certain key accents because accents were unknown to Plato, and the very attempt to supply them involves interpretation: it requires a choice between ἔστιν as existential or predicative, and ἕν as predicate or subject. That is, there is a choice between a disjunction of the form, "whether it is one or not one," or of the form, "whether one is or one is not."[71]

We are hypothesizing 'the one itself,' to keep to transliteration rather than translation, and if we read, "whether it is one or not one," we immediately want to know what the antecedent of *it* is: what 'one itself' are we are hypothesizing? If we keep to the text of the *Parmenides*, we are not here faced with an embarrassment of ambiguous riches, but a choice between alternatives. Parmenides has said that he will begin with his own hypothesis: at 128a 8, Socrates said that Parmenides held that the All is one, and this is explicitly stated to be his hypothesis by Zeno at 128d 5-6. On this reading, then, the antecedent of *it*, the meaning of "the one itself," is the All, the universe, the sum of things, and the deductions that follow trace the consequences of the hypothesis that the All is one and its denial — the consequences, that is, of assuming or denying Parmenides' One Being.

But Parmenides' One Being can scarcely be the subject of Parmenides' present hypothesis. In the first place, the One Being cannot be participated in because there is nothing else besides it, but the subject of the hypotheses that follow can be participated in: it is an Idea. Second, the One Being precludes the possibility of 'others,' whereas the exercise to follow assumes that they may exist. Again, the denial of the One Being is taken as equivalent to the assertion of plurality, but the denial of Parmenides' present hypothesis does not require this result.

Much has happened in the *Parmenides* between Stephanus pages 128 and 137; specifically, Socrates has put forward the theory of Ideas, and Parmenides, after offering criticisms he himself claims to be answerable, has accepted the theory, along with its attendant pluralism (135a-c). Among the Ideas present, if not accounted for, is Unity, and Parmenides, in saying that his hypothesis is about "the one itself" can only, in context, be understood to mean the Idea of Unity, (see, for example, 129b 5-7, c 2, d 7-e 1, 130b 5, 136a 6), as indeed his language itself suggests. That Unity is the subject is further required by the fact that Parmenides has just said that the subject of the exercise should be an Idea (135d-e), a suggestion confirmed by the use of such examples as Likeness and Unlikeness, Motion and Rest, mentioned as Ideas at 129e, and Generation and Destruction and Being and Not-being. So the antecedent of *it* must be, not the All, but the Idea of Unity.[72] The disjunction, then, must mean, "whether Unity is one or not one."

Alternately, however, ἕν may be subject and ἔστιν existential, for the neuter singular adjective, with or without agreeing article, may have the force of an abstract noun. It has that force, and prominently so, at 130b 5, where ἕν and πολλά are used in direct apposition with αὐτὴ ὁμοιότης: the passage mentions Unity, Plurality, and Likeness itself.[73] Since Parmenides is hypothesizing about Unity, his hypothesis, read existentially is, "whether Unity is or Unity is not."

That the existential meaning is primary is shown by 135e-136a; and the existential meaning is fertile, in that it implies the predicative reading. It is true of every Idea that it is, a claim later taken to imply that it participates in Being (142b-c); it is also true of every Idea that it is one; indeed, Parmenides will affirm that to be and to be one are coimplicatory. That Unity exists, therefore, implies that Unity is one. It may be observed, however, that the Idea of Unity is one in no ordinary way: it is *just* one, as excluding plurality, for no Idea can be qualified by its own opposite (129b-e). This point is crucial to the incompatible deductions that follow.

The existential reading is also fertile with respect to Parmenides' One Being: for the One Being also must both be and be *just* one (cf. *Phys.* I 186a 32-34), and it is therefore in this respect exactly homologous to the Idea of Unity. It follows that any results that follow from the premise that Unity is *just* one will apply, *mutatis mutandis*, to the One Being. So Parmenides' present hypothesis, that Unity exists, subsumes what is essential to his initial hypothesis. The ambiguity in the formulation of that hypothesis points to this clustered, but ordered, set of meanings. The exercise that follows has sometimes been understood as a criticism of the historical Parmenides; this is not mistaken so long as we remember that it is true only *per accidens*, true only in so far as Parmenides' One Being is homologous with the Idea of Unity.

A Point of Translation

That the subject-matter of the deductions is an Idea is required by 135d-e. Parmenides tells Socrates, "I admired it when you said, and said to him, that you would not allow inquiry to wander among the things we see, nor even within their domain, but rather in the field of those things there, which one would most especially grasp by rational account and believe to be characters." That 'the One' is an Idea is not left to inference: Parmenides says it in so many words.

Cornford, however, translating the passage, offered this (*PP* 104, my italics): "There was one thing you said to him which impressed me very much: you would not allow the survey to be *confined* to visible things or range *only* over that field; it was to extend to those objects which are specially apprehended by discourse and can be regarded as Forms." That is, according to Cornford's translation, the inquiry in the deductions which follow will range *both* over sensibles *and* over Ideas. With deference, I submit that this is not in the Greek. The passage says that the inquiry will *not* range over sensibles, but *will* range over Ideas.

No doubt Cornford distorted the Greek because he did not otherwise see how this passage could be squared with the fact that certain of the deductions which follow show that 'the One' is in time, has shape, and is in motion. These characteristics, after all, pertain to what we see, not to Ideas. It seems therefore that the inquiry must extend to the domain of the visible after all.

The true solution, as will be shown in what follows, is this. The hypotheses proceed on the assumptions, incompatible, as we shall find, in the case of an Idea of Unity, that (i) there are Ideas, and (ii) that "you and I and the other things we call many"—sensibles, in short—participate in them (129). But by the Dilemma of Participation (131a-c), participation is to be construed as a part/whole relation, and this implies that the inner nature of Ideas is infected by sensibles, and infected in the most fundamental respects. It is for this reason that, if there is an Idea of Being, and if sensibles partake of it, to be is to be in time.

The discourse, then, ranges only among Ideas. But Ideas are to be understood in terms of what has gone before: Aristotles and Parmenides do not write on a clean slate, and for this reason, Ideas turn out to have many of the characteristics appropriate to sensibles, and to replicate the most general features of the sensible world. This is specifically true in respect to the subject of all the hypotheses, namely, the Idea of Unity.

Structure and Ambiguity

To say that Parmenides formulates his hypothesis ambiguously is not to say that there are multiple subjects of the hypothesis. On the contrary: if the subject of the hypotheses which follow is the Idea of Unity, then there is one and only one subject of the hypotheses.

This view was rejected by Proclus, who maintained that the word 'one' in what follows is trebly ambiguous, as between a One which is superior to being, a One inferior to being, and a One of the same order as being; and that 'not being' in what follows, is doubly ambiguous, as between what in a way is and in a way is not, and what in no way is. The result, for Proclus, is a scheme of nine hypotheses, serially ordered, which exhibits the metaphysical foundations of Neoplatonism:[74]

> In the first, he inquires how the One which is superior to being is related to itself and to the others; in the second, about the one coordinate with being; in the third, how the One which is inferior to being is related to itself and to the others; in the fourth, how the others which partake of the One are related to themselves and to the One; in the fifth, how the others which do not partake of the One are related to themselves and to the One; in the sixth, how the One, if it is not as in a way being and in a way not being, is related to itself and to the others; in the seventh, how the One, if it is not as in no way being, is related to itself and to the others; in the eighth, how the others are related to themselves and to the One which is not, when it in a way is

and in a way is not; in the ninth, how the others are related to themselves and to the One, when it in no way is.

Cornford, accepting the ambiguity theory but eschewing the Neoplatonic metaphysics that first led to it found eight hypotheses, with an addendum to the second.[75]

The ambiguity theory, and the serial order of hypotheses it requires, is defective in that it distorts the structure of everything that follows. So far from resting on a textual base, it is inconsistent with that base: it requires that the conclusions Parmenides explicitly draws at 160b and 166c, which are contradictory, be dismissed as merely ostensible; it requires that the initial arguments of each deduction, which are presented as inferences from the same hypothesis, be treated as disguised definitions marking off different hypotheses; it requires that Parmenides' own introduction to the exercise, and his own statement of what is to be examined, namely, the Idea of Unity, be ignored; and finally, it requires that the clearly demarcated and antithetical structure of what follows be dismissed, and a serial structure not present be substituted in its place. With deference to and immense respect for two of the greatest Platonists who have ever written on the *Parmenides*, we must conclude that the ambiguity theory is not an interpretation but a failure to interpret, for it ignores structure.

Parmenides offers two, and only two, hypotheses: that Unity is, and that Unity is not. Those two hypotheses are considered, respectively, from the point of view of consequences for Unity itself, and consequences for the others. For convenience in exposition, and only for convenience, the fourfold division that results will be treated as offering four hypotheses:

Hypothesis I: if Unity is, what follows for Unity (137c-157b).
Hypothesis II: if Unity is, what follows for the others (157b-160b).
Hypothesis III: if Unity is not, what follows for Unity (160b-164b).
Hypothesis IV: if Unity is not, what follows for the others (164b-166c).

It is to be remembered that this is merely a division of convenience: Hypotheses I and II rest on the same assumption, namely, that Unity is; Hypotheses III and IV rest on the same assumption, that Unity is not. The difference between I and II, and III and IV, is simply that they trace the consequences of the same hypothesis for Unity and the others, respectively.

So far, we have been led to expect only four main divisions in the exercise. In fact, the scheme is more complex. The first hypothesis, that Unity is, yields three deductions in respect to Unity (Hypothesis I), and two deductions in respect to the others (Hypothesis II); the second hypothesis, that Unity is not, yields two deductions in respect to Unity (Hypothesis III), and two deductions in respect to the others (Hypothesis IV). The deductions from each hypothesis are mutually contradictory, and Deduction 3 of Hypothesis I, which combines results drawn from Deductions 1 and 2 of that hypothesis, reaches results that are internally contradictory. The conclusion drawn from the first hypothesis, that is, from Hypotheses I and II, is stated at 160b: "If Unity exists, Unity is both all things and not even one (or, nothing), both relative to itself and to the others." So the assumption that Unity is leads to multiple contradictions. It remains only to add that the assumption that Unity is not also leads to contradictions, both in Hypotheses III and IV. Thus the general conclusion of both assumptions stated at 166c: "Whether Unity exists or does not exist, both Unity and the others are and are not, and appear and do not appear to be, all manner of things in all manner of ways, relative to themselves and to each other." In short, it is impossible either to affirm or to deny the existence of Unity.

This structure, it will be observed, is explicit.[76] It is a chief reason for the ambiguity theory, and a sufficient reason against it. It is a chief reason *for* the theory because the structure implies that contradictions may be deduced both from the affirmation of a proposition and its denial; this uncomfortable result can be avoided if we vary the meaning of the two assumptions with the deductions, and thus render the deductions as independent hypotheses. But the structure is a sufficient reason *against* any such theory, precisely because it makes Plato's choice of structure, clearly marked and obviously intended, unintelligible.

The ambiguity theory assumes that the exercise which follows is a specimen of the fallacy of equivocation: it is thus a species of that broader genus of interpretations which represent the exercise as an exercise in the detection of fallacies. In support of this it is often remarked that Parmenides describes what is to follow as an 'exercise,' and calls his traversal of the ocean of arguments a 'laborious game' (137b). But if we sometimes exercise for practice, we also exercise to win, and the need for exercise to attain the highest knowledge is explicit in the *Republic* (VI 503 e 3, cf. 504b 2, cf. *Timaeus* 90b), while legislation is a game of reason in the *Laws* (VI 769a, cf. III 695a, IV 712b, along with VII 803c-804b). There is much that seems fallacious in the exercise which follows, and some of it is funny, presenting that logical passage into illogic which is characteristic not of humor but of wit. Yet the exercise, the dialectical game, is presented as deductive, and it is impossible to treat it as an exercise in the detection of fallacies without destroying its character, and thereby its explicitly drawn conclusions, notably those at 160b and 166c. The fallacy theory, like the ambiguity theory, which is a species of it, must treat the deductive form and its conclusions as merely ostensible. Once again, a chief reason for the fallacy theory is also a sufficient reason against it: it renders the structure unintelligible.

It may be urged that the structure *is* unintelligible. Parmenides suggests that both denial and affirmation of a hypothesis must be examined, and the result is not, in any ordinary sense, a reductio. Given a proposition, P, and proof that P implies absurdity—say, Q and not-Q—it follows that not-P. The contradictory of self-contradictory propositions is true, and this principle is basic to all indirect proof. But that principle is violated in the exercise which follows, for contradictions are deduced both from the proposition that Unity is and that

Unity is not. The result has been likened by Ryle to Russell's Paradox, which led to the invention of the Theory of Types: if the set of all sets that are not members of themselves is a member of itself, it is not a member of itself; and if it is not a member of itself, it is a member of itself. The peculiarity of this paradox, and related paradoxes, which distinguishes it from a logical falsehood, is that mutually contradictory propositions are equivalent, as implying each other. In what follows, that Unity is not implies that Unity is (162a-b), and that Unity is implies that Unity is not (141e), though these results are reached by means other than those of set theory.

More generally, they are reached by means other than those of formal logic. The exercise presents, not a single contradiction, but contradiction piled on contradiction. The multiplicity of contradictions does not derive from the theorem of the propositional calculus that a contradiction implies anything, that if P and not-P then R, for any R. That theorem requires a truth-functional logic unknown to Plato. The exercise that follows uses logical methods, that is, methods of inference, as does any form of reasoning. But contradictions are derived intensionally, from the meaning of the terms used, and the reasoning, it may be added, is sometimes self-referential, as at 160d. The multiplicity of contradictions, in short, cannot be mechanically derived, and close scrutiny of the text is needed if they are to be understood. It will then be seen that the results at 160b and 166c in fact follow.

Dialectical Deduction

The results at 160b and 166c are reached by precisely the method Parmenides prescribes. That method, generalized, is to consider the consequences that follow for an Idea when it is hypothesized to be, or not be, or to have any other qualification whatever, relative to itself and to the others, and to examine the others relative to themselves and to the Idea hypothesized, whether it is hypothesized as being or as not being (136a-b). The results of Parmenides' own hypothesis about Unity are of ultimate generality: for when you have mentioned Unity and the others, everything has been mentioned (159b-c). We deal here with terms of unrestricted application. The exercise is indeed a passage and wandering through everything (136e), and the metaphor of wandering also foreshadows the inconsistency to come.

What is to be understood by 'the others'? The phrase has recurred often in what has gone before, usually in reference to other things, which partake of Ideas, but sometimes in reference to things that are simply different from a given Idea.[77] Since it has been assumed that sensible participants in Ideas may have a substantial existence of their own, it follows that the Others may be considered either in their character as participants, or in their character as other, apart from participation. The phrase 'the others' is thus ambiguous, but the ambiguity is systematic, predicated on Socrates' own admissions, and its effect in what follows is a direct function of the consequences for Unity that are adduced.

The exercise presents nine main Deductions, when Parmenides' description of method would lead us to expect only four. But the Deductions are tightly paired: they contradict each other within the same Hypothesis and follow from the same Hypothesis with respect to the same thing, so that it is possible to treat the pairs as distinct and incompatible movements within a single argument. The tightness of the pairing, its contradictory unity, if you will, is neatly brought about by I.3, which combines results obtained in I.1 and I.2, which are incompatible, and reaches results which are themselves internally inconsistent and homologous with III.1. The multiplicity of Deductions derives from their inconsistency. Though the Hypotheses conform exactly to Parmenides' description of proper method, that description does not, before the Idea to be hypothesized is chosen, indicate the manifold inconsistency that the exercise will expose.

That the deductions are dialectical is indicated, in the first place, by dramatic form: Parmenides acts as questioner, and the young Aristoteles (later one of the Thirty, and *not* the philosopher), who is younger and will give least trouble, is the respondent. No doubt Parmenides' questions are leading, and Aristoteles gives no trouble at all.[78] Yet it is important to remember that we are dealing with a dialogue, not a treatise, with the eliciting of agreement rather than the didactic demonstration of truth.[79]

The deductions are dialectical in a deeper way. Parmenides does not—he could not—logically derive a set of implications from the bare propositions that Unity is and that Unity is not. He rather considers the bearing on Unity, conceived as being or as not being, of a set of qualifications, all of them highly general and some of the highest generality. The list presented in I.1 includes Part/Whole, Limited/Unlimited, Shape, In Itself/In Another, Motion/Rest, Same/Different, Like/Unlike, Equal/Unequal, Older/Younger/Same Age. It is shown that none of these qualify Unity, except for lack of limit. In II.2, all of them qualify Unity, along with Contact/No Contact, which now applies because Unity has shape and is in another. This list reflects the Eleatic tradition, and may indeed conform to the principal divisions of Zeno's book.[80] But it was chosen, surely, not for its historical antecedents but for its generality—the generality that attaches to the Eleatic tradition.

In later Deductions the list is shortened, because the argument takes for granted results established before. But especially in I.1 and I.2, Parmenides will introduce definitions and arguments that draw on Academic mathematics and physics, especially in relation to place, time, motion, number, and infinity; the force of those arguments can often be recovered by reference to the physical works of Aristotle. The exercise does indeed indicate a passage and wandering through everything, since the qualifications examined in relation to Unity and the others represent the most general features not only of the intelligible but of the sensible world. The deductions are dialectical, then, in that they consist in examination of hypotheses in connection with other propositions assumed and not demonstrated to be true.

This raises a crucial point. The examination not only assumes propositions in Academic mathematics and physics, but also propositions to which Socrates has already agreed. Carried on for Socrates' benefit, the examination is dialectical as proceeding according to Socrates' own admissions. Among the relevant admissions are the following:

There are Ideas. Assumed at 128e-130b, 130e; used at 142c, 143a-144e, 146d-147a, 149e-150c, 158a-b.

There are sensibles, and they partake of Ideas. Assumed at 129a-e; used at 142a, 143a, 157-e-158b. An important premise for establishing that to be is to be in time (141e, 152a, 155d), and its direct consequence that to be is to be somewhere (145e, 151a).

Ideas are not qualified by their own opposite. Assumed at 129a-e; used at 137c-d, 159c-d.

If anything partakes of an Idea, part of the Idea is in it. Assumed at 131c, used at 144c-d, and required for the results mentioned under the second admission.

If something partakes of an Idea, the part of the Idea in it is part of the participant. Assumed at 131a-c; used at 142d-e, cf. 137c-d. Presupposed by the preceding proposition (see especially 131c 7).

At least some participants are separate, as having a reality apart from Ideas. Assumed at 130d; used at 159c.

What can be thought of must be something which is. Assumed at 132b-c; used at 160c, 161e, 166a-b.

These results, reached in the first and second parts of the *Parmenides*, are vital to the interpretation of the third. Applied to the Idea of Unity, they will, when combined with premises drawn from Academic physics and mathematics, prove fertile — too fertile, since the result will be multiply inconsistent. The exercise that concludes the *Parmenides*, like what has gone before, is aporetic: the wrong admissions have been made. But the *Parmenides* does not undertake to do work meant for the reader, and determine which admissions are wrong. The exercise is meant to make the young Socrates, and the reader, a better philosopher (135c-d), and to engender intelligence and truth (136e); it does so by yielding flatly impossible results at the uttermost level of generality. Perplexity arising from mistaken admissions cannot be restricted to an isolated domain: it extends to all that is, and to the very possibility of understanding.

The Neoplatonic Interpretation of the Parmenides

The structure of the concluding portion of the *Parmenides* is absurd, and since it is not subtly but blatantly absurd, we are surely meant to understand it so. Both the assumption that Unity is and its denial lead to multiple contradictions. In short, it is possible neither to affirm nor to deny the existence of Unity.

This account is incompatible with the Neoplatonist interpretation of the

Parmenides; an interpretation of importance not only because it has persisted for nearly two thousand years, but because it has exercised a profound, if not always benign, influence on the history of metaphysical reflection. It is a pleasant peculiarity of this honored misinterpretation that the ambiguity theory, which should make the dialogue trivial, transposes into a revelation of an Unknown and Unknowable God. E. R. Dodds remarked ("The *Parmenides* of Plato and the Origin of the Neoplatonic 'One'", *C.Q.* XII (1928), at 133):

> Read the second part of the *Parmenides* as Plotinus read it, with the single eye of faith; do not look for satire on the Megarians or anybody else; and you will find in the first hypothesis a lucid explanation of the famous 'negative theology,' and in the second (especially if you take it in connection with the fourth) an interesting sketch of the derivation of the universe from the marriage of unity and existence. What you will find in the remaining hypotheses I cannot so easily predict; even within the Neoplatonic school there were violent differences of opinion about them.

By the "first hypothesis," Dodds means what is here called Deduction 1 of Hypothesis I, the 'second hypothesis' Deduction 2, the 'fourth hypothesis' Deduction 2 of Hypothesis II. The Neoplatonic interpretation requires that the order of the deductions be taken as serial, and their incompatibility as only apparent owing to ambiguity. Given this assumption, Plotinus was free to suppose that I.1 reveals an ultimate principle of reality beyond being, beyond knowing, ineffable, (*Enn.* V. iv. 1). This God beyond Being Plotinus identified not only with the One of the *Parmenides* but with the Good of the *Republic*: it is the ultimate cause of the unity, the goodness, and the being—three terms Plotinus thought strictly equivalent—of all things which are.

Plotinus found more than his God in the *Parmenides*. He also found the three successive hypostases that emanate from God: Intellect, Soul, and Nature (*Enn.* V. i. 8). Intellect, he supposed, includes the Platonic Ideas, that is, νοῦς is both τὸ νοοῦν and τὸ νοούμενον; Soul includes the Demiurge of the *Timaeus*; Nature includes Aristotelian matter, potentiality, which is also treated as the same as not-being, privation, στέρησις, which is also mysteriously the same as ἀνάγκη, the Necessity of the *Timaeus*. God is set over all three Hypostases as utterly transcending them, so much beyond them that God cannot be said to be: Plotinus's God, like Bradley's Absolute, is, "too rich, not too poor, for division of its elements." As Proclus was afterward to explain, it is accurate to say that God is *not* good, is *not* one, does *not* exist, so long as one understands the sense of the negation: it is that the application of the predicates is inadequate to the unity of the subject.[81]

Plotinus was a mystic. According to Porphyry, who edited Plotinus' work after his death into six books of nine chapters each—hence 'Enneads'—Plotinus was in a state of ecstasy four times during the six years Porphyry was his pupil.

Because he was a mystic, Plotinus' theory of God has often been treated as though it were not the product of rational reflection, not philosophy, but a product of psychopathology — though no doubt of an appropriately rarified kind. The truth, however, is that Neoplatonic metaphysics rests not on revelation but reflection, and that the premises of that reflection are rooted firmly, not in Hellenistic syncretism, but in Plato's and Aristotle's own account of what it is to be real.

Both Plato and Aristotle suppose that to be real is to be intelligible, and that to be intelligible is to be, or to be possessed of, essence or form.[82] They also suppose that to be real is to be independent and ontologically prior, that is, able to exist apart from other things.[83]

These two claims dwell peacefully together until a third is added, whereupon they war. Suppose that determination is negation, that is, that what a thing is is the totality of what is it not. If this is so, then nothing intelligible, and therefore determinate, can exist apart from what it is not; therefore, nothing intelligible and determinate is independent. And given that whatever is is intelligible, it must follow that nothing independent of anything which is can be.

Here, then, is the step Plotinus took. God cannot be identified, as the Stoics had done, as Spinoza and Hegel were later to do, with the sum of things, the concatenated chain of beings, which are what they are in and through each other: for those things, he argued, collectively and distributively require a source or principle, an ἀρχή, and that principle must be distinct from and prior to them. That is, it must be independent of them. But if independent, then not intelligible, and beyond Being. What is and is intelligible in the primary sense, Intellect, the realm of essences or Ideas, is not independent, but exists wholly in and through its transcendent source, as Soul and Nature exist in turn through it.

The principle that determination is negation, then, is explosive, the faithful attendent of monism and its incongruous counterpart, negative theology. The principle is also more ancient than Plotinus, for Aristotle knew a theory very like it (*Posterior Analytics* II 97a 6-19):

> To define and divide one need not know the whole of existence. Yet some hold it impossible to know the differentiae distinguishing each thing from every single other thing without knowing every single other thing; and one cannot, they say, know each thing without knowing its differentiae, since everything is identical with that from which it does not differ, and other than that from which it differs. Now first of all this is a fallacy: not every differentia precludes identity, since many differentiae inhere in things specifically identical, though not in the substance of these nor essentially. Secondly, when one has taken one's differing pair of opposites and assumed that the two sides exhaust the genus, and that the subject one seeks to define is present in one or other of them, and one has further verified its presence in one of them, then it does not matter whether or not one knows all the other subjects of which the differentiae are also predicated. For it is

obvious that when by this process one reaches subjects incapable of further differentiation one will possess the formula defining the substance.

If we are to give the author of the theory Aristotle is criticizing a name, it should be Speusippus, and it is the theory that determination is negation phrased in other terms. Aristotle's reply in terms of division and definition *per genus et differentiam*, apparently irrelevant, is in fact tightly connected. If it is true that determination is negation, then the categorial distinction between essence and other properties, like the distinction within categories between essence and things that have essence, [84] is destroyed. No doubt it is different, but surely not different in kind, to be a horse and to be this horse, to be this horse and to be a man: what each is is defined solely in terms of what it is not. The denial of any distinction between essence and accident is at the heart of Bradley's paradoxes of relation and predication in *Appearance and Reality*, as it is also at the heart of the account of predication Russell constructed in response to Bradley: neither supposed any important difference between "Socrates is a man" and "Socrates is just." Aristotle's response to Speusippus in terms of definition *per genus et differentiam* is a response that defends ontological independence of plural substances by admitting a distinction between definable essence and other attributes.

Speusippus, then, appears to have come very near to formulating the principle that determination is negation, and may indeed have supposed that there is a One which is beyond Being, and that it is a First Principle or *arche*.[85] If this is so, the foundations of Neoplatonism lie deeper than the Hermetists, or Philo, or Albinus and the Middle Academy, or Nicomachus and the Neopythagoreans: they lie in the Early Academy, in the first generation of Platonic epigony.

But if Plato's nephew anticipated Plotinus, it by no means follows that Plato himself founded negative theology. Plotinus based that claim on two texts, the *Parmenides* and the account of the Good in Book VI of the *Republic*.

Plotinus's account of the Good, if it were correct, would lend weight to his account of Unity in the *Parmenides*. Cornford, indeed, argued that (*PP* 133):

> The equation of the Good with the bare unity of Hyp. I is in flat contradiction with the text. That Unity has no second character; therefore we cannot say that it is good or the Good. It has no sort of being; therefore, if this is the Good, the Good does not exist, is not real, is not even an entity. . . . The Neoplatonisers may fairly be asked to explain why he (Plato) said that you cannot truly assert that the One is anything whatsoever, when he means that you can truly assert that it *is* beyond being, and *is* good, and *is* a god.

This is a fair example of the speechlessness to which English-speaking critics are often reduced by claims of ineffability. Plotinus certainly thought that you can say (truly) of the first principle that it *is* One, and Good, and God, and beyond Being, but that you could also say that it is *not* one, and *not* good, and *not* God, precisely because it is beyond being. You could say both sets of things because they are not incompatible, since the affirmations involve identity and the negations do not. I can identify the first principle with Goodness, and call it good, precisely because it is the source of all goodness in the universe; and to be and to be good, Plotinus thought, are equivalent. I can identify the first principle with Unity, and call it one, for the same reason. We deal here with what in medieval discussions of the Divine Names became known as analogy of attribution or proportion. It is similar to Plato's own account of assertion of the phenomena of this world, with this difference, namely, that whereas analogy of attribution predicates through a cause, it cannot accurately be said to predicate through an exemplary cause or essence. The Christian God differs from Plotinus's God not only in that He exists, but that he is existence: "I am who am."[86] But God and the One are alike in that they are one and good as cause of the unity and goodness of those things that exist because of them.[87] They are not, however, exemplary causes: that is, they cannot be what it is to be one and what it is to be good, since, if they were, unity and goodness would be identical, whereas they are not identical. It is possible, then, to reinstate Cornford's point —but with a difference.

It will be argued that the Neoplatonic interpretation of the *Parmenides* is possible because the Neoplatonic interpretation of the *Republic* is necessary. Socrates is made to say of the Good that (*Republic* VI 509b): "Since the Good is not Being, but even beyond Being, surpassing it in dignity and power." The Good is an unhypothetical first principle (510b). So, the Neoplatonists argue, we must admit that Plato accepted a first principle that is beyond being, and this for a very good reason: he *says* so, and in so many words.

Does he? There is plainly an immense leap in inferring that because the Good is beyond Being in that it surpasses it in dignity and power, it is therefore beyond Being in that it does not exist. As Shorey remarked, "The practical ethical outcome of all this . . . is merely that goodness is more precious than any knowledge or intellectual faculty." And Shorey went on to add ("The Idea of Good in Plato's *Republic*," *Studies in Classical Philology* i (1895), 188-239 at 197, 198):

> (T)he idea of Good is the cause of the goodness of all good things, as the idea of three is the cause of the threeness of all triads, the idea of white the cause of all whiteness. And if we read into Plato the Neo-Platonic or modern fancy that evil is purely negative and that things exist only in so far as they are good, we may make the Idea of Good the cause of all existence.

Shorey assumes, of course, that the Good is an Idea, whence it must follow that it is and is knowable, as other Ideas are. Certainly there are very good grounds for this assumption. That the Good is an Idea is stated or implied several times (*Republic* 508e 3, 517c 1, 534c 1); as such, it is intelligible and can be known,

(517c, 504d, 3, 508a, 518c-d, 534c, e), grasped by a logos (511b, 534c), and distinguished from other Ideas (534b); and, of course, as an Idea, it is a thing which is (526c, cf. 517c). It is also on the same level as the Beautiful (507b, cf. 532b), which Plotinus acknowledged to be a thing which is and an object of knowledge. In view of this, Cornford was surely correct in commenting on *Republic* 509b (*PP* 132):

> But can it be proved that these words mean anything more than that, whereas you can always ask the reason for a thing's's existence and the answer will be that it exists for the sake of its goodness, you cannot ask for a reason for goodness; the good is an end in itself; there is no final cause beyond it?

The Good is beyond Being because it surpasses Being in dignity and power. It surpasses Being because both good things and evil things participate in Being, whereas only good things participate in Goodness insofar as they are good. This presupposes, of course, that evil is not merely the privation of goodness, and this presupposition is accurate for Plato, who acknowledged the existence of Ideas of various kind of evil as the opposites of various kinds of good,[88] just as the theory of Ideas Socrates puts in the *Parmenides* (128e-130a) requires. Plotinus, on the other hand, supposing that evil is purely privative and that whatever is is good, inferred that if the Good is not Being and is beyond Being, surpassing it in dignity and power, it must surpass it in and through not being. That is, the Good does not exist by reason of its excellence. It is a lovely piece of what, in psychological terms, is called projection, but which has no precise name in the study of the history of philosophy because it goes so largely unrecognized. Plotinus's result, of course, is neither stated nor implied by Plato's text, which shows, on the contrary, that he would have regarded it as nonsense. And since the Good is the First Principle of explanation, it must follow that not all things that exist can be (purposively) explained. In this, then, the *Republic* is on the same ground as the doctrine of Necessity in the *Timaeus* (cf. *Republic* II 379b).

For the sake of argument, I have supposed that the Good of the *Republic* and the Unity of the *Parmenides* are connected. Plotinus, indeed, thought they were identical, and identical with God. But of course they are not: for what it is to be good is not identical with what it is to be one; otherwise, it would be the same to be good and be one. Plotinus' One and Good is not an exemplary cause. Nor does Plotinus's scheme, despite stout asseveration to the contrary, and reasoning by modern commentators of such tortuousness as to defy analysis, fit the *Parmenides*.

This is clear for reasons we have already seen. Even in respect of the 'first hypothesis,' there are clear disparities. It is true that Unity, in I.1., is neither in motion nor at rest, neither in place nor time, neither the same as itself nor different from other things, that it is unknowable, an object neither of perception, knowledge, nor account, and that (triumphantly) it does not exist. And yet even here where the case is strongest, the analogy fails: for the nonexistence of

Unity in Deduction I.1 is derived from the premise that to be is to be in time, a premise which both Plato and Plotinus thought false.

Plotinus found in the 'second hypothesis' the account of a Unity that contains in itself the basis of all plurality, a Unity that in conjunction with Being produces a Many, and in conjunction with that Many produces motion and rest, place and time, identity and difference. But in fact, the Unity of the 'second hypothesis,' I.2., does not fit any of the three main hypostases of Plotinus; it is not Intellect, Soul, or Nature. Unlike Intellect, it is divisible and in time; unlike Nature, it contains Ideas; unlike Soul, it is not a designing intelligence or Demiurge. It does, however, contain numerous conclusions Plato meant us to recognize as absurd.

In general, the Plotinian scheme of hypostases does not fit the structure of the *Parmenides*, and the very deductions to which the Neoplatonic interpretation is most apt remain unfit. But the sovereign, fundamental objection to the Neoplatonic interpretation is, as we have seen, that it falsifies the structure of the *Parmenides*, that it reduces the neatly balanced and inconsistent antitheses of the concluding part of the dialogue to a sanitized serial order, that it is compelled to dismiss the true order as "merely ostensible."

Aristoteles as Respondent

The third and final part of the *Parmenides* is distinguished from what has gone before not only by its subject-matter but by its speakers. In the first part, Socrates had replied to a paradox offered by Zeno against plurality. In the second, Socrates was questioned about his theory of Ideas by Parmenides. Now, in the third and concluding part, Parmenides questions the young Aristoteles.

Coincidence of name has suggested that the young Aristoteles, companion of Socrates, is meant to represent Aristotle the philosopher, pupil of Plato, born fifteen years after Socrates' death. Thus for example, the late Professor Ryle wrote in 1965 (*SPM* 146):

> In Part II of the *Parmenides* old Parmenides demonstrates the two-way Zenonian method of argumentation, dressed up in questioner-answerer style. If, as I now think, it was Aristotle who in his early teaching years, introduced the teaching of dialectic into the Academy, partly as a training-exercise for future philosophers, then, some way on in the 350's Plato designed Part II of the dialogue as a pedagogic exemplar for Aristotle's *Topics* classes. It is no accident that Parmenides' young interlocutor is a namesake of the author of the *Topics*.

There are times when even an argument may wish to hurry past with eyes averted, its face muffled in its cloak; but certainly one must admit that if *a* is the namesake of *b*, it is not accidental, but in some sense logically necessary, that *a* has the same name as *b*. On the other hand, from the mere fact of having the same name, it does not follow that *a* was named for *b* — or *b* for *a*. Ryle's inference without evidence was exploded in advance by Cornford in 1935 (*PP* 109 n. 1):

> The persistent notion that Aristoteles is a mask for the young Aristotle seems to me fantastic. It is quite probable that the *Parmenides* was written before Aristotle joined the Academy in 367 or 366 B.C. at about the age of seventeen. His early works indicate that for years afterwards he was, as we should expect, a faithful adherent of the theory of Forms, under the overwhelming influence of his master. The objections to the theory are advanced by Parmenides, not Aristoteles, who has nothing to say for himself.

Cornford's conclusion is proved by this fact alone: Aristoteles, the character of the *Parmenides*, is identified as a historical figure known to Plato's audience. He is that Aristoteles who became one of the infamous Thirty Tyrants (127d).

Why Plato chose this particular man to be the respondent we can scarcely now say. He may well have been in youth a friend of Socrates, a member of the same circle that contained Critias and Charmides, Plato's kinsmen, friends of Socrates, and members of the Thirty. Plato's choice may have a basis in biographical fact. Still, the *Parmenides* is fiction, meant to be understood as such. For present purposes it is more important to understand, not why this particular person was chosen, but what sort of part in the dialogue he plays.

Here the evidence of the text is, so far as it goes, dispositive. It is that, although Socrates is young and relatively inexperienced in dialectic, in need of the training this section is meant to provide, Aristoteles is younger and still more inexperienced. Because of his youth, he will give least trouble as a respondent in the laborious game now to be played, and be most likely to say what he really thinks (137b-c). As it turns out, what he really thinks involves multiple contradictions (160b, 166c).

We know something else about the young Aristoteles. The laborious game that follows is concerned, not with sensibles, but with the Ideas (135d-c). The choice of Aristoteles as respondent implies that he is familiar with the theory of Ideas, so that he can examine hypotheses that involve it — this, no doubt, because Socrates has already discussed the theory with him (135d).

Why then should a youth who will not give trouble, who will say what he thinks, and who is familiar with the theory of Ideas be made respondent in a discussion concerning Ideas? The question answers itself. The young Aristoteles is chosen, surely, because he represents a naive understanding of the theory combined with a readiness to follow where Parmenides leads. In confirmation, it may be observed that Aristoteles is exercised as an example to Socrates (135d), and the exercise leads Aristoteles to accept absurdities at which Socrates, a more mature philosopher, would have balked, whether or not he could identify their source. Socrates can lift his eyes from a path to see where it is taking him (130d), and has shown consistent unwillingness to accept absurdity (131c, e, 132b, d,

134c). Aristoteles, the ideal respondent for Parmenides' purposes, never balks, however outrageous the consequence.

We might have expected, after all, that Socrates would be the respondent. It is his theory under discussion (135b-c, d-e), and the exercise is meant for his benefit (135d, 136a, c). Instead, he is made to listen while a less experienced man is examined—and allowed to reflect on admissions that lead to the absurdities of 160b and 166c. There is, as it were, a trick of perspective in the concluding portion of the *Parmenides*, which Plato as an artist uses for purposes of philosophy. The reader—who must in first intention have been, not a farmer from Thrace, but a trained member of the Academy thoroughly familiar with the theory of Ideas—is offered the same point of view as Socrates himself, a point of view different from that of Aristoteles: what the young Aristoteles is led to infer from Parmenides' questions is not what Socrates and the reader will be led to infer from those questions combined with Aristoteles' answers. Thus, for example, Aristoteles accepts the conclusion of the affirmative hypotheses at 160b, and of all the hypotheses at 166c. Yet those conclusions are absurd, and Socrates and the reader are meant to understand that they are absurd. The youth and inexperience of Aristoteles, his willingness to say what he thinks and not give trouble, indicate a willingness to follow the argument where it leads, undeterred by absurdity. In this Aristoteles differs from Socrates, from members of the Academy, and from many subsequent readers of the dialogue.

It is interesting to observe, in this connection, that Parmenides himself sometimes afterwards provides reasons for admissions that Aristoteles had before made without reasons. The third part of the *Parmenides* is dialectic, proceeding according to what the respondent admits, and it is therefore mistaken to force a rigidly deductive scheme on Parmenides' proofs.

Cornford, translating the last part of the dialogue, dropped most of Aristoteles' responses. Since those responses consist mainly in Yes, No, and Maybe, it may be asked why Plato did not drop the dialogue form altogether—why, instead of choosing a passive respondent, Plato did not rather allow Parmenides to offer, as Cornford in fact makes him do, a connected discourse.[89]

The answer seems clear. In general, one vouches the truth of what one asserts; but no philosopher, and certainly not Parmenides, could vouch the truth of 166c. Neither Socrates nor the reader can accept that result, nor reasonably suppose that Parmenides does. The perspectival difference between Socrates, and us with him, and Aristoteles, is preserved by the dialogue form. If it be replied that 166c may be understood as a reductio without voucher of truth, the short answer is that it is not a reductio, since it asserts both the proposition to be reduced and its denial.

Cornford, having cast the form of the third part into a discourse, inspected the result at 166c and concluded that, had Plato believed it, he must have burnt his books and lapsed into unbroken silence. This is a natural inference, if the final portion of the *Parmenides* is a treatise. In fact, it is not a treatise, but dialectic, and shows a conclusion to which skillful questioning dealing with a putative Idea of Unity may lead. We are meant to ask, not whether the conclusion is true, for it cannot be true, but which among the admissions that produced it must be rejected. We are meant to ask, in short, what went wrong.

The exercise that concludes the *Parmenides*, then, is aporetic: mistaken admissions have beem made. But the *Parmenides* does not undertake to do work meant for the reader, and state which admissions are wrong. It is not a dogmatic statement of doctrine. Aristoteles, young and without caution, is a very symbol of perplexity.

Aporia and Education

In the third and lengthiest part of the *Parmenides*, Parmenides illustrates a method of inquiry using the young Aristoteles as respondent. The method is hypothetical. The subject-matter is the Idea of Unity. The inferences Aristoteles draws under Parmenides' questioning lead to absurdity.

Not surprisingly, those inferences have been read in a multitude of ways. They are not logical but metaphysical: they exhibit the Unknown God beyond Being, or perhaps a proto-Hegelian dialectic of Being, Not-being, and Becoming, or Unity in Difference. On the contrary, they are not metaphysical but logical: they offer an exercise in the detection of fallacies, perhaps especially fallacies involving ambiguity; or perhaps they anticipate Russell's Paradox and the Theory of Types; or perhaps they are a *tu quoque* argument against the Eleatics and Megarians; or perhaps they are a joke. The concluding part of the *Parmenides* recommends a method; it does not recommend a method; it contains positive doctrine; it does not contain positive doctrine. Assertion meets denial in a welter of strife. Twenty-five hundred years after it was written, the *Parmenides* remains a puzzle for ordinary readers, and for scholars whose business it is to understand it, a scandal.

If we are to understand the concluding part of the *Parmenides* in all its bewildering reticulation, we must look to its structure; that is, we must assume that Plato as a competent philosopher and artist has said what he meant, and that we, by attending to what he has said and the way he has said it, can understand it. His chosen method of expression remains the dialogue, not the treatise, and his use of dialogue is consistent with a characteristic theory of instruction (*Republic* VII 518b-d, trans. Cornford):

> Education is not what it is said to be by some, who profess to put knowledge into a soul which does not possess it, as if they could put sight into blind eyes. On the contrary, our own account signifies that the soul of every man does possess the power of learning the truth and the organ to see it with; and that, just as one might have to turn the whole body round in order that the eye should see the light instead of darkness, so the entire soul must be turned away from this changing world, until its eye can bear to contemplate reality and that supreme splendour which

we have called the Good. Hence there may well be an art whose aim would be to effect this very thing, the conversion of the soul, in the readiest way; not to put the power of sight into the soul's eye, which already has it, but to ensure that, instead of looking in the wrong direction, it is turned the way it ought to be.

The aim of eduction is not to impart information, but to turn the eye of the soul in the right direction, so that we may see clearly what before had been obscure. By the time Plato wrote the *Parmenides*, he had come to believe that one way in which this can be done is by the construction of aporiai, perplexities, on fundamental issues in philosophy. In the concluding part of the *Parmenides*, this is precisely what we find. The structure is not that of a reductio ad absurdum: indirect proof rests on the logical principle that the contradictory of a self-contradictory proposition is true. The structure of the *Parmenides* implies that contradiction can be deduced both from a proposition and its denial, and this extreme of absurdity is, in respect to aporiai, a species of perfection in the art of their statement.

This is a laborious game played for a serious purpose.[90] The method may best be compared, not to developments in modern logic, but to the search for Elements in Greek mathematics, for a self-consistent set of axioms, definitions, and postulates from which the known theorems of mathematics could be derived — a serious intellectual concern in Plato's time. The reader is offered multiple proofs and asked to isolate their assumptions. If those assumptions yield inconsistency, there is latent inconsistency in the foundations of his science, and he must be prepared for further inquiry: which among his assumptions must be rejected, and why, and with what result?

I.1. First Hypothesis, First Deduction (137c-142a)

The First Deduction of Hypothesis I follows from the assumption that the Idea of Unity excludes its opposite, Plurality, a point Socrates has already granted (129b-c, 129e-130a). Therefore, Unity cannot be many.

The Deduction that follows may be divided into five main sections. (1) It is first shown that Unity cannot be many, and therefore cannot be a whole or have parts. (2) This conclusion is then used as a premise to prove that Unity cannot have a limit or boundary, have any shape or figure, be in place, or be in motion or at rest. (3) It is then shown that Unity cannot be qualified by any member of three sets of highly general relational terms, namely sameness and difference, likeness and unlikeness, and equality and inequality; the arguments here appeal to the premise that Unity cannot be a whole or have parts, whence it is inferred (cf. 139c, e) that Unity, since it excludes plurality, can neither be nor have any second character. (4) It is then proved that Unity cannot be older, younger, or the same age as anything, whence it is inferred that it cannot be in time. (5) Assuming that anything that partakes of Being must be in time, it is inferred that Unity cannot partake of Being, and therefore, cannot so much as be one: this implies that it cannot be named or spoken of, that it is neither an object of knowledge, opinion, or perception.

The results established for Unity in this Deduction follow validly from the assumptions that Unity admits no plurality, and that any assertion about it implies that it is a whole of parts, and therefore many. The premises of the arguments offered often use definitions that may be glossed from Euclid and Aristotle, and the arguments themselves, when they touch on physical qualifications such as place, time, and motion, may often be explicated by reference to Aristotle's *Physics*. I.1 introduces definitions that must have been or become common coin in Academic physics and mathematics, whence Aristotle derived them.

The arguments of this Deduction, taken by themselves, seem inelegant. Its conclusion might have been derived more perspicuously from the assumption that Unity can neither be nor have any second character on pain of being many. Again, the particular characters chosen for examination, despite their generality and intrinsic interest, may well seem chosen arbitrarily, in that other characters might also have served.

But in fact, there is nothing arbitrary about the list of exclusions in the First Deduction, since the characters involved are among the most general features of the world. Nor is the argument inelegant: what may seem superfluous argumentation for the First Deduction taken by itself will prove to be vital argumentation for the final part of the *Parmenides* as a whole: the First Deduction is meant to lay a foundation for the other Deductions which are to follow.

i. Part and Whole (137c-d)

Since the Idea of Unity excludes qualification by its opposite, Plurality, it cannot be many. It therefore cannot be a whole of parts. For by definition, a whole is that from which no part is absent; and parts are parts of a whole. In either case, Unity would be many, not one. But Unity is not in the least many, but *just* one. Therefore, if Unity is one, it will not be a whole or have parts.

This inference is not a disguised definition, indicating the sense in which 'Unity' or 'one' is to be taken in this Deduction (see 137b). It is a valid inference from the assumption that the Idea of Unity exists, and therefore excludes Plurality; Unity can no more be many than Largeness can be small or Beauty ugly.

It is suggested at *Sophist* 245a that a thing that has parts may *have* the character of Unity, and be in that way a sum or whole, but that Unity itself, rightly marked off, must *be* altogether without parts. The definition of a whole as 'that from which no part is absent' is repeated at *Theaetetus* 205a, and was accepted by Aristotle, who followed the Second Deduction of Hypothesis I in defining a part as that into which anything can be divided (see *Meta.* V 1023b 26, V 1023b 13). Parmenides' argument here parallels Aristotle's claim that (*Meta.* X 1054a 20ff.):

The one and the many are opposed in several ways, of which one is the opposition of the one and plurality as indivisible and divisible; for that which is either divided or divisible is called a plurality, and that which is indivisible or not divided is called one.

The inference that Unity cannot be a whole of parts has an important consequence. It had earlier been assumed, in the Dilemma of Participation (131a-c) that if there is participation, things that participate receive as their share either the whole of an Idea or part of it. It is a direct inference, and one repeatedly made in the Deductions that follow,[91] that what falls to the share of the participant is part of the participant, which must then be a whole of which that part is part. Given this assumption, the denial that Unity is a whole of parts implies that it does not participate in anything; the affirmation that it participates in something, namely Being, will be taken in I.2 to imply that it is a whole of parts.

ii. Limit and Unlimited (137d)

Since Unity is not a whole of parts, it can have neither beginning, middle, nor end; for those things would be parts of it. Therefore, Unity is unlimited, as having no limits. To borrow from Aristotle, Unity is unlimited in that it is incapable of being gone through because it is not of its nature to be gone through, unlimited in the sense in which the voice is invisible.[92] The argument anticipates Aristotle's definition of limit as, "the last point of each thing, i.e., the first point beyond which it is not possible to find any part, and the first point within which every part is."[93] Euclid I, Def. 13 defines a boundary as that which is the limit or extremity of anything.

iii. Shape (137d-138a)

If Unity is without parts, it is without limits, and if it is without limits, without shape. For if Unity had figure or shape, it would have either straight shape or round; both imply extremes and middle; but what has extremes and a middle has parts, and Unity has no parts. Therefore, Unity has no figure or shape.

In the *Meno*, one definition of figure is "that in which a solid terminates," that is, "the limit of a solid" (76a). As Heath remarks,[94] this makes figure practically equivalent to surface.[95] The argument here marks an advance: it anticipates the Euclidean definition of a figure as that which is contained by any boundary or boundaries (I. Def. 14); its definition of straight is repeated by Aristotle in the *Topics* (VI 148b 27), and is taken by Heath[96] to be the origin of the Euclidean definition of a straight line as "a line which lies evenly with the points on itself" (Book I, Def. 4). The definition of round anticipates the definition of circle offered at *Epistle VII* 342b and of sphere at *Timaeus* 33b. Its sense is repeated, though in more complex formula, by Euclid's definitions of circle (Book I, Def. 15) and sphere (Book XI, Def. 14).

iv. In Itself, In Another (138a-b)

If Unity is without parts, without limit, and without shape, it cannot be (a) in itself, or (b) in another. So it is nowhere.

a) Unity cannot be in itself because, if it were, it would contain itself and be contained by itself, in which case, as both container and contained, it would not be one but two, and thus many.[97] As Aristotle remarks, the only circumstance in which a thing can be said to be in itself is when it is a whole of parts (*Phys.* IV 210a 25 ff.); but nothing can be said to be in itself in virtue of its own nature (*Phys.* IV 210b 1 ff.).

b) Unity cannot be in another because, if it were, it would be contained in a circle by what it was in, and touch what contains it with many parts at many places. Parmenides here assumes that if Unity had a shape, that shape would be circular or spherical. Since it does not partake of Circularity and has no parts, it cannot be in another.

This is equivalent to a proof that Unity cannot be in place. As Aristotle remarks (*De Gen. et Corr.* II 322b 34 ff.):

> 'Contact' in the proper sense applies only to things which have 'position.' And 'position' belongs only to those things which also have 'place.' . . . Assuming therefore, that 'to touch' is—as we have defined it in a previous work (*Phys.* V 226b 21)—"to have the extremes together," only those things will touch each other which, being separate magnitudes and possessing position, have their extremes 'together.'

In the *Physics* (IV 212a 20, cf. V 226b 21 ff.), Aristotle had said that, "the innermost motionless boundary of what contains is place."

Parmenides' proof of (b) would be unexceptionable, had he argued that if Unity were in another, it would have some perimeter, and touch that in which it is in many places with many parts. But he further supposes, without apparent reason, that if Unity were in other it would have a specific kind of perimeter, namely that of a circle or sphere.[98] Once again, Aristotle throws considerable light on the inference (*De Caelo* II 286b 34):

> If, again, one orders figures according to their numbers, it is natural to arrange them in this way. The circle corresponds to the number one, the triangle, being the sum of two right angles, to the number two. But if one is assigned to the triangle, the circle will not be a figure at all.

The reason for associating the circle with unity and the number one had been given earlier (*De Caelo* II 286b 13):

> Let us consider generally which shape is primary among planes and solids alike. Every plane figure must be either rectilinear or curvilinear. Now the rectilinear is bounded by more than one line, the curvilinear by one only. But since in any kind the one is naturally prior to the

many and the simple to the complex, the circle will be the first of plane figures. Again, if by complete, as previously defined (*Phys.* III 207a 8), we mean a thing outside which no part of itself can be found, and if addition is always possible to the straight line but never to the circle, clearly the line which embraces the circle is complete. If then the complete is prior to the incomplete, it follows on this ground also that the circle is primary among figures. And the sphere holds the same position among solids. For it alone is embraced by a single surface, while rectilinear figures have several. The sphere is among solids what the circle is among plane figures.

The circle is bounded by one line as the sphere is bounded by one surface; it is for this reason that Parmenides assumes that if Unity had shape, that shape would be round. The completion and perfection of circular shape may also play a role in this assumption: in the *Timaeus* (33b), the Demiurge gives spherical shape to the body of the World, not only because "the fitting shape would be the figure which comprehends in itself all the figures that there are," but also because this figure is, "the most perfect and uniform of all; for he judged uniformity to be immeasurably better than its opposite." If Unity, what is *just* one, had a shape, that shape would be circular. But since Unity can have no parts, it can have no shape. So Unity cannot be in place, since it cannot be in something that contains it.

v. Motion and Rest (138b-139b)

If Unity is without parts, without limits, without shape, and without place, it can neither be (a) in motion, nor (b) at rest.

If (a) Unity were in motion it would either (i) change in character, and so not be what it is, Unity, or (ii) change place, either by moving from place to place or by revolving in the same place. In either case, Unity would necessarily have parts and be many, and therefore Unity cannot be in motion.

a) The division between (i) change in character and (ii) change in place is repeated at *Theaetetus* 181d. The[99] division is restricted to physical motion: it includes the nine kinds of other-moved motion listed in the *Laws* (X 893c-894a), but not that self-moving motion, which in the *Phaedrus* (245c-246a) and *Laws* (X 896a) is said to be the essence and definition of soul. (i) Unity cannot move by changing character, since if it were to change character, it would be other than what it is. This reasoning is anticipated in the *Cratylus* (439e), and has much in common with Aristotle's claim that though there is motion in respect to quantity, quality, and place, there is no motion in respect to substance.[100] Generation and destruction, that is, are not motions, and are distinguished from alteration and locomotion below at 156a-b. (ii) Nor can Unity change place by revolving in a circle, for this would imply that it revolves on its own axis, and what revolves would be parts of it; since Unity has neither middle nor parts, it cannot change places by revolving. Neither can Unity pass from place to place, for this would imply that it can come to be in something. But what is coming to be in something can be neither wholly in it nor wholly outside it; part must be within and part outside. Since Unity can be neither in itself nor in another, it cannot be in a place; since it cannot be in a place, it cannot—*a fortiori*, it would seem—come to be in a place. Why, then, is it necessary to argue that coming to be in a place is possible only for a thing which has parts?

The answer is that the argument rules out two accounts of local motion; local motion analyzed as a sequence of discrete positions, and local motion analyzed as continuous becoming. The discussion parallels that of time which follows.

Since Unity has no parts, it cannot come to be in something, and therefore cannot move by changing places. The sense of this argument is repeated by Aristotle (*Phys.* VI 234b 10ff.):

> Everything which changes must be divisible. For since every change is from something to something, and when a thing is at the goal of its change it is no longer changing, and when both itself and all its parts are at the starting-point of change it is not changing (for that which is in whole and in part in an unvarying condition is not in a state of change), it follows, therefore, that part of that which is changing must be at the starting-point and part at the goal; for as a whole it cannot be in both or in neither. . . . It is evident, therefore, that everything which changes must be divisible.

This accurately represents Parmenides' analysis of coming to be in something.

b) The proof that Unity cannot be at rest is less perspicuous than the proof that it cannot be in motion. Rest is that state in which a thing is 'in the same' (cf. *Theaetetus* 182d). Since Unity is neither in itself nor in another, it cannot be 'in the same,' and therefore cannot be at rest. The argument appears to be purely verbal, but in fact it is not. We are tempted to object that since Unity is an Idea, and no Idea can change, Unity must be at rest; and that even though the denial that Unity can be in itself or in another excludes sameness of place, and therefore rest with respect to character. But this assumes that Unity can be characterized by Sameness, which is mistaken (see below, 139b-e). It also assumes that rest may be identified with changelessness, and this also is mistaken. Thus in the *Sophist* (252d, cf. 254d), Rest and Motion, though both combine with Being, do not combine with each other; that is, the Idea of Motion cannot be said to be at rest, though it is undoubtedly changeless. So it is that Aristotle remarks that, "Not everything that is not in motion can be said to be at rest, but only that which can be moved, though it actually is not moved" (*Phys.* IV 221b 12ff.). Rest is the opposite of motion, and only those things are at rest which are in principle capable of being moved. That which admits of motion and thereby of rest with respect to change of character must be in a place.[101] Therefore, the fact that Unity can be neither in itself nor in another only that it cannot be at rest with respect to place, but that it cannot be at rest with respect to change of character. As Cornford saw (*PP* 122), what is neither in itself nor in another can neither be in the same place nor the same condition. More generally, for a characteristic or Idea to change in character would imply its destruction; but rest is not the opposite of generation or destruction.

vi. Same and Different (139b-e)

Up to this point, Unity has been found to have no geometrical or physical characteristics, a thing not surprising in any Idea, though the proof has proceeded through the denial that Unity is a whole of parts. But Parmenides will now deny that Unity can be the same as or different from anything, and this, in addition to the denials of likeness and unlikeness and equality and inequality, which are to follow, is consciously if not avowedly paradoxical. Aristotle remarks (*Meta.* V 1021a 10 ff.):

> The equal and the like and the same . . . all refer to unity. Those things are the same whose substance is one; those are like whose quality is one; those are equal whose quantity is one; and 1 is the beginning and measure of number, so that all these relations imply number, although not in the same way.

But in this Deduction, Unity is disjoined from Sameness, as it will later be disjoined from Likeness and Equality, and *a fortiori* from Number.

The ground on which it is maintained that Unity can neither be the same as nor different from anything else is simple, clear, and cogent—given the premises on which this Deduction depends. The claim that Unity cannot be the same as another or different from itself might have been accepted as obvious; but in fact, a reason is given for it, namely, that in either case Unity would not be one. That reason is needed, for the denial of sameness is meant to exclude, not only numerical identity, but sameness in any respect.

This is important to the proof that Unity cannot be the same as itself or different from another. Unity cannot be different from anything. For a thing cannot be different by virtue of being one, but only by virtue of being different. Therefore, if Unity were different, it could be so only by virtue of Difference, not by virtue of Unity. But Unity is one, not many, and cannot be anything except in virtue of what it itself is. Put otherwise, it is not a whole of parts.

It follows, and for exactly the same reason, that Unity cannot be the same as itself. The argument at this point carefully distinguishes Unity from Sameness by reason of the connection of Sameness with plurality: when a thing comes to be the same as many, it does not come to be one.[102] So Unity cannot be the same or different by virtue of its own nature; and it cannot be the same or different by virtue of Sameness or Difference, because then it would not be one. Parmenides' argument assumes that to possess a character implies plurality on the part of the possessor, and that Unity excludes any sort of plurality. Put alternately, it has been assumed that to possess a character implies that the possessor is a whole of parts; but Unity cannot be a whole or have parts, and therefore cannot possess any further character.

vii. Like and Unlike (139e-140b)

Unity cannot be (a) like itself or another, or (b) unlike itself or another.

a) Unity cannot be like itself or another because to be like is to be qualified by the same characteristic (or, by Sameness), and since Sameness is not the same as Unity, Unity, if it were qualified by Sameness or any other character would be more than one. The previous proof has shown that Unity cannot be the same as or different from anything because it could be neither of those things in virtue of its own nature: it cannot *have* a second character, because then it would be many; it cannot *be* a second character, because then it would be other than what it is. The present argument is simply a corollary.

Parmenides' explication of likeness in terms of sameness is repeated at greater length by Aristotle (*Meta.* V 1018a 15 ff.):

> Those things are called 'like' which have the same attributes in every respect, and those which have more attributes the same than different, and those whose quality is one; and that which shares with another thing the greater number or the more important of the attributes (each of them one of two contraries) in respect of which things are capable of altering, is like that other thing. The senses of 'unlike' are opposite to those of 'like.'

b) By parity of reasoning with the proof of (a), Unity cannot be characterized by Difference, since it would then be many, not one. But if to be like is to be characterized by Sameness, or the same character, to be unlike is to be characterized by Difference, or a different character. Since Unity cannot be characterized by Difference, or by any character different from itself, it cannot be unlike itself or another.

viii. Equal and Unequal (140b-d)

Unity cannot be (a) equal to itself or another, or (b) unequal to itself or another.

a) Unity cannot be equal to itself or to another because to be equal is to have the same measures, and since Unity is not characterized by Sameness and has no parts, it cannot have the same measures as anything.

b) Unity cannot be unequal to itself or to another because to be unequal is either to be commensurably or incommensurably greater or smaller than something, and thus either to have more or fewer measures, or larger or smaller measures.[103] But if Unity had more or fewer, or larger or smaller, measures, it would have parts and be many. It has already been shown that it cannot have one measure, since it would then be equal to itself.

The definitions of commensurability and incommensurability here offered are similar to Euclid's—not surprisingly, since Euclid's was probably first stated by Theaetetus before the *Parmenides* was written:[104]

> Those magnitudes are said to be commensurable which are measured by the same measure, and those incommensurable which cannot have any common measure.

Parmenides' claim that incommensurable magnitudes have larger or smaller measures, as distinct from having no common measure, appears to be an inference from the principle that all magnitudes have a measure and that common measures are equal, with the result that measures that are not common must be unequal, and thus larger or smaller.

It will be observed that the denial of equality in this proof is made to follow indirectly from the denial of sameness, whereas the denial of inequality is made to follow directly from the denial of divisibility, that is, the denial of possession of parts.

The issue of incommensurability bears on the analysis of the infinite and Zeno's paradoxes, and both those topics are important to the remainder of the exercise to follow. Incommensurability implies the infinite divisibility of any magnitude, and the proof that there are magnitudes that have no common measure is paradoxical, in the literal sense that it is contrary to received opinion. As Aristotle remarked (*Meta.* I 983a 16-20):

> It seems wonderful to all who have not seen the reason, that there is a thing which cannot be measured even by the smallest unit. . . . (Yet) there is nothing which would surprise the geometer so much as if the diagonal turned out to be commensurable.

And Aristotle refers to a well-known proof by reductio that, if the diagonal of a square were commensurable with its side, odd numbers would be equal to even numbers (*Prior Analytics* I 41a 26-28). The proof is interpolated into the text of Euclid's *Elements* as X. 117. Two lengths are commensurable if their ratio can be expressed as a ratio of integers, and any ratio of integers can be reduced to lowest terms, having no common divisor except 1. It follows that a ratio in lowest terms must contain at least one odd number, since all even numbers contain 2 as a common divisor.

Assume then that AC, the diagonal of a square, is commensurable with AB, its side. Then if AC is commensurable with AB, AC : AB : : m : n, where m and n are integers and their ratio is in lowest terms. Thus, either m is odd or n is odd.

Now, $AC^2 = 2AB^2$, since the diagonal is the hypotenuse of an isosceles right triangle, and the square of the hypotenuse is equal to the sum of the squares of the sides. Therefore, $m^2 = 2n^2$.

Now, since $2n^2$ is even, m^2 is even. Therefore, m is even, since the square of any odd number is odd.[105] Therefore, n is odd.

But since m is even, it is of the form 2k. Therefore, $4K^2 = 2n^2$ and $2K^2 = n^2$.

Therefore, n^2 is even. Therefore, n is even. But n was odd, which is impossible. Therefore, the diagonal AC cannot be commensurable with the side AB, for AC does not have to AB the ratio of a number to a number.[106]

This result may also be put in terms of reciprocal subtraction, as in Euclid X.2:

> If, when the lesser of two unequal magnitudes is continually subtracted
> in turn from the greater, that which is left over never measures the one
> before it, the magnitudes will be incommensurable.

This result is an extension of reciprocal subtraction to determine what numbers are prime to each other, or their greatest common measure.[107] It implies that incommensurable magnitudes have no common measure, however small, and therefore that all magnitudes are infinitely divisible:[108]

> The Pythagoreans were first to address themselves to the investigation of
> incommensurability, having discovered it as the result of their obser-
> vation of numbers; for, while the unit is a common measure of all
> numbers, they were unable to find a common measure of all magni-
> tudes . . . because all magnitudes are divisible *ad infinitum* and never
> leave a magnitude which is too small to admit of further division, but
> that remainder is equally divisible *ad infinitum*.

Parmenides' definition of incommensurability in terms of larger and smaller measures reflects this point: for any integral measure of a magnitude, however small, there is another magnitude whose measure is greater or less than the assigned measure, and reciprocal subtraction will go on to infinity because of the difference in units of measurement. The definition implies a distinction between incommensurability and irrationality: for incommensurability is an inherent relation between magnitudes implying larger and smaller measures, whereas irrationality is an assigned property based on choice of given measure. If the leg of an isosceles right triangle is allowed to correspond to a unit of measure, the hypotenuse will correspond, as we should say, to the square root of two; but alternately, if the hypotenuse is allowed to correspond to a unit of measure, the leg will correspond to the square root of two over two. Greek mathematicians could not have put the matter this way, because they identified number with the integers, and did not suppose that the square root of two, or fractions, were numbers; but they saw the point. Euclid's first and third definitions in *Elements* X, a book that summarizes the work of Theaetetus, distinguish irrationals from incommensurables on the ground that irrationals are incommensurable with an *assigned* straight line. The first scholium on Book X traces this distinction to the Pythagoreans: "(They showed that) all magnitudes can be rational and all irrational in a relative sense; hence the incommensurables would be for them *natural* (kinds), while the rational and irrational would rest on *assumption* or *convention*" (Trans. Heath, *TBEE* iii. 1). Parmenides' formulation implies that both of two incommensurables have some number of measures, and different units of measurement.

Perhaps a late date should be assigned to the discovery of incommensurability on the ground that it implied a "crisis in the foundations" of Pythagorean ontology. Aristotle testifies that the Pythagoreans supposed that the real nature of things is number, and that they constructed the whole universe out of numbers, conceived as magnitudes. But the discovery of incommensurability is the discovery of irrationality, of the fact that no ratio of integers can express the ratio of diagonal and side. If this is true, how can an ontology be erected on the claim that the real nature of things is number? That this question is not recent is shown by ancient traditions that the Pythagorean school undertook to keep the discovery of irrationality a secret, and that those who revealed it to the world met an untimely death, or, more vividly, were drowned at sea.

Yet in view of the definition of incommensurability offered by Parmenides here, the problem seems unreal: for the diagonal and the side both admit integral units of measurement, and therefore both may be regarded as composed of numbers; it is only that the units are different. The claim of a crisis in the foundations seems to neglect the distinction between incommensurability and irrationality — the latter existing by convention, not by nature. Incommensurability, no doubt, forced a wedge between purely arithmetical relations and geometrical relations, a wedge exhibited in the distinction between the rational theory of proportion of Euclid VII-IX and the general theory, embracing both rationals and incommensurables, of Euclid V; and Euclid V, it is generally agreed, is the later work, the work of Eudoxus. This is usual in the development of mathematics; truths are found governing special cases and then extended to a more general theorem. Incommensurability implies, not a "crisis in the foundations" of Pythagorean ontology, but a mathematical problem to be solved. The recognition of incommensurability may, of course, long have antedated the discovery of a theory of proportion adequate to it.

When was incommensurability discovered? Heath put the date early (*HGM* i. 168), and if so, it may well be supposed that it was in or before Zeno's time. In the *Laws* (VII 819d-820c), written mainly or wholly in the 350s, the Athenian Stranger remarks that he learned only recently about certain discoveries concerning incommensurability still not generally known; and indeed, his respondent, Clinias, betrays an unfortunate ignorance in the matter. But those discoveries have to do with the incommensurability of lines, planes, and *solids*, that is, solid geometry or stereometry, and we know from the *Theaetetus* that Theaetetus explored the incommensurability of solids around the year 400. The passage in the *Laws* implies nothing about the date of discovery of the theorem in plane (rather than solid) geometry that the diagonal is incommensurable with the side.

The *Theaetetus* (147d-148b) is more informative. It implies that the Greek treatment of incommensurability had, at the date of writing, passed through at least three stages. The third, due to Theaetetus himself, gave a general account of incommensurability by classifying square and oblong numbers, the former of which can and the latter of which cannot be obtained by multiplying a number by itself, and extended the result to solids. Theaetetus built on the work of his teacher, Theodorus, who had proved in the second stage that the sides or roots of squares representing three, five, and so on, up to seventeen square feet, are incommensurable with the unit line. We do not know when Theodorus worked out his proofs, only that he has recently provided Theaetetus with them, and that the dramatic date of the *Theaetetus* is 399. Nor do we know when the first stage occurred. As Heath remarks (*HGM* i. 155, cf. *TBEE* ii. 288):

> (T)he passage which states that $\sqrt{3}, \sqrt{5}$, etc., are incommensurable says nothing of $\sqrt{2}$. The reason, no doubt, is that the incommensurability of $\sqrt{2}$ had been proved earlier, and everything points to the probability that this was the first case discovered.

Certainly, it is the simplest case, since it does not even require the generalized proposition of Euclid I. 47, that the square on the hypotenuse of *any* right triangle is equal to the sum of the squares of the sides, the so-called Pythagorean Theorem. A special case of this theorem, the 3-4-5 triangle, must have been known, but not proved, in Egypt; it is used to make right angles with a knotted string and a rule by carpenters and shipwrights today. The special case of the isosceles right triangle is hardly more complex: the result can be proved, though not thereby deduced from elements, by superposition of congruent triangles and simple counting. The problem of doubling the square, by which the slave-boy is introduced to geometry in the *Meno*, leads directly to this result. We need then ask only the question of the ratio of the diagonal to the side to set the problem Euclid X. 117 so elegantly solves by reductio.

We know too little about the history of mathematics in the fifth century to speak with confidence, but there is no compelling reason to assign a date late in that century to the discovery of incommensurability, and quite a good reason for supposing that it was known by about 465, and perhaps earlier. For if the *Parmenides* is to be dated around 450, and if Zeno at that date was nearing forty, and if Zeno wrote his book in his twenties, then 465 would seem to be an approximate *terminus ad quem* for the discovery of incommensurability, *if* Zeno's work betrays familiarity with it. Now, Zeno's Fragment 3, to take but one example, argues that things that are are infinite, since there are always other things between things that are, and again others between them, and this implies a relatively precise concept of the infinite divisibility of magnitudes, and of the property of density, as we should call it, which attaches to such divisibility. But infinite divisibility is an intelligible, not a perceptual, property, and it is difficult to see how Zeno could have known of it unless he had a mathematical proof of it; that proof must surely have been the proof of incommensurability, which implies of any magnitude that it has no least measure. It may well be, indeed, that a proof of incommensurability along the lines of Euclid X. 117 may have given not only Zeno but Parmenides their confidence in reductio ad absurdum, their faith in reason, and their equally strong distrust of the senses and common opinion. If this were so, then Parmenides must have known the proof when he wrote the *Way of Truth*, putting the terminus ad quem of the discovery perhaps as early as 485.

ix. Older, Younger, Same Age (140e-141d)

Unity can be neither older, younger, nor the same age as anything. It cannot be the same age because it would then partake of Likeness and Equality with respect to time, and it has been shown that Unity cannot partake of Likeness or Equality. To this it might have been added that time, like magnitude, admits of measure (Cf. *Timaeus* 37e, 47a). Since Unity has no parts, it does not admit of measure, and therefore cannot partake of Unlikeness or Inequality with respect to time. So it cannot be older or younger than anything. It follows that it cannot be in time at all.

The argument proceeds, as all others have, from the specific nature of Unity. But like the earlier denials of motion and geometrical characterization, it might have proceeded from the bare fact tht Unity is an Idea. Thus, for example, it is held at *Timaeus* 38a that,

> That which is forever in the same state immovably cannot be becoming older or younger by lapse of time, nor can it ever become so; neither can it have been, nor will it be in the future; in general nothing belongs to it of all that Becoming attaches to the moving things of sense: but those have come into being as forms of time, which images eternity and revolves according to number.

Time is an element in the rational structure of the world; but Ideas, the ultimate principles of that structure, are not in time. Parmenides, however, goes around a longer way.

The proof that Unity cannot be in time rests on a general analysis of what it means to be in time, and the cogency of that analysis can scarcely be said to leap to the eye. It is assumed that what is in time is becoming older than itself, and that what is becoming older than itself is becoming younger than itself. Older and younger are opposite and correlative, so that if x becomes older than (double of, larger than) y, y becomes younger than (half of, smaller than) x (cf. *Republic* IV 438b-c). Furthermore, everything that comes to be comes to be for a time equal to itself; therefore, it must have the same age as itself. So everything in time is older, younger, and the same age as itself.

But why is it to be assumed that if x is in time, x is becoming older than x, x is becoming younger than x, and x is the same age as x? Cornford explained this as follows (*PP* 128, italics Cornford's):

> The above argument is not a 'sophism.' Whatever exists in time must be of a *different* age at every moment from its age at any earlier moment; and the lengthening interval between its younger self and its older self must always be the same as the interval between its older self

and its younger self. But we have seen that no propositions involving the terms 'same' and 'different' can be true of the One we have defined.

This provides a reason for saying, what is certainly true, that what is in time is older than it was, and becoming older than it is; but it provides no reason whatever for saying that what is in time is becoming both older and younger than itself. It does not, in fact, so much as provide a meaning for that phrase.

A thing becomes older than it was at every successive stage of its existence in time; but alternately, it may also be said to be older than every subsequent stage of itself, which may thus be described as younger or newer — the Greek νεώτερον has both meanings. Thus in the *Symposium* (207d), though a man is called the same, he never has the same things: he is always becoming young, or new (νέος), by reason of replacement of hair, flesh, bones and blood, which are ever being destroyed. Plato uses the concept of Time as Destroyer, marked by Aristotle in the *Physics* (*Phys.* IV 221a 3 - b 2, 222b 17-25); but gives equal weight to the work of Time the Builder. Like the *Symposium*, the *Timaeus* (38a) holds that things become older and younger through time: older as having existed longer, younger as being ever new. In estimating the force of these expressions, it is helpful to remember that in Greek the future is often described, not only as what lies ahead, but also as what lies behind us, ὄπισθεν, for we cannot see it. Shakespeare refers to "the dark *backward* and abysm of time,"[109] and Sophocles tells of "day following day, drawing toward and drawing back from death."[110]

So what is in time is becoming both older and younger than itself, depending on what perspective you choose, and is of the same age as itself.

By Plato's own account of time in the *Timaeus*, time came to be with the Heavens: it is, in effect, not movement, but movement in so far as it admits of numeration (*Timaeus* 37c-d, cf. *Physics* IV 219b2-3):

> Now the nature of that Living Being was eternal, and this character it was impossible to confer in full completeness on the generated thing. But he took thought to make, as it were, a moving likeness of eternity; and, at the same time that he ordered the Heaven, he made, of eternity that abides in unity, an everlasting likeness moving according to number — that to which we have given the name Time.

The "moving likeness of eternity" is, of course, circular motion about a fixed axis, exhibited by the heavens. The poetry should not conceal that this is a highly mathematical account of time as proportional measure or ratio of motion to motion. Speaking dogmatically, there is no clear anticipation in Plato of the conception of Time as a river, carrying objects on its broad bosom to float and sink. The river of time, purified of its poetry and channeled to the prediction of natural events, issues in the Scholium to the initial definitions in the *Principia*. Newton comments:[111]

Absolute, true, and mathematical time, of itself, and from its own nature, flows equably without relation to anything external, and by another name is called duration: relative, apparent, and common time, is some sensible and external (whether accurate or unequable) measure of duration by the means of motion, which is commonly used instead of true time; such as an hour, a day, a month, a year.

Absolute time, duration, is measured by clock-time, relative motion. That is, where Plato and Aristotle had conceived of time as the measure of motion, Newton conceived motion as the measure of time, which is duration. And Newton gave a significant and interesting reason for this assumption:[112]

Absolute time, in astronomy, is distinguished from relative, by the equation or correction of the apparent time. For the natural days are truly unequal, though they are commonly considered as equal, and used for a measure of time; astronomers correct this inequality that they may measure the celestial motions by a more accurate time. It may be, that there is no such thing as an equable motion, whereby time may be accurately measured. All motions may be accelerated and retarded, but the flowing of absolute time is not liable to any change. The duration or perseverance of the existence of things remains the same, whether the motions are swift or slow, or none at all: and therefore this duration ought to be distinguished from what are only sensible measures thereof; and from which we deduce it, by means of the astronomical equation.

Time must be equable in its flow; but each motion by which time is measured admits of unevenness; therefore every motion by which time is measured admits of unevenness; therefore, we must distinguish apparent time from absolute time, duration as such. The argument is analogous to the Cartesian *cogito*, which proceeded from the possibility of error in any case to the possibility of error in every case, and inferred a single principle, the doubting self, about which one could not be mistaken. In like manner, Newton, proceeding not from the possibility of error but from the possibility of inequable variation, infers the existence of a principle, which shall be free of any possibility of variaton. Like the *cogito*, Newton's postulate of absolute time involves a fallacy of composition of a sort that had deep roots in the theology of the middle ages: Anselm had argued that if all beings are contingent, in the sense that it is possible for them not to be, then being itself would be contingent, and that since being itself is not contingent, there is and must be a necessary being. Newton's time, like the *cogito*, is open to the objection that variation in measure can be determined only relative to some other measure, as falsity in judgment can be determined only relative to some other judgment, which need not be unshakably true but only assumed to be true relative to the argument in which it occurs as a countervailing premise.

As becoming older than itself by passage of time, Unity will also become younger than itself. What is relative is correlative. So in the *Charmides* (168c), what is more than itself will be less than itself, and what is older than itself will be younger than itself; for if a thing has its own power relative to itself, it will then have the nature and reality (οὐσία) in relation to which that power exists. Since Unity is not a whole of parts, and admits neither Sameness, Difference, nor Equality, it cannot be in time.

x. Conclusion (141d-142a)

If Unity is not in time, it does not exist, and what does not exist cannot be even to the degree of being one. So there will be neither name nor account, knowledge, opinion, or sensation of it, and Unity cannot so much as be named or spoken of.

The conclusion of the First Deduction of Hypothesis I formally contradicts its own premise, that Unity is and is one. But if it is a valid inference that, if Unity is then Unity is not, it would seem that Unity is not is a necessary truth.

Yet the argument by which this result is established is again peculiar. Parmenides might have drawn the conclusion that Unity does not partake of Being directly from the fact that Unity can neither be nor have any second character, on pain of being many, as he will infer in the Second Deduction of Hypothesis I that Unity must be a whole of parts and have multiple characteristics from the fact that Unity has a share of Being. Instead, he here derives the conclusion that Unity can neither be nor be one from the premises that it cannot be in time, and that to be is to be in time. But the proposition that to be is to be in time, restated at 151e-152a, contradicts known tenets of the theory of Ideas. That theory requires that Ideas be eternal and unchanging;[113] they are not *in* anything.[114] So far is it from being true that, for Platonism, what is must be in time, what truly is cannot be in time at all. Why then does Parmenides assume, and assume without argument, that to be is to be in time?

Cornford offered the following account (*PP* 130):

> Neither of the two inferences: (1) that the One does not exist, (2) that the One is not even an entity and therefore cannot be the subject of a true statement that it is one, appears to follow from the previous conclusion that the One is not in time. A Platonic Form is an entity that is not, and does not come to be, in time, and yet has many characters and can be known. . . . Plato is content to draw a true conclusion from premises that hardly sustain it. But the premises themselves are true; and to represent a true conclusion as following from true premises, which do not by themselves entail it, is not sophistry in the usual sense. It is rather taking a short-cut, to avoid entering on explanations which will be more in place elsewhere.

Waiving questions of sophistry, this explanation offers no account of why the proposition that to be is to be in time should be accepted, or why the proposition that Unity both is and is one should be rejected on the basis of it. The proposition is unusual, and one that the theory of Ideas does not admit. What then explains it?

The answer lies in the Dilemma of Participation (131a-c). Parmenides' criticisms proceeded on the premise that sensibles exist, and exist separately from Ideas. But if sensibles exist, and are separate from Ideas, they must participate, along with Ideas, in Being. But Being is itself an Idea. Deny that there is participation by sensibles in it—push the Hinge outward—and sensibles can no longer be said to be or be separate from Ideas. So there must be participation in Being by sensibles, and since participation implies participation in parts of Ideas, it implies participation in parts of Being—that is, Being is a whole, some of whose parts are in sensible participants, since those participants are.

But sensibles are in time, and come to be and pass away. Therefore, some parts of Being must come to be and pass away with the sensibles they are in, for each sensible has its own part of Being. Given that a whole is that from which no part is absent, generation or destruction of parts of Being implies change in Being itself, since Being is a whole consisting of its parts. But Being, if it changes in this way, admits a before, an after, and a now, and therefore is in time. Therefore, to be is to be in time, since to be is to partake of Being, and Being is in time. This result, wholly unacceptable to Platonism, is the conclusion of an aporetic structure that requires us to look to the premises that generated it.

It remains to add only that Unity, since it in no way is, cannot be a subject of discourse or an object of apprehension. So it is that in the *Republic* (V 477a-b), what simply and solely is not corresponds to sheer ignorance. So it is that in the *Sophist* (238c), "One cannot legitimately utter the words, or speak or think of that which just simply is not; it is unthinkable, not to be spoken of or uttered or expressed."

Aristoteles' agreement that this cannot be true of Unity is well founded. It cannot even attain to the dignity of being false.

I.2. First Hypothesis, Second Deduction (142b-155e)

The First Deduction has proved that if Unity is not a whole of parts, no characteristic belongs to it. The Second Deduction will prove that if even one characteristic belongs to it—the bare characteristic of being—Unity is a whole of parts; this result will be found to imply precisely the characteristics denied of Unity in the First Deduction.

The propositions that if Unity is not a whole of parts, no characteristic belongs to it, and that if a characteristic belongs to it, it is a whole of parts, are transpositionally equivalent and assume that assertion of a characteristic of a subject implies the relation of part and whole. This is neither ordinary Greek nor ordinary Platonic idiom. There can be but one justification for it within the body of the *Parmenides*, and that is the Dilemma of Participation (131a-c), which construes participation in terms of the relation of part and whole, and implies that if there is participation it must be of parts. That implication is assumed both in the First Deduction, and in the detailed argumentation of 142c-145a.

Introduction (142b-c)

Parmenides begins with a proof that 'to be' and 'to be one' have different significations: if the Idea of Unity is, that Idea partakes of Being.

The Proof that Unity and the being of Unity are not identical is a complex instance of modus tollens. If the being of Unity were the same as Unity, then (i) the being of Unity would not be the being *of* it (but rather, it would *be* Unity); (ii) Unity would not partake of that being (but rather, it would be that being); (iii) the statements "Unity is Unity" and "Unity is" would be identical in meaning, since there would be no distinction between the being of Unity and Unity. It is assumed that these connected consequences are false, since the statements are not identical in meaning, and 'is' signifies something different from 'is Unity' (or, 'is one'). So if Unity is, that must mean that Unity partakes of Being.

It will be observed that the hypothesis here is exactly the same as that of the First Deduction: we have returned and are to go over it again from the beginning. But whereas in I.1 we were led to a Unity which excluded all plurality, we are now to attend to the important fact that Unity has been assumed to exist.

i. Part and Whole (142c-d)

Since Unity partakes of Being, it must be a whole and have parts. For it both is and is one, and its unity and being are parts of it. Since parts are parts of a whole (137c), anything that is one must be a whole and have parts.

A salient feature of this argument is its ambiguity: both grammatically and in terms of sense, its subject may be abstract, Unity or the property of being one, or it may be distributively generic, what(ever) is one. The ambiguity is intentional: it is essential to the argument that follows that Unity be itself one thing. But that the primary subject of the argument is Unity is shown by the fact that what has been hypothesized is coordinate with Being, and is distributed to the numbers (144c-d), which partake both of Being and Unity. But although Unity is the primary subject of the argument of 142c-d, the argument is so constructed as to apply generally to anything which is and is one. Thus it is that τὸ ἓν ὂν at 143a is equivalent to τὸ ὂν ἓν at 144e 5.

In treating Unity as itself one, the argument suggests a Third Man. Good reason is given for the assumption. It is that being and unity are coextensive: whatever is one is, and whatever is is one. Since, by hypothesis, Unity is, Unity is one.

The claim that unity and being are coextensive was assumed in the First Deduction (141e 9-12), and is later restated with greater explicitness (144c-3); it was accepted by Aristotle, who gave as a reason for saying that unity and being are in a sense the same that, "to be one is just to be a particular thing."[115] Earlier in the *Metaphysics* he had explained the point (*Meta.* IV 1003b 22-34):

If, now, being and unity are the same and are one thing in the sense that they are implied in one another as principle and cause are, not in the sense that they are explained by the same definition . . . 'one man' and 'man' are the same thing, and so are 'existent man' and 'man,' and the doubling of the words in 'one man and one *existent* man' does not express anything different . . . ; and similarly *'one* existent man' adds nothing to 'existent man,' so that it is obvious that the addition in these cases means the same thing, and unity is nothing apart from being; and if, further, the substance of each thing is one in no merely accidental way, and similarly is from its very nature something that is: — all this being so, there must be exactly as many species of being as of unity.

Aristotle, though he supposed that being and unity were *in a sense* the same, as being coextensive, did not suppose that they were the same. He commented of the historical Parmenides that, "It is necessary for him, then, to assume not only that 'being' has the same meaning of whatever it is predicated, but further that it means (1) what just is and (2) what is just one" (*Phys.* I 189a 33 ff., cf. *Sophist* 224b-c). But the Platonic Parmenides, like Aristotle, distinguishes: 'to be' signifies something different from 'to be one' (142c 4-5, d 2-3).

This bears on the fact that the being and unity of Unity are *parts* of Unity, a claim that must be understood through Parmenides' inference at 142b-c that if Unity partakes of Being, the being of Unity is not identical with Unity. There is, then, a distinction between Being and the being *of* something, and this distinction is confirmed at 144b-c in the case of the being of numbers (cf. *Sophist* 225c-d). In a similar way, Socrates had earlier granted a distinction between Likeness itself and the likeness we possess. (130b, cf. *Phaedo* 102d, 103b). It is consistent with this that Cornford should have suggested that the term 'part' should be so construed as to include "any and every diversity of aspect or character" (*PP* 116). This is not false, but unless carefully qualified, it is likely to be misleading. In the first place, the term 'part,' if it does not have two senses, surely has two uses: at 142b-c, f is part of x if x partakes of F-ness, and this leads to a dense infinity of parts; at 144b-c, f is part of F-ness if x has f, and this leads to a discrete infinity of parts; thus the being of Unity (to choose an example) may be regarded both as a part of Unity, and as a part of Being. In the second place, the use of 'part' for diversity of character or aspect is neither ordinary language nor ordinary Platonic Greek. It derives directly from the Dilemma of Participation stated at 131a-c. Thus at 142b-c it is inferred that if Unity partakes of Being, it partakes of its own being (142c 1), and that the signification of 'is' in the statement 'Unity is' is not Being, but the being of Unity. The argument here is to be distinguished from that of the Eleatic Stranger in the *Sophist* (255c-d), since it is meant, not merely to distinguish Unity from Being, but from *its own* being. Unless the latter distinction is taken as self-evident, it is unintelligible apart from the Dilemma of Participation.[116]

If to say that Unity is is to say that Unity partakes of Being, and if this implies that the being of Unity is a part of Unity, the claim that Unity is a whole, of which the being of Unity is part, becomes intelligible. Part and whole had earlier been defined in terms of each other: parts are parts of a whole, and a whole is that from which no part is absent.[117] This account implies both containment and dependence: a part, to be a part, must be part of some whole; a whole, to be the whole that it is, must contain the parts it contains. Parmenides assumes that this definition is satisfied by the relation between Unity and its own being: the being of Unity cannot exist apart from Unity, nor can Unity exist apart from its own being. This reciprocal dependence involves containment: as parts are parts of a whole, so the whole contains its parts (144e 9).[118]

Given the Dilemma of Participation and appropriate definitions, Parmenides' inference that Unity, if it is, is a whole and has parts, is valid. It implies that Unity, since its own unity is part of it, partakes of Unity — that is, that Unity is itself a member of the class of things it characterizes. This premise, however, is not stated but implied. By a Third Man Argument, Parmenides might have gone on to prove an infinite multiplicity of Unities; instead, he proves that Unity has infinitely many parts. The peculiar and aporematic quality of this reasoning is shown by the fact that it is debarred in the First Deduction of Hypothesis II, which corresponds to the Second Deduction of Hypothesis I in that it considers the consequences for the Others of a Unity which is, and maintains that each of those others, as one, will be other than Unity, since otherwise they would not *partake* of Unity but rather *be* Unity, whereas nothing but Unity itself can be Unity. This implies that since Unity itself is Unity, it cannot partake of Unity; it is not one among many things which are one (158a).

iia. Limit and Unlimited: First Argument (142d-143a)

In the First Deduction, that Unity was not a whole of parts was immediately taken to imply that it is unlimited, in the sense that it is without limits. The argument of the Second Deduction is more complex. Parmenides attempts to prove that Unity, if it is and thus partakes of Being, is one and many, whole and parts, limited and unlimited in multitude. His argument, as we have seen, begins with a proof that Unity, if it is, is a whole whose parts are being and unity (142c-d). This conclusion will now be shown to imply that Unity is infinitely divisible, each part containing being and unity as parts (142d-143a). But a new principle of division will next be introduced: Unity, considered in abstraction from its own being, will be found to be different from that being (143a-b). Unity, conceived apart from its own being, will be shown to imply the existence of the numbers, which are infinite in multitude (143c-144a). Since Being is distributed to all of the numbers, Being has infinitely many parts (144a-c). But since Unity is coextensive with Being, it too must have infinitely many parts (144c-e). And since Unity is a whole that contains its parts, it is limited with respect to its wholeness; therefore, it is part and whole, one and many, limited and unlimited in multitude (145a).

There are a variety of puzzling features about this argument. One of them is its apparent redundancy. Parmenides' initial division provides him with an infinite plurality of parts. He might therefore have given an existence proof of infinitely many numbers, conceived as pluralities of units according to the Euclidean definition, by means of this division. Instead, he introduces a new principle of division for the purpose. Again, he derives the conclusion that Unity has infinitely many parts from the infinity of number, but he has already shown that Unity is infinitely divisible into parts consisting of being and unity. In short, the new principle of division introduced for number seems unnecessary, and Parmenides twice shows that Unity has infinitely many parts.

One way of explaining this redundancy would be to claim that the meaning of 'Unity' has shifted: the Greek expression 'one' or 'the one' is after all multiply ambiguous. The Unity which is shown to have infinitely many parts consisting of being and unity is a Unity which is, τὸ ἓν ὂν (142d). But the Unity which is shown to have infinitely many parts distributed in correspondence to the numbers is a Unity considered apart from its own being (143a). There is, then, a distinction between τὸ ὂν ἕν and αὐτὸ τὸ ἕν, and that distinction is put in stated terms at 144e 5-6. The existence of this distinction, however, does not explain why Parmenides should use two arguments to prove that Unity is unlimited in multitude, since it implies no ambiguity in the meaning of 'Unity.' The distinction rests only on abstraction (143a 7), and the force of this is indicated by the fact that to consider Unity apart from its own being implies that it is different from its own being (143b), a premise that lays a foundation for the First Deduction of the Third Hypothesis, that Unity, if it is not, can be spoken of and is different from other things, and thus in some sense possesses being (160c-d, 161e-162b). Parmenides is not dealing with different Unities, but with the same Unity conceived in different ways. It is the same thing that is twice proved to be unlimited in multitude. Despite the difference in the way in which Unity is conceived in the two proofs, then, apparent redundancy remains.

That redundancy, however, is apparent, not real. Parmenides is dealing not with one but two kinds of infinity: a dense infinite allied to that of continuity, typical of extensive magnitudes, and the infinity of succession, typical of number. These kinds of infinity were distinct in Greek mathematics in a way in which they are not in our own, since the Greeks, identifying number with the positive integers greater than 1, and thus lacking both rationals and reals, had no concept of number as continuous or dense, and no notion of isomorphism between numbers and lines or other continua. Unity will be proved to have infinitely many dense parts, and infinitely many successive parts, and its simultaneous possession of these different kinds of parts explains the apparent redundance of the account. As a dense infinite, Unity is proved to be a whole of parts through its participation in Being. As a successive infinite, it is proved to be a whole of parts, not through its participation in something else, but through the participation of infinitely many things, the numbers, in it.

The proof that Unity, if it is, has infinitely many parts, follows from what has gone before in a simple and cogent way. Whatever is is one, and whatever is one is. Therefore, the two parts of Unity, namely its being and its unity, must respectively be and be one. Thus, by the same argument that showed that Unity, if it is, has unity and being as parts, each of those parts, since they are and are one, must have unity and being as parts, ad infinitum. Assuming the transitivity of the *part of* relation, so that, for example, the unity of the being of Unity is part of Unity because it is part of the being of Unity, it follows that Unity has infinitely many parts.

The conclusion that Unity is "unlimited in multitude" is ambiguous between a process and a product. Does Parmenides mean that Unity has infinitely many parts, that it is infinitely divided so that the act of distinguishing parts is merely recognition of this distinction? Or does he rather mean that it is (not infinitely divided but) infinitely divisible, that the *process* of division can be carried out on any part, however small? Ignoring the specifically Aristotelian connotations of the terms, this distinction is the distinction between an actual and a potential infinite.

Aristotle, it may be observed, distinguished his notion of a potential infinite from his usual notion of potentiality (*Phys.* III 206a 14-21):

> We must keep in mind that the word 'is' means either what *potentially* is or what *fully* is. Further, a thing is infinite by addition or by division. Now, as we have seen, magnitude is not actually infinite. But by division it is infinite. (There is no difficulty in refuting the theory of indivisible lines.) The alternative then remains that the infinite has a potential existence. But the phrase "potential existence" is ambiguous. When we speak of the potential existence of a statue we mean that there will be an actual statue. It is not so with the infinite. There will not be an actual infinite. The word 'is' has many senses, and we say that the infinite 'is' in the sense in which we say 'it is day' or 'it is the games,' because one thing after another is always coming into existence.

Aristotle returns to this distinction between the actual and a potential infinite which cannot be actualized, later in the *Physics*:[119]

> To the question whether it is possible to pass through an infinite number of units either of time or of distance we must reply that in a sense it is and in a sense it is not. If the units are actual, it is not possible: if they are potential, it is possible.

This is the core of Aristotle's reply to Zeno.

The Actual Infinite

Actuality and potentiality are, of course, technical terms in Aristotle's metaphysics and philosophy of nature, and Aristotle's terms for actuality, in this case ἐντελέχεια, are all his own. But his concept of potentiality in the infinite is the exact opposite of his usual concept of potentiality, which precisely *can* be actualized, and it is probable that he borrowed this bit of vocabulary from the mathematicians. In mathematics, δύναμις meant power, usually the second power, or square.[120] By a natural extension, Theaetetus applies the term to square roots of numbers that are not perfect squares, that is, to incommensurables;[121] and it is but a slight further extension to speak of what is infinite in power in order to designate what is indefinitely capable of further division, or addition, though not of course infinitely added or divided.

Unity is infinitely divisible. Is it so only potentially, only in that, for any distinction between its being and its unity, further distinction is possible? Or does every such distinction require the prior presence of parts?

If this question is to be answered by analogy with Greek mathematics, as known to us through Euclid, writing about 300 B.C., there is a strong case for treating Unity as a potential infinite. *Elements* X. 1. states that:

> Two unequal magnitudes being set out, if from the greater there be subtracted a magnitude greater than its half, and from that which is left a magnitude greater than its half, and if this process be repeated continually, there will be left some magnitude which will be less than the lesser magnitude.

This theorem, which later came to be called the Postulate of Archimedes, is the foundation of much Greek mathematics. Euclid's analysis of incommensurability and irrationality in *Elements* X, and the great Method of Exhaustion expounded in Elements XII, which anticipated the calculus,[122] both rest on it. It was known to and probably first formulated by, Plato's contemporary and colleague in the Academy, Eudoxus, who may, however, have been anticipated by Theaetetus. It will be observed that the theorem's treatment of infinity is purely potentialist: the theorem does not state that any magnitude is infinitely divided; it only states that any magnitude is infinitely divisible, as having no parts that do not admit the process of division. As with magnitude, so with multitude. Euclid's proof that, as we should be pleased to put it, there are infinitely many primes, states rather that, "Prime numbers are more than any assigned multitude of prime numbers."[123] Aristotle correctly reported the best mathematical thinking of his time when he said that the mathematicians "do not need the (actual) infinite and do not use it" (*Phys.* III 207b 29).[124] It is worth adding that an actual infinite is not implied by Plato's account of (phenomenal) infinity at *Philebus* 24a-25a, and may well there be precluded. Presumably, then, Plato's own treatment of infinity was potentialist.

But an actual infinite does seem implied by Parmenides' account here. Importantly, although Unity has in effect been proved infinite by division, there is no reference to the *process* of division; there is only mention of parts. Then again, it is said that the least part[125] comes to be from or is composed of two parts,[126] and that whatever comes to be a part contains or holds (ἰσχει 142e 4, 6, 7) two parts, namely, unity and being. This suggests, not that the presence of parts derives from the process of division, but that the process of division is possible because of the presence of parts. It suggests, in short, an actual rather than a potential infinite, and this suggestion is confirmed by the fact that there are infinitely many numbers, each of which has being (144a-c).[127]

Cornford suggested that the infinity proved in Parmenides' argument is somehow mental rather than real: it is shown that we can *think* of Unity as infinite, not that it *is* infinite (*PP* 139). But this is founded on nothing in the text, and would appear to be mistaken. Parmenides claims, not that it may be thought of Unity that it has infinitely many parts, but that it may *truly* be thought of Unity that it has infinitely many parts; and this was precisely Aristotle's reason for denying that the infinite is somehow mental. Indeed, Aristotle knew as an argument for an actual infinite that, "it never gives out in thought."[128] That is, the mental act of distinguishing parts is merely recognition of their distinction.

Density and Continuity

Parmenides' proof that Unity has infinitely many parts satisfies one of Aristotle's definitions of continuity: "By continuous I mean that which is divisible into divisibles that are infinitely divisible."[129] This definition implies, as Aristotle points out, that no two divisions in a continuum can be in succession; that is, given a point of division, there is no next or consecutive point of division, since between any two points of division there is a further point of division. As Aristotle puts it (*Phys.* VI 231b 6-9):

> Nor, again, can a point be in succession to a point or a moment to a moment, in such a way that length can be composed of points or time of moments: for things are in succession if there is nothing of their own kind intermediate between them, whereas that which is intermediate between points is always a line and that which is intermediate between moments is always a period of time.

This account of continuity in terms of infinite divisibility emphasizes its plurality. Aristotle gives another account, which emphasizes its unity (*Phys.* V 227a 10-15):

> The 'continuous' is a subdivision of the contiguous: things are called continuous when the touching extremities of each become one and the same and are, as the word implies, contained in each other; continuity is impossible if these extremities are two. This definition makes it plain that continuity belongs to things that naturally in virtue of their mutual contact form a unity.

Although Aristotle argues that sameness of extremity implies lack of successiveness (*Phys.* VI 230a 24-29, *et seq.*), he nowhere argues that lack of successiveness implies sameness of extremity. But since both of these formulae are stated as definitions, and definitions of the same thing, Aristotle presumably supposed them to be equivalent.[130]

It is easy to construct an argument to show that they are not equivalent, since infinite divisibility is implied by but does not imply continuity. If—to use language no Greek could have used—the points on a given line are allowed to stand in one-to-one correspondence to the rational and real numbers, then the rational points on the line, corresponding to the Cantorian sequence 1, 2, 1/2, 1/3, 3 . . . , will be dense on that line; that is, between any two rational points there will be rational points. But density is not equivalent to continuity, since there are also irrational points on the line, points corresponding, for example, to the square roots of the primes; and as it happens, the irrational points are also dense on the line. Thus, infinite divisibility according either to a rational principle of division or an irrational principle of division does not imply continuity: continuity requires, minimally, that both kinds of division be possible.

As a criticism of Aristotle's equivalence between continuity and infinite divisibility, this argument is beside the point. Aristotle lacked the notion of a number continuum, and could not have put the point numerically. But the geometry of his time was fully adequate to establish its analogue: Aristotle knew that a line could be divided infinitely according either to a rational or an irrational proportion, that is, divided in a proportion which is that of an integer to an integer or in a proportion which is not. But to put the point thus geometrically is to alter it. Aristotle, and Greek mathematicians generally, would have understood that rational fractions, and *a fortiori* irrationals, are not numbers but ratios; they correspond, not to points on a line, but to ratios of lengths of lines. Thus Aristotle does not say that points are dense on a line, but that points are never in succession because there are always lines between them. Any line, of course, may be divided according to any ratio. Infinite divisibility, then, implies continuity because it implies division according to a ratio of things that are continuous. It follows that infinite divisibility is not the essence of continuity, but a convertible property of it. Aristotle's alternate formula, "things are continuous whose extremities are one" (*Phys.* VI 231a 21), though it has other difficulties, is perhaps a better candidate for definition.

Aristotle, in discussing continua, has in view extensive magnitudes such as space, time, and motion, and Parmenides will shortly go on in this Deduction to prove that Unity occupies space and time, and is in motion. Shall he then be supposed to have here proved that it is continuous?

Unity has not been shown to be continuous in the sense that the touching extremities of its parts are one and the same, for its parts have not been shown to have extremities, let alone identical extremities. But Unity has been shown to be divisible into parts that are infinitely divisible. This, by Aristotle's account, is both a necessary and sufficient condition for continuity. It should follow that Unity, satisfying this condition, is continuous.

However, it does not follow. Aristotle, dealing with extensive magnitudes, could assume that if they were divisible in a rational proportion, they would be divisible in an irrational proportion. But Parmenides, who has not yet shown that Unity is an extensive magnitude, provides an analysis restricted to two terms, being and unity, and limited to division answering to the simplest of rational proportions, the ratio of 1 to 2. The parts of Unity, therefore, stand to each other only in the ratio of a number to a number; the infinity derived is the infinity of multitude, not magnitude. A. E. Taylor, indeed, claimed that, "The 'rational fractions' are, to be sure, not a continuum, but they satisfy the only conditon for a continuum known in Plato's time, that between any two a third can always be inserted."[131]

But this objection is not, perhaps, dispositive, since there is reason to suppose that, assuming infinite division to have been carried through, anything infinitely divisible according to a rational proportion is infinitely divisible according to an irrational proportion. This assumption appears to be stated and criticized in several arguments of the pseudo-Aristotelian treatise *On Indivisible Lines*[132] and may well have fifth-century roots.[133] It turns on the further assumption that infinite divisibility implies an actual infinity of parts, that is, that the act of distinguishing parts is merely recognition of their distinction, and an actual infinity of parts appears to be assumed in the proof that Unity is infinitely divisible: for it is said that the least part is composed of two parts,[134] and that whatever comes to be a part contains or holds (ἴσχει 142e 4, 6, 7) two parts, namely its unity and being. This suggests, not that the presence of parts derives from the process of division, but that the process of division is possible because of the presence of parts. It suggests, in short, an actual rather than a potential infinite, and this is confirmed by the fact that each of the infinitely many numbers is said to have being (144a-c).

Given an actual infinite, and the further assumption that if *A* is an infinite plurality, no plurality is greater than *A*, it may be supposed that division according to any ratio will yield at infinity, that is, when the division is conceived to have been completely carried through, parts equivalent to division according to any other ratio.[135] It would follow that whatever is infinitely divisible according to a rational ratio is infinitely divisible according to an irrational ratio. Since this satisfies the only criteria for continuity known to Greek mathematics, whatever is infinitely divisible is continuous. This, then, is a reason for supposing that since Unity is infinitely divisible according to a rational ratio, Unity is continuous. That is, it satisfies the formal conditions proper and peculiar to an extensive magnitude.

iib. Limit and Unlimited: Second Argument (143a-145a)

Since Unity is, it has a share of being, and is therefore many. But if we consider Unity apart from that of which it has a share, will it still be many, or only one?

The question here raised is pursued without interruption to the end of the discussion at 145a. As a thing which is, Unity has already been shown to be many as containing infinitely many parts: it has the dense plurality characteristic of a continuum, though it has not itself been proved continuous. But that argument rests on the assumption that, because Unity partakes of its own being, it is not the same as its own being (142b 8 - c 1, cf. 158a), which is part of it. We are now asked to consider Unity in abstraction from its own being, and to determine whether, so conceived, Unity is one or many. The argument that follows will prove that it is many: it has the plurality proper to what possesses infinitely many discrete parts. The method of proof is to show that to distinguish Unity from its own being implies the existence of number; to infer that the numbers, of which there are infinitely many, exist or have being; that they therefore must have unity; and to conclude that Unity, considered apart from its own being, is distributed to all the numbers, and hence has infinitely many parts. It will be seen that the abstraction of Unity from its own being anticipates the reasoning of the First Deduction of Hypothesis III, where it is argued that in speaking of a Unity which is not, we speak of something knowable and of something different from other things (160c-d), and that such a Unity must therefore in some sense be (161e-162b).

The claim is first stated at 139c that Unity, as such, cannot be different from anything, since it does not pertain to a thing qua one to be different from anything, but only to a thing qua different. Hence, since Unity is not Being, but shares in it, its being is different from it; but it does not pertain to a thing qua being, any more than it pertains to a thing qua one, to be different; it pertains only to a thing qua different, and what is different is different by virtue of Difference (143b 5).[136] This account may be compared with the arguments by which Being, Sameness and Difference are distinguished in the *Sophist* (255b-d), where, in conclusion, the Eleatic Stranger says of Difference that, "this nature pervades all the Forms; for each is different from the rest, not by virtue of its own nature, but because it partakes of the character of Difference" (255e).

Parmenides next proceeds to show that Unity, taken apart from its own being, implies number (143c-d).

The exact force of his argument cannot be reproduced in English. Greek possesses, as English does not, a dual as well as a singular and plural. When Parmenides argues that since it is possible to mention Unity and to mention Being, 'each of two' has been mentioned, the English 'two' is more explicit than the text, which contains only the genitive dual, αὐτοῖν. It is from this feature in the syntax of his language that Parmenides goes on to infer that both have been mentioned, and that since both have been mentioned, two have been mentioned.[137]

Euclid defines number as "a multitude of units,"[138] and though the *Elements* dates from approximately 300 B.C., this definition, or congeners of it, all treating number as a plurality, is certainly much earlier. It represents Aristotle's treatment of number,[139] and Aristotle was abreast of the mathematics of his time. Iamblichus, indeed, attributed a kindred definition to Thales, "following the Egyptian view."[140] This is unlikely, but since the contents of *Elements* VII had probably been fixed in main outline by the latter part of the fifth century, the notion of number as a plurality of units may be taken to date at least from that time.

The definition has consequences. In the first place, it excludes zero as a number.[141] It is natural to think of number as what answers to the question, "How many?" and if you are asked how many books are on the table, the answer "none" is quite as appropriate as the answer "ten." The modern mathematician will think of "none" as by implication introducing zero, an interesting number with important properties. The Greek mathematician, along with untutored common sense, will think of "none" as denying that there is any number of books on the table—not even one. It is not by accident that the verb *arithmein*, corresponding to the noun *arithmos*, number, means "to count." Zero, since it is not a counting number, is not a number.

The definition has other consequences. If number is a plurality of units, fractions will not be numbers: 2/3 represents the ratio of two to three; it cannot represent a number smaller than one, the unit, for the unit is indivisible[142] —another way of saying that the number series begins with one, and the unit has neither part nor parts.[143] Irrationals, which differ from fractions in that they cannot be expressed as the ratio of an integer to an integer, will also be dealt with in terms of ratios; since they are not pluralities of units, they are not numbers. Without a zero, there will be no negative numbers; *a fortiori*, there will be no complex numbers. By modern mathematical standards, the Greek concept of number was considerably impoverished.

There is a further consequence of the definition of number as a plurality of units, and it is a surprising one. It is that one, the unit, is not a number, since it is not a plurality.[144] Aristotle, reflecting the mathematical tradition of his time, held that one is the beginning and measure of number, rather than a number, and explained this as follows (*Meta.* XIV 1088a 5-7, cf. V 1016b 18ff., 1021a 13):

> 'The one' means the measure of some plurality, and 'number' means a measured plurality and a plurality of measures. (Thus it is natural that one is not a number; for the measure is not measures, but both the measure and the one are starting-points.)

This does not mean, of course, that one was not used in mathematical operations: 6 + 1 = 7 is taken, not as the addition of a number to a number, but of a unit to a number. Plato consistently defines arithmetic as the science of odd and even,[145] and though he nowhere explicitly states that one is not a number, this is implied by the present passage.[146] Two is the first number:[147] and it is by establishing that there are items numerable by the first number, rather than by one, that Parmenides begins his account.

Plato defined mathematics as the science of odd and even numbers.[148] Parmenides, having shown the existence of the first odd and even numbers, proceeds to prove the existence of the rest.

The initial numbers in Parmenides' classification are 4, the first even-times even number, 6, the first even-times odd or odd-times even number, and 9, the first odd-times odd number. The measure of number, 1, the first even number, 2, and the first odd number, 3, have already been given.

These numbers, and the classification they introduce, were of considerable importance to Greek number theory;[149] they were also of importance in the theory of proportion. Archytas of Tarentum, in a fragment of his lost work *On Music* preserved by Porphyry,[150] distinguished three means: the geometric, a : b = b : c, the arithmetic, a-b : b-c = a : a = b : b = c : c, and the harmonic, a-b : b-c = a : c. The numbers Parmenides gives are primary examples of these proportions: 1, 2, and 4, and 4, 6, and 9 are in geometric proportion; 2, 4, and 6 in arithmetic proportion; 2, 3, and 6 in harmonic proportion. According to Pythagorean theory, 1, 2, 3, and 4, whose sum is 10, constitute the "tetractys of the decad," and as the Pythagoreans also knew, the ratios of those numbers define the perfect consonances of music: the octave is 2:1, the fifth, 3:2, and the fourth 4:3. These ratios, along with the theory of proportion, provide the basis for the generalized science of harmonics projected by Plato in the *Republic* (VII 530c-531c), a science he connected with astronomy. As the theory of proportion was connected with music, so it was also connected with cosmology. In the *Timaeus* (31c), continued geometrical proportion is said to be the most perfect of bonds, and Greek number theory took it to be the most perfect and primary proportion.[151] It is for that reason that the Demiurge uses it in the construction of the World's body, using the theorem that two mean proportionals are required to connect cubics, and thus solids, whereas only one mean is required to connect squares, and thus planes (32a-b). The proportions in question are $p^2 : pq = pq : q^2$ and $p^3 : p^2 q = p^2 q : pq^2 = pq^2 : q^3$. The first proportion is satisfied by the numbers Parmenides has provided: 6 is the mean proportional between $4 = 2^2$ and $9 = 3^2$. The second proportion, which Nicomachus called "a Platonic theorem,"[152] requires, in addition to the numbers Parmenides has provided, $8 = 2^3$ and $27 = 3^3$, i.e., twice twice two and thrice thrice three. It is cited by Theon[153] as the "second tetractys," subsequent to the first, or Pythagorean, tetractys summing at 10.

Parmenides' classification of the numbers has often been supposed to be equivalent to an account of their generation.[154] This claim appears to be as old as Aristotle;[155] it is, however, mistaken.

The term 'number,' as Aristotle points out, has two senses: that by which we count, and that which is counted or countable.[156] Parmenides, if he were a Platonist (cf. 135b-c), would suppose that that with which or by which we count are Idea Numbers such as Two, Three, Four, and so on,[157] a serial plurality which is itself countable. These Ideas are not pluralities of units, but the number-properties of such pluralities; they cannot be generated by arithmetical operations such as addition and multiplication, since such operations presuppose their existence. Indeed, as Ideas, they cannot be generated at all.

Parmenides, then, proceeding by addition and multiplication, has not generated numbers as properties that numbered pluralities possess; has he, then, generated numbers as pluralities that possess those properties? The answer is that he has not. If a given number is a plurality of units, then to derive that number is to show that there are as many units as that number. The multiplication used in 'twice two' requires an existence assumption, namely, that four is a number, that is, that there are four units; four cannot be three units one of which is counted twice. But Parmenides, deriving numbers successive to three by simple multiplication, does not attempt to show that there are pluralities of units corresponding to the products of multiplication. He might easily have done so if he wished, for he has available his previous proof that Unity has infinitely many parts, and what is infinitely divisible is infinitely numerable.

The truth is that Parmenides has presented, not a generation, but an existence proof, resting on the assumption that if m and n are integers, the product and sum of m and n are integers.[158] It will be seen that any of Parmenides' methods —multiplication of even numbers, of odd numbers, or of odd and even numbers —will suffice to prove the existence of any number, since any of these methods, by repeated application, will prove the existence of a number larger than any number desired. Parmenides introduces four methods, rather than one, in order to provide not only an existence proof of numbers, but a classification of them.[159] Nothing in this argument indicates that numbers can be constructed or derived from simpler constituents, or generated in any way. Parmenides' argument is compatible with the view that numbers are timeless objects neither generable nor destructible; it is also compatible with the view that numbers are simple essences incapable of analysis into ontologically (as distinct from numerically) prior and posterior elements. The purpose of Parmenides' argument is to provide not a *ratio essendi* for number, but a *ratio cognoscendi*. If Unity exists, then, since it can be considered apart from its own being, it implies the existence, not only of Being, but of Difference. There is, then, a plurality with these members; and to recognize the existence of that plurality is to commit oneself to the truths that $2 = 2 \times 1$ and $2 + 1 = 3$. But to accept any mathematical truth is to accept every mathematical truth; the existence of any number implies the existence of every number. Therefore, the existence of a plurality with three members implies the existence of plurality with infinitely many members, namely, the plurality of numbers. The effect of Parmenides' argument is to establish precisely the implication that Proclus, long afterward, claimed for it: "If One exists, number will exist, from which it follows that (infinite) plurality exists."[160] This implication is explicitly stated in the *Sophist* (238a-b, cf. *Theaetetus* 185d). In short, the hypothesis that Unity exists implies the existence of the number series; but an existence proof is not a generation.

Aristotle in the *Physics* maintains that "Everything that is infinite may be so in respect of addition or division or both" (*Phys*. III 204a 7, cf. 206a 15). By what is infinite by division Aristotle understands, as we have seen, what is continuous, divisible into divisibles that are infinitely divisible. He nowhere explains what he means by the expression 'infinite by addition,' but it clearly applies to the infinity that is characteristic of numbers. This is confirmed by his claim that the infinite by division and the infinite by addition are in a sense the same:[161]

> In a way the infinite by addition is the same thing as the infinite by division. In a finite magnitude, the infinite by addition comes about in a

way inverse to that of the other. For in proportion as we see division going on, in the same proportion we see addition being made to what is already marked off. For if we take a determinate part of a finite magnitude and add another part determined by the same ratio (not taking in the same amount of the original whole), and so on, we shall not traverse the given magnitude.

That is, what is infinitely divisible is infinitely numerable; to the series of divisions there corresponds the series of numbers. It will be recalled that 'number' means the natural numbers, exclusive of one (except for counting) and zero; and if number is so defined, the number series is not continuous, but rather, as Aristotle points out (*Phys.* V 227a 20, *Meta.* XIII 1085a 4), successive or discrete. A thing is in succession when (*Phys.* V 226b 34 - 227a 2, cf. *Parmenides* 149a):

> it is after the beginning in position or in form or in some other respect in which it is definitely so regarded, and when further there is nothing of the same kind as itself between it and that to which it is in succession.

Thus for example, there is no natural number between any two natural numbers that are in succession. Parmenides will now go on to show that Unity has parts corresponding to each of the numbers, and this is equivalent to showing that Unity has infinitely many discrete parts.

Numbers and 'Intermediates'

We have here the probable source of Aristotle's claim in *Metaphysics* I. vi. that Plato posited mathematical intermediates between sensibles and Ideas, differing from sensibles in that they were eternal and unchangeable, and from Ideas in that there were many alike, whereas each Idea is unique. The reason usually given for this strange doctrine, though not by Aristotle, is that it is meant to account for the possibility of arithmetical operations: '2 + 2 = 4' uses two 2s, and Twoness plus Twoness amounts neither to Fourness nor 4. Aristotle's testimony on this has often been accepted as primary evidence of and for Plato's "unwritten doctrines"; there is better reason to suppose that it is merely an interpretation of a text open to our own inspection, namely, this section of the *Parmenides*.[162]

Aristotle himself believed that mathematics implies a special mathematical matter (*Meta.* XI 1059b 14 ff.), derived by abstraction from sensibles, which strips away everything except the quantitative and continuous (*Meta.* XI 1061a 29 - b 25). On his view, then, mathematical objects are genuinely intermediate, in that they can neither be identified with sensibles nor yet exist apart (*Meta.* XIII 1077b 11 ff):

> It has, then, been sufficiently pointed out that the objects of mathematics are not substances in a higher degree than bodies are, and that

they are not prior to sensibles in being, but only in definition, and that they cannot exist somewhere apart. But since it was not possible for them to exist in sensibles either, it is plain that either they do not exist at all or exist in a special sense. . . . For just as the universal propositions of mathematics deal not with objects which exist separately, apart from extended magnitudes and from numbers, but with magnitudes and numbers, not however *qua* such as to have magnitude or to be divisible, clearly it is possible that there should also be both propositions and demonstrations about sensible magnitudes, not however *qua* sensibles but *qua* possessed of certain definite qualities. . . . Thus since it is true to say without qualification that not only things which are separable but also things which are inseparable exist (for instance, the mobiles exist), it is true also to say without qualification that the objects of mathematics exist, and with the character ascribed to them by mathematicians.

The abstractive distinction between arithmetic and geometry is then stated as follows (*Meta.* XII 1078a 20-31):

Each question will be best investigated in this way—by setting up by an act of separation what is not separate, as the arithmetician and the geometer do. For a man *qua* man is one indivisible thing; and the arithmetician supposed one indivisible thing, and then considered whether any attribute belongs to a man *qua* indivisible. But the geometer treats him neither *qua* man nor *qua* indivisible, but as a solid. For evidently the properties which would have belonged to him if perchance he had not been individual, can belong to him even apart from these attributes. Thus, then, geometers speak correctly: they talk about existing things, and their subjects do exist; for being has two forms—it exists not only in complete reality but also materially.

Mathematical matter here has nothing to do with potentiality: it is the result of abstraction, and means what is quantitative or continuous. It was on this meaning that the Seventeenth Century was later to fix. Importantly, Unity in I.2 of the *Parmenides* will in this sense prove material, even as it has already been proved infinite by division and by addition. Aristotle, conceiving number as a plurality of units, those units distinguished by the fact that they are considered *qua* indivisible even though the geometers consider them in precisely the opposite way, need only have recognized, in reading the *Parmenides*, that the divisions of Unity implied an actual infinite; he might then have concluded that Plato was committed to the existence of mathematical intermediates. If number is a plurality of units, if those units represent actual divisions of Unity, then, in the *Parmenides*, number implies the existence of things that are neither Ideas nor sensibles and that, as actual, exist 'apart.'

Aristotle's account has found favor with several recent commentators, for example, Anders Wedberg,[163] who maintains that the intermediate (or 'mathematical') numbers are aggregates of ideal units, each unit, since it is one and nothing else, being a perfect exemplification of Unity.[164] There is no text in the dialogues that states or implies that this is Plato's view, whatever some texts may have been taken under Aristotle's inspiration to suggest. There is, however, a text that makes it certain that it is not Plato's view, for the difficulties Socrates finds in the notions of addition and division at *Phaedo* 96e-97b[165] apply, not only to number conceived as a plurality of sensible units, but to number conceived as any sort of plurality of units at all, whether sensible or ideal.

To this it may be added that the assumption that there may be perfect as well as imperfect exemplifications of an Idea is unexampled in the dialogues; on the contrary, since each of the numbers is one, and all exemplifications of number are many, all exemplifications are inherently deficient. Again, the assumption that there is an infinite plurality of simple ideal units, which are one and have no second character, is meaningless: nothing can be *merely* one, except perhaps Unity itself, and two things cannot each merely be one and still be different, as the *Parmenides* so carefully shows. But perhaps it is enough to remark that Professor Wedberg constantly mixes Aristotle's testimony about Plato with Aristotle's testimony about Speusippus and Xenocrates, and produces a *mélange*.

The true view of Plato's arithmetic, wholly ignored by Wedberg, was stated by Cook Wilson in 1904. It is perhaps worth quoting at some length, since it has been so generally and widely ignored:[166]

> Plato's ἰδέα is of course the Universal. We are not concerned here with what is peculiar to his view of its nature, but with a part of it, which all must accept, and upon which Plato laid great stress: namely, the assertion that the Universal is one—a unity, that is, in contrast with the manifold to which it corresponds. This means that whereas there are many circles, for instance, Circularity, the Universal, is one—there is only one Circularity. It is not necessary to repeat the familiar *reductio ad absurdum* of the hypothesis that there could be more than one. 'The circle,' with the definite article, is an equivalent expression for circularity, and even if we give several definitions of 'the Circle' we suppose them all definitions of one and the same thing. 'The number Two,' as we call it, is a Universal: it is 'twoness' in general, and there is only one 'twoness.' It is because there is only one that we use the definite article in the expression '*the* number Two.' Now, 'the number Two' thus accurately understood cannot enter into a process of summation like a particular two. 'Two and two make four' means two things (= a particular two) added to two other things of the same kind amount to four things. The proposition is a universal one because it stands for 'any two things added to any other two things, etc., etc.,' but not because it means an addition of universals. It does not mean, that is, that twoness added to twoness is fourness.... Thus 'the number Two,' 'the number

Three,' etc., that is the universal twoness, the universal threeness, etc., or, in popular language, the abstractions of twoness and threeness, etc., do not consist of units and are not capable of numerical addition in the same sense as a two and a three, by the combination of units. And thus if we call them Numbers (we call them the Numbers) they are certainly numbers which are not addible. This is exactly the Platonic doctrine; for if the ἰδέαι or Universals of number are called ἀριθμοί they must be ἀριθμοὶ ἀσύμβλητοί.

Geometry of course affords an exact parallel. . . . Circularity cannot intersect circularity, for there is only one circularity.

Cook Wilson, it will be observed, treats mathematical number as a plurality of units, and the Idea numbers, which are unaddable, as the properties of those pluralities. But this need involve no ontological commitment to mathematical numbers as pluralities of units distinct from Ideas and sensibles. Mathematical statements may be treated as hypothetical: 2 + 2 = 4 means that if any group of two things is added to any other group of two things, the resulting group contains four things. If this treatment leaves the operations of addition and division undefined, and in terms of the *Phaedo* and its criticism of any treatment of number as a plurality of units, undefinable, we may recall that Number Ideas stand to each other in an order of prior and posterior, as the *Phaedo* (104a-b) implies and Aristotle himself repeatedly states (for example, at *E.N.* I 1096a 17-19). Professor Harold Cherniss has kindly communicated to me unpublished notes on Plato's philosophy of mathematics, which suggest how mathematical operations may therefore be analyzed. Granting the existence of the series of integers,[167] arithmetical propositions express relations between the numbers placed in that series. Thus, for example, 2 < 5 does not imply that there are fewer units in 2 than in 5, since each of those numbers is itself a single unit (cf. *Republic* VII 525c-526a, *Philebus* 56d-e). It rather expresses the fact that 2 is prior rather than posterior to 5 in the series of integers. It implies, of course, that there are fewer units in a plurality that partakes of 2 than in a plurality that partakes of 5 for 2 and 5, remember, are Ideas—but it is the order of priority and posteriority, of position in the series, that explains arithmetical operations. To add x to n, begin with the place after n in the series and count x places forward; to subtract x from n, begin with the place before n and count x places back. To multiply n by x, count n x number of times; thus, to multiply 2 x 4, begin with 2 as one and count four places of the same kind to arrive at 8. To divide n by x, begin with x and count the number of places of the same kind from x to n inclusive; thus, to divide 8 by 2, begin with 2 as one, count every other place (2, 4, 6, 8), and 4 is the answer. Thus $n + x$ is the xth position after n; $n - x$ is the xth position before n (since there are no negative numbers, there may of course be no such position); n x x is the number reached by counting n x number of times; $n \div x$ is the number of times x is counted in reaching n. It is not, of course, to be supposed that the mathematician realizes that his whole

enterprise proceeds from Ideas, through Ideas, and ends in Ideas when he performs arithmetical operations; that is for the dialectician, inquiring into the foundations of mathematics, to teach him.

Infinity and Parts

Unity has infinitely many discrete parts. This result is now used to prove that
Being has infinitely many parts (144a-b). Since number is unlimited in multitude
and has a share of Being, each number has a share of Being. Since Being is distributed to all of the things which are, it is divided infinitely, and there are parts
of it without limit.

This argument is valid. It has already been proved that if Unity exists, it has a
share of Being, and that therefore Unity and the being of Unity are different. A
parallel argument can be constructed for anything which is, and specifically for
each of the numbers that have been proved to be. Alternately, being is lacking to
nothing which is; since numbers have Being and are unlimited in multitude, and
since the being of each thing is a part of Being, the parts of Being are unlimited
in multitude.

This use of the concepts of part and whole is paralleled by *Sophist* 257c-258a.
The Eleatic Stranger there claims that the nature of the Different is divided up
like Knowledge: Knowledge is one, but each separate part of it that deals with
something is named after that thing, and we therefore speak of many kinds of
knowledge (cf. *Parmenides* 134a). The same is true of Difference: part of the
Different is different from the Beautiful, part different from the Just, part different from the Tall, and so on.

The main point of this argument is simple. As we may speak of Knowledge as
one and yet distinguish between knowledge of geometry and knowledge of cob-
bling, so we may also speak of Difference as one and yet distinguish between
difference from Beauty and difference from Justice. The *Sophist's* vocabulary
of parts and division matches Parmenides' account here. Being and Difference,
however, are different kinds of terms. Difference is a term that "is always said
in relation to something else" (*pros alla, Sophist* 255c). That is, Difference, like
Knowledge, is a relative, something whose nature is to be *of* something or *than*
something (cf. *Republic* IV 438b-d, *ACPA* n. 188): if *x* is different, *x* is different
from something. Being is unlike Difference in that it is said *both* in relation to
something else *and* in respect to things by themselves (*kath' hauta*). It can
scarcely be that this implies a distinction between the 'is' of existence as distinct
from the 'is' of predication or the 'is' of identity: for the latter distinction implies
ambiguity, whereas we here deal with Being as single, same and therefore unambiguous. The Stranger's meaning is made clear by the *Parmenides*. If Unity is or
partakes of Being, it does not follow that Unity is or has Being *of* or *than* or
in relation to something else; it does follow, however, that we may speak of the
being of Unity. So 'being' used in the second way is a relative: that is, it is *of*
something, whereas 'being' in the first use is not a relative. Nor is the term

thereby ambiguous, even though it may be both relative and nonrelative.[168] It should be observed that if this analysis in terms of part and (by implication) whole has the result that part and whole are reciprocally dependent, then the Form of Difference, to be the Idea it is, must contain difference from Beauty, difference from Justice, and so on, as parts. This would indicate that Difference is not simply a common character, but more like a "concrete universal," a system internally related to its instances as incapable of existing apart from them, as they are from it.

To say that number is unlimited in multitude is, of course, compatible with the claim that number is potentially infinite in that for any number chosen there is a greater number. Granting that there is an unlimited plurality of numbers, the question arises whether there is a number of that plurality, i.e., an infinite number. Aristotle provides evidence that someone in the Academy had formulated this conception;[169] nevertheless, it is not to be found here. Parmenides does not refer to an infinite number, but to number unlimited in multitude (144a 6). It is not self-contradictory to suppose that there are infinitely many numbers, each of which is finite, unless one supposes that 'infinite' is itself a number adjective, which is precisely the point at issue. Again, it is not self-contradictory to suppose that a thing has infinitely many parts, but no parts that are 'infiniteth' in order of distinction.

The conclusion that the parts of Being, since they are unlimited in number, are most multitudinous ($\pi\lambda\epsilon\hat{\iota}\sigma\tau\alpha$, 144c 1, 2), suggests a question. The conclusion is not directly derived from the premise that Being is not lacking to anything which is (144b 3-4), since that premise is used in a sub-argument to show that Being is not lacking to any of the numbers, of which there are infinitely many (144b 4-6), and it is from the latter that the conclusion that the parts of Being are most numerous is derived. The conclusion, that is, appears to be derived *simply* from the infinity of number, despite the fact that the existence of other things besides number—Being and Difference, for example—has already been proved. Again, the parts of Being are distinguishable from the numbers whose being they are by the same reasoning that allowed Unity to be distinguished from its own being. This raises the question whether Parmenides, in inferring that the parts of Being are *most* multitudinous, is assuming that if X is an unlimited or infinite plurality, no plurality is greater than X.[170]

If the infinite involved here were actual, rather than potential, this assumption would imply a paradox: the paradox, to express it in set-theoretical language, that an infinite set may be equivalent to a proper subset of itself, as the set of integers is equivalent to the set of even integers, or the set of points on a line equivalent to the set of points on the half-line. That there should be pluralities which may be matched member for member, and yet which are in the customary sense of containment unequal, is an implication of an actual infinite, and a paradox without analogy to the behavior of finite (and familiar) groups. It was not until the nineteenth century that this paradox was relieved of the appearance of absurdity.[171] Thus it is that Plutarch can state as an objection against the Stoic doctrine[172] of infinite divisibility that, if it were true, it would imply that[173]

> the man is not composed of more parts than the finger, nor the universe of more parts than the man, for physical division goes on to infinity; but among things infinite there is neither a greater nor a less.

This implication is rejected as obviously absurd, and, though the texts are silent, this helps to explain why it was the potential infinite that made its way in Greek mathematics. The potential infinite is not a dogma in metaphysics, but a solution in mathematics: for example, if it is absurd to say that the half-line has as many parts as the line, it is not absurd to say that any operation of division carried out on the line may proportionally be carried out on the half-line. The stone that was to become the foundation of the modern treatment of infinity was originally rejected by the builder.[174]

If Parmenides is here assuming that there is no plurality greater than an infinite plurality, this would explain why he takes such pains to stress that the parts of being are *most* multitudinous. The Greek superlative, no doubt, is often merely equivalent to a strong comparative.[175] It is to be observed, however, that the force of πλεῖστα, with its repetition, is emphatic (144c 1, 2, cf. 144d 6).

Questions of infinity aside, perhaps the most arresting feature of Parmenides' argument is the shift it involves in the use of the word 'part.' Previously, if Unity partook of Being, its own being was part of it. We now find a use in which a given number is part of number, and the being of that number part of Being. These are distinguishable uses. For plainly, 'all number' at 144a 8, which is equivalent merely to 'number' at 144a 4, is not the characteristic of being a number; it is the number series itself. But the basis of the inference that Being is distributed to the numbers, and therefore has parts, is the proposition that, "if all number partakes of Being, each part of number will partake of it too" (144a 6-8), where each part of number means the individual numbers. This conclusion can follow only from the Dilemma of Participation, which implies that the being of any number is not only part of that number, but part of Being.

Having shown that the parts of Being are "most multitudinous," Parmenides goes on to infer (144c-d) that those parts must be one. For a thing which is must be one (*hen*) since it cannot be nothing (*ouden*); as Aristotle remarks, "to be one is just to be a particular thing" (*Meta.* X 1054a 18). But Unity cannot be in many places at once as a whole, and therefore it is divided; only as divided can it be present to all the parts of Being at once. In short, Parmenides here presents the second horn of the Dilemma of Participation.

It will be observed that it is not here claimed that, since Unity and Being are coordinate and each of the numbers is, therefore each of the numbers is one. The numbers are not parts of Being: it is the being of each of the numbers that is part of Being. The parts of Unity here involved, then, are not the unity of the numbers, but the unity of the being of the numbers. Parmenides has not chosen between numbers as Ideas and numbers as pluralities of units: it would seem a contradiction to claim that seven, if it is a plurality of units, is one, when it is seven. The argument is so formulated that *however* number is conceived, it will be true of the numbers that Unity is divided in correspondence with them, since it is divided by Being. These parts of Unity, namely, the unity of the being of each of the numbers, will be equal to the parts of Being.

The Dilemma of Participation implies that if there is participation, it must be of parts. This explains why, if Unity partakes of Being, it partakes of its own being, which is part of it, and why the signification of 'is' in the statement "Unity is" is not Being, but the being of Unity. It explains why Being is distributed to the numbers and divided, and why Unity as a whole cannot be in many places at once, but is present to all the parts of Being only as divided. Finally, it explains why the term 'part' has a double force, so that the being of Unity can be treated both as a part of Unity and as a part of Being, and the being of a number both as a part of Being and as a part of that number. In short, the implication is repeatedly assumed as a premise in the detailed argumentation of 142c-145a, and at 144c-d made explicit.

Since Unity is distributed to every part of Being, Unity is unlimited in multitude, even considered apart from its own being (144d-e).

The type of infinity here in view is allied, obviously, to the successive infinite of number—allied but not identical. Aristotle gives two criteria of successiveness: items in succession are ordered according to position, form, or some other principle; and there is nothing of the same kind between them. The numbers, standing in an order of prior and posterior, satisfy both requirements. But the being and the unity of the numbers, considered as parts of Being or parts of Unity, do not stand in an order determined by position or form: they are not in succession directly; rather, that to which they belong is in succession. As the being or unity of things that are in succession, however, there is nothing of the same kind between them. Parmenides' earlier account of the infinite by division seemed to imply not continuity but density; the account here of the infinite by addition seems to imply not successiveness but discreteness.

The conclusion of this argument, that not only is the Unity which is (or the being which is one) unlimited in multitude, but also that Unity itself, i.e., considered apart from its own being (cf. 143a), is unlimited in multitude, may well seem strange and paradoxical. It has been shown that to hypothesize a Unity which is, and then to consider it apart from and thus as different from its own being, implies the existence of the numbers, and that the numbers, because they partake of Being, partake of Unity; yet this can hardly be said to imply that Number, in partaking of Unity, partakes of Unity apart from its own being. But the aim of the argument is not to show that if the numbers are one, they partake of Unity conceived apart from its own being. It is to show that Unity, conceived apart from its own being, has parts if the numbers are one. In short, if Unity is participable, it is partable, whether or not it is said to exist. This again is a direct consequence of the Dilemma of Participation.

Parmenides now draws the conclusion that because parts are parts of a whole,

Unity will be limited with respect to its wholeness, since parts are contained by the whole, and what contains is a limit. Thus Unity is whole and parts, limited and unlimited in multitude (144e-145a).

This conclusion is stated generally, as a consequence that obtains not only for Unity as a thing which is, but for Unity itself, that is, conceived apart from its own being. Unity as a participant was shown to be a whole of parts at 142c-d. It has now been shown to be a whole of parts as participable. As we have seen, this involves a shift in the use of the word 'part,' in that the part of Being or Unity that anything has is now regarded as a part of the participant. The coextensiveness of Being and Unity implies that anything which is, is one; but anything which is one partakes of Unity, and thus has a part of Unity. Unity is therefore a whole from which no part is absent, since there is nothing which is that does not have a part of it. Thus both as participable and participant, Unity is many, is a whole, and has parts; it is both limited and unlimited—limited, as being a whole, and unlimited as containing infinitely many parts.

So far we have followed a complex and tangled way to a decidedly queer result. The Form of Unity has been shown to be in two ways a whole of parts, respectively dense and discrete. This accords with the remark in the *Sophist* that, "If a thing is divided into parts, there is nothing against its having the property of unity as applied to the aggregate of all the parts, and being in that way one, as being a sum or whole."[176] The whole is taken to be a limit of its parts, as containing them, a result that anticipates Aristotle's dictum that the infinite is not what contains, but is contained (*Phys.* III 208a 4, cf. 207a 8-14). Insofar as we deal here with a thing merely taken as one and whole, there is no more difficulty in this than in Socrates' earlier claim (129c-d) that he is both one and many, an apparent paradox dismissed in the *Sophist* (251a-c) and described in the *Philebus* (14d) as childish.

But it is otherwise if the thing taken to be one and whole is the Idea of Unity itself; for the *Sophist*, in the same passage in which it is said that a thing divided into parts may be one and whole, also says, "Surely Unity in the true sense and rightly defined must be altogether without parts" (*Sophist* 245a), whence it follows that a whole of parts can have but cannot be Unity. Yet that we deal in 142b-145a with Unity is shown in that we deal with the characteristic anything has that is said to be one. There is no ambiguity between the subjects of the first and second arguments, since the second argument consists merely in considering the subject of the first argument apart from its own being.

It follows, however, that the deduction in 142c-145a is of a highly unfortunate character, given that its subject is the Idea of Unity. Socrates had earlier said that though he saw no difficulty in claiming that the things we see are both one and many, like and unlike, he would be astonished if it were shown that Unity is many or Plurality one (129b-130a). Parmenides has given ample reason for surprise. The First Deduction of Hypothesis I proved that if Unity is not many, it can have no parts (137c-d), whence it is deduced that it cannot be even to the degree of being one, that nothing can be said of it, and that it is not an object of discourse (141e-142a) — a conclusion which ill comports with it (to misspeak) being an Idea. Parmenides has now shown that if Unity partakes of Being it has infinitely many parts, and infinitely many parts even if taken separately from its own being. The inference that Unity may be a whole of parts, and thus many, contradicts Socrates' original theory, and is itself contradicted by *Sophist* 245a. The contradiction occurs again in the body of the *Parmenides* itself: for in the First Deduction of Hypothesis II (158a-b) it is argued that since a whole is one whole and each part one part, they partake of Unity and therefore cannot be Unity, but are other than Unity. This implies that Unity cannot be a whole of parts. To this it may be added that if the infinity of number is potential, Unity cannot be a whole because it is ever incomplete. We are asked, in 142c-145a, to examine the logic of the argument and to inquire what it assumes; we are not asked to accept the truth of its conclusion, any more than we are expected to accept the truth of the ultimate conclusion of all the Hypotheses at 166c.

There is a further peculiarity. Parmenides has concluded that Unity is a whole of parts, and that those parts are contained by the whole, which is limited in respect to its wholeness. This is no trifling inference, since he will next argue that if Unity is a whole it must have extremities, and therefore beginning, middle, and end; so Unity has shape. The minimal condition on which Unity can have shape is that it is a continuous and extensive magnitude. There is nothing in 142c-145a to directly justify this claim; the argument so far has shown only that Unity must have multitude, not magnitude. If the inference is to be justified, it must be latent in premises other than those by which this argument explicitly proceeds. Yet the consequences of denying that Unity is many have not proved felicitous in I.1.

It may be added with respect to the first argument, that Unity is both limited and unlimited (142d-143a), that the results reached are ultimately general: the subject of the hypothesis is Unity, but the pattern of analysis in respect to its unity and being will apply to anything which is and is one. As containing parts, everything and anything will contain infinitely many parts, and so be unlimited, though since parts are parts of a whole, it will also be limited.

iii. Shape (145a-b)

Parmenides argues that since Unity is limited, it has extremes, and since it is a whole, it has beginning, middle, and end. This implies that Unity must have shape, whether straight, round, or a mixture of both.

There is an element of play in this inference. The historical Parmenides had held that his One Being was motionless within the limits of mighty bonds (*DK* 8.26), and that it is bounded on every side, equally balanced in every direction from the center like the bulk of a well-rounded sphere (*DK* 8.42-44). The Platonic Parmenides argued in the First Deduction that Unity, if it had a shape, would be spherical or circular, but that since it has no parts, it can have no shape. Parmenides now argues that Unity has shape, but that shape need not be spherical or circular, presumably because Unity now has parts and is many.[177]

But the proof is puzzling. There is nothing in 142b-145a directly to justify the claim, for that argument has not shown that Unity must have magnitude. Neither is there anything to justify the claim that what is limited must have extremities, or that a whole must have beginning, middle, and end. Thus for example, if virtue is a whole of which courage is a part, this would hardly justify an inquiry into the location of virtue's middle. Nor is limit taken to imply extremities in the *Philebus* (e.g. 16c-17a, 18a-b).

The fact is that Parmenides is here assuming a proposition that will later be made explicit: that to be is to be somewhere (143e), that is, in a place. Given that Unity is, it is somewhere. Given that as a whole, it is limited and in a place, its limitation implies extremities: an extended whole cannot be unlimited just insofar as it is whole. But if Unity is limited and in place, it must have beginning, middle, and end (cf. 137c). But this is to imply that Unity is an extensive magnitude, and partakes of some shape.

This result is absurd. Why then should it be derived?

It follows, in fact, from the earlier agreement that if Unity is not in time, it does not exist; if so, then if Unity exists it is in time. Since Unity has now been proved to be and to be a whole it is in time: it has beginning, middle, and end, and therefore some shape. That is, it is a finite extensive magnitude, though as far as the argument so far has shown, that magnitude is temporal rather than spatial. A temporal finite magnitude, unlike any spatially finite magnitude that is not a mere abstraction, such as a line or a plane, has only one dimension: time has no width.

But to say that Unity has temporal shape is to suggest that it has spatial shape as well; for time is a measure of motion. Ideas, of which Unity is one, are no doubt ontologically prior to phenomena, being eternal causes whose existence is a condition for the becoming of their sensible likenesses in space. Given the doctrine of the *Timaeus* (48e-52c) that a participant must be *of* something other than itself and *in* something other than itself, and that what it is *in* is space, as it is *of* the external Ideas, a further consequence follows. If space is a condition for the existence of participants, and if parts of the Idea depend for their existence on participants, then Ideas, as wholes from which no part is absent, depend for their existence on space, and parts of Ideas may be located by reference to the location of the participants they are in. Conversely, if space is a condition for the existence of participants, and Ideas are participants, Ideas are in space. But Unity, by hypothesis, is a participant in Being. It follows that Unity, limited with respect to its wholeness, is spatially limited, and that is has spatial extremities; because it is a whole of parts, it is an extended magnitude, has shape, and has not only temporal but spatial shape. It is somewhere.

The deduction of 142b-145a follows as a result of the application of the Dilemma of Participation to the Idea of Unity, and the deduction of 145a-b follows from that of 142b-145a with the additional assumption that space is a condition of participation, which may be taken as a precondition of the claim that to be is to be in time. Unity, which is an Idea, has also, in the language of the *Timaeus*, become an image.

Here is a further argument that also applies.

We may begin with the proposition that if Unity partakes of Being, participation is possible. If participation is possible, then if anything partakes of Being, it partakes of Unity. So if Unity is, Unity is participated in; it is participated in, for example, by all the parts of itself, each of which is one, and by all the numbers.

Now, it has been agreed by Socrates, as a dialectical admission on which Parmenides' deduction now proceeds, that at least some sensible participants, for example, hair, mud, and dirt, are separate, in that they have a nature and reality of their own. Therefore, by the account offered at the beginning of I.2, they participate in Being. Therefore, they participate in Unity, since whatever is, is one. Therefore, there are parts of Unity in sensible participants, and sensible participants and Unity share common parts.

Now, sensible participants are extended magnitudes. But any part of an extended magnitude is an extended magnitude. Therefore, the parts of Unity are extended magnitudes, because they are parts of sensible participants, and the specific extension involved is spatial extension. But if Unity is a continuous whole, which has parts that are spatially extended magnitudes, Unity is a continuous spatially extended magnitude. Since then it is limited, as one and whole, it must have some shape.

Now, it is easy to claim that this argument is confused. The characteristics of extended magnitudes, 'predicates,' are radically different in kind from the extended magnitudes of which they are characteristics: the argument equivocates on the word 'part,' ignoring the distinction between the parts into which an extended magnitude may be divided to yield an extended magnitude, and the parts which answer to characteristics of extended magnitudes. That distinction is precisely one that the theory of Ideas was introduced to explain.

But it would appear that the distinction has collapsed. We may say, if we please, that the Idea of Unity is what it is to be one. But it has also been shown that the Idea of Unity is one in exactly the same sense that anything else which is is one: if anything participates in Unity, part of the participant is part of Unity. Once Ideas and sensibles are assumed to have common parts, the ground for distinguishing the characteristics of extended magnitudes from the extended magnitudes of which they are characteristics has been cut from beneath our feet. So it is that Parmenides will later (150a) argue that if Unity partakes of Smallness, Smallness must be stretched out evenly with it, or be contained by it.

Did the historical Zeno argue that if many is, the same things both have and do not have shape? If so, we have no record of it, but the building-blocks of the argument lay ready to hand. If there is plurality, things which are are limited; therefore, they have shape. But by *DK* 1 and 2, they are also so large as to be infinite, so small as to be nothing at all; therefore, they do not have shape.

iv. In Itself, In Another (145b-e)

Unity must be (a) in itself, and (b) in another.

a) Unity is in itself because it is a whole that contains all its parts. Indeed, it *is* all its parts, and because this is so, Unity is contained by Unity, and is in itself.

In the First Deduction, it was proved that Unity cannot be in itself, since if it were, it would both contain itself and be contained by itself, in which case it would be, not one, but two. The sense of this dark saying is considerably illumined by Aristotle, who concludes that there is one circumstance in which a thing can be said to be in itself, namely, when it is said to be so, not qua itself, but qua being a whole of parts:[178]

> When there are parts of a whole — the one that in which a thing is, the other the thing which is in it — the whole will be described as being in itself. For a thing is described in terms of its parts, as well as in terms of the thing as a whole, e.g., a man is said to be white because the visible surface of him is white, or to be scientific because his thinking faculty has been trained. The jar then will not be in itself and the wine will not be in itself. But the jar of wine will: for the contents and the container are both parts of the same whole.
>
> In this sense, then, but not primarily, a thing can be in itself, namely as 'white' is in body (for the visible surface is in body), and science is in the mind. It is from these, which are 'parts' (in the sense at least of being 'in' the man) that the man is called white.

This explains the sense in which Unity, as all the parts, contains itself and is contained by itself: it is one whole and all the parts, and may therefore be considered as the sum of its parts. Considered as a whole, it contains all its parts; considered as all the parts, it is contained by the whole. So it both contains and is contained by itself.

b) In the *Theaetetus*, the identification of the whole with the sum of its parts is taken to prove that a whole cannot be different from all its parts.[179] Parmenides now constructs an argument that contradicts that conclusion. The whole cannot be in all the parts, since it cannot be in any one part, the greater in the less, and therefore cannot be in all. In short, because the whole cannot be in any of its parts, it cannot be in all its parts — an apparent fallacy of composition. But the argument, it will be observed, takes 'all the parts' distributively rather than collectively, and requires that the concept of a whole be applied collectively rather than distributively. Once again, a parallel point is made by Aristotle. He has remarked that though a thing can be in itself, it cannot be in itself primarily; he next goes on to show that nothing can be in itself in virtue of its own nature (*Phys.* IV 210b 8 ff):

> Thus if we look at the matter inductively we do not find anything to be 'in' itself in any of the senses that have been distinguished; and it can be seen by argument that it is impossible. For each of two things will have to be both, e.g. the jar will have to be both vessel and wine, and the wine both wine and jar, if it is possible for a thing to be in itself; so that, however true it might be that they were in each other, the jar will receive

the wine in virtue not of *its* being wine, but of the wine's being wine,
and the wine will be in the jar in virtue not of *its* being a jar but of the
jar's being a jar. Now that they are different in respect of their essence
is evident; for 'that in which something is' and 'that which is in it'
would be differently defined.

Substitute 'whole' for 'jar,' as container, and 'part' for 'wine,' as contained, and
the conclusion follows that Unity, *qua* whole, cannot be in any part or in every
part, *qua* part. Put otherwise, Unity cannot be in all the parts of itself because
all the parts are in the whole that contains them; and the whole cannot be in the
whole because it cannot be both container and contained.[180] It is the nature of a
whole, as a whole, to contain; it is the nature of a part, as a part, to be contained;
and the whole, as whole, cannot therefore be any or every part of itself. Therefore, Unity, as a whole, cannot be in itself.[181]

This gives adequate ground for claiming that Unity, as all its parts, is in itself, and that Unity, as a whole, is not in itself. But it does not give adequate
ground for the further inference that if Unity as a whole is not in itself, it must
be in something other than itself, since if it were nowhere it would be nothing.
This assumes that to be is to be somewhere, a proposition that, like the kindred
proposition assumed in the First Deduction that to be is to be in time (141e),
Plato explicitly rejected.[182]

As with the proposition that to be is to be in time, the assumption that to
be is to be somewhere, and that what is nowhere is nothing, is a legitimate inference from the Dilemma of Participation, which has just been explicitly recalled
(144c-d). Being is a whole some of whose parts are distributed to sensibles (130b,
136b). Those parts, by the Dilemma, cannot exist independently of the sensibles
they are in. Since Being is a whole, and a whole is that from which no part is absent (137c), its parts are essential to it; it follows that Being cannot exist independently of the sensibles its parts are in. Since sensibles are by their very nature
in place or space, it follows that Being cannot exist apart from things in place or
space, and therefore cannot itself exist apart from place or space; it further follows that Being is located by reference to the sensibles it is in. If then we assume
that to participate in or have a share of something that is located is itself to be
located, it follows that to be is to be somewhere, and that what is nowhere is
nothing, that is, has no share of Being. Since Unity is a whole, it is not in itself;
since to be is to be somewhere, it must therefore be in something else. We have
already seen that it must be in time. We now see, and see again, that it must be
in place or space.

This result will imply contact (148d-149d). Why is it not derived simply from
the agreement that Unity has shape? For it would surely seem that a continuous
magnitude that has shape must be somewhere.

The truth is that Plato in the *Timaeus* assumes, and Aristotle explicitly argues,
that this proposition is false in at least one case. That is, there is at least one continuous magnitude that has shape and that is not somewhere.

Place, Aristotle holds, is the innermost motionless boundary of what contains, that is, the boundary of a containing body that is in contact with a contained body (*Phys.* IV 212a 20). As such, place is separable from the body that is in it, and therefore distinct both from the shape and inner extension of the contained body: "Insofar as it (place) is separable from the thing, it is not the form: *qua* containing, it is not the matter" (*Phys.* IV 209b 30). Aristotle is thereby led to conclude that the Heaven, the οὐρανός, which perhaps is the All, the common place of all things as distinct from the special place of any, has itself no place except accidentally, through its parts (*Phys.* IV 212a 31 - 212b 1, 8-21), since nothing is outside it to contain it: "If then a body has another body outside it and containing it, it is in place, and if not, not" (*Phys.* IV 212a 31-32). The universe is finite, but to ask its location, as distinct from the location of its parts, is nonsense.

This conclusion, as distinct from the analysis in terms of containing body that supports it, may have been as old as the Eleatics: Parmenides' Being has nothing outside it, and yet is likened to a sphere. In the *Timaeus*, Plato holds that the world's body is spherical, and that nothing material is outside it, a fact taken to explain why it is free from age and illness (*Timaeus* 32c-33b). It would seem that Plato, no less than Aristotle, thought the question, "Where is the world?" to be nonsense, and would therefore have denied that the world is in a place.

Why, then, does Parmenides suppose that Unity as a whole, if it is, is somewhere, that it is in something other than itself? The simplest answer is that to participate in Being is to be somewhere, and Unity as a whole participates in Being; therefore, it is somewhere. But this implies, by analysis of place already offered, that Unity is in another and contained by what it is in, touching it at many places with many parts of itself (138a).

Once again, we know that the historical Zeno constructed paradoxes involving place, perhaps using the opposition of In Itself/In Another. Aristotle remarks (*Phys.* IV 209a 28-30),

> Further, if it (place) is itself an existent, where will it be? Zeno's difficulty (ἀπορία) demands an explanation: for if everything that exists has a place, place too will have a place, and so on *ad infinitum*.

If this difficulty comes from the book mentioned in the *Parmenides*, Zeno must have argued that if plurality is, the same things both are in place and are not in place. Plurality implies divisibility. If something is in place, and many, then by Fragment 3 there must be something between its parts, or other members of the plurality. This answers, it would appear, to Aristotle's suggestion that place is a διάστημα, an interval or extension of magnitude. But that extension, by Fragment 3, must be infinitely divisible: there must be an infinity of places in the same thing, and each of those places is in a place that contains it (cf. *Phys.* IV 211b 19-20). Aristotle meets this with the distinction between a potential and an actual infinite (*Phys.* IV 212b 4-7):

> Some things are potentially in place, others actually. So, when you
> have a homogenous substance which is continuous, the parts are poten-
> tially in place: when the parts are separated, but in contact, like a heap,
> they are actually in place.

In short, if we regard place as an attribute of body, and if body is potentially
but not actually divisible ad infinitum, place will be potentially but not actually
divisible ad infinitum, as the potential limit of potentially containing bodies.
Each actual body will be in place as bounded by a bodily container, and each
place may be said to be in place as the inner limit of a body itself outwardly
limited by a further body. Thus, to apply the potential infinite to place requires
containment of bodies, and this is the ultimate solution to Zeno's paradox (*Phys.*
IV 210b 22-27, cf. 212b 27-29):

> Zeno's problem — that if Place is something it must be in something — is
> not difficult to solve. There is nothing to prevent the first place from
> being 'in' something else — not indeed in that as 'in' place but as health
> is 'in' the hot as a positive determination of it or as the hot is 'in' body
> as an affection. So we escape the infinite regress.

Place is a relational qualification of what is contained. In Aristotle's terms, it
is a category, in a subject *not* as a part, and incapable of existing separately
from what it is in (*Categories* 1a 24-25). But Zeno's difficulty about place would
seem to apply to Unity in precisely the terms in which it is stated. If Unity is,
and to be is to be somewhere, Unity is somewhere; therefore, it is in place. But
if place is, and to be is to be somewhere, then place is somewhere; that is, it is
in place. And so ad infinitum. It must further follow that the place in which
Unity is, is one, since the place is; therefore it must contain part of Unity.

v. Motion and Rest (145e-146a)

The First Deduction analyzed motion as change of character and change of place
(138b). It is now shown that Unity is (a) at rest and (b) in motion.

a) The proof that Unity is at rest conforms to the First Deduction. It was
there held that what is not in the same thing is not at rest. The converse is now
stated: what is in the same thing is at rest. So rest is equivalent to being in the
same thing. Unity, as all the parts, is in Unity as a whole. Since Unity is in itself, it is at rest; that is, it is in the same place as itself, considered as all the
parts of a limited whole.

b) The proof that Unity, because it is in something different, changes, is put
almost perfunctorily. In I.1., motion was found to imply change of place or
change of character (138b), and change of place is possible only for something
that has parts (138c-d). Unity has now been shown to have parts, to be in itself
as all the parts and in another as a whole, and to be an extended and limited
magnitude, possessed of shape.

The conclusion that Unity changes derives directly from these results. As a whole, Unity contains all its parts and is in something other than itself, which contains it. What Unity is in, as container, must be; therefore, it must be one; therefore, by the Dilemma of Participation, there must be parts of Unity in what contains Unity. Therefore, part of the container is part of Unity, and the limits of Unity, as a whole, must be conceived as continually expanding: for any limit taken, Unity must have further parts beyond its limit. So Unity must be conceived as continually coming to contain parts beyond those it is conceived to contain; it is, as it were, continually spilling over its own boundaries. It has already been proved infinite both by addition and division; now, by division, it contains just the parts it contains, and is at rest; by addition, it must continually be said to contain parts other than those already contained by it.

So Unity must be said not only to *be* in something other than itself, but to *come to be* in something other than itself. Unity is not yet in its container, as having no parts it does not contain; Unity is no longer outside its container, since the container is and is one. The necessary conditions for coming to be in something attach to Unity; and those conditions are jointly sufficient.

Since becoming implies an *already* and a *not yet*, Unity must be in time because it is in place. And since the analysis attaching to Unity attaches equally to Being, Being is in time. It had earlier been suggested that to be is to be in time because sensibles participate in Being; but it now appears that this result may also follow because Being is a whole of continually increasing parts. It is possible to argue that because Unity is, and to be is to be in time, Unity changes, since to be in time is to change. But it is now also possible to argue that Being must be in motion as Unity is in motion, and therefore, that to be is to be in time because Being changes. A result originally established by appeal to sensibles may now be taken to follow from analysis of Ideas in themselves.

The conclusion that Unity is moved contradicts a set of well-known Zenonian proofs that there is no motion (*Phys.* VI, ix). It is worth remarking, however, that the account offered here agrees with Zeno's Fragment 4, meant to prove that motion is impossible: "What is moved moves neither in a place where it is nor in a place where it is not." Unity is never in the same place, since it continually expands to encompass what contains it; but of course, it is not in a place where it is not. So Zeno's paradox, directed against the possibility of motion, is here implied by the analysis of motion. This account, generalized to the issues of being, not-being, and becoming, will later lead to an analysis of the instantaneous, which is in no time at all (156d-e).

vi. Same and Different (146a-147b)

Unity must be (a) the same as itself and (b) different from itself and (c) different from the others and (d) the same as the others.

Those who have been so fortunate as to have acquired an aesthetic delight in paradox will find this a remarkably pretty proof. For it establishes, among other things, that the Idea of Unity must be the same as other things that have no unity at all. Parenthetically, it also anticipates consequences for the Others in Deductions to follow.

The proof turns on a lemma, stated with Eleatic generality: if *x* is related to *y*, then either *x* is the same as *y*, or *x* is different from *y*, or, if neither the same nor different, *x* and *y* are related as part to whole or whole to part. This lemma is founded on the Dilemma of Participation; for it assumes that assertion of a subject is founded on sameness, difference, or the relation of parts and whole. But further, the argument that has established that Unity is a limited extensive magnitude implies that anything which is is a limited extensive magnitude; so the lemma exhausts the possible relations between limited extensive magnitudes, considered as such.

a) It is not taken as merely obvious that Unity is the same as itself. That proposition is derived from the lemma: Unity is not part of itself, and thus does not stand to itself as whole to part or part to whole; this follows from the fact that Unity, qua Unity, is not in itself. Again, Unity is not different from itself, because it is not different from Unity, or one.[183] Thus by disjunctive syllogism, Unity is the same as itself.

b) But Unity is in a certain respect different from itself. For it is both in itself and in another, and therefore is in the same thing, namely itself, and also in a different thing, place. In that respect, it is different from itself.

c) Unity is also different from the others. For as many things as are not Unity (or one) are different from Unity, and Unity is different from things that are not Unity (or one).

d) Unity is also the same as the others. The proof of this proceeds by showing (i) that Unity is not different from the others, and (ii) that Unity does not stand to the others as whole to part or part to whole, whence it follows by the lemma and disjunctive syllogism that Unity is the same as the others.

e) Sameness and Difference are opposites. Therefore, Difference can neither be nor partake of Sameness, whence it follows that Difference cannot be the same as anything. But if Difference were participated in it would, by the Dilemma of Participation, be a whole of parts, and as a whole of parts it would, like Unity, be both in itself and in another (145b-e). But if it were in itself, it would be in the same thing, namely in itself (145e-146a), whence it would follow that Difference would be the same as itself, and thus the same. Again, to be is to be in time, and what is in time is the same age as itself (141d). Therefore, if Difference were in anything for any time whatever, during that time Difference would be in what is the same, and thus be qualified by Sameness. This is tantamount to a proof that Difference cannot be participated in, and more generally, that there can be no such Idea as Difference, since to be is to be in time. This result, absurd in itself, is incompatible with (a) and (b) above. It might have been proved, on the same grounds, that Sameness cannot be participated in.

If Difference cannot be participated in, it follows that if Unity is different from the others, it cannot be different by virtue of Difference; nor can Unity and the others be different by virtue of themselves. So Unity is not different from the others, nor they from it.

ii) It remains to show that the others — things that are not Unity — are not related to Unity as part to whole or whole to part. Things that are not Unity are here understood to be things that are not one: they cannot have a share of Unity, since if they did, they would in a sense be one. This assumption is a consequence of the separation of sensibles from Ideas. Simmias, we have said, has a substantial existence apart from any Idea. What sort of existence has he got apart from the Idea of Unity? Put in the context of the Dilemma of Participation, Simmias, if he is one, has a part of Unity in him. If that part is in Simmias as incapable of existing apart from him, Simmias is a bearer, a substrate; and insofar as that substrate is not identical with Unity or any part of Unity, it is not one. Participants, conceived apart from their own unity, are neither one nor have a number. Unity cannot contain the others, conceived in this way, since parts must be one if they are to be, and a whole is as many as its parts (144c-d). Nor can the others, lacking all unity, be a whole that contains Unity as a part, since to be a whole is to be one.

By disjunctive syllogism, then, Unity, since it is not different from the others, and is not related to the others as a whole to part or part to whole, is the same as the others — the same, that is, as things that have no unity at all. The absurdity of this result is manifest. Indeed, given the equivalence between being and unity, it is tantamount to a proof that the others have no existence, and therefore that Unity, since it is the same as the others, has no existence. Assuming that Unity partakes of Being, we have been led to a Way that Is Not.

vii. Like and Unlike (147c-148d)

Unity is (a) like the others and (b) unlike the others and (c) like itself and (d) unlike itself.

a) Unity has been proved to be different from the others, and they from it. But if different, then by Difference, the nature or Idea of which 'different' is the name. Now, to be like is to be qualified by the same characteristic.[184] Therefore, since Unity and the others are qualified by the same characteristic, namely Difference, they are like each other. So Unity is like the others just insofar as it is different from them.

It will be observed that this is incompatible with 146d-e, which assumed that Difference can never be the same. If the nature of which 'different' is the name is the same on varying occasions of use of the name, then this is a linguistic reason for saying that Difference is the same as itself, and thus qualified by Sameness. So in the *Cratylus*, it is assumed that names must have a fixed reference which is ever the same (439d).

b) If Unity is like the others because it is different from the others, and Likeness and Unlikeness and Sameness and Difference are opposites, so that being the same as the others is opposite to being different from the others, then insofar as Unity and the others are the same, they are unlike. But Unity has just proved to be the same as the others (147b). Therefore, it must be unlike the others.

This argument appears to assume that if one opposite introduces another then the opposite of the first will introduce the opposite of the second. This seems almost a parody of the account of *Phaedo* 103c ff., where opposites such as hot and cold and odd introduce characters such as fire and snow and three, and those characters are excluded by the presence of the opposite of the introducing opposite. Socrates there limits this account to *some* cases (103e 2), and its generalized use here appears to lead to a blatantly fallacious result. As Cornford points out, "Since likeness means having an identical character, and two things are alike if they both have an identical character, and two things are alike if they both have the character 'different' (as has just been proved), they are also alike, not unlike, if they both have the character 'same.'" And Cornford goes on to remark, correctly, that this is stated at 148c 4.[185] But in this case, the apparent premise holds, and the result, though inconsistent and absurd, is not fallacious. Unity has been proved to be the same as the others, which have no unity at all. Therefore, if to be unlike is to be qualified by a different characteristic, and Unity is one, Unity is unlike the others (and itself) just insofar as it is the same as the others (and itself). In short, the premise that Unity is the same as the others refers us back, not only to the premise that it is the same because it is different, but to the previous result that it is the same because it is not different (147b), just as the agreement that Sameness and Difference are opposite (148a) refers us back to the leading premise of the previous proof.

(a) and (b). Parmenides next provides opposite grounds for the same conclusion. To be qualified by the same characteristic is not to be qualified as of another sort; what is not qualified as of another sort is not unlike; and what is not unlike is like. So Unity is like the others because it is the same as the others. In a parallel way, to be qualified as other is to be qualified as of another sort, and what is qualified as of another sort is unlike. So Unity is unlike the others, which have no unity at all. We are, then, given multiple and inconsistent grounds for the same conclusion. Unity is both like and unlike and the others because it is the same as the others, which are without unity.

(c) and (d) Unity is like itself and unlike itself, both because it is the same as itself and because it is different from itself. The grounds for this have already been given (146c).

viii. In Contact, Not in Contact (148d-149d)

Unity (a) touches the others and (b) touches itself and (c) does not touch itself and (d) does not touch the others.

This proof breaks the formal symmetry of the First and Second Deductions. But it is directly connected with the proof in I.1 (138a-b) that Unity, if it has no parts, can neither be in itself nor in another. It was there suggested that if Unity were in another, it would be contained in a circle (as perfectly one) by what it was in, and touch it in many places with many parts. In I.2 it has been proved that Unity has parts, has shape (not necessarily circular), and is in another

—the latter result assuming that to be is to be somewhere, and that to be in something is to be in some place.

a) Unity touches the others because it is in an other (145b ff.). If Unity, as whole, is in something other than itself, and if it has shape and is somewhere, it must touch or have contact with what it is in. Therefore, what it is in must be an extensive magnitude, as Unity is an extensive magnitude, and as such, divisible. So Unity, if it is in something other than itself, touches many parts of what it is in with many parts of itself. That is, as in another, it touches others.

b) Unity also touches itself, since it is in itself as a whole. But as in itself, it cannot touch the others.

Unity touches itself because it is a continuous magnitude and as continuous, all of its parts, taken distributively, touch other parts of itself: for continuity is to be analyzed in terms of identity of touching extremities (cf. *Phys.* V 227a 10-13), and continuity implies succession and contact (cf. *Phys.* V 227a 17-19). Considered as all its parts, Unity does not touch other things outside it, because all the parts are contained by the whole, and therefore nothing outside the whole is one. Because Unity is in itself, the others have been shown to have no unity, that is, not to be one or have any number; given the equivalence between being and unity, this implies that the others have no being, that is, that they do not exist.

c) Unity does not touch itself. For what touches must lie in succession to what it is to touch (cf. *Phys.* V 227a 17 ff.), occupy a place contiguous to the thing it touches. But Unity cannot be in succession to itself, for it cannot be two, and so be in two places at once. The same thing at the same time cannot both contain itself and be contained by itself (138b), and Unity has been proved to be the same as itself. So Unity, as the same as itself, does not touch itself. This result contradicts that of (b), and implies that Unity can have no extensive magnitude. Since the proof that Unity is an extensive magnitude followed directly from the assumption that Unity participates in Being, this implies that Unity has no being, that is, does not exist.

d) Neither can Unity touch the others. For if it touched the others, it would be separate from and in succession to the others that it touched. Thus there is some number, n, of terms or parts of Unity and of the others it touches, and the contacts between those elements will be of the number $n - 1$. But it has been shown that the others do not partake of Unity, and that there is therefore no number of them (147a). So the necessary condition for contact, namely, numerability of elements in contact, is not fulfilled. Unity cannot touch the others. The argument makes explicit the assumption underlying the claim in (b) that if Unity is in itself, it is kept back from touching the others.

The theorem that the ratio of elements in contact to contacts is superparticular—that is, the ratio of $n : n - 1$—might have been used to construct a general proof that nothing is in contact with anything. If something is in something else, as contained to container, it has a shape and therefore a perimeter, and touches in many places with many parts of itself. But that perimeter is infinitely divisible, and this implies infinitely many parts of the container in contact with infinitely many parts of the contained. By the theorem, the corresponding ratio is that of $n : n - 1$. There is no such (cardinal) number, and no such ratio.

There is, however, some evidence for the development in the early Academy of a doctrine of infinitesimal parts. Aristotle in the *Metaphysics* (I 992a 20-22) says that Plato rejected the point as a fiction of the geometers, and held that the beginning (or principle) of the line was indivisible lines. One might suppose that what Plato actually held was that the principle of lines is the Line, Linearity, which is indivisible as being a unique and self-subsistent Idea; alternately, he may have meant that points have no independent existence, in that they are definable in terms of potential divisions in lines, which are thus prior in definition. But neither of these is the meaning Aristotle takes. That *someone* in the Academy maintained a doctrine of indivisible lines is suggested by the Peripatetic treatise *On Indivisible Lines*, and Aristotle himself refers to those who held this view.[186] There is evidence in Aristotle, and testimony in Proclus, Themistius, Simplicius and Philoponus, that this is the doctrine of Xenocrates.[187] That Xenocrates held it, if he did, does not of course preclude that Plato stated it in the *Parmenides*.[188]

These indivisible lines could not have been of finite length, since division according to a rational proportion will not at any finite stage yield an irrational ratio, or vice versa. The author of *On Indivisible Lines* assumed that those lines are of finite length, and concluded, not surprisingly, that the doctrine "conflicts with nearly everything in mathematics." Since members of the Academy were not geometrical illiterates, and understood the fact of incommensurability,[189] it is a reasonable inference that if anyone in the Academy maintained a doctrine of indivisible lines, those lines must have been, not merely "mighty small," but infinitely small, minimal, or infinitesimal parts conceived as indivisible on the ground, presumably, that what is infinitely small admits no smaller. Minimal parts, so conceived, would not measure a magnitude, since if anything measures a (finite) magnitude, that magnitude is an integral multiple of it,[190] and an integral multiple of an infinitesimal is infinitesmal. A theory of minimal parts, so conceived, would be consistent with Euclid X. 1., since it is a sufficient condition for the truth of that theorem that every finite division be divisible. It would also be consistent with the fact of incommensurability, since infinitesimal parts do not measure a magnitude.[191] It remains the case that if a doctrine of infinitesimals was formulated in the Academy, it was decisively rejected by subsequent Greek mathematics.[192] Still, it may well be answered at *Parmenides* 149a-c. If so, the concept of number must admit an infinite cardinal, for a doctrine of the infinitely small logically requires a prior conception. As the form of the word indicates—compare 'decimal'—'infinitesimal' stands for an ordinal, analogous to 'third,' 'tenth,' or 'hundredth.' But to formulate the notion of an infinitesimal as an ordinal requires the use of an infinite number as a cardinal: Euclid expresses the distinction between ordinals and cardinals in terms of a part called by the same name as a measuring number, and a number called by the same name as the measuring part.[193]

That *someone* in the Academy may have supposed that there is (not an infinite number of things but) an infinite cardinal number is indicated by a criticism lodged by Aristotle against those — they are Platonists — who think that number is 'separated' from material things.[194] Aristotle argues that number must be either finite or infinite; that it cannot be infinite, since number is either odd or even (a constant assumption of Plato's), whereas infinite number can be neither odd nor even. Many things about this argument are obscure; in particular, it would be good to know what arguments Aristotle would have given for the conclusion that infinite number can be neither odd nor even. But the point seems plain: if you regard the numbers as separate, that is, as actually existing apart from numbered objects, then you must either regard number as finite, in which case there is an odd or even number than which there is no greater number, which is absurd; or you must regard number as infinite, in which case there is a number which is neither odd nor even, which is equally absurd. If we are entitled to assume that there is no number greater than an infinite cardinal number, the basis for the claim that an infinite number can be neither odd nor even is clear; for the addition of 1 to an infinite cardinal number produces the same number, whereas the addition of 1 to an odd number produces an even number, and of 1 to an even number an odd number, and odd and even numbers are not the same.

There is no evidence that Parmenides at any point assumes the existence of infinite cardinals or ordinals.[195] But it seems clear that the treatise *On Indivisible Lines* should be read against the background of *Parmenides* 144a-e — the background of the actual infinite.

The alternative, and the inference the reader is perhaps more clearly meant to draw, is the reinstatement of Zeno's paradoxes against plurality. Fragment 1 argued that plurality implies that things which are are so large as to be infinite; Fragment 2, that things which are are so small as to be nothing. Without a doctrine of infinitesimals, these are direct consequences for Unity from the argument on Contact, given that Unity is a continuous magnitude. The argument further revives Zeno's Fragment 3, already alluded to at 144c-d: If things are many, they must be as many as they are, neither more nor less; if they are as many as they are, they are limited; but if things are many, they are unlimited, for there will always be different ones between things which are, and different ones again between those; so things which are are unlimited.

The argument on Contact may show that, besides lack of a zero, the Greek mathematicians refused to extend the concept of number from the integers to the rationals, to treat rational ratios as rational numbers, because of the density or compactness property that the rationals have and the integers do not have. Zenonian perplexities result.

ix. Equal and Unequal (149e-151e)

Unity is (a) equal to the others and (b) equal to itself and (c) larger and smaller than itself and (d) larger and smaller than the others. The proof of this is replicated, first for magnitude and then for multitude.

Magnitude

a) If Unity were larger or smaller than the others, it could not be so either by virtue of its own nature or by virtue of the nature of the others as other than Unity; it must be so by virtue of Largeness and Smallness (cf. 146e - 147a, 147c-d). Largeness and Smallness must therefore exist, since they are opposite to each other and come to be present in things which are, namely, in the Idea of Unity and the Idea which things have as other than Unity (cf. 158c), that is, the Idea of Plurality, here identified with other things as simply other than Unity, the opposite of plurality.

Now, to be is to be somewhere, and thus in something. Apply this to Small-ness. If Smallness is present in Unity, it is present in the whole of Unity, or in part of Unity. Suppose it is in the whole of Unity. Then either it is coextensive with Unity, or it contains Unity. For to say that Smallness is present to Unity is to say that it is and is one, and therefore is an extensive magnitude. Since Unity is an extensive magnitude, Smallness must be everywhere that Unity is, if Unity is small; otherwise, it is something other than Unity that is small. If then Unity is small, Smallness must either extend evenly with Unity, in which case it is equal to Unity, or contain Unity, in which case it is larger than Unity. But Smallness cannot be equal to or larger than anything, since it would then do the work of, act the part of, Equality and Largeness, not its own. This principle, established by Socrates' admissions at 129c-130a, 131d-e and applied at 148b-c, has already been used to prove that Difference cannot be in anything (146d-e).

Again, Smallness cannot be in part of Unity. For it cannot be in all of a part, on pain of being equal to or greater than that part; therefore it cannot be in any part, however small. The pattern of reasoning there is interesting: it is akin to mathematical induction, which is not a normal device of Greek mathematics.

The conclusion is that Smallness can never be in anything, since if it were, it would be equal or large; therefore, nothing can be small except Smallness. If that is so, then Largeness cannot be in anything, and this for neatly incompat-ible reasons. If Largeness is in Unity, there will be something else larger than it, namely, that in which Largeness is present: if F is in a, F in whole or part is part of a, and the whole is greater than its part. This result directly contradicts the pattern of argument just used for Smallness. Using that pattern, and appealing to the fact that Largeness and Smallness are correlatives, Largeness cannot be in anything: for whatever is large must be larger than something smaller, and so, since Smallness is not in anything, Largeness cannot be larger than anything but Smallness, and conversely. This conclusion matches the claim that correlative Ideas have their power or significance (150d 1) only relative to each other, and not to things in our world (133c-e). Significantly, it here is derived from proof of the impossibility of participation, conceived as a relation implying magnitude not only of participant but of what is participated in.

Given that Unity and Otherness or the others are, they must be somewhere.

Given that they are magnitudes, and that they are not larger or smaller than each other, they must be equal. So Unity is equal to Otherness or the others.

b) Unity is equal to itself. For it can have neither Largeness nor Smallness in it, and therefore cannot exceed or be exceeded by itself. But a magnitude that neither exceeds nor is exceeded by itself is equal to itself.

c) Unity is both larger and smaller than itself. For it is in itself, as a whole that contains all its parts; furthermore, it is all its parts (145b-c). Therefore, it touches itself, lying in succession to itself (148d-e). So it is larger than itself as containing itself and smaller than itself as being contained by itself. So Unity is unequal to itself, being larger and smaller than itself.[196]

d) Unity is both larger and smaller than Otherness or the others. For there is nothing besides Unity and the others; what is must be somewhere; what is somewhere is in something, and contained by what it is in; what contains is larger than what is contained. Since Unity is, it must be in something; therefore, it must be in the others. That is, Unity must be contained by the Idea of Otherness, and may be said to be other than something. Since the others are, and to be is to be in something, the others must be in something; given that they are in Otherness, as a whole of which they are parts, Otherness must be in something; and there is nothing for Otherness, and thereby the others, to be in except Unity: Otherness can be said to be one. Alternately, the others, insofar as they are, are one, and therefore contain parts that are parts of Unity. They therefore are in Unity as Unity is in them. So Unity is smaller than the others, since it is in them, and larger than the others, since they are in it. So Unity is not only equal to, but larger and smaller than the others as a whole, that is, Otherness. So it is both equal and unequal to the others.

Multitude

In the First Deduction, it was proved that Unity can be neither equal nor unequal to itself or to another. If equal, it would have the same measures. If larger or smaller, it would have, if commensurable, more or fewer measures, and if incommensurable, larger or smaller measures. But Unity there had no measures, for if it did it would have as many parts as measures, and the Unity of I. 1 has been proved to have no parts. But the Unity of I. 2 does have parts, and because it is a magnitude, admits of measures. As equal in magnitude to itself and to the others, it has as many measures as itself and the others, and as of measures, so of parts. Because it lies in succession to itself it is greater than itself, and therefore has more measures as it has more parts; as containing the others it is greater than the others, and again has more measures as it has more parts. As smaller than itself it has parts in contact with what contains it, and therefore is smaller than itself; as contained by the others, it is smaller than the others, and has less measures and parts. That is, since Unity is equal to, larger than and smaller than both itself and the others, or Otherness, it must have more, fewer, and equal measures as itself and the others, or Otherness. It is inferred from this that it is of more, fewer, and equal number as itself and as the others, or Otherness, and so similarly with parts. The argument might have been generalized to show that all magnitudes are equal, and that no magnitudes are equal.

It remains only to add that the proof that Unity and the others are both equal and unequal to each other in magnitude and multitude follows from the premises provided for it, and that the conclusion is absurd. Academic readers must surely have again recalled Zeno's argument that if plurality is, the same things must be so small as to be nothing, so large as to be infinite. The argument implies that this must be true of Smallness itself. It has been shown that nothing can be small except Smallness, with the direct implication that Smallness can have no parts; since those parts would be, as parts, smaller than Smallness (cf. 131d); but if this is so, Smallness can neither be nor be one, and Smallness is so small as to be nothing. Again, if Smallness is coextensive with or contains Unity, and Unity is such that it has parts distributed to others outside it, Smallness must be large, and so large as to be infinite, as the container of an infinitely expanding whole. This matches the result of Fragments 1 and 2 of Zeno. It is not funny but witty—the intellectual wit of incongruous surprise.

x. Older, Younger, Same Age (151e-155c)

Unity is (a) becoming older and younger than itself and (b) is older and younger than itself and (c) neither is nor becomes older nor younger than itself and (d) is older and younger than the others and (e) is neither older nor younger than the others and (f) does not become older and younger than the others and (g) becomes older and younger than the others. So Unity both is and comes to be older and younger than itself and than the others, and neither is nor comes to be older or younger than itself and than the others.

a) (151e-152b) Since it is one, Unity is. But to be is to share in Being in present time, just as *was* and *will be* are in intercourse with what has passed and what is to come. That is, if to be is to be in time (141e), then to say that a thing *is*, as distinct from saying that it was or will be, is to say that it has a share of Being in present time. The hypothesis that Unity is, therefore, implies that it partakes of Being in present time.

This analysis should be contrasted with that of *Timaeus* 37e-38a where it is claimed that days, months and years,

> are parts of Time, and 'was' and 'shall be' are forms of time that have come to be; we are wrong to transfer them unthinkingly to eternal being. We say that it was and is and shall be; but 'is' alone really belongs to it and describes it truly; 'was' and 'shall be' are properly used of becoming which proceeds in time, for they are motions.

In the *Timaeus*, Plato reserves 'is' for timeless being: what is in time cannot be said to be, but only to become. But the *Parmenides* assumes that to be is to be in time, whence it follows that to be is to be in present time: for what is future is not (yet) and what is past is not (any longer). But the concept of the present, we shall find, is not without its peculiarities.[197]

Time passes. Therefore, if Unity always has a share of Being in present time, and Time passes, Unity is always growing older than itself, since it advances with time. This need be taken as no more than the common-sense point that a thing becomes older than it was at every successive stage of its existence in time.

Alternately, however, a thing may be said to be older than every subsequent stage of itself, which may thus be described as younger or newer—the Greek *neoteron* has both meanings.

As becoming older than itself by passage of time, Unity will also become younger than itself (cf. 141b-c). What is relative is correlative. So in the *Charmides* (168c), what is more than itself will be less than itself, what is heavier than itself will be lighter than itself, what is older than itself will be younger than itself; for if a thing has its own power relative to itself, it will then have the nature and reality in relation to which that power exists.

Cornford found in this argument a special concept of time: that of the 'ever-flowing stream' on which things are borne forward. But Parmenides merely says that time passes or travels, a word that leaves open the question of whether the future lies ahead of us or overtakes us from behind. Poetry aside, if the metaphor of the ever-moving stream implies that time is a container existing independently of its contents, the suggestion is inappropriate. For Plato, time is relational and, in its numbering of days and years, part of the rational structure of the world. It does not flow "equably without relation to anything external," as Newton maintained in the Scholium to the initial definitions in the *Principia*; rather, time came to be with the heavens. It is a function of the motion of the heavens, whose motions proide the measure by which other motions are numbered and measured. As Aristotle was later to put it, "Time is not movement, but only movement in so far as it admits of enumeration" (*Phys.* IV 219b 2-3). That is, time is a measure of relative change.

But this has not here been introduced. We deal only with is, was, and will be. Unity, having regard to temporal succession, is becoming older and younger than itself.

b) (152b-e) Having shown that Unity is *becoming* older and younger than itself, because it partakes of Being in present time, and time passes, Parmenides next shows that Unity *is* older and younger than itself. This is done by adding to the fact of temporal succession the 'now.' Unity, in passing from past to future will occupy a place between them, and what stands between past and future is the now. This now, as the end-point between past and future, must be indivisible: there is no 'specious present,' a now with duration and thus a before and after (cf. *Phys.* VI 233b 33 - 234a 4). Insofar as Unity has reached the now, it is not *becoming* older but *is* older than itself, and therefore younger than itself. That is, if what was at T_1 is at T_2, it is older than it was by virtue of the fact that it exists later, and younger or newer than it was by virtue of the fact that it exists after what existed before.

This leads to a contrast between being and becoming. To be is to be in the now. But to come to be is to come to be between the now and the after. This suggests that becoming is primitive and continuous, so that between any now and any after there is an interval, potentially divisible but never exhaustively divided: there is no *next* now (cf. *Phys.* VI 231b 6-9). If this is so, becoming, and that image of becoming that is the passage of time, may be compared to a continous line, and the nows located in it to points on the line. The analysis suggests Aristotle's analogy between stretches of time and lines, and moments or nows and points (*Phys.* IV 222a 10-16):

> The 'now' is the link of time . . . (for it connects the past and future time), and it is a limit of time (for it is the beginning of one and the end of the other.) But this is not obvious as it is with the point, which is fixed. It divides potentially, and in so far as it is dividing the 'now' is always different, but in so far as it connects it is always the same, as it is with mathematical lines.

The application of this to passage in time is direct (*Phys.* VIII 262a 28-32):

> When its motion is continuous A cannot either have come to be or ceased to be at point B: it can only have been there at the moment of passing, its passage not being contained within any period of time except the whole of which the particular moment is a dividing point.

The now is a limit of becoming, and when Unity reaches it, it ceases to become and then is. But it becomes as leaving the now and grasping the after, which introduces a fresh now, a fresh limit to be left behind.

The claim that becoming takes place between the now and the after may be read as an argument against the unreality of time. Recall, for example, the classic statement by Augustine (*Confessions* XI. xiv., trans. Pine-Coffin):

> What, then, is time? I know well enough what it is, provided that nobody asks me; but if I am asked what it is and try to explain, I am baffled. All the same I can confidently say that I know that if nothing passed, there would be no past time; if nothing were going to happen, there would be no future time; and if nothing *were*, there would be no present time.
>
> Of these three divisions of time, then, how can two, the past and the future, *be*, when the past no longer is and the future is not yet? As for the present, if it were always present and never moved on to become the past, it would not be time but eternity. If, therefore, the present is time only by reason of the fact that it moves on to become the past, how can we say that even the present *is*, when the reason why it *is* is that it is *not to be*? In other words, we cannot rightly say that time *is*, except by its impending state of *not being*.

What is past is no longer; what is future is not yet. The present merely bounds two things which are not, and itself has no duration. So there is no duration, and no time. The answer is that there is continuous duration, and that the now merely marks a limit in it, analogous to a point on the line. But since Unity *is* only in the now, its becoming must be prior to its being, as the line is prior to the point.

c) (152e) Unity neither is nor becomes older or younger than itself. For it neither comes to be nor is for a longer period of time then itself. Therefore, it has the same age as itself. But what has the same age as itself neither is nor is becoming older or younger than itself.

d) (153a-d) Unity is both older and younger than the others. For the others are others, not an other, and so are plural, and have a number. This result, which contradicts the treatment of the others at 147a-b, where they were found to be without unity or number, is entailed by 151b-c, where Unity is more, fewer, and equal to the others in number, a result which is required if the others are, since Being and Unity are coextensive, and which implies that there is a plurality of others.

There is, then, some number of others, corresponding to the measures of Unity. But of a number, that is, a plurality of units, the lesser comes before the greater, and the least first. But the least is one. So Unity, the property that the first unit of the others must have, must come to be before all that has number. Therefore, the others are younger than Unity, and Unity older than the others.

We want to object that though Unity is ontologically prior to any plurality of units, this in no way implies that it is temporally prior. Nor is there any reason why less of a plurality must come to be before more of it; a total plurality might come to be all at once.

But this neglects the assumption that to be is to be in time. If this is so, and if *a* is prior to *b*, the only sense that can be given to priority is temporal priority. As this applies to Unity in its priority to any number of things, each of which is one, so it applies to the numbers themselves. If 8 is greater than 7, then 7 is numerically prior to 8; but if numerically prior, then prior, and if prior, then prior in time. The result is absurd, and meant to be; it is brought out by the punning use of the words 'prior' and 'posterior.'[198]

Parmenides next argues that Unity is younger than the others, and the others older than Unity. It is important to remember, in examining this proof, that the others are things other than Unity, and that the parts of Unity are different from Unity (143a-b), and therefore other than Unity. It is also important to remember the analysis of becoming offered at 141a in the First Deduction: if Unity is coming to be in time, then part of it must already have come to be, and part of it must not yet have come to be.

Unity cannot come to be contrary to its own nature; that is, it cannot come to be other than one. And since it is a thing which is, it is, as one, one whole consisting of all its parts. But because Unity has parts, it proved to have beginning, middle, and end; and since to be is to be in time, the beginning must be understood as a temporal beginning, and the end as a temporal end. So if Unity is a whole, it must come to be as a whole simultaneously with the coming to be of its last part, since a whole is that from which no part is absent (137c). Thus, if Unity cannot come to be contrary to its own nature, and if in coming to be it comes to be both one and whole, it comes to be last among the others, including other parts of Unity.

There will be no others that come to be after Unity, since when Unity has once come to be, time will be no more: the completion of Unity will take place in the last now. This implies either that the universe is not infinite in time, or that Unity does not exist as one and whole, because it is forever incomplete, without end. But if Unity comes to be last of all the others, including all parts of itself, it is younger than the others.

e) (153d - 154a) But Unity is neither older nor younger than the others. The beginning and every other part of Unity, given that it is part and not parts, is one.[199] But unity, since it is coextensive with Being, is present to everything which is, including the others. So Unity will come to be along with the first part, and the second, and the third, and so on through to the end, and will be lacking to no one of the others that come to be. And this will be so until it has passed through to the end and become a whole one, or one whole. Thus it will be of the same age as all its parts and of the others taken collectively—all of the others, as distinct from each of the others (cf. 153c, e). Thus it is neither older nor younger than the others, since it is of the same age as they. The same argument might have been used to show that it is neither older nor younger than itself, conceived as all its parts.

f) (154a-c) Unity does not become older or younger than the others. For it has been proved that Unity is older than the others (153a-b). But if A is older than B, it remains older by the same amount during its entire career in time. Therefore it *is* older, and is not *becoming* older, and, since their difference in age is constant, the others are not becoming younger than it. The reason is that adding equals to unequals always makes the sums different by the same amount. That is,

If a > b, then a + m > b + m,

and, (a + m) - (b + m) = (a - b),

where a and b are ages, and m is any period of time. This proposition was later suggested as a general axiom by Pappus, and rejected by Proclus and Simplicius, who showed that it could be proved.[200] It produces an arithmetical progression, in that each successive term in the sequence differs by a constant amount from its predecessor. It is general in that it permits the introduction of any numbers or magnitudes so long as the resulting sequence is related by a constant difference of inequality. That constant of difference may, but need not, be representable by a number. Given that time is continuous, and given a body traversing the side (s) and the hypotenuse (h) of an isosceles right triangle at the same speed, then s: h = T_1 : T_2, whence it follows that the ratio of T_1 and T_2 is irrational, not to be expressed by a number. So the constant of difference in Parmenides' progression need not be a number, and it will be observed that he carefully states his theorem in terms of constancy of difference without assigning a numerical value to that difference or suggesting that it is always possible to do so. Archytas[201] defined arithmetical proportion as containing three terms, which are to each other such that the first exceeds the second by the same amount that the second exceeds the third: that is, (a − b) = (b − c); he compares arithmetical to geometrical proportion, (a:b) = (b : c), on the ground that arithmetical proportion introduces equality with respect to sameness of difference, while geometrical proportion introduces equality with respect to sameness of ratio; and he observes that in arithmetical proportion, the ratio between the greater terms is smaller, and between the smaller terms greater. Parmenides' arithmetical progression introduces inequality rather than equality while maintaining sameness of difference, and his next proposition will introduce the Archytean property of decreasing inequality with respect to ratio. It has been said that Plato was not an original mathematician. But it is worth remarking that the theorems he here uses are not attested before Hellenistic times.

g) (154c - 155c) Unity becomes but never is older and younger than the others. It has been proved both that Unity is older than the others, and that the others are older than Unity. But if Unity is older than the others, this implies that Unity has come to be for a time greater than the others. If, however, equal time is added to a greater and a lesser time, the greater will differ from the lesser by a smaller proportional part at every subsequent time. Therefore, since Unity takes time equal to the others, as well as more time, the ratio of its age to the others is constantly diminishing, and so it is becoming younger than the others, as the others are becoming older than it.

This account involves a sequence, geometrical in that it involves comparison of ratios, which specifies a further property of the arithmetical progression Parmenides has already constructed. If we take the terms of that progression, not in respect of their sameness of difference in age, but in respect of the ratio of their successive ages, we find that as the ages increase, the successive ratios diminish. If Jones is ten years older than Smith, then when Jones is thirty, Smith is twenty, and when Jones is fifty, Smith is forty: the ratio of 5 to 4 is smaller than the ratio of 3 to 2. Put generally,

If a > b, then (a + m) : (b + m) < (a : b).

This property was noticed much later by Theon and Nicomachus in respect to numbers, and again in the fourteenth century, in the dawn of modern mathematics.[202] The result is interesting; it is neither a progression nor a series, but a sequence whose ratios are defined by a progression, and a sequence that does not terminate. Parmenides' emphatic claim that Unity is always *becoming* but cannot *be become*, that is, cannot finally become, younger than the others, since then it would no longer be becoming but would *be* younger, is an explicit rejection of the claim that the sequence has a limit: though it continually approaches the ratio of equality, that ratio cannot be part of the sequence.[203] This is in contradiction to 153c-d.

Since Unity is not only older than the others, but the others also older than

Unity (153d), the same reasoning will prove that the others are ever becoming but never are younger than Unity. So Unity becomes older and younger than the others, and the others older and younger than Unity.

xi. Conclusion (155c-e)

The conclusion of the First Deduction contradicted its own Hypothesis: Unity could not be even to the degree of being one. The conclusion of the Second Deduction does not labor under this defect, but under others.

The Second Deduction concludes, contrary to the assumption underlying Socrates' original challenge to Zeno (129e - 130a), that as things are with the things we see, so they are also with what we apprehend by reflection. Unity is an Idea, and exists or partakes of Being. Because it exists, it can be named and spoken of, and things can belong to it and be of or related to it. As an Idea, Unity is intelligible. But it is also perceptible, that is, of a sort able to be perceived, because it is and becomes in time and place, has figure and is subject to change. It is an object of opinion as satisfying a defining property of opinion offered in the *Republic* (V 479e-480a), namely, that it is qualified by opposites, and subject to becoming. Parmenides' remark that everything of the sort that pertains to the others also pertains to Unity is significant: for the others are participants, and in the Second Deduction, we have been led to conclude that Unity, what it is to be one, is itself one thing in the same way that the others are one: it has the unity of a participant.

If the conclusion of the Second Deduction of the First Hypothesis does not formally contradict its own Hypothesis, it formally contradicts the conclusion derived from that same Hypothesis in the First Deduction, and itself exhibits multiple contradictions in the course of its own argument. The young Aristoteles accepts its conclusion: "That is completely true." His consent is no more revealing as to the logical acceptability of the result than his earlier denial of the conclusion of the First Deduction, expressed at 142a. More accurately, his earlier doubt and his present assent both go to results that follow from the same Hypothesis, and to Deductions each of which generate inconsistencies and absurdities. This fact is itself an exhibition of the dialectical situation. We deal with a respondent who has agreed to contradictory reasoning, and is not in logical harmony with himself. He is, if he did but know it, in aporia, perplexity.

Perhaps as just a comment on the Second Deduction as may be found was made, in a quite different context, by Aristotle, in a passage already quoted (*Topics* II 113a 24-32):

> Or again, look and see if anything has been said about something of such kind that if it be true, contrary predicates must necessarily apply to the same thing: e.g. if he has said that the 'Ideas' exist in us. For then the result will be that they are both in motion and at rest, and moreover that they are objects both of sensation and of thought. For according to the views of those who posit the existence of Ideas, those

Ideas are at rest and are objects of thought; while if they exist in us, it is impossible that they should be unmoved: for when we move, it follows necessarily that all that is in us moves with us as well. Clearly also they are objects of sensation, if they exist in us: for it is through the sensation of sight that we recognize the Form present in each individual.

I.3. First Hypothesis, Third Deduction (155e-157b)

The First Hypothesis differs from those to follow in that it contains a third Deduction. There is an element of play in this. The historical Parmenides had distinguished the Way that Is from the Way that Is Not, and then had gone on to distinguish a third Way, a Way that Is and Is Not, and shown that it reduced to the Way that Is Not. The Platonic Parmenides proceeds in a similar manner. In I.1 he has proved that Unity neither is nor is one (141e). In I.2 he had proved that Unity both is and is One (142b-c). Given these results, Parmenides now, in I.3, undertakes to combine them.

I.3 does not follow from an independent hypothesis, as Proclus supposed:[204] we are taking up the same hypothesis for the third time (155e). Nor is the argument simply a corollary of the Second Deduction, as Cornford supposed (*PP* 194): for it combines results derived in the previous deductions, producing the new conception of unqualified becoming. I.3 is simply a third Deduction, combining results derived from the previous two. This is legitimate, since the previous Deductions, incompatible as they are, derive from one and the same hypothesis, that Unity is. Therefore, any consequence so far adduced may be applied.

Being and Not Being in Time (155e)

If I.1 is to be reconciled with I.2, Unity must sometimes have a share of Being, since it is, and sometimes not have a share of Being, since it is *just* one. This defines coming to be and ceasing to be: for to come to be is to get a share of Being, and to cease to be is to get rid of it or lose it. Thus, since Unity both takes and lets go of Being, it comes to be and ceases to be (156a-b). The language here parallels the description of coming to be in time as letting go of the now and grasping the after (152c). But letting go of the now is an element in coming to be; letting go of Being defines ceasing to be. Once again, there is an element of play in this. But it is an element which distinguishes the now, which is in time, dividing past and future, from the instant, which will prove not to be in time at all.

The claim that Unity becomes because it is at one time but not at another is itself implicitly contradictory. We may say that Socrates is and is not, in that he exists at one time but not at another; but to extend this to Unity raises immediate difficulty. If there is a time such that Unity does not have Being at that time, then that time is; therefore, it is one. So Unity must be if the time when it is not is, and the argument of 152e-153b applies. So Unity must be when it is not, and the argument thus anticipates the result derived in III.1 at 162a: Unity, if it is not, is, and if it is, is not. This consequence had already been adumbrated in I.2: for Unity was there proved to be the same as the others, which have no unity at all, and by implication, no being (147b).

Becoming and Perishing (156a)

In I.2, Unity, as a thing which is, was proved to come to be in time. It is now shown to become a thing which is. Therefore, the present account implies that there is a becoming of becoming. Put otherwise, we deal here with becoming in an unqualified sense, sheer coming into being of what is not, whereas becoming in time is the most general kind of becoming in a qualified sense, becoming one thing after having been something else. Unqualified becoming is introduced to heal the contradiction between I.1 and I.2. But the contradiction infects the solution. Getting a share of Being implies letting go of Being, since Unity is not; letting go of Being implies getting a share of Being, since Unity is. To claim that a thing that both is and is not comes to be is equivalent to claiming that it perishes.[205] Cornford remarked that we should not be led to imagine that this passage, "offers some sort of Hegelian synthesis reconciling an antinomy" (*PP* 195). Quite so, for the 'synthesis' is no less logically defective than the incompatible elements it putatively reconciles.

Qualified Becoming and Perishing (156b)

Parmenides has defined a kind of coming to be and perishing that Aristotle was later to describe as unqualified, as distinct from the particular coming to be and perishing that occurs when a thing changes in respect to some character (*Phys.* V 225a 12-19), that is, a character distinct from being and not being. Parmenides, having derived unqualified becoming and perishing for Unity, proceeds to derive particular kinds of becoming and perishing. It has been agreed that Unity is both one and many, and that it comes to be and ceases to be. From this it is inferred that when Unity comes to be one it ceases to be many, and when it comes to be many it ceases to be one.

This is an unexpected result. Why are we to suppose that Unity ceases to be many in becoming one, or ceases to be one in becoming many?

Parmenides is assuming the principle enunciated in the *Phaedo* that everything that has an opposite can come to be only from its opposite:[206] given that one and many are opposites, they come to be from each other. A specific example is found in the treatment of Unity and time in the Second Deduction. Unity has come to be first of all the things that have number; therefore, those things must come to be later. But all of them, as having number, are one, and so contain parts of Unity; so in respect of continual generation of new parts, Unity is continually becoming many and just in that respect it is ceasing to be one (153a-b). On the other hand, since Unity has parts, it must come to be after all the other parts of it: out of many parts it comes to be one and whole (153c-d). So it becomes one and ceases to be many, and becomes many and ceases to be one.

Unqualified becoming of a thing that inherently becomes implies qualified becoming. To come to be Unity implies coming to be one, and anything that comes to be one in a qualified sense must have been many; alternately, if it ceases to be one, it must become many. Thus in I.2, Unity has come to be first of all the things that have number; but all of them, as having number, are one and thus contain parts of Unity; so in respect of continual generation of new parts, Unity is continually becoming many, and just in that respect, ceasing to be one (153a-b). On the other hand, since Unity has parts, it must come to be after all the other parts of it (153c-d). So it becomes one and ceases to be many, and becomes many and ceases to be one. If the Unity of I.2 becomes in an unqualified sense, what becomes implies qualified becoming, becoming in respect to change of character.

Yet it may be doubted that this reaches the core of the present inference. Parmenides has proved that there is unqualified becoming and perishing, and now infers a type of particular becoming and perishing, namely becoming one from many and many from one. This follows from the premises from which unqualified becoming and perishing were derived. Unity is an Idea. As an Idea, it excludes its own opposite, Plurality, and is therefore *just* one. As an Idea, it partakes of Being, and is therefore not only one but many. Since I.1 and I.2 both derive consequences for the Idea of Unity, those consequences being incompatible, it may be inferred that if an Idea of Unity comes to be, it comes to be *just* one, and that if it comes to be it comes to be many. If this contradiction is to be mediated by the introduction of time, it must follow that when Unity comes to be *just* one it ceases to be many, and when it comes to be it comes to be many and ceases to be *just* one. So it comes to be many as it ceases to be one, and comes to be one as it ceases to be many. If this is absurd—and it is—it is an absurdity that derives from the conjoint affirmation of I.1 and I.2. Unity combines qualified and particular becoming because it ever is just one and ever is both one and many, and ever is not and ever is in time.

Parmenides next infers that since Unity comes to be one and many, Unity must combine and separate. This implies reference not to time but to place (cf. *Phys.* VIII 260b 11-14): to be is to be somewhere, and therefore to come to be is to come to be somewhere. Unity, in becoming one, comes to be in one place: it is drawn together. Unity, in becoming many, comes to be in many places: it is drawn apart. So Unity both combines, as being drawn together, and separates, as being drawn apart, and both of these processes must be understood as going on together, reciprocally and in opposite senses. The comparison with Heraclitus is clear: "They do not realize that in being drawn apart from itself it is drawn together with itself; there is a back-stretched connection, as in the bow and the lyre."[207] But the jointure suggested here has in it little enough of the lyre: it is absurd, the product of contradiction. The world of I.3 is the world of Cratylus,[208]

> who finally did not think it right to say anything but only moved his finger, and criticised Heraclitus for saying that it is impossible to step twice into the same river; for *he* thought one could not do it even once.

Similarly, since Unity is both like and unlike (147c-148d), it must come to be like and unlike, and larger, smaller, and equal (149e-151e), whence it follows, since it combines and separates, that it grows and diminishes and is made e-qual.[209]

Motion and Rest (156c)

Furthermore, Unity must be both in motion and at rest (145e-146a), and the passage from rest to motion or from motion to rest implies change. When it is changing, Unity can be in neither state: it cannot change so as to be in motion while it is at rest, nor so as to be at rest while it is in motion (cf. *Phys.* VI 234a 34 - b 4). If something in time must be either in motion or at rest (cf. *Phys.* VI 234b 9), it must follow that Unity, when it changes, is not in time.

Given that motion and rest must be understood to occur together, recipro-cally and in opposite senses, this contradicts the claim that to be is to be in time, and Unity, at every stage of its existence, is not in time; for at every stage of its existence it is both in motion and at rest, and therefore changes. To introduce time as a mediator of the contradictions adduced in I.2 is to learn that time can-not mediate them. If to be is to be in time, Unity, if it is, is not.

The Instant (156c-e)

Assuming that Unity changes, since it is both in motion and at rest, when does it change? Not while at rest, nor while in time; for motion and rest occupy time (cf. *Phys.* VI 234b 9) but the change from motion to rest or rest to motion can occupy no time at all. Unity, therefore, must change at an instant, defined as that from which and that into which what is moved or at rest changes. In Aris-totle, the instant is a *limit* of motion and rest; it is here treated as that *in* which change occurs.

Aristotle defines the instant as specious: 'instant' refers to what has departed from its former condition in time imperceptible because of its smallness (*Phys.* IV 222b 15). That is, the Aristotelian instant is an extremely small duration, and thus in time, and a part of time. Aristotle rejects the concept of the instant as a primary *when* from which change begins: there is no such thing as a begin-ning of a process of change (*Phys.* VI 236a 14-15), since any first part of change assumed is divisible. So Aristotle dispenses with the instant by appeal to the potential infinite; to suppose that instants exist is to suppose that an infinite division has a last term, that it can be completed. This is consistent with Aris-totle's denial that change between contradictories implies a state that is both or neither (*Phys.* VI 235b 13-19, cf. VIII 262a 30-b 22). There is no moment at which the change occurs, only a period of time that may be as small as you please. But the Platonic Parmenides' account of the instant implies an acual infinite, for it implies that division can be carried through so as to determine a *first* part of an infinite sequence from which change proceeds. The Aristotelian account might have been framed with the argument of I.3 explicitly in mind.

Parmenides' account differs because it must. The qualified becoming involved in change between motion and rest derives from unqualified becoming involved in transition from being to not being and vice versa. That transition cannot be continuous, and qualifies Unity at every stage of its career.

The account Parmenides offers of the instant is in fact closely similar to Aristotle's account of the now. Aristotle, though he admits a specious instant, denies the specious present (*Phys.* VI 234a 1ff., 11ff.): the now is indivisible, that is, not a duration, since it is the extremity of the past, no part of the future being on that side of it, and the extremity of the future, no part of the past being on the other side of it. If the now were a duration, part of the past would be in the future and part of the future in the past. The now is the limit of past and future, and since it is so essentially, the now is indivisible. Because the now is a limit of time, time cannot be a series of moments or nows: for a limit implies something limited distinct from its limits (cf. *Phys.* VI 231b 7 ff., VIII 262a 30ff.). Therefore, nothing can be in motion or at rest in a now; indeed, if a thing could be either, it could be both (*Phys.* VI 234a 24ff., 234a 32 ff.). In a similar vein, Parmenides infers that nothing can be at rest or in motion at an instant. The instant, as distinct from Aristotle's specious instant, is a now in which change is supposed to occur.

The result is a restatement, at a level of ultimate metaphysical analysis, of a Zenonian paradox, which Aristotle presents as the Arrow:[210]

> Zeno's reasoning, however, is fallacious, when he says that if everything when it occupies an equal space is at rest, and if that which is in locomotion is always occupying such a space at any moment, the flying arrow is therefore motionless. This is false, for time is not composed of indivisible moments any more than any other magnitude is composed of indivisibles.

But by Parmenides' account, the arrow is neither in motion nor at rest in the instant, the now in which change occurs. If, then, time is composed of instants, the arrow when it is in motion is not in motion, and when it is at rest is not at rest. Aristotle locates the nub of the paradox precisely in the assumption that time is composed of moments, a claim he denies on the basis of his analysis of infinity as ever potential and never actual.[211] Parmenides' analysis implicitly contradicts that account, for unqualified becoming precludes continuity.

Neither because Both (156e-157b)

Unity changes from rest to motion in an instant; it is not then in time, nor is it in motion or at rest. The same analysis applies to all other changes. When Unity changes from being to ceasing to be, or from not being to coming to be, it is between certain kinds of motion and rest, and then neither is nor is not, and neither comes to be nor ceases to be. A way that both is and is not has issued in a way that neither is nor is not.

The analysis is extended: Unity is neither one nor many, combined nor separated, like nor unlike, becoming like nor unlike, large nor small nor equal, grows nor diminishes nor becomes equal.

The initial deduction in I.3 is overdetermined, in the sense that it can be derived either from the conjunction of I.1 and I.2, or from I.2 alone. If derived from the conjunction, the conclusion of I.3 shows that time will not mediate the contradiction, given an actual infinite. If derived from I.2, the conclusion of I.3 shows that I.2 implies the results of I.1, given an actual infinite.

II.1. Second Hypothesis, First Deduction (157b-159b)

We are now to consider what follows for the others, if Unity exists. It was proved in I.2 that things other than Unity exist, since Unity, if it is, is in another (145d-e, cf. 148d). So the existence of others follows from the hypothesis that Unity is. Since to be and to be one are equivalent, things other than Unity, since they are, must be one; therefore, they participate in Unity. II.1 will show that the others satisfy a necessary condition of participation, because they are, collectively and distributively, a whole of parts. Yet is also has been agreed that other things, if they participate in Unity, are separate from it; that Unity, because it is what it is to be one, excludes its own opposite, Plurality; and that participation implies that Ideas must be in their participants in whole or in part. The combination of these agreements will lead to incompatible deductions in II.1 and II.2.

II.1 proves that things other than Unity have the properties attributed to Unity in I.2. Unity was there proved to be, not only what it is to be one, but one thing, a whole of parts (142c-d). It is now proved that the others are wholes of parts, and participate in Unity.

Part and Whole (157b-158a)

Since the others are other than Unity, Unity is not the others; but the others must partake of Unity, because they have parts. For if they did not have parts, then, since they are and therefore are one, they would be completely one, and so not other than Unity. At 158a-b it is shown that if the others were without parts, they would be Unity.

That things other than Unity have parts is a direct consequence of I.2: if other things are, they are one (142c-d), are different from Unity (146d), and have more, fewer, and equal measures to Unity (151b-e).

Parmenides proceeds to argue that the whole of which the parts are parts must be one thing composed of many parts; for each part must be part of a whole, not of a plurality. This proposition might have been taken as true by definition: parts are parts of a whole and a whole is that from which no part is absent (137c-d). Instead, the proposition is here established by indirect proof, a proof whose function is to introduce a concept of plurality that is devoid of wholeness and therefore of unity. That concept will prove important in what follows.

Assume that there is a part that is part of a plurality but not of a whole. If it is part of a plurality, it is part of *all* of that plurality. But if it is part of all of a plurality, it is part of itself, and this is impossible.

The argument appears to involve a blatant fallacy of division, proceeding from "part of all" to "part of each." In fact, it does not and indeed cannot involve such a fallacy, since the plurality in question, ex hypothesi, is not a whole, and therefore cannot be taken collectively. If x is part of *all* of a plurality, and if that plurality is devoid of wholeness, then that plurality must be taken only distributively; but then, x must be part of *each* member of the plurality if it is part of all. It follows that x is part of itself, since to say that x is part of a plurality is to say that x is a member of that plurality. The argument is similar to that of 145c-d, where it was shown that Unity as a whole cannot be *in* all its parts, since (if we abstract the character of wholeness from all the parts) all the parts are simply every part, and Unity as a whole cannot be in every part because it cannot as a whole be in any part. In general, the notion of a plurality without wholeness implies a multitude of which nothing can be a part. Therefore, things other than Unity cannot be parts of such a plurality. The argument may be compared with that of the *Sophist* (235d, trans. Cornford):

> Whenever a thing comes into being, at that moment it has come to be as a whole; accordingly, if you do not reckon unity or wholeness among real things, you have no right to speak of being or coming-into-being as having any existence. . . . And further, what is not a whole cannot have any definite number either; for if a thing has a definite number, it must amount to that number, whatever it may be, as a whole.

Parmenides goes on to suggest that since the parts of things other than Unity are not parts of a plurality, nor of an 'all' construed distributively, then are parts of a single Idea, the Idea of Wholeness. So things other than Unity, insofar as they have parts, partake of Wholeness and Unity (cf. *Sophist* 245a-c), and since they cannot be members of a bare plurality, they must admit of being taken collectively, as one complete whole.

Everything other than Unity, and therefore every part of everything other than Unity, has a share of Unity. For if it did not have a share of Unity, it would, as one, be Unity, and nothing but Unity itself can be Unity. In short, to be is to be one; to be one is either to be what it is to be one — that is, Unity — or it is to have what it is to be one—that is, to partake of Unity. If a plurality of things have a character, they cannot be that character. Since Unity, as an Idea, excludes its own opposite, it cannot be many. If things other than Unity are one, they must also be many, since if they were not, they would be just one, and there could then be no difference between them and what it is to be one. It follows that the others have parts, and those parts must be one no less than the wholes of which they are parts: for to be and to be one are equivalent. In short, things other than Unity are one, in whole and in part. Thus the others, both as wholes and part by part, have a share of Unity.

Limit and Unlimited (158b-d)

Since the others partake of Unity, they are different from Unity, and therefore many; if they were neither one nor many, they would be nothing. This is incompatible with 146e-147b.

From this it is inferred that the others must be unlimited in multitude, and this in virtue of their own nature. For if the others participate in Unity, the Dilemma of Participation implies that Unity, in whole or in part, is in them. If then we inquire what the others are just in themselves, apart from what they participate in, we find an element that is not one and, by the very terms in which the analysis proceeds, has no share of Unity. This element has been foreshadowed in the analysis of a plurality without wholeness or Unity at 157c-d.

Put briefly, things that participate in Unity must also participate in Plurality, and if we consider them apart from Unity, only bare plurality is left. (cf. 143a)

The abstraction produces surprising results. If by reflection we subtract the fewest we can from the resulting multiplicity—a subtraction performed *per impossibile*—we find what is left to be pure multitude without any unity at all. That is, we are left with a multitude without parts or members, a multitude that cannot itself be a whole. It is unlimited, but its unlimitedness is of no ordinary kind: for it cannot be infinite either as continuous or successive, since both kinds of infinity imply unity and wholeness. The unlimited multiplicity of II.1 may be compared with the unlimitedness of Unity in I.1 (137d): it cannot be gone through because it is not of its nature to be gone through, as the voice is invisible. The otherness of things other than Unity, as it turns out, is strictly analogous to the unity of what is one and nothing else.

But if the others, considered as "the nature different from the characteristic" of Unity, are unlimited in multitude, they are, as parts of a whole, limited relative to that whole, as the whole is limited relative to them. Limit is a product of unity and difference. So it is that, for things other than Unity, their communion with—that is, their participation in—Unity produces in them something that provides a limit for them relative to each other. Their own nature provides unlimitedness.

So things other than Unity, as wholes and part by part, have a share of Limit and Unlimited.

This account, it will be observed, suggests that otherness is indeterminate matter, to which Unity, as a principle of determination, stands as form. It is the root of Aristotle's claim that Plato adopted a Dyad, of the Great and the Small, as matter.

Likeness and Unlikeness (158e-159a)

Things other than Unity are both like and unlike each other and themselves. Insofar as they are limited and unlimited, they are in both respects the same and therefore like. But limit and unlimitedness are opposites, and most unlike. Therefore, in respect to limit and unlimitedness taken singly, the others are like each other and themselves; in respect to both taken together, the others are unlike each other and themselves, as qualified by opposites. The argument may be compared with 139e-140b.

Other Characters (159a-b)

Because the others are both like and unlike, they are same and different, in motion and at rest, and qualified by all opposite affections; a fuller list will be found at 160a, in the denial of this result in II.2. The arguments for the result in II.1 may be supplied from I.2.

Aristotle and the Parmenides

It is at this point apposite to remark that perhaps the single most fundamental and striking of Aristotle's reports about Plato's doctrines was drawn from the *Parmenides,* and specifically, from the discussion of Unity, or 'the One,' in its relation to the Others. At *Metaphysics* I 988a 8-13, Aristotle reports of Plato:

> It is evident from what has been said that he has used only two causes, that of the essence and the material cause (for the Forms are the causes of the essence of all other things, and the One is the cause of the essence of the Forms); it is evident what the underlying matter is, of which the Forms are predicated in the case of sensible things, and the One in the case of the Forms, viz. that this is a dyad, the great and the small.

Now, the first thing to be observed about this passage is that it is not a reference to the *Philebus,* a suggestion at least as old as Porphyry.[212] At *Philebus* 23c-30e, Socrates offers a doctrine of Four Kinds of things in the All: Limit, Unlimited, the Mixture of these, and the Cause of the Mixture. The Unlimited, τὸ ἄπειρον, is a principle that everywhere admits the More and the Less as its distinguishing feature, and that contains such indeterminate principles as the hotter and colder, wetter and drier, quicker and slower, greater and smaller, and so on (25c, df. 24c-d). The Unlimited appears to be unlimited both internally and in extent: between any two divisions a third is possible, and there is an extreme beyond any extremity. For example, there is no highest or lowest temperature, and between any two temperatures there is a temperature. Limit stands as the opposite of the Unlimited. It is, "Equality and the equal, the double, and anything which is a number relative to a number or a measure to a measure." (25a-b). Limit and Unlimited combined to produce the Mixed Class, (27b). To illustrate: a temperature of 75 degrees is a member of the Mixed Class: it derives from the hotter and colder and from limit, that is, number and measure.

The More and the Less of the *Philebus* plainly has a merely verbal resemblance to Aristotle's reference to the Great and the Small. The *Philebus* says nothing about Ideas, or their essence, being caused by the One. The class defined by the More and the Less is quantitatively indeterminate, but qualitatively determinate: it answers to continua of temperature, speed, size, and so on. Therefore, the More and the Less does not match Aristotle's Great and Small in respect to its most crucial characteristic: its thoroughgoing indeterminism, its lack of any characteristics at all. Equally important, Aristotle in the passage quoted claims that Plato recognized only the formal and material causes, and by implication denies that he recognized any others—that is, denied that he recognized efficiency and finality. Aristotle could hardly therefore have had in mind the *Philebus*, where one of the Kinds is the Cause of the Mixture, and explicitly identified as Wisdom, Mind, and Soul (30c).

Aristotle claims that Plato thought that the material principle of *all* things —both of Ideas and phenomena—was the Great and the Small, a Dyad. So both Ideas and phenomena have a substrate, and it is the same substrate. In the *Physics* (*Phys.* IV 209b 5 - 210a 1), Aristotle says that, for Plato, the participant was matter, which in the *Timaeus* is identified with space, but in the "unwritten doctrines" with the Great and the Small. The passage is important enough to quote at some length (*Phys.* IV 209b 5 - 210a 1):

> Now if place is what primarily contains each body, it would be a limit. . . . If, then, we look at the question in this way the place of a thing is its form. But if we regard the place as the *extension* of the magnitude, it is the matter. For this is different from the magnitude: it is what is contained and defined by the form, as by a bounding plane. Matter or the indeterminate is of this nature; when the boundary and attributes of a sphere are taken away, nothing but the matter is left.
>
> This is why Plato in the *Timaeus* says that matter and space are the same; for the 'participant' and space are identical. (It is true, indeed, that the account he gives there of the 'participant' is different from what he says in his so-called 'unwritten teaching.' Nevertheless he did identify place and space.)
>
> Plato . . . ought to tell us why the forms and the numbers are not in place, if 'what participates' is place—whether what participates is the Great and the Small or the matter, as he called it in writing the *Timaeus*.

It would appear that, although the *Timaeus* is taken to identify the participant with space, the "so-called unwritten doctrines" identified the participant as the Great and Small, or the Dyad, which is matter to which the One stands as form (*Phys.* I 187a 17). Elsewhere in the *Physics* (I 192a 6-12), Aristotle both distinguishes the Great from the Small and claims that whether taken separately or together, they are to be identified with not-being. The distinction between them is explicated by his later remark that they are two infinites (*Phys.* III 203a 16, cf. 206b 27), and this is based on *Parmenides* 142c-145a. The infinity of the Small is the infinity of what is divisible into divisibiles that are infinitely divisible, the infinite partibility of Unity; the infinity of the Great is the infinity of Unity corresponding to the infinite and ever-increasing succession of Numbers; and to both these infinites, Unity stands as a whole and limit, stands, in short, as form. The fact that there are two infinites is by itself sufficient to explain Aristotle's description of a Dyad; but two or the dyad, δυάς, is put in opposition to Unity and treated as a condition of the existence of things other than Unity in I.2; for example, at 143c-d and in the deduction on Contact at 149c-d. In respect to 143c-d, we recall Aristotle's remark that, "The units in 2 must each have come from a prior 2, but this is impossible."[213] Plato's reason for making the other entity beside the One a dyad was due to his belief that the numbers, except for the primes, could be produced out of the Dyad as out of some plastic material (987b 33 ff.); so, cooky-cutter implications apart, *Parmenides* 143a ff., *if* taken as a generation of number, does not produce the primes, and requires the notion of duality to proceed. Aristotle later objects that, "the very elements—the great and the small—seem to cry out against the violence that is done to them; for they cannot in any way generate numbers other than those got from 1 by doubling";[214] so in *Parmenides* 142c-e, the division produces parts only of the order of $1/2^n$. The fact that Unity has parts that are or correspond to the numbers, and this in the context of a discussion limited to Ideas (135d-e), doubtless led Aristotle to his conclusion that Ideas are numbers (*Meta.* I 991b 9-20), and his consequent assimilation of Platonism to Pythagoreanism (*Meta.* I 987b 22-30), which explains his denial, in the teeth of the evidence, of efficiency and finality in Plato's philosophy. Indeed, Aristotle, relying on the *Parmenides,* appears to have anticipated the ambiguity theorists in his interpretation of it. "Evidently, if there is a One-itself and this is a first principle, 'one' is being used in more than one sense; for otherwise the theory is impossible" (*Meta.* I 992a 9).

We have already seen that Aristotle's criticisms of Plato derive in large measure from the *Parmenides*; that is why they swing like a gate between the claim that the Ideas, being separate, are unknowable and irrelevant to the sensible world, and the claim that they are themselves in sensibles and therefore are a kind of sensible. The hinge of that gate is the Dilemma of Participation. Plato's formulation of that Dilemma was aporematic: but minimally, when thought through, it indicates that participation cannot be a relation between substantially independent terms. Aristotle, assuming the independent and primary reality of the sensible world, and facing a theory he knew to require separated and self-subsistent Forms, found that the knots could not be untied.

But beyond his criticisms, Aristotle's reports about Plato's beliefs respecting the One and the Great and the Small derive from the *Parmenides* as well, a fact that has been overlooked because the concluding part of the *Parmenides* has been persistently misunderstood when it has not been insistently ignored. The result has been a perverse tendency to claim that Plato privately taught a kind of esoteric doctrine quite unlike anything exhibited by the dialogues. But the final part of the *Parmenides* differs from the doctrines of the dialogues, not because it is esoteric, but because it is aporematic. This is why Aristotle at one point in the *Physics* (IV 109b 14-15) refers to the "so-called unwritten doctrines"—so-called because, Aristotle thought, the *Parmenides* does not state a doctrine but implies a doctrine, and Aristotle, interpreting the dialogue, tells us what that doctrine is.

To this it must be added that there is much truth in Aristotle's interpretation—certainly much more than is to be found in the work of interpreters who have lacked a gift for metaphysics. Let it be supposed that any given participant, whether sensible or Idea, has a character by reason of its participation in an Idea, and exists separately from that Idea. It follows that each participant, whether sensible or Idea, must have a core of independent reality apart from its participation; in short, each participant, whether sensible or Idea, must be very like what Aristotle called matter in the sense of substrate.

But this raises an interesting problem. If Being and Unity are, as the *Parmenides* supposes, themselves Ideas of which other things partake, it must follow that the substrate, if it is, is one, and that if it is not one, it is nothing. Here is the basis of Aristotle's insistent claim that the Dyad is not-being, a claim well-founded on passages in the *Parmenides*.[215] The *Timaeus* solves the problem for the relation of sensibles to Ideas, as Aristotle in the *Categories* and *Metaphysics* never succeeded in doing. But it can scarcely be said that the solution of the *Timaeus*, which consists in denying the substantiality of sensibles, can be extended to Ideas. Nor can it be said that the *Sophist* solves the problem for the relation of Ideas among themselves. But it may well be said that the necessity of the ontology of the *Timaeus* is given indirect proof in the hypotheses that conclude the *Parmenides*; and if Plato did not write the *Philosopher*, we may well suppose that the *Parmenides* contains news about what the philosopher cannot say.

In any case, Aristotle got a great many important things right. The Great and the Small is the participant of the *Parmenides*: it is things other than Unity which, if they are to be, must have Unity. There is indeed a difference between that participant and the Space of the *Timaeus*, which is (not matter, but) the eternal Receptacle that mirrors forth the eternal Ideas. The Great and the Small is a substrate. It participates in 'the One.' It is matter, to which Unity stands relatively as limit or form. It is not-being, though not in the sense of privation. And the substrate of Ideas and the substrate of sensibles is, since indistinguishable, the same. Aristotle, one may respectfully suggest, was a good deal closer to understanding the *Parmenides* than any important commentator since.

II.2. Second Hypothesis, Second Deduction (159b-160b)

II.1 proved that Unity, as an Idea, can be participated in by things other than Unity. But if Unity excludes plurality, it cannot be participated in. The consequences of this for the others are now adduced. II.2 is the counterpart of I.1, as II.1 was the counterpart of I.2.

Unity must be separate from things other than Unity, and the others separate from it. For there is nothing other than Unity and other than the others (cf. 151a); therefore, there is nothing different from them, in which same thing Unity and the others can be. At 151b, this was a reason for holding that Unity and the others must be in each other, and so not separate. It is here offered as a reason for holding that Unity and the others are never in the same thing, and therefore separate. This follows from 139a-b; Unity cannot be in the same thing because it can neither be in itself nor in another. For the Idea of Unity is *just* one.

It follows that the separation between Unity and the others is radical. Since Unity excludes all plurality, it cannot be in anything, in whole or in parts. But by the Dilemma of Participation, Unity, if it is participated in, must be in its participants in whole or in part. Since the others are separate from Unity (cf. 130a-b), they cannot participate in Unity and are in no way one.

Since the others are not one, neither are they many: for each would be one part of a whole if they were many (157c-d). This implies that the absence of Unity deprives the others of limit: they constitute a multiplicity, which cannot be many as either continuous or successive, and therefore cannot be or have a number (158c-d). Number, that is, is a plurality of units, and the others cannot be understood to be many ones; this conclusion was first drawn at 147a-b, where, if the others had a number, they would not completely be not one. But the conclusion was there derived because the others are not different from Unity and so not separate from Unity; it is derived on just the opposite ground here.

Things other than Unity are neither like nor unlike either Unity or themselves. If they were, they would have two opposite characteristics, and it is impossible for what does not have a share of Unity to have a share of two things; that is, if things other than Unity do not have a share of Unity, they cannot have a share of anything. If they had a share of anything, they would have a share of Unity; the argument, it will be observed, is a reductio. It implies that things other than Unity have no share of anything at all.

That is, the consequences that follow for things other than Unity in II.2 are precisely those that follow for Unity itself in I.1. Things other than Unity cannot be even to the degree of being many, because they cannot be to the degree of being one.

Conclusion of the First and Second Hypotheses (160b)

This conclusion is not merely ostensible, or the result of ambiguity. It literally follows, and is genuinely paradoxical.

Unity is all things relative to itself, for in I.2 Unity proved to have all of a list of highly general and opposite characters, and to be the same as things other than itself. Unity is not even one, or nothing, relative to itself, for in I.1 Unity proved neither to be nor be one. Unity is all things relative to things other than Unity, for in II.1 those things are shown to have all the opposites that Unity in I.2 had; as many things as pertain to the others do indeed pertain to Unity (155e), and things other than Unity in II.1 are equivalent to Unity in I.2. Finally, Unity is not one, or nothing, relative to things other than Unity, for in II.2 things other than Unity are equivalent to Unity in I.1, and have no characteristics whatever, since they are not one.

This structure is contradictory and absurd. It is determined by the explicit premise that an Idea of Unity exists, and by the assumptions, first put earlier, that no Idea can be qualified by its own opposite, that if there is participation there is participation in the whole of an Idea or part, and that given multiple participation, parts of Ideas are in participants. Given the exclusion of opposites, Unity, what it is to be one, cannot be many; given the Dilemma of Participation, it cannot then be participated in nor can it participate. But given that Unity is, it participates in Being, and whatever is is one. Therefore, Unity is many, and has the unity appropriate to a whole of parts, since part of Being is part of it, and every part which is is one part. I.1 and II.2 exhibit the result of applying this account of participation to an Idea that excludes plurality. I.2 and II.1 show the result of applying this account of participation to an Idea that does not exlude its opposite. The resulting contradiction is coimplicatory, since I.1 both implies and is implied in I.2: an Idea of Unity must be what it has and have what it is, if the Dilemma of Participation is true. In the same way, I.1 and I.2 severally imply and mutually contradict II.1 and II.2, which contradict each other. Since the existence of things other than Unity is implied by the existence of Unity, those things must be one if Unity is; since things other than Unity cannot participate in what it is to be one and admits no plurality, things other than Unity cannot be one.

The point of this structure, so stated, is relatively clear; yet it has often been misunderstood or ignored. The reason lies in I.2, and the baffling variety and complexity of its arguments. I.2 offers, in effect, a Transcendental Deduction, proving that Unity, if it participates in Being and is thus a whole of parts, has the most general characteristics of an object in the sensible world: it has shape and place, is in motion and in time.

Yet despite its complexity, I.2 serves a simple, and important, dialectical purpose. The argument of the physical deductions respecting shape, place, motion, and time depends on the Dilemma of Participation, a dilemma which was first introduced in criticism of the theory of Ideas and which issues in the proposition that to be is to be in time. Underlying that Dilemma is the assumption that participation, if it is possible, is a relation between substantially independent entities, a result implied initially by the agreement that sensibles are just what we see them to be. Because hair, mud, and dirt are worthless and trivial, they are endowed with independent and substantial reality. The assumption of distinct and independent reality is, of course, more applicable to the relations of Ideas to sensibles, just as Aristotle says (*Meta.* VII 13). The concluding portion of the *Parmenides* raises the aporiai put by Parmenides in criticism of the participation of sensibles in Ideas to the participation of Ideas among themselves.

I.2, proceeding from the Dilemma of Participation, proves that Ideas, and specifically the Idea of Unity, if they have independent and substantial existence and yet participate in each other, have the sort of reality appropriate to sensibles: they are in place, in time, subject to change. But even if the Dilemma of Participation were removed, even, that is, if the claim that the part/whole relation is needed to explicate the relation of Ideas to sensibles or of Ideas to Ideas, as a real relation binding distinct entities, the contradiction involved in positing the existence of an Idea of Unity would remain. If the Idea is what it is to *be* one, in a way that excludes all plurality, it seems clear that it cannot participate or be participated in, whether or not participation is construed as a relation of part and whole. If the Idea is one in such a way as to *have* unity, Zeno's paradoxes are unresolved, and this at the most general level of discourse, because Unity is one thing among many things which are one.

But this result is not stated: it is shown. The structure of the concluding part of the *Parmenides*, like the structure of the dialogue as a whole, is aporetic. It is meant to force the reader to isolate and reflect on the assumptions that have produced such cumulative absurdity.

The obvious course is to deny the hypothesis on which the Deductions proceed: that Unity is. If I.2 is taken in conjunction with I.1, neither Ideas nor, by derivation in II.1 and II.2, sensibles can have any reality at all.

But denial of the fundamental hypothesis will prove no more tenable than its affirmation. This need hardly be surprising, since I.1 explicitly implied that Unity, if it is, is not, and I.2 implied that Unity, if it is, is the same as things other than Unity that have no unity at all and, given that to be and to be one are equivalent, therefore are not. It is a law of logic that the contradictory of self-contradictory propositions is true; there, the contradictory of a self-contradictory proposition will be shown to be self-contradictory. The structure of the Hypotheses is genuinely paradoxical, in the sense that whether the hypothesis that Unity is is affirmed or denied, the result is absurdity. The solution of the massive perplexity here offered must lie elsewhere. It is not part of the business of the *Parmenides* to supply it.

III.1. Third Hypothesis, First Deduction (160b-163b)

The assumption that Unity exists has led to multiple contradictions, summarized at 160b. It would seem therefore to follow, and follow logically, that Unity does not exist. That is, if the hypothesis that Unity is implies contradictions that, Unity is not is a necessary truth: for the contradictory of a self-contradictory proposition is necessarily true. But here the result is otherwise.

Not-being as an Idea

Parmenides had begun the dialectical exercise by suggesting that various Ideas might be fit subjects of hypothesis, that is, might be assumed either to be or not to be, with consequences reckoned for themselves and for the others. Parmenides has chosen Unity, but he mentions other candidates as well: Plurality, Likeness, Unlikeness, Motion, Rest, Coming to be, Ceasing to be, Being and Not-being (136a-b). These terms are Ideas (135e-136a), and at this point, all of those Ideas have been proved to be partaken of by Unity, if Unity is. The multiple contradictions that have been derived are due ultimately to the fact that Unity, as an Idea, is what it is to be one and therefore excludes all plurality, and yet also as an Idea exists: for by the governing theory of 129, to say that Unity exists is to imply that it participates in Being (142b-c), a consequence that in turn implies that it is subject to the Dilemma of Participation (144c).

The conclusion of the affirmative hypotheses at 160b really does follow, and really is absurd. The logical result, according to any normal form, is that there is no Idea of Unity; but this admirable result falls foul of the fact that, just as the existence of Unity implies participation in the Idea of Being, the nonexistence of Unity implies participation in Not-being. In consequence, denial of the existence of Unity will turn out to be no less absurd than its affirmation.

That an Idea of Not-being is required if there is an Idea of Being follows not only textually (136b) but dialectically: Being and Not-being are opposites; where things are qualified by opposites, those opposites are Ideas; and Unity, if it is, both is and is not. So if Unity is, Unity has a share of Being; therefore, if Unity is not, Unity has a share of Not-being. This explains why Not-being is mentioned as an Idea at 136b.

The notion that there should be an Idea of Being is at least plausible. In the *Sophist* (243d-244b), the Eleatic Stranger criticizes the Pluralists of the fifth century on just this point. Suppose you say there are two real things, for example, the hot and the cold. What do you mean by 'is'? If you call one of the two things 'being,' both cannot be real, for then there will be only one real thing and now two; but if you call both together 'being,' then the two would be one. But if Being is a third thing beside the other two, then the All or sum of things is not two but three. That this is the Stranger's own solution is indicated by his doctrine of the Communion of Kinds. Being is a kind that communes or mingles with other kinds, and is distinct from them (154d, 257a). The argument, *mutatis mutandis*, is the One over Many.

But if an Idea of Being, what it is to be, *ens commune*, seems straightforward enough, an Idea of Not-being as its opposite seems downright absurd. That Idea, since it is not what it is to be but what it is not to be, must, it would seem, exclude Being; that is, it cannot be qualified by its opposite. So Not-being is not. On the other hand, ex hypothesi, it is an Idea; to be an Idea is to be; therefore, Not-being is. In the result, the assumption that Unity is not will be found to replicate the assumption that Unity is.

We are now to ask, if Unity is not, what follows for Unity Hypothesis I, examining the consequences for Unity if Unity is, had issued in a Parmenidean structure. I.1 resulted in a Way which Is Not; I.2 in a Way which (putatively) Is; I.3 in a Way which Is and Is not. In III.1, that Unity is not will be found to imply that Unity is, by arguments parallel to those in I.2. But given that Unity is not, this implies that Unity both is and is not, by reason of participation, with results similar to those of I.3. III.2, on the other hand, will show that to deny being to Not-being is to embrace the meaningless.

That 'Unity is not' either does or does not admit of significant denial. It it does, Hypothesis III implies that Unity is, and therefore both is and is not; thus III.1. If it does not, Hypothesis III shows that it is meaningless; thus III.2. In short, Hypotheses I and III are either equivalent or equally meaningless.

Existence as a Predicate

If the force of the hypotheses that follow is to be felt, it is necessary to remove grounds for misunderstanding. An Idea, it will be said, is a predicate; existence is not a predicate; therefore, whatever else the negative hypotheses of the *Parmenides* indicate, they indicate a sequence of confusions about existence that may be resolved by elementary quantification theory.

The claim that existence is not a predicate is not a claim about surface grammar: the statement "Lions exist" links a grammatical subject to a grammatical predicate in just the same way as "Lions run." But whereas it makes sense, logically, to ask the quantity of "Lions run"—all of them, or only some?—we feel as if we have somehow missed a step if we are asked whether all lions exist, or only some. And on reflection, we see why. That lions exist is equivalent to "There are lions," which is in turn equivalent to "Something is a lion." In the latter statement, 'lion' appears, not as grammatical subject, but as predicate, and we are not in the least tempted to ask the quantity of the statement because it is already quantified. "Something is a lion" is equivalent to the claim that the predicate 'lion' is true of at least one thing. "Nothing is a lion," *per contra*, is equivalent to the claim that the predicate 'lion' is not true of at least one thing. As Russell remarked, the notion of existence is derived immediately from the notion, "sometimes true."[216]

This is the basis of Russell's theory of descriptions, a theory fashioned to refute the Meinongian claim that there must be tame Tigers in Tennessee if we say of them that there aren't. It is also an important foundation of linguistic philosophy and the abandonment of metaphysics: if existence is analyzed in terms of the truth of predicative statements, there is scant reason to pursue the invitation of Aristotle's claim that there is a science that studies being qua being and the attributes that essentially pertain to it. Yet Aristotle himself pointed out that one sense of being is truth; he also suggested that if is a derivative sense (*Meta.* VI. 4):

> That which is in the sense of being true, or is not in the sense of being false, depends on combination and separation. . . . But since the combination and separation are in thought and not in the things, and that which is in this sense is a different sort of 'being' from the things that are in the full sense, that which is in the sense of being true must be dismissed. . . . Let us consider the causes and principles of being itself *qua* being.

The issue of the causes and principles of being is the issue of ontological priority, and of what there is. For Aristotle, what is in the primary sense is substance, for Plato, Ideas. For both Plato and Aristotle, what is and is ontologically prior is individual. A Platonic Idea is no more a 'predicate' than an Aristotelian substance: it is neither said of something nor is it the ontic shadow of what is said of something. It is not a spiritualized donut with a hole in its middle, waiting to be saturated or filled or 'instantiated'; it exists in its own right, without reference to the things that participate in it.

The quantificational account of existence implies that no individual can meaningfully be said to exist or not to exist. On this view, then, neither the hypothesis that Unity is or that Unity is not makes any sense at all. But that this conception of existence is too restrictive may easily be shown: there is a sense of existence or reality that applies to individuals; and it is prior to the quantificational sense in that it is a criterion for its use.

The point may be brought out by example. It is surely true that some Greek gods were adulterous. For example, Zeus was adulterous. It would seem then that,

(∃x) (x was a Greek god and x was adulterous)

But this commits us to,

(∃x) (x was a Greek god)

that is, to the claim that Greek gods once existed. And we presumably need to be able to deny this even while affirming that they were adulterous.

Suppose then we try another form. We might say,

(x) (x is a Greek god ⊃ (∃y) (y is a Greek god and y is adulterous))

The horseshoe relieves us of existential commitment — but why do we use it? We use it precisely because we do not believe that Greek gods exist; we would reject it as too weak for the claim that some Greek men are adulterous precisely because we believe that there are Greek men. In short, we use a conception of existence or reality as a criterion for determining when we will use the existential quantifier *simpliciter* and when we will condition it. And that is equally so when we say that "Some Greek gods were adulterous" is "true in Homer," but not really true; or that a genuine existential claim must allow of instantiation with genuine proper names—that is, names with real bearers, and dismiss Zeus. The existential quantifier cannot be identified with existence or reality because existence or reality is a criterion for its use. The denial that Greek gods exist implies that no real thing exists because of or by reason of a Greek god: they do not affect the career of the world. The issue is one of "the causes and principles of being."

The problems of Not-being that trouble the concluding hypotheses of the *Parmenides* will not vanish on an instant when quantification theory appears. They represent metaphysical cruces requiring solution—and are not here solved.

Two Concepts of Truth

III.1 will undertake to prove that Unity, if it is not, is, a proposition that follows both dialectically and from the fact that Unity is an Idea, an essence or nature, what it is to be one. In this connection it is helpful to observe that Aristotle distinguishes two concepts of truth, combination and contact, whose opposites are respectively falsehood and ignorance. This distinction bears directly on the negative hypotheses in the *Parmenides*, though it is nowhere mentioned there. Aristotle's reason for denying that negation can be identified with falsehood derives from the *Sophist* (263b-d) (*Meta.* IX 1051a 34- b5):

> The terms 'being' and 'non-being' are employed firstly with reference to the categories and secondly with reference to the potency or actuality of these or their non-potency or non-actuality, and thirdly in the sense of true and false. This depends, on the side of the objects, on their being combined or separated, so that he who thinks the separated to be separated and the combined to be combined has the truth, while he whose thought is in a state contrary to that of the objects is in error.

So with respect to composite things, truth consists in combination and separation, and its opposite is falsehood. It is otherwise, however, with that truth which consists, not in combination and separation, but in contact (*Meta.* IX 1051b 18 - 1052a 4):

> But with regard to incomposites, what is being or not being, and truth or falsity? A thing of this sort is not composite, so as to 'be' when it is compounded and not to 'be' if it is separated, like "that the wood is white" or "that the diagonal is incommensurable"; nor will truth and falsity still be present in the same way as in the previous cases. In fact, as truth is not the same in these cases, so also being is not the same; but (a) truth or falsity is as follows—contact and assertion are truth (assertion not being the same as affirmation), and ignorance is non-contact. For it is not possible to be in *error* regarding what a thing is, save

in an accidental sense. . . . it is not possible to be in error, but only to
know them or not to know them. But we do inquire what they are, viz.
whether they are of such and such a nature or not. (b) As regards the
'being' that answers to truth and the 'non-being' that answers to falsity,
in one case there is truth if the subject and the attribute are really combined, and falsity if they are not combined; in the other case, if the object is existent it exists in a particular way, and if it does not exist in
this way it does not exist at all. And truth means knowing these objects,
and falsity does not exist, nor error, but only ignorance—and not an
ignorance which is like blindness; for blindness is akin to a total absence
of the faculty of thinking.

The source of this is *Republic* V: the opposite of truth and reality is not falsehood but ignorance, which corresponds to not-being, lack of any object for the
mind to grasp. The converse of this is the claim of the *Parmenides* (132b-c)
that a thought, to be a thought, must be of something which is. If then we assume
that Unity is an Idea, an essence or nature, to think of Unity that it is not is to
think—confusedly perhaps, unclearly it may be, but to think—of what is. To
show that there is no Idea of Unity would require a reductive analysis, an analysis that would exhibit that the work done by this putative Idea is in fact done
otherwise. A similar sort of reductive analysis is implied, of course, in the typical
claim of the early and middle dialogue that Virtue is Knowledge.

Not-being and Difference

It is sometimes suggested that the *Parmenides* generally, and the negative Hypotheses in particular, raise problems which are solved in the *Sophist*, especially by
the doctrine that Being has no opposite and that Not-being is Difference. This is
untrue. In the first place, the *Sophist* does not solve problems of negation but
poses them, since its account of Not-being is incoherent. In the second place,
even if that account were not incoherent, it could not be applied to the *Parmenides*.

That the *Sophist* is incoherent on the subject of negation follows from its
identification of Not-being and Difference: for from this it follows that the negative existential and negative predicative statements must be analysed in terms of
negative identity statements. Perhaps, inelegantly, Theaetetus is not flying reduces to Theaetetus is different from everything which is flying. No such verbal
legerdemain will reduce "Unity is not." Nor is there anything but paradox in the
Sophist's claim that Being is not Sameness, that Sameness is the opposite of
Difference, and that Difference is Not-being; for incompatibility is a primitive
fact of negation, and this analysis cannot account for it.

The problems of Not-being in the *Parmenides* are not the same as those of
the *Sophist*. And the *Sophist*, no less than the *Parmenides*, is an aporetic dialogue (cf. 249d, 250e), with problems of contextual interpretation which have
yet to be solved. The attempt to find in it dogmatic assertions of doctrine with
respect to Being and Not-Being is a mistake.

i. The Nature of the Hypothesis (160b-d)

That Unity is not, εἰ ἓν μὴ ἔστιν, is different from and completely opposite to 'not Unity is not,' εἰ μὴ ἓν μὴ ἔστιν. How is this expression to be understood?

The subject is not "not-one = no-thing," as Cornford suggested (*PP* 219). This fits nothing in the context, and "Nothing is not" is compatible with, not opposite to, Unity is not. Again, εἰ μὴ ἕνα μὴ ἔστιν is not an ordinary way of expressing double negation, "Not the case that Unity is not": nor does this fit the context, which illustrates the point being made by contrast of the opposites Largeness and Smallness, rather than statement negation.

It would seem, then, that the expression μὴ ἕν means not-Unity (or not-one) in the sense which Aristotle characterizes as 'indefinite,' and thereby opposite, like not-man and not-just.[217] Presumably, not-Unity differs from Plurality in that it is more inclusive. Professor Ackrill remarks[218]

> While a number must be either equal or unequal to another Aristotle recognizes that there is an intermediate condition between justice and injustice (*Categories* 11b 38 - 12a 25). This would suggest the possibility that by 'not-just' he means (not 'unjust,' but) 'either unjust or in the middle condition between being just and being unjust.' Correspondingly, 'not-white' would mean (not 'black,' but) 'of some colour other than white.'

There is an intermediate condition between being one and being many, namely, coming to be one or coming to be many. One should not hasten, however, to suggest an analogy with the 'not-beauty' of the *Sophist* (257b), since the latter is part of the Different found among things which are.

"Unity is not" is a significant assertion, and this is exhibited by comparison. To say that Largeness is not and that Smallness is not is to say in each case that a different thing is not.[219] In the same way, "Unity is not" means something different from saying that other things are not, and we know what is meant. So what is meant is something knowable, and different from the others, whether it is said to be or not to be. These consequences are deduced from the bare claim that "Unity is not" is a meaningful or intelligible statement.

This account coheres with I.2. At 147d-e, meaning was analyzed in terms of naming: to use a name such as 'same' or 'different' is to use a name *for* something, and to name that of which it is the name and nothing else. So, in denying that Unity is, the word 'Unity' must name something even though Unity is said not to be. At 143a-b, Unity was conceived in abstraction from its own being, and found to be different from its being by virtue of Difference. This implied that Unity, Being, and Difference had been mentioned (143c), that they were numerable, and that as numerable they implied the existence of the numbers. Since each of the numbers is one, it was found to follow that Unity itself, conceived apart from its own being, was distributed to infinitely many things (144c-e).

ii. The This and the That (160d-161a)

Begin again from the beginning: if Unity is not, there must be knowledge of it, for otherwise, when someone said that Unity is not, we would not know what he meant—sound without sense. Next, since other things are different from Unity, Unity must be different from the others (cf. 146d). Therefore, Unity partakes of Difference, for when one says that Unity is different from other things, he does not mean the difference of the others, but the difference of *that*, Unity, from them.

"Unity is not" and "Largeness is not" deny the existence of different things, deny the existence of *this* rather than *that*. It follows that Unity partakes of Difference, and therefore of *this, that*, and so on. Cornford pointed out[220] that Parmenides here speaks (as it happens, ungrammatically when translated into English) in terms of possession or participation to avoid the natural locution, that Unity *is* these things—a locution that would suggest, contrary to hypothesis, that Unity is. But the periphrasis itself implies that Unity participates in Ideas such as Difference, and Unity has already been found to be knowable. In this III.1 contradicts I.1 and agrees with I.2.

iii. Likeness and Unlikeness (161a-c)

If Unity is not, it has unlikeness to the others and likeness to itself. It has unlikeness to the others because they are other in kind than it is, and things other in kind are unlike. It has likeness to itself because it has sameness in kind to itself. It will be observed that the others are said to be unlike Unity not only as *having* a different character, but as *being* of a different character.

The argument represents, in effect, a claim of the discernibility of non-identicals, and the identity of indiscernibles.

iv. Equal and Unequal (161c-e)

Unity is not equal to the others, for it if were, it would be like them with respect to equality, and Unity cannot be like or equal to anything, since it is not. This follows the careful and artificial separation of being and having that has been observed thus far in III.1.

Since Unity is not, it is not equal to the others, so the others are not equal to Unity. Therefore, they are unequal to Unity. Given that the others are, Unity must partake of Inequality, relative to which the others are unequal to it.

The passage from not being equal to being unequal is strange: Parmenides, after all, is quite capable of distinguishing the two, for he did so at 140b-d. But the present inference is justified by 151a-b. Outside of Unity and the others there is nothing; to be is to be somewhere; the others are; therefore they are somewhere; they are not in themselves, therefore they are in Unity. Since the others are in Unity, they are contained by Unity; therefore, they are smaller than Unity. Alternately, they are many; but Unity is not a multitude, so it is fewer than the others, and they are greater than Unity in multitude. So Unity must have inequality with respect to them.

But Largeness and Smallness belong to Inequality. Therefore, if Unity has Inequality, it has Largeness and Smallness. This result follows from the conjoint grounds by which it was established that Unity has inequality.

Now, Largeness and Smallness exist, since they are contrary, and in something (149e). But to be is to be somewhere, and logical opposition therefore implies spatial distinction: if Largeness and Smallness are opposites and, as Ideas, cannot qualify each other, they must be far apart from each other, that is, not in the same place. One may compare the identification of numerical and temporal priority at 153a-b, which followed from the claim that to be is to be in time. Now, since Equality is logically intermediate between Largeness and Smallness, and since logical distinction implies locative expression, Equality must be located between Largeness and Smallness. This implies that whatever has Largeness and Smallness in it must have Equality, as between the two: for in locative terms, whatever has two things that are far apart must have what is between them as well. So Unity, if it does not exist, has Equality, Largeness, and Smallness in it.

The argument serves further to remind the reader of the complexity of the notion of opposition. Equality has an opposite, namely, Inequality, which reduces to the conjunction of Largeness and Smallness; but there, Largeness and Smallness are opposite, with Equality intermediate between them.[221] The result, already prefigured in the Paradox of Divisibility (131c-e), provides a foundation for Aristotle's claim in ethics that although virtue is a mean between excess and defect, it is itself an extreme with respect to better and worse.

But complexity of opposition extends further. We might hope to set up a square of opposition for Ideas analogous to the square that applies to A-, E-, I-, and O-propositions in traditional logic:

	Subalterns	*Subalterns*
Contraries	A: All S is P.	E: No S is P.
Subcontraries	I: Some S is P.	O: Some S is not P.

A and E are contraries: not both can be true, but both can be false. I and O are subcontraries: both can be true, but, waiving existential import, not both can be false. Contradictories, AO and EI, are diagonally opposite in the square: not both can be true, and not both false. And A and E propositions, which are universal, are taken to imply their respective particular subalterns, I and O.

The analysis provided by the square is, it is interesting to observe, truth-functional. But it does not seem unreasonable to undertake to extend the structure of the analysis in respect to contrariety, subcontrariety, and contradiction to Ideas and the things that have them. When this is done, it is quickly apparent that logical relations differ according to the Ideas chosen, that is, according to intensional relations of Ideas among themselves.

Take, for example, Likeness and Unlikeness. Since anything that has Likeness has Unlikeness, and vice versa, these Ideas are, in respect to *having*, subcontraries: that is, the same things are both like and unlike, though at different times, in different respects, and so on. On the other hand, since Likeness cannot be unlike nor Unlikeness like, these Ideas, with respect to *being* as distinct from *having*, are contraries. Clearly, Unity and Plurality are in this respect like Likeness and Unlikeness. So too are Equality and Inequality. Largeness and Smallness can be reduced to the scheme only be reducing them to Inequality, since there is no provision for Equality as a middle or mean.

Now consider Oddness and Evenness. Nothing which in the primary sense has oddness has evenness, or vice versa: these Ideas in respect of *having* are not subcontraries. They are, however, contraries in respect of *being*. Oddness cannot be even nor Evenness odd. It is reasonable to describe Ideas that are contraries and do not admit of subcontraries as contradictories, if and only if everything which is must have or partake of one or the other of them. This is true of Oddness and Evenness, since it is true of number. And given this account, it would seem that Being and Not-being, unlike Unity and Plurality, are not merely contraries but contradictories.

There is an intensional element even in indefinite terms, since they indicate contradiction or subcontrariety according to the sense of the term they negate.

v. Being and Not-being (161e-162b)

Unity must in some way partake of Being: for it must be as we say it is. Otherwise, we would not speak truly in saying that Unity is not. So Unity, if it is not, is; for if it is not a thing which is not, it is a thing which is.

We wish to reply with Aristotle that, "It is not true to say that what is not, since it is thought about, is something that is; for what is thought about it is not that it is, but that it is not."[222] But the assumption that Not-being is an Idea precludes this result, as shown in the present passage. Being and Not-being were identified as Ideas at 136b, and to assert that something is or is not is to assert participation in them.

What is not must be in order not to be, and what is must not be in order to be, since what is must not be a thing which is not if it is to be, and what is not must be a thing which is if it is not to be.

This result follows and is flatly absurd; the absurdity is not relieved by supposing, with Cornford, that, "With astonishing lucidity, Plato has distinguished existence from the being which belongs to any entity which can be thought or spoken of" (*PP* 231). This neatly Meinongian conclusion does not fit the text: Being and Not-being are treated as single Ideas; that no distinction between being and existence is intended is sufficiently indicated by the fact that whereas we may claim (fallaciously) that what is not is, on the ground that what is not has being but does not exist, we can scarcely claim that what is is not on the ground that what is exists but does not have being, or that what exists does not exist.

A similar point applies to the Meinongian counterpart in grammar, which insists on a sharp distinction between the existential and the so-called 'verdictive' *is*. In Greek, to say what is true is to say what is, and to say what is false is to say what is not. In sophistic hands, this led to the claim that to think the thing which is not is to think nothing, and therefore not to think, so that false speech or thought is impossible.[223] It helps to explain why Aristotle treats being as truth,[224] though he is careful to observe that this is a derivative sense of being (*Meta*. XI 1065a 21-25, IX 1051b 17-33). But this does not fit the present passage. We might claim that what is not is on the ground that it is true that it is not; we can scarcely claim that what is is not on the ground that it is false that it is. The claim that we can truly say that what is not is because we can truly say that it is not is based, not on a 'verdictive' *is*, but on the possibility of significant denial, following the argument of 160c-d.

The consequence that what is not is, and that what is is not, is a legitimate inference from the assumption that Being and Not-being are Ideas. If Unity, or anything else, is not, then it is other than Not-being and partakes of Not-being. Now, by the Dilemma of Participation, if Unity partakes of Not-being, Not-being must be in Unity in whole or in part. If then by reflection we abstract Not-being from what it is in, there must be a remainder; Unity, after all, and anything else, must be different from Not-being. That remainder, since Not-being has been abstracted from it, must be something, as containing Not-being. Therefore, it is.

That what is is not follows from precisely the same account, substituting Being for Not-being. So Unity, if it is not, is; and if it is, is not. In III.1, Unity began as equivalent to Unity conceived apart from its own being in I.2; it has now proved equivalent to the Unity which both is and is not in I.3. Similar consequences will follow from change and generation and destruction.

vi. Motion and Rest (162b-e)

Unity both is and is not, and it is possible for a thing both to be and not to be only if it changes. Change implies motion. So Unity must move, as changing from being to not-being. A similar argument had already established that Unity, if it is, must come to be and cease to be, and thereby change (155e-156c).

Motion implies change of place or change of character (138b), and either of these implies that Unity is: for if Unity is to change, it must be somewhere, and be in time.

But since Unity is not, it is nowhere, so it cannot move by changing place; for place must be, and what is not cannot be in something that is (cf. 138c-d). Nor can Unity alter character, since the account would not then be about Unity but something else (cf. 138e).

So Unity does not change; since it is not, it is; since it is, and is motionless, it is at rest. Once again the inference seems fallacious: Parmenides knows well enough that what is not in motion is not thereby at rest (cf. 139a-b). But this neglects context. Precisely because Unity is not, it is; because it is, it is some-where; because it is not, it is motionless, or without motion; and what is both somewhere and motionless is at rest. As in I.3, to undertake to mediate the con-tradiction that Unity both is and is not by appealing to motion is to permit the contradiction to recur in the putative solution.

III.1 and I.3 are in fact neatly parallel. If Unity is, it is both in motion and at rest in such a way as to combine being and not-being. If Unity is not, it is both in motion and at rest in a way that combines both being and not-being. Parmen-ides in 162a-b so speaks as to emphasize the parallelism.

vii. Generation and Destruction (162e-163b)

Since Unity is moved, it must alter character; insofar as Unity is not moved, it does not alter character. So Unity both does and does not alter character.

Once again, the pattern of reasoning is similar to I.3 (156a-c). There Par-menides had inferred from becoming to change of character, to motion, to change; here Parmenides has inferred from change to motion, to change of character, to becoming. The conclusion, which is contradictory, is derived from a contradiction.

III.2. Third Hypothesis, Second Deduction (163b-164b)

In III.1 Unity began as equivalent to Unity conceived apart from its own being, as in I.2, and ended as equivalent to that Unity which both is and is not in I.3.

Now, in III.2, Unity, if it is not, is equivalent to the Unity of I.1: it is a Unity that can neither be nor be one, a Unity to which nothing can belong, of which nothing can be said. This Unity has (to misspeak) the not-being rejected as un-intelligible in the *Sophist* (238c): "One cannot legitimately utter the words, or speak or think of that which just simply is not; it is unthinkable, not to be spoken of or uttered or expressed." That is, the hypothesis that Unity is not in III.2. is in a strict sense meaningless. Yet it is implied by I.1 (141e), and further by the contradictions in I.3 and III.1.

Proclus and Cornford found here an ambiguity in the expression 'is not.' But this merely trivializes what is in fact serious and vicious. As in the thought of the historical Parmenides, the Way that Is and Is Not has reduced to the Way that Is Not: III.2 follows systematically from what has gone before, and also implies it, insofar as it is equivalent to I.1. The truth-values of "Unity is" and "Unity is not" are the same: they have no truth-value. If Unity is not, it can stand in no relation, cannot be an object of knowledge, opinion, or perception, cannot be named or accounted for. The conclusion is exactly that put at 142a, where it followed from the hypotheses that Unity is.

If Unity is not, this implies absence of being from what we say is not: for 'is not' does not mean a thing which somehow both is and is not, but means with-out qualification what in no sense is. So if Unity is not, it is impossible for it to be in any way at all.

The further deductions follow from this conception of absolute nonentity. Unity, conceived in this way, can stand in no relation, and cannot be the object of knowledge, opinion, or perception, cannot be named, accounted for, or spoken of. The conclusion, it will be observed, is exactly that of I.1 (142a), which was derived from the hypothesis that Unity is. Contradiction is piled on contradiction.

IV.1. Fourth Hypothesis, First Deduction (164b-165c)

We are now to consider what follows for the others if Unity is not. Things other than Unity were shown in II.1 to be unlimited multiplicity when considered apart from their participation in Unity, which provided them with limit. In II.2 they were wholly without qualification, since Unity could not be participated in. We have already found II.1 and II.2 to be tightly paired with I.1 and I.2. In the same way, IV.1 and IV.2 will prove to be tightly paired with III.1 and III.2. Unity, if it is not, has been shown to be insofar as its existence admits of significant denial; thus IV.1. But Unity, if it is not, cannot be in any sense at all; thus IV.2.

As in III.1, if Unity is not, there are things other than Unity; for we could not speak of them unless they were. This result follows from 160c in conjunction with 161e. The existence of things other than Unity is implied whether Unity is (I.2) or is not (III.1).

If the others are other than Unity, they are different from Unity; for to be other implies being different. Once again, this result derives from 160c. Therefore, they must be different from something, and since they cannot be different from Unity, since it is not,[225] they must be other than each other.

If the others are other than each other, and Unity is not, they must be other, not as other ones, but as quanta in which there is no unity. The word 'mass' is chosen, for want of a better term, to describe a multiplicity in which there is no unity; the Greek ὄγκος, like our 'mass', may mean either bulk or weight, and as a medical term tumor or tumidity.[226] Once again, we have reached the sheer multiplicity of II.1 (158b-c).

These masses must appear to be one, since they are other than each other; but they cannot be one, since there is no Unity. And as other than each other, they will also appear many. There will thus seem to be some number of them; 'number' here is to be understood as a plurality of units, and since diverse multitudes, however small, divide into still smaller multitudes, some will seem odd, some even, without actually being so since there is no unity in them. And having the appearance of number, we may pick out some that appear to have the least number. Since they are others, the least number of them will seem to be two (cf. *Phys.* IV 220a 27).

The others cannot have parts or be a whole, since they have no unity. But they will appear to have the infinite divisibility attributed to Unity in I.2 (142e-

143a), and they will appear so because of their otherness or difference. From this it is inferred that the masses will seem large and small and equal, without being so, and relative to each other they will appear to have a limit; but if by reflection we take any of them, as by reflection we took Unity apart from its own being at 143c, we shall find no limit because of the absence of Unity. And if Unity is not, this will be so of whichever of the others one may take; so though the masses appear one, each on close inspection proves unlimited in multitude, since it is deprived of Unity. Observe the lovely inversion of 143c: there we abstracted Unity from its own being; here we consider any given thing as being, apart from its own unity. In general, the others will appear to have the characters attributed to Unity in I.2, and to the others which are parts of Unity in II.1; but these masses are unlimited because Unity is not.

Once again, it is tempting to associate this result with the Four Kinds of the *Philebus* (23c ff.), and specifically with the Unlimited, the class of things stamped with the seal of the More-and-Less. But the continua of the *Philebus* are qualitatively, though not quantitatively, limited, as may also be true of the discordant powers in the Receptacle in the *Timaeus* (52d). But the others under discussion in IV.1 are limited in no way at all; they have only the appearance of limit, and they are not even continua, for that would imply the presence of Unity. Nor are they, as in the *Philebus* and *Timaeus*, restricted to sensibles, but are of utmost generality. Yet in their indeterminancy they suggest once more substrate and matter—suggest, since the least number of them is two, Aristotle's doctrine that the Great and Small was matter for the Ideas in cooperation with the One, that it was not-being, and that it was an Indefinite Dyad.

But if Aristotle so read the passage, we must recall that it will be contradicted in the next Deduction; and properly so, for the very concept of such things is vicious. The sole ground on which the others are conceived to be in IV.1 is that we are speaking of them.

IV.2. Fourth Hypothesis, Second Deduction (165e-166c)

If Unity is not, the others will not be either one or many. Neither will they appear one or many, for Unity, if it does not exist, cannot seem to be present to anything or be conceived by anything. And since the others cannot appear or be conceived to be one, they cannot appear or be conceived to be many. It follows that they can have no other characters. In sum: if Unity is not, nothing is.

Conclusion

It is important to see that the conclusion of the *Parmenides* is not merely ostensible, but required by the structure and argument of all that has gone before. The *Parmenides* has presented a complex, reticulated aporia, and the impossibility in which it issues requires close reflection on the premises by which it proceeds.

At 160b, Parmenides summed up the results of Hypotheses I and II, and the summary involved flat contradiction. It should follow, by the logical principle on which all reductio ad adsurdum proof rests, that Unity does not exist. But in III and IV that claim too is shown to imply contradiction: if Unity is not, it both is and is not, and just simply is not; and the others are correspondingly affected.

The inner structure of the four hypotheses is broadly coimplicatory. Whether Unity is or is not, it can have no characteristics (I.1, III.2), and must have all characteristics (I.2, I.3, III.1). Whether Unity is or is not, things other than Unity must have all of a specific list of characteristics (II.1, IV.1) and can have no characteristics (II.2, IV.2). Since these results follow both from the assumptions that Unity is and that Unity is not, Unity, if it is not, is, and if it is, is not. That III deals with having rather than being, and IV with appearing rather than being, does not violate the symmetry of this arrangement; for the arguments used in III and IV to establish and deny having and appearing might as easily have been developed in I and II. The final result is perfection of aporetic structure.

***

At the conclusion of an analysis that has eschewed speculation in favor of code-cracking, a brief bit of speculation may perhaps be indulged. The *Parmenides* is aporetic, not dogmatic: it presents metaphysical perplexities, not positive doctrine. To undertake to solve the problems it raises without close attention to Plato's later dialogues in their relation to it would be like trying to reconstruct Aristotle's metaphysical views from Book B alone. Nevertheless, there are certain things that may be inferred with reasonable probability.

The first is that there are deep-seated, serious, perhaps insoluble problems involved in applying the theory of Ideas to unrestricted terms such as being, unity, and difference. The *Parmenides* would seem to explode the possibility of an Idea of Unity that is one in a way that excludes all plurality; it would seem also to explode the possibility of an Idea of Being that implies the existence of Not-being. That Being has no opposite is explicitly (though perhaps not coherently) claimed in the *Sophist*, which also introduces Kinds such as Sameness and Difference, which are qualified by their own opposite. Very simply, this is not the theory of Ideas Socrates put at *Parmenides* 129, and not the theory of the *Phaedo* and the *Republic*. There is no abandonment of the theory of Ideas in dialogues later than the *Parmenides*; but we must expect issues involving unrestricted terms to arise, which the theory does not of its own force solve.

The problem of unrestricted terms is connected but not identical with further problems involving substrate. There is a common aporetic difficulty underlying Parmenides' initial criticisms of the theory of Ideas and arguments in the Hypotheses; intriguingly, it is a common problem arising from apparently diverse sources. Socrates, when first questioned, was certain of the existence of Ideas of Unity and Plurality, Likeness and Unlikeness. He was equally certain of the non-existence of Ideas of Hair, Mud, and Dirt. But as the lack of Ideas for existing sensibles implies sensible substrate, so the presence of Ideas of unrestricted terms implies ideal substrate: if there is a real distinction between things and the being and unity of those things, we must conceive that there is a remainder after being and unity have been abstracted.

In both Parmenides' criticisms and the hypotheses, participation is a real relation between things that are distinct, and the Dilemma of Participation is a derivative but crucial result. In this, Plato laid a main foundation for Aristotle's criticism of the theory of Ideas, as he also laid the foundation for a key concept of Aristotle's own thought: matter as substrate, not primarily of change but of predication, matter as opposed to substantial form. This result, unhappy in its intricate confusion, arose because Aristotle supposed that sensibles are primarily real — in short, substantial.

Plato's own solution to the problems of substrate in respect to sensibles is indicated in the *Timaeus*: there is no sensible substrate if sensibles are purely relational entities, if their whole being is such as to be *in* something other than themselves, namely, space and *of* something other than themselves, namely, the eternal Ideas.

But Plato nowhere indicates a solution to the problems of substrate posed by assuming the existence of such Ideas as Being and Unity, distinct from other Ideas which are and are one. For reasons that cannot now be recovered, he did not choose to write the *Philosopher*. But suppose, as a matter of least change and greatest simplicity, that the theory of Ideas does not extend to such unrestricted terms. We are then left with a metaphysical position that for want of a better name, and quite unoriginally, we may call essentialism: the view that to be is to be somewhat, that on ultimate analysis what is and what it is are identical, one and the same. If this is so, being and unity are not common terms predicated of Ideas, as one over many. On the contrary, they are apprehended in the apprehension of every Idea, that is, in the apprehension of what it is to be each thing, the apprehension of essence. If this is a true interpretation, Plato anticipated Aristotle in recognizing that being is not a genus, and more generally, that unity and difference are not genera either. On this hypothesis, Plato saw that it is nonsense to speak of what it is to be being, or what it is to be different, or what it is to be one, apart from determinate essences, which are and are one and are different from each other. Being, unity, difference are not definable essences, not genera, but unrestricted in scope, the transcendentals and syncategorematic terms of later metaphysics.

So Platonism rejects unrestricted terms as Ideas, and thereby rejects substrate for essences. In this way it preserved, as an inheritance for future generations, the legacy of Father Parmenides: that what is is intelligible.

Appendix

Appendix. The Set-Theoretical Analysis of Infinity

Many arguments in the *Parmenides* are concerned with or involve the infinite, and those arguments are often among the most difficult to interpret. Neither of these facts should occasion surprise. The infinite was forced on the attention of Greek mathematicians and physicists by the discovery of incommensurability, but its nature was not finally clarified until Cantor's work in the nineteenth century. To understand the *Parmenides*, it is helpful to have at least a skeletal notion of the modern treatment.[227] The distinction between set-inclusion and set-equivalence is fundamental.

Set Inclusion

A set X is included in (or a subset of) a set Y if and only if every element of X, that is to say, every member of the set, is also an element of Y. It follows from this that every set is included in (or a subset of) itself: thus, for example, the set of even integers is a subset of the set of integers; it is also a subset of itself. Since the empty set or null set, $\emptyset$, has no members, every member of $\emptyset$ is a member of every set, and therefore the null set is a subset of every set. So every set includes itself and the null set as subsets.

Given set inclusion, it is possible to define set identity. Two sets X and Y are identical if and only if X includes Y and Y includes X, that is to say, if and only if every element of X is an element of Y and every element of Y is an element of X. In short, sets are identical if and only if they have the same members: thus for example the set of integers greater than 6 and less than 8 and the set of primes greater than 5 and less than 11 are identical, and identical to the set whose only member is 7.

Given membership, inclusion, and identity, it is possible to define proper inclusion: a set X is properly included in (or a proper subset of) a set Y if and only

293

if X has at least one element and X is included in Y and X is not identical to Y. Thus for example, though the set of even integers is a proper subset of the set of integers, it is not a proper subset of itself, even though it is a subset of itself. Nor is ∅ a proper subset of any set of which it is a subset.

Set Equivalence

Two sets X and Y are equivalent if and only if there is a biunique (or one-to-one) correspondence between their elements or members. That is, they are equivalent if and only if the elements of each set may be paired in such a way that to each element in X there corresponds one and only one element in Y, and to each element in Y there corresponds one and only one element in X. Thus, for example, the set of horses is equivalent to the set of heads of horses, the set of circles is equivalent to the set of centers of circles, and in countries where monogamy is required by law, the set of husbands is equivalent to the set of wives.

In respect to finite sets, set equivalence corresponds to our ordinary notion of equality in number: the elements in two sets can be paired one-to-one if and only if those sets have the same number of elements. Indeed, set equivalence is the basis of counting: for to count the elements in a set is to establish a one-to-one correspondence between those elements and the successive elements in the set of positive integers beginning with 1. This is a deep truth behind Plato's view in the *Phaedo* that numbers are prior to operations such as multiplication and division.

In this connection, one may introduce the notion of the cardinal number of a set, as that which a set has in common with all equivalent sets and no others. The cardinal number of a finite set is n if the set is equivalent to the set of the first n integers.

Finite and Infinite Sets

It follows from the definition of proper inclusion and equivalence that no finite set, that is, no set whose cardinal number is an integer, can be equivalent to a proper subset of itself. This corresponds to the characteristic claim of Greek geometry, and our own ordinary intuition based on dealing with finite pluralities, that the part cannot be equal to the whole.

The case is fundamentally different, however, if the notion of set equivalence is extended to infinite sets. Thus, for example, the set of even integers is a proper subset of the set of integers, being included in it and not identical to it. But as there are infinitely many integers, so there are also infinitely many even integers, and because this is so, the set of integers is equivalent to a proper subset of itself. This equivalence may be shown by simple pairing:

1	2	3	4	5	. . . . . .n. . . . . .
↕	↕	↕	↕	↕	↕
2	4	6	8	10	. . . . . $2n$. . . . . .

Because each member of the set of integers can be put into biunique correspondence to a member of the set of even integers, the set of integers is equivalent to a proper subset of itself.

The paradoxical character of this result may be brought out by observing that, in ordinary terms, it is true both that there are *more* integers than even integers, since there are also odd integers, and that there are *as many* even integers as integers, since they can be matched one-to-one. The whole is "greater than" some of its parts, and yet also "equal to" some of its parts. This appears absurd; but it appears so because our ordinary notions of equality and inequality, fitted as they are for use with finite pluralities, cloudily combine two distinct concepts, inclusion and equivalence. The study of the infinite was troubled for over two thousand years by a lack of clear conceptions, mainly owing to the imprecision of ordinary language.

The result that an infinite set may be equivalent to a proper subset of itself is not an accidental feature of some infinite sets: Cantor suggested that it in fact defines an infinite set. A set is infinite if and only if it is equivalent to a proper subset of itself.

There is nothing in this result that lies beyond the power of Greek mathematics: the point has been here put in terms of numerical conceptions to which the Greeks had attained; it might also have been put geometrically, in terms of the equivalence of divisions on the line and divisions on the half-line. To have done this, however, would have been to abandon the potential infinite for the actual infinite, with Zenonian paradoxes left unsolved.

Succession, Density, and Continuity

The integers form a successive series: if *n* is in succession to *m*, there is no integer such that it is less than *n* and greater than *m*. The Greeks, identifying number with the positive integers or natural numbers, supposed that all number is successive.

Modern mathematics treats the positive integers as a proper subset of the rational numbers, that is, those numbers that may be expressed as the quotient of two integers. The rational numbers are not successive, but dense: that is, for any two rational numbers *m* and *n* such that *n* is greater than *m*, there is a rational between *m* and *n*, that is greater than *m* and less than *n*. Put otherwise, given any rational number, there is no *next* rational number, since between any two rational numbers there is a rational number. If the rational numbers are paired with points on a line, then the rational points are dense on that line: there are rational points within any rational interval, however small. Thus, between 1/4 and 1/2 and their corresponding points, there is 3/8 and its corresponding point; between 3/8 and 1/2 and their corresponding points, there is 7/16 and its corresponding point; and so ad infinitum.

The Greek mathematicians, for reasons having to do with the fact that they did not regard zero as a number, treated the quotient of two integers not as a number but as a ratio. Their geometry, however, was fully adequate to express this result, and Aristotle regards density (in effect) as a defining property of continuity.

It happens, however, that although every continuous infinite is dense, not every dense infinite is continuous. Furthermore, the infinity of continuity is of a different and higher order than the infinity of density. The latter point lies beyond the range of Greek mathematics: proof of it requires the real numbers, and was first offered by Cantor. The Greek mathematicians knew that any continuum was infinitely divisible according either to a rational or an irrational proportion; they could not have known the complexities in the nature of the infinite that this fact entails.

The set of real numbers is the union of the set of rational numbers and the set of irrational numbers, the union, that is, of those numbers that cannot be expressed as the quotient of two integers and those that can be so expressed. The union of two sets X and Y is the set containing all and only members of X and Y. The rational numbers constitute a denumerable infinite; the irrational numbers constitute a nondenumerable infinite; therefore the real numbers, the union of the rationals and irrationals, constitute a nondenumerable infinite.

To say that the rational numbers are denumerable is to say that they are equivalent to a given proper subset of themselves, namely the positive integers. This equivalence cannot be established by ordering them according to their magnitude, because they are dense. But if one disregards relative magnitude, it is possible to order the rational numbers in a single row, $R_1, R_2, R_3 \ldots R_n$ . . . which will stand in biunique correspondence to the integers. Specifically, the following array will generate all of the rational numbers:

$$
\begin{array}{cccccc}
1 \rightarrow 2 & 3 \rightarrow 4 & 5 \rightarrow 6 & \cdots \\
1/2 & 2/2 & 3/2 & 4/2 & 5/2 & \cdots \\
1/3 & 2/3 & 3/3 & 4/3 & \cdots \\
1/4 & 2/4 & 3/4 & \cdots \\
1/5 & 2/5 & \cdots
\end{array}
$$

By ordering these numbers according to the diagonal procedure shown, and cancelling all quotients that have a common divisor and thus are not in lowest terms, we obtain the Cantorian sequence,

$$1, 2, 1/2, 1/3, 3, 4, 3/2, 2/3, 1/4, 1/5, 5, 6 \ldots$$

This sequence will contain every rational number once and only once. Since the elements of this set can be put in one-to-one or biunique correspondence to the positive integers, the set of rational numbers is denumerable.

Cantor proceeded to show by reductio ad absurdum that the real numbers are nondenumerable. In following this proof, it is helpful to recall a fact about the rational numbers, that the decimal expression of any rational number is periodic: after some finite set of digits has appeared initially, the same digit or group of digits will repeat itself infinitely often thereafter. Thus for example, 1/2, is .5000 . . . , 1/3 is .33333 . . . , 1/6 is .166666 . . . , 1/7 is .142857142857 . . .

and so on. Cantor's proof assumes that any digit may be substituted in any decimal place, an assumption true of real but not of rational numbers.

The proof that the real numbers are nondenumerable begins by assuming that the real numbers are denumerable. If this were so, it would be possible to arrange the real numbers in a table of infinite decimals:

1st Number	$N_1 . a_1 a_2 a_3 a_4 \ldots$
2nd Number	$N_2 . b_1 b_2 b_3 b_4 \ldots$
3rd Number	$N_3 . c_1 c_2 c_3 c_4 \ldots$

The capital letters indicate integers occurring before, and small letters integers occurring after, the decimal point. Since the real numbers are assumed to be denumerable, this table must in principle list all the real numbers. To show that the real numbers are nondenumerable, therefore, it is necessary to show only that there is a real number that does not occur in this list. This can be done by choosing a first digit a which differs from a_1, a second digit b which differs from b_2, and third digit c which differs from c_3, and so on. By this means it is possible to construct an infinite decimal z such that $z = 0. abcdefg \ldots$. But z is different from any number occurring in the table: it is not equal to the first because it differs in the first digit after the decimal point; it is not equal to the second because it differs in the second digit after the decimal point; nor can it be equal to the nth number in the table, because it differs in the nth digit. Thus the set of real numbers is nondenumerable, since the assumption that it is denumerable leads to contradiction: the real numbers, corresponding to rational and irrational divisions in the continuum, are not equivalent to the rational numbers, which are an infinite proper subset of themselves. Since the real numbers are the union of the set of rational numbers and the set of irrational numbers, and since the union of two denumerable sets is denumerable, it follows that the irrational numbers are nondenumerable: the set of rational numbers is not equivalent to the set of irrational numbers.

Transfinite Numbers

As Cantor extended the notion of equivalence from finite to infinite sets, so he also extended the notion of the cardinal number of a set from finite to infinite sets. Two sets have the same cardinal number if they are equivalent. Therefore, all sets equivalent to the set of integers—that is, all denumerable sets—have the same cardinal number, which Cantor designated Aleph-zero. The arithmetic governing this, the first transfinite cardinal number, is remarkably different from the arithmetic of finite numbers, for it implies the following equalities: Aleph-zero = Aleph-zero + n = Aleph-zero x n = Aleph-zero^n, where n is any natural number. In short, the sum and product of Aleph-zero and any natural number, and Aleph-zero raised to any natural power is Aleph-zero.

Cantor went on to hypothesize that if Aleph-zero is the cardinal number of the denumerable infinite, $2^{\text{Aleph-zero}}$ is the cardinal number of the real number continuum, and $2^{\text{Aleph-zero}}$ is greater than Aleph-zero. It has only recently been shown that $2^{\text{Aleph-zero}}$ is Aleph-one, that is, the transfinite number next in succession to Aleph-zero: there is no set whose cardinality is greater than Aleph-zero but less than $2^{\text{Aleph-zero}}$.[228]

These beautiful results were inaccessible to Greek mathematicians because of their impoverished conception of number. But it is well to recall that the Greeks, by the time of Plato or within a few years of his death, had arrived at the general notion of a transfinite cardinal and had anticipated the paradoxical equalities which hold for its arithmetic, and that Aristotle had rejected those results on grounds which presuppose the potential infinite.[229]

Notes

Notes

1. No division of speakers, following TWY and Proclus against B.
2. Cf. 136d 1.
3. A. E. Taylor and F. M. Cornford read <οὐ> πολλούς 'a few,' suggested by 129d 1, 136d 6-7, 137a 7. There is no manuscript support for this, and it is difficult to suppose that Plato wrote, μετ᾿ αὐτοῦ οὐ πολλούς, κ.τ.λ.
4. Compare *Sophist* 243a-b, *E.N.* I 1095a 26.
5. A proverbial expression, found in Pindar, Fr. 106.
6. Or, 'if the All is one' (128b 1); alternately, 'if one is' or 'if unity is' or 'if there is (only) one' (128d 6). The expression is syntactically amphibolous: 'one' may be taken as predicate with 'is' copulative, or as subject with 'is' existential; in the latter case, it may have the force of an abstract noun, 'unity.'
7. That is, 'if it is many' or 'if things which are are many' (127e 1-2), or 'if the All is many' (128b 1); alternately, 'if many is' or 'if plurality is' or 'if there are many (things).' Syntactical amphiboly as in preceding note.
8. Reading ταὐτά in 129d 3.
9. Following, with Cornford, Diès's conjecture, ὃν ἄλλο αὐτῶν οἵων ἡμεῖς, κ.τ.λ.
10. The conditional is future most vivid, the protasis expressing something undesired or feared, and the apodosis a threat or a warning.
11. Giving ἀνόητα its passive meaning. Alternately, with active meaning, "that being thoughts they do not think."
12. See below, n. 66.
13. The antecedent is presumably Pythodorus (127c, 130a), but may perhaps be Antiphon (127a, 136e).
14. ἐναντίον λέγειν: "discuss in presence of" or "discuss in opposite manner." Cf. 128d-e.
15. The poem is extant: Ibycus, Fr. 6 (Mosino).
16. Or, "if unity is one." Unity, of course, is what it is to be one.
17. The argument through this passage resembles Zeno Fr. 3: if things are many, they must be as many as they are, and there is neither more of them nor less. If they are as many as they are, they would be limited. But if things are many, they are unlimited, for there will always be different ones between things which are, and different ones again between those. And thus things which are are unlimited. See 161d below.

18. The expression translated "in something different," ἑτέρωθι, particularly refers to difference in place or in time.

19. ὡς ἄρα epexegetic, as at *Theaetetus* 152d 2. But there are overtones of skepticism as to the conclusion: cf. Smyth 2798, Denniston pp. 38-39.

20. Professor Cherniss has kindly communicated to me the following in correspondence: "The text of 148e 7 is manifestly corrupt. The exact correspondence of e 8-9 (εἰ μέλλει... κατέχον ἐκείνης) with e 4-6 (πᾶν τὸ μέλλον... ἢ ἂν μετ' ἐκείνην) shows that what followed μετ'ἐκείνην there must have defined ἐκείνην, as in 9-10 ἐν ᾧ αὐτό ἐστιν defined ἐκείνης there. Whatever the wording really was, <ἐν> ᾗ ἂν ἕδρᾳ κέηται <οὗ> ἅπτεται gives the sense that must have been expressed; but I confess that no emendation known to me seems to me paleographically persuasive."

21. Cf. *Phys.* V 227a 6: "A thing that is in succession and touches is 'contiguous.' "

22. 'Numbers' here means pluralities of units, that is, things numerable. The units here are the terms in contact.

23. This is the proportion *epimorios* or *superparticularis*, the ratio of N + 1 : N, proved by Archytas to admit no geometrical mean. For the proof, see Heath, *HGM* i 215.

24. δυάς, repeated below, d2. This is the number two (cf. *Phaedo* 101c 5), though number is here conceived as a plurality of units rather than as a number property. It is also Aristotle's word for the 'Dyad' (e.g. at *Phys.* I 192a 10, III 203a 15, 206a 25, *Meta.* I 987b 33, XIII 1081a 14, Alexander, *in Metaphy.*) though Aristotle often uses it simply for the number two (e.g. *Phys.* IV 220a 27).

25. The locution is explained by Euclid VII, Propositions 37 and 38, where to have a part called by the same name as a measuring number expresses a fractional ordinal, and to call a number by the same name as a measuring part expresses a cardinal. Parmenides' expression covers both cases: the point is that we cannot speak, for example, either of a tenth of the others or of ten others.

26. εἴδει 149e 7; the argument contradicts 131e 1. Taylor, followed by Cornford, remarks that the proper translation is "Entity — the Greek word is εἶδος, used, as often in Plato, colourlessly, with little more meaning than 'something or other.' " And not only colorlessly, but misleadingly, given that we have just had οὐσία in the sense of essence or nature (149e 4), and will immediately have εἴδη in the sense of characters or Ideas (149e 9). Nor are there examples in Ast or *LSJ* where εἶδος means 'entity' or 'thing.' See also 157d, 158c, 159e, 160a, below and *PP* 207 n.2.

27. That is, Largeness and Smallness.

28. There is a pun in "whatever is" (τό γε ὂν ἀεί): whatever is, or what *always* is.

29. 141a-c.

30. Not, "later than all the others," since its end is one of the others.

31. Or, "a whole one."

32. Reading τοῦ ἑνὸς ὄντος in 154b 7 with BTY. τὸ ἓν... ὂν in c 3 puts the converse of the relation; cf. 142d 1. W reads τοῦ ἑνος, and nothing supports Schleiermacher's τοῦ ὄντος, followed by Burnet, or Dies's οὐδ ενὸς ὄντος.

33. See above, 159e, 158c, 157d, 149e.

34. Sc. a thing which is not.

35. Construed following Shorey, *Class. Philo.* xii (1891), pp. 349-53, whose emendations are adopted by Burnet.

36. Reading ὑπό with all manuscripts. Among the others, it may be recalled, are things which are or have minds. See 142a, 132c. On the other hand, conceiving can take place *by* conception: "Knowledge and the knowable are opposed as relatives, and knowledge is called just what it is, of the knowable, and the knowable too is called just what it is, in relation to its opposite, knowledge; for the knowable is called knowable by something — by knowledge." (*Categories* 11b 27-31, trans. Ackrill. See 132c, 134b.)

37. Thus in the *Menexenus*, a satire on Pericles' Funeral Oration, Socrates refers to events down to the time of the King's Peace in 387, twelve years after his own death. The *Gorgias* is so riddled with anachronism that no dramatic date can be assigned to it; that this is intentional is shown, not only by the fact that many of the anachronisms are blatant, but also by 521d, where Socrates is made to claim, uncharacteristically, that he is the only true statesman in Athens, and by the repeated prophecies of his trial and death. For further discussion, see Cornford's translation of the *Republic*, p. xxii and n. 1., and Dodds's edition of the *Gorgias*, pp. 17-18.

38. Thus at *Euthydemus* 273a, Ctesippus of Paeania is described as "insolent due to his youth."

39. So Diès, *Parménide* 14-19, followed in a qualified way by Cornford, *PP* 67-68, *PTK* 177.

40. I follow Zeller and Raven in treating *Fr.* 1 and *Fr.* 2 as different parts of one argument.

41. A term Zeno probably borrowed from the mathematicians; *Meno* 86e. It is used at 127d to mean, not only an assumption to be tested, but also the consequences that follow from that assumption. At 128d, it appears to mean only the assumption itself. Simplicius (*Phys.* 139.5, *DK* 256.4,5) substitutes the term ἐπιχείρημα, which is presumably to be taken in its Aristotelian sense, to mean dialectical as opposed to syllogistic proof, s.v. *LSJ* II.

42. Heath suggests that the substance of Euclid, *Elements* VII-IX, which relies on indirect proof in many places goes back to the Pythagoreans, and that there is clear indication that number theory had been reduced to elements by the time of Archytas (c. 430-365 B.C.). *TBEE* ii, 294-95.

Indirect proof is used, for example, in VII, 1 and 2, which are essential for finding greatest common measure and reduction to lowest terms.

43. "If someone were to attack your hypothesis, you would refuse to answer him until you had considered the consequences which follow from it, to see whether they agreed or disagreed with each other" (*Phaedo* 101d, after R. Hackforth). At 102a, Echecrates, who is probably a mathematician, interrupts Phaedo's account to express his approval of this description of proper argumentative procedure.

44. "Things are said to be 'like' which have the same characteristic (τὰ . . . ταὐτὸ πεπονθότα) in all respects, or more characteristics the same than different, or whose quality is one." *Meta.* V 1018a 15 ff.

45. Compare the use of ὅμοια at *Phaedrus* 261d 7 with ὁμοιοῦν at 261e 3 and ὁμοιότητα at 262a 6.

46. The reference is commonly supposed, though on slender evidence, to be to Antisthenes. *PTK* 254.

47. Plato's example of something both in motion and at rest is a spinning top, or any other instance of axial rotation about a fixed point, as in the motion of the fixed stars. See *Republic* IV 436d.

48. *PTK* 44, cf. *PP* 78n. 1. We are later told that, "It would never occur to a modern writer on Logic to wonder whether 'head' or 'hand' must be relative terms because such a thing must belong to someone" (*PTK* 283). This remark is not without irony. The calculus of relations is required to prove so deceptively simple an inference as that, since horses are animals, heads of horses are heads of animals.

49. αὐτὰ τὰ ὅμοια (129b 1). The neuter plural is generic, as it is in αὐτὰ τὰ ἴσα at *Phaedo* 74c 1-2. Socrates is stating a general truth about anything that can be said to be *just* like, and not unlike. The context implies that this is true of Likeness. At *Phaedo* 102c ff., it is also true of the characters of Ideas immanent in things.

Phrases such as αὐτὰ πέντε καὶ δέκα (*Theaetetus* 196a), αὐτὰ τὰ δώδεκα (*Theaetetus* 196b), and αὐτὰ τὰ δέκα (*Cratylus* 432a) are only verbally similar. They express numbers—

five, seven, twelve, and ten — as distinct from sets of things numbered, and they are plural because the nouns that occur in them have no singular. Indeed, it is only in a limited sense that they are even verbally similar, since they are noun and not adjectival constructions.

50. Reading τῷ . . . τῷ in 74 b 8-9. τότε . . . τότε, which has good manuscript support, is ruled out by ἐνίοτε. That the rendering should be "appear equal to one thing but not to another" rather than "appear equal to one man but not to another" is implied by the parallel datives in 74a 10, and supported by the argument of *Republic* V 479a-c and VII 523a ff. The evidence of *Symposium* 211a is nugatory, since it supports any of these renderings. It is to be remembered that φαίνεσθαι, though it sometimes has the subjective force of seeming as opposed to being, is in fact a stronger verb than δοκεῖν or εἰκέναι: its basic sense is 'to come to light,' and it is often best rendered in English, not by 'appear,' but by 'prove' or 'turn out to be.' For the sake of uniformity, 'appear' has been used in the present translation.

51. Translation by Cherniss, *SPM* 361. As Cherniss there points out, this exactly repeats the thought and language of the *Phaedrus* (see 250a-d, 249b, 263a-b), where "the most precious entities which have no perceptible images" are identified as justice, temperance, and so on (150b, d). G. E. L. Owen "Plato on the Undepictable," *Exegesis and Argument* (ed. Lee, Mourelatos, Rorty, [Assen, 1973,] 349ff.) denies the parallel on the ground that the *Politics* passage refers to human artifacts (p. 355).

52. *Theaetetus* 185c-186a; see Campbell's note on 185c 4-5. Cornford suggested that, "The terms are 'common' . . . in the sense in which a name is common to any number of individual things . . . these common terms are, in fact, the meanings of common names — what Plato calls 'Forms' or 'Ideas.'" (*PTK* 105) This will not do. 'Bright,' 'loud,' 'sweet,' and 'hard' are common names, applying to a host of individual things. Yet such terms, in the idiom of the *Theaetetus*, are not common but special, for the reason that (not they but) their instances are proper and peculiar to a given sense.

53. *Meta.*, XII 1070a 19-20, cf. I 990b 28. For fuller discussion of Aristotle's views on extent, see Robin, *La Théorie Platonicienne des Idées et des Nombres d'après Aristote*, Paris, 1908, pp. 173-98; Cherniss, *ACPA* i, 226-318; W. D. Ross, *Plato's Theory of Ideas*, Oxford, 1951, ch. xi.

54. As Cornford pointed out, *PP* 84, n. 2. Compare *Phaedo* 102b 2 and *Parmenides* 130e 5.

55. Compare Aristotle's distinction between difference and otherness, *Meta.* X 1054b 23-27.

56. Compare 145b and *Phys.* IV 210a 15, along with 142e and *Meta.* V 1023a 14-17, 24-25. At 159b-c, it must first be proved that Unity is not in the others to prove that Unity is separate (χωρίς) from the others and the others from Unity.

57. Euclid, *Elements* I, Axiom 5. See below. 145d. That the Paradox of Divisibility admits an extensive reading, however, is shown by 150a-c.

58. Aristotle remarks that mathematicians use common axioms only in a special application; the investigation of common axioms is also important to metaphysics. Cf. *Meta.* XI 1061b 18, IV 1005a 18ff., *Post. Anal.* I 76a 4 - b 2.

59. Cf. 149e, 150b-c, and *Phaedo* 100c-101b, 102a-d, especially 102b 4-6. Note that the above argument presents the kernel of the Largeness Regress that follows (131e-132b).

60. It may be observed in this connection that the opening question of the argument, τί δὲ δή is a formula of transition (Denniston, *The Greek Particles*, 2nd ed., [Oxford, 1954] p. 176), but one that sharpens a contrast or stresses an addition (Denniston, p. 460). Dodds (*Plato's Gorgias*, [Oxford, 1959] p. 202) calls it "a surprised question" — the surprise there being conditioned on what has gone before. In general, the expression is used as a formula of transition between different branches of the same argument. This is so on other occasions of use in the *Parmenides*: 132c 9, 148d 5, 153d 5. See also *Gorgias* 452c 3, *Apology* 24e 10, *Republic* V 470e 4, VII 523e 3, *Laws* XI 935d 3. For uses of τί δή in the *Parmenides*,

see 137c 6, 138b 8, 139a 5, 139d 3, 140e 2; for uses of τί δέ see 140e 1, 130c 1, 131d 4, 132a 6, 141e 1, 143d 8, 143e 5, 145a 5, 146a 3, 146c 4, 147a 6. These lists are not exhaustive.

61. ἓν in ἓν τὸ μέγα . . . εἶναι (132a 3-4) is in predicate, not attributive, position. Therefore, ἕν in εὖ ἕκαστον εἶδος . . εἶναι (132a 1) is also predicate, since the former generalized must yield the latter. The εἶναι, of course, is emphatic: the Idea is ἕν τι or μία τις, and Unity and Being are coextensive (142c-d, 144c).

62. *In Metaph.* 80.10-11: "and there is not in the case of any of them anything that itself is predicated of itself."

63. If we ground (2) on 130b 2-3 and the proposition that Largeness cannot be what it has, the inconsistency will recur.

64. The complexity of this passage leads me to doubt the parallel suggested by D. J. Allan, following Hick, to *de Anima* 429b 22-29, which in any case concerns Anaxagoras. See *Aristotle and Plato in the Mid-Fourth Century* (ed. Düring and Owen), Goteborg, 1960, p. 140ff.

65. Reading εἴδους in e 1 with all manuscripts and Proclus. Burnet and others have excluded it because they supposed that, unless this is done, 132d 9 - e 1 and 132e 3-4 must be redundant — an unexpected result in so tight and economical an argument. Given the exclusion, there is then a transition from sharing in one and the same (thing) to sharing in the Idea itself. But this, besides being textually unwarranted, neglects the purposeful ambiguity of the argument.

66. If ὧν = ἐκείνων ὧν in 133d 1 (cf. H. F. Cherniss, *SPM* 364, n. 1.), then Ideas have their being relative to themselves, but "not relative to those things among us, whether likenesses or whatever they are assumed to be, of those things of which we have a share and from which we get our several names." This would be a fair enough statement of the theory of Ideas in the *Timaeus*. But it seems doubtful that the passage should be so construed. In the first place, likeness is a relative, and the argument requires that sensibles are not in any way relative to Ideas. In the second place, this requirement arises from denial of participation in Ideas.

67. See *Sophist* 255c: "Among things that exist, some are always spoken of as being what they are just in themselves, others as being what they are with reference to other things" (trans. Cornford). Like Difference, Mastership and Slavery are terms of the latter sort. So is Knowledge. See below, 160d-e, 164c. See also *Charmides* 168b-169a, *Theaetetus* 160b.

68. γιγνώσκεται . . . ὑπ' αὐτοῦ τοῦ εἴδους τοῦ τῆς ἐπιστήμης, κ.τ.λ. 134b 6-7. The construction is parallel to that of the pleonastic nominative at 132c 4, except that it is now the verb that is pleonastic. The claim that Knowledge knows is another way of saying that Knowledge is what it is of (i.e., relative to) other Ideas, as Mastership is what it is of (i.e., relative to) Slavery.

69. 134d 9-10, c 11, ἀκριβέστερον, c 7. Cf. Alexander, *in Metaph.* 83.17-21; other arguments for Ideas only establish that there is something common to individuals, whereas the 'more exact' arguments establish that what is common is a paradigm. Parmenides' statement that there is 'most exact' knowledge and mastership repeats the claim that Mastership and Knowledge are what it is to be master and what it is to be knowledge (133d 8, 134a 3).

70. *In Metaph.* 83.16. Ross emended to παραδειγματικὸν ὄν in the Oxford Translation, vol. XII, p. 128 n.1, but returned to the manuscript reading in *Aristotelis Fragmenta Selecta*, p. 125, 1.9. Professor Owen, *SPM* 295, does not translate this clause.

71. See *PED*, pp. 245-6.

72. In this context, Zeno's hypothesis, if many is (136a), must be understood to mean, or include, "if Plurality is." Thus πολλά at 130b 5 is equivalent to πλῆθος at 129d 8, and is the Idea of Plurality.

73. As has just been observed, πολλά at 130b 5 is equivalent to πλῆθος at 129d 8; for

other examples of neuter adjective with abstract force, see 135c 9, 136b 3.

74. *In Parm.* 1040. 1-16. Cf. Plotinus, *Enneads* V.i.8, E. R. Dodds, *C.Q.* XXII (1928), pp. 129ff.

75. *PP* 109-15, cf. *PED* 268-74. Cornford argued that the subjects of Hypothesis I and II are not the same, on the ground that the subject of Hypothesis I is a bare unity, which is in every sense one and in no sense many, whereas that of Hypothesis II is plural as being an entity (*PP* 109, 117, 135, 203-4); he explicitly rejected the suggestion that the subject of both hypotheses is the Form of Unity (*PP* 112, and n. 1). Without here undertaking an estimate of his interpretation generally (on which see *PED* 168-74), it may be observed that his interpretation violates the text of Hypotheses I and II in two ways: it treats as disguised definitions what are clearly deductions (*PP* 111, 114, 117, 136) and treats the derivation of physical attributes in Hypothesis II not as proving that Unity *has* those attributes, but as proving that there is no reason why it should *not* have them (*PP* 115, 146, 203-4).

But the explanation of the difference between Hypotheses I and II is precisely that their subject is the Form of Unity. As a Form, Unity excludes its own opposite, and therefore can in no sense be many (129c-e, 131d); this yields Hypothesis II, given the Dilemma of Participation and concomitant physical attributes it supplies. That the subject of *all* the hypotheses will be a Form is implied by 135d-e.

76. I.1. (137c-142b): εἰ ἕν ἐστιν.

    I.2. (142b-155e): ἓν εἰ ἔστιν, 142b 3, 5, εἰ ἓν ἔστιν, 142c 3, proceeding again from the beginning.

    I.3. (155e-157b): τὸ ἓν εἰ ἔστιν, 155e 4, proceeding for the third time.

    II.1. (157b-159b): ἓν εἰ ἔστιν, 157b 6.

    II.2. (159b-160b): ἓν εἰ ἔστιν, 159b 3, 5.

    III.1. (160b-163b): εἰ ... μὴ ἔστι τὸ ἕν, 160b 5, εἰ ἓν μὴ ἔστι, 160b 7, ἓν εἰ μὴ ἔστι, 160d 3.

    III.2. (163b-164b): ἓν εἰ μὴ ἔστι, 163c 1, returning once more to the beginning.

    IV.1. (164b-165e): ἓν εἰ μὴ ἔστι, 164b 5, starting again.

    IV.2. (165e-166c): ἓν εἰ μὴ ἔστι, 165e 2-3, returning once more to the beginning.

The difference in word-order used in formulating the hypotheses is nugatory (see *PED* 245-46), and there is no difference in meaning between ἐν and τὸ ἕν. It is consistently stressed throughout that the same two assumptions are being dealt with.

77. See, for example, 129a 3, 130e 6, 132a 6, c 9, d 2, 3. At 133a 5 and 134c 8, the reference is to other Ideas.

78. R. S. Brumbaugh, *Plato on the One*, New Haven, 1961, suggested that Aristoteles' answers provide a kind of code for deciphering the logical modality of Parmenides' questions or the acceptability of his conclusions; this is not in fact verified by the text. To take but one example, Aristoteles denies that the conclusion of I.1 can be true of Unity (142a), and this has been taken to indicate Plato's own view of the unacceptability of the result. But Aristoteles also accepts as true the conclusion of I.2 (155e), which is no less absurd, and agrees to the conclusion of I.3 (157b), the result of a deduction that is internally self-contradictory. He accepts the conclusion of I and II at 160b, and remarks of the conclusion of all the hypotheses, which is radically contradictory, that it is "quite true" (166c). Aristoteles is younger even than Socrates, philosophically untrained, and without independent insight.

79. Perhaps more accurately, we are dealing with something intermediate between dialogue and treatise. Cf. Sophist 217 c-d.

80. Cf. 127e. The list is fully represented in Parmenides' poem: Part/Whole, Fr. 8. 22; Limited/Unlimited, 8.30-33, 8.49; Shape, 8.43; In Itself/In Another, 8.29, cf. 8.22-26; Like/Unlike, 8.5, 8.22-26; Equal/Unequal, 8.23-24, 8.44-48; Older/Younger/Same Age, 8.5; Contact/No Contact, 8.6, 8.26. This list is representative, not exhaustive. There are other opposites in the poem important to the Deductions that follow: Growth/Diminution, 8.7;

Generation/Destruction, 8.3, 8.11-14, 8.19-21, 8.40; and of course Being/Not Being, Frr. 2, 6, 7, 8.2, 8.40.

The situation with Zeno is less clear: we have lost the book. Certainly he constructed paradoxes involving Motion and Rest, Unity and Plurality, Limit and Unlimited, Like and Unlike, In Itself and In Another, and almost certainly Contract and No Contact. It is unprovable, but certainly not impossible or even unlikely, that the list of terms in the exercise to follow closely coincided with the topics of his book.

81. See W. F. R. Hardie, *A Study in Plato*, Oxford, 1936, 123-24.

82. See, for example, *Republic* V 477a, the true Parmenidean legacy.

83. See, for example, *Meta.* V 1019a 1ff., *PTF* 132-33.

84. On which see *Topics* I, ix.

85. See *Meta.* XIV 1092a 11-15, and Dodds, "The *Parmenides* of Plato and the Origin," at 140.

86. *Exodus* iii. 14. See Augustine, *Civ. Dei.* VII, vi, xi.

87. See Augustine, *Confessions* VII, xii, xiii.

88. See, for example, *Republic* V 475e-476a.

89. Compare *Sophist* 217c-e.

90. Cf. *Phaedrus* 277e-278a, *Laws* VI 769a, VII 803c, *Politics* 288c, *Alcibiades* I 132b, *Epistle* VI 323d.

91. For example, at 139b ff., 142b-c.

92. Cf. *Phys.* III 204a 3 ff., *Meta.* XI 1066a 35 ff.

93. *Meta.* V 1022a 3 ff. It is a fallacy of accident to take Parmenides' argument here as a rejection of geometrical points. But see *Meta.* I 992a 20-22, and Alexander, *in Metaph.* 120.4-6 (Hayduck).

94. *HGM* i 293.

95. Cf. Euclid XI Def. 2, *Meta.* X 1066b 23 ff.

96. *HGM* i 293, cf. *TBEE* i 165-66.

97. The argument was anticipated by Gorgias, who claimed that nothing can be in itself, since the same thing will be container and contained, and thus be two things; for the container is place, and the contained body. *DK* B3, 11. 17 ff.

98. Cornford (*PP* 119) translated 138a 3-4 as, "If it were in another, it would be encompassed all round by that in which it was contained." This would not be a mistranslation of the sentence if it did not mistake its context: Parmenides has just defined Circularity (137c), and offers as a reason why Unity cannot be in another that it does not partake of Circularity. Also, Cornford's remark (*PP* 120) that, "Plato is evidently thinking of Parmenides' Sphere; hence the specific denial of roundness," is mistaken: the passage does not merely claim that Unity *cannot* be round, but that if it were in another, it *would* be round.

99. See also the account of alteration below at 156b, and *Phys.* V 226a 17.

100. *Phys.* V 225b 10, cf. 226a 17, and *Theaetetus* 181d.

101. This is why Aristotle maintains that, "'Motion,' in its most general and primary sense is change of place" (*Phys.* IV 208a 32). If local motion is the primary motion, local rest is the primary rest. Cf. *Phys.* VIII 260b 1 ff.

102. The connection between sameness and plurality is stressed by Aristotle: "Clearly, therefore, sameness is a unity of the being either of more than one thing or of one thing when it is treated as more than one, i.e., when we say a thing is the same as itself; for we treat it as two." *Meta.* V 1018a 7 ff.

103. As Proclus suggests (*in Parm.* 1026.8-11), the incommensurable may have the same number of different measures.

104. X. Def. 1. For other references to incommensurability in Plato, see *Theaetetus* 147d-148b, *Laws* VII 819e-820c.

105. *Elements* IX. 29. The account here follows, with minor changes, that of Health, *HGM* i. 91. For the modern formulation, see Russell, *Introduction to Mathematical*

Philosophy, London, 1919, p. 67.

106. Cf. Euclid X.8.

107. Euclid VII 1,2.

108. Scholium on Euclid X, cited and translated by Heath, *HGM* i 154.

109. *The Tempest* I. ii. 49. For the more usual metaphor, see *Troilus and Cressida* III. iii. 145-6: "Time hath, my lord, a wallet at his back,/ Wherein he puts alms for Oblivion." Here the wallet is the past. Compare ὄπισθεν with the English 'after'; after means later, but the afterdeck is to the rear.

110. *Ajax* 475-76, after Jebb.

111. *Principia*, vol. i. (trans. Motte, Cajori), Berkeley, 1971, p. 6.

112. *Principia*, pp. 7-8. Cf. *Physics* IV 218b 14-18.

113. See, for example, *Timaeus* 37c-38a, 27d-28a, 52a-c.

114. *Timaeus* 62a, *Symposium* 211a-b.

115. See *Meta*. X 1054a 13-19, VII 1040b 16, XI 1061a 15-18.

116. The ground for the inference that if Unity partakes of Being, it partakes of its own being is Parmenides' earlier argument at 131a-c that if things partake of characters they cannot partake of the whole character, with the result that part of the character must be in them. This implication is restated at 144c 8 - d 4. If the line of argument is pursued, the being of Unity is not only a part of Unity but also a part of Being – the use of 'part' found at 144c. See also *Sophist* 257c-158c.

117. 137c, cf. *Theaetetus* 205a, and *Meta*. V 1023b 26, *Phys*. III 207a 10.

118. If this is a correct account of Parmenides' use of the part/whole distinction here, it prompted debate in the Academy, echoes of which may be overheard in Aristotle's remark at *Categories* 1a 24-25 that by "in a subject" he means what is *not* part of a subject and cannot exist separately from what it is in. Note that an Aristotelian substance cannot be a whole of which items in categories other than substance are parts, since if part and whole are interdependent, change in the parts implies change in the whole – a doctrine compatible with perpetual flux, but not with the notion of substance as self-subsistent substrate of change.

119. VIII 263b 3-6, cf. Simplicius, *in Phys*. 1290.21-24 (Diels) on *Phys*. 263a 4, and 1013.26-27.

120. Euclid X Def. 2, *Timaeus* 54b 5, cf. 32a 1.

121. *Theaetetus* 147d.

122. For a clear and concise statement of the connection – and the differences – between the calculus and the Method of Exhaustion, see C. B. Boyer, *The Concepts of the Calculus*, New York, 1949, pp. 33-37.

123. *Elements* IX. 20.

124. In its finitism, Greek mathematics may be compared with the Intuitionism of Brouwer and Heyting (See Russell, *Principles of Mathematics*, London, 1919, p. vi; Kneale and Kneale, *The Development of Logic*, Oxford, 1964, pp. 675 ff.) The foundations, however, are very different. Intuitionism refuses to admit any existential proposition that cannot be demonstrated by constructing an instance, and therefore rejects, not only infinite sets of objects, but also unrestricted Excluded Middle. Its impulse is in Kant, and mathematical verifiability in relation to forms of intuition. Greek mathematics, to the contrary, rests throughout on indirect proof, and therefore on Excluded Middle, and its finitism appears to represent a mathematical solution to Zenonian problems.

125. The Greek superlative is often equivalent to a very strong comparative, as indeed is true in English. There is no contradiction in saying that the least part has parts, understanding by this that the very smallest part *taken* has parts.

126. For parallel construction with similar implication, see *Philebus* 27a 11, *Sophist* 263d 3.

127. The *Parmenides* thus provides a conditional metaphysical proof of Russell's Axiom of Infinity, that if *N* is any finite cardinal number, there is at least one class having *N* members. Russell finally supposed that this could not be logically derivable, owing to type difficulties (*Introduction to Mathematical Philosophy*, pp. 134-35).

128. *Phys.* III 203b 22-25, with 208a 15-19.

129. *Phys.* VI 232b 24-25, cf. 231b 15-16, I 185a 10 *de Caelo* I 268a 6-7. For argument that infinite divisibility implies continuity, see *de Gen. et Corr.* I 317a 14-18. Compare also the definition of a part as that into which any thing can be divided, *Meta.* V 1023b 13.

130. One might argue that, so far from being equivalent, they are incompatible. For infinite divisibility implies continuity, and continuity implies the denial of successiveness, whereas sameness of extremity is taken to be a species of contiguity, and contact is defined as a species of succession (*Phys.* V 227a 9, cf. 17-24, *Meta.* XI 1068b 26 - 1069a 15). The explanation is that Aristotle uses "in succession" in a strong and a weak sense. In the weak sense, two things are in succession if they may be taken in any order of prior and posterior; in the strong sense, that order must be a discrete order of prior and posterior. See *Phys.* V 226b 34 - 227a 6, 20.

131. *Plato*, New York, 1950, p. 511, n. 1.

132. *de Lineis Insecabilibus* 968b 4-10, 16-21, 969b 6-12, 970a 1-4.

133. See C. B. Boyer, *The Concepts of the Calculus*, 20-21.

134. For parallel construction with similar implication, see *Philebus* 27a 11, *Sophist* 263d 3.

135. It will be recalled that the distinction between the dense but denumerable infinity of the rational numbers and the nondenumerable infinity of the reals was unknown before Cantor, and certainly not anticipated in Greek mathematics. No plurality was greater than an infinite plurality.

136. On this foundation, Parmenides will later erect an argument that since Unity is different from the others, and the others different from Unity, Unity is in this respect the same as the others and the others the same as Unity (147c). The argument is superficially paradoxical, but sound nonetheless; things are said to be the same when they partake of the same character. Unity and the others partake of the character of Difference; they are thus in this respect the same; they therefore also partake of Sameness. Similarly, Parmenides has argued in Hypothesis I (139d-e) that Unity cannot be the same as itself, since if it were, it would not be (just) one; Unity, if it has no parts, cannot partake of Sameness. Mr. Richard Robinson (*PED*, pp. 248-49) dismisses both arguments as willful sophisms. Both in fact depend on the assumption that Sameness and Difference are characteristics distinct from Unity.

137. It is from 143c-d and what follows, I believe, that Aristotle derived his distinction between the Indefinite Dyad and the number 2, a distinction that presupposes a generation of number. Here is Robin on the distinction: "Il ne faut pas confondre la Dyade indéfinie avec le nombre deux, et cette confusion est surtout dangereuse sinon se représente en réalité ce nombre sans sa forme arithmétique. Ce qu'il y a dans la Dyade, c'est une puissance indéterminée de multiplication . . . Mais il ne peut être question de multiplier ce qui n'est pas une quantité, mais un principe, et l'Un, bien loin d'être un terme, en quelque sorte passif, sur lequel agirait le puissance multiplicative de la Dyade, est tout au contraire l'agent par lequel la puissance multiplicative de la Dyade produit un nombre, c'est-à-dire une multiplicité réelle. En d'autres termes, la Dyade est multiplicative en elle-même et par elle-même. Par conséquent, la première fois que l'Un exerce sur elle son action déterminante,

le produit engendré se trouvera être quelque chose qui reproduit la Dyade, puisque ce quelque chose en est la puissance actualisée. C'est le Nombre Deux, dans lequel nos retrouvons le plus et le moins, mais non pas un plus et un moins illimités." (Robin, *Idees et Nombres*, pp. 444-45.)

138. *Elements* VII Def. 2.

139. *TBEE* ii. 280.

140. *HGM* i. 70.

141. A. E. Taylor (*Plato*, 6th ed., New York, 1950, pp. 505-6) attempted to give Plato the zero, and claimed to find the real numbers at *Epinomis* 990c-991b (p. 501, n. 1), a passage that in fact limits number to the odd and the even. The evidence for this and other treasures is on a level with Taylor's gift to Plato of Dedekind cuts (p. 511).

142. *Meta.* 1089b 35, cf. 1016b 25.

143. Cf. *Elements* VII Defs. 3, 4.

144. The first person to treat one as a number, as distinct from *using* it as a number, appears to have been Chrysippus, who may, however, have been anticipated by Speusippus: see *ACPA* n. 202, Ross, *Aristotle's Physics*, Oxford, 1936, p. 604.

145. *Theaetetus* 198a, *Gorgias* 453e, cf. *Phaedo* 104a-b.

146. Cf. *Republic* VII 524d, *Phaedo* 104a-b, 101c. *Hippias Major* 302a treats one as an odd number, but this is dialectical and does not imply a commitment to the proposition that one is odd as a matter of abstract number theory.

147. Cf. *Meta.* XIII 1085b 10; *ACPA* 202. Even here, the ancients were not unanimous, sometimes regarding two not as a number, but as the beginning of even number. See *HGM* 70-71. One argument for this was that it is characteristic of numbers that their product is greater than their sum, whereas $2 + 2 = 2 \times 2$, and 1×1 is less than $1 + 1$. See M. L. D'Ooge, *Nichomachus: Introduction to Arithmetic*, New York, 1926, p. 116 ff.

148. For example, at *Theaetetus* 198a, *Gorgias* 453e.

149. See Euclid VII, Defs. 8-10; for further discussion, see *HGM* i 71-72, *TBEE* ii 281-84.

150. *in Ptol. Harm.* 93.5 (Düring), *DK* Archytas B.2.

151. *PC* 45, citing Adrastus on the authority of Theon.

152. *Arith.* II xxiv 6 (D'Ooge).

153. *Plato Arith.* 94, 11-14 (Hiller).

154. For further discussion, see "The Generation of Numbers in Plato's *Parmenides*," *Class. Philol.* LXV (1970), pp. 30-34.

155. *Meta.* I 987b 32-34, cf. *ACPA* n. 106. At XIII 1084a 2-6, Aristotle gives an account of the generation of number that echoes Parmenides' argument, and is a misinterpretation of that argument.

156. See *Phys.* IV 219b 5-8.

157. See *Phaedo* 96e-97b, 101b-c, 104a-b (comparing with the latter *Post. Anal.* II 96a 24 - 96b 14). See further J. Cook Wilson, "On the Platonist Doctrine of the ἀσύμβλητοι ἀριθμοί" *Class. Rev.* XVIII (1904), pp. 247-60; *ACPA* 300-305 and Appendix VI.

158. The objection that Parmenides' procedure does not generate the primes, which is as old as Aristotle (*Meta.* I 987b 33), neglects the fact that multiplication is abbreviated addition (*Elements* VII, Def. 15, cf. *TBEE* ii 287) and also the fact that no generation is here involved. Cornford's explanation of the point is mistaken: "The objection that prime numbers cannot be obtained by multiplication is invalid, since Plato evidently includes addition and starts with that when he *adds* one term to another to make two, and two to one to make three. Moreover, primes were sometimes regarded as odd multiples of an odd number, 1 being treated for this purpose as odd: $5 = 5 \times 1$" (*PP* 141, n. 2). Cornford goes on to cite Theon (*Plat. Arith.* 23, 14) in support of the last remark. But he forgets that one was *not* added to one to make two, two rather being derived from the dual and shown to imply two ones; that the passage from Theon he cites also says that a prime is "measured

by no number, but by a unit alone" (23, 9-10); and that to analyze 5 as the product of 5 and 1 requires a number system that already contains 5.

159. The classification is not exhaustive, since it does not classify the primes, and not exclusive, since even-times odd and odd-times even numbers are the same, and some numbers may be both even-times odd and even-times even: $12 = 2 \times 6 = 4 \times 3$. There was, however, an ancient tradition that even-times even numbers are always (in effect) numbers of the form 2^n: see *TBEE* ii 282.

160. *in Parm.* 1261, 18-21 (Cousin).

161. *Phys.* III 206b 3-10. Heath (*Mathematics in Aristotle*, Oxford, 1949, p. 106, cf. 108-9) translated this passage in such a way as to imply, not the infinite divergent series of the natural numbers, but an infinite convergent series such as, $1/2 + 1/4 + 1/8 \ldots + 1/2^n + \ldots = 1$. But if this were so, it would assume that Aristotle had the concept of the sum of an infinite arithmetical series as the limit toward which that series tends. This conception, though it has analogues in Greek geometry in the method of exhaustion, is unexampled in Greek arithmetic, the reason being, perhaps, that fractions were treated not as numbers but as ratios, and an infinite series of ratios does not sum at a number. It is, then, unlikely that Aristotle understood his "infinite by addition" to include infinite convergent series, and his Greek, surely, admits the sense of the Oxford translation here quoted. I owe this point to Professor Marshall Clagett.

162. For further discussion see *REA* 33-37, *ACPA* 300-305 and App. VI, and Paul Shorey, *The Unity of Plato's Thought*, 82-85. Also see *Class. Philol.* xxii (1972), 213-18, for Shorey's criticism of J. Adam's treatment of mathematical intermediates in *The Republic of Plato* (2nd ed.), 159-63.

163. *Plato's Philosophy of Mathematics*, Stockholm, 1955.

164. Wedberg, p. 118, cf. p. 66.

165. Cf. 101b-c.

166. "On the Platonist Doctrine of the ἀσύμβλητοι ἀριθμοί, *Class. Rev.* XVIII (1904), pp. 249 ff.

167. See *REA*, pp. 35-36.

168. It will follow that terms such as Difference are doubly relative: x, if it is different, is different from something, and we may therefore speak of the difference *from* something *of* x.

169. *Meta.* XIII 1083b 37- 1084a 9, cf. *Phys.* III 206b 7-9. If Xenocrates formulated a doctrine of infinitesimals, the conception should be attributed to him, since infinitesimals logically presuppose an infinite (ordinal) number.

170. Notice that 149b-c does not contradict this assumption, since it deals with some *number* of measures, which may be as many as you please, marking off a perimeter.

171. See B. Bolzano, *The Paradoxes of the Infinite* (trans. D. A. Steele), London, 1948, pp. 98 ff.

172. Perhaps that of Chrysippus. See Diog. Laert. VII, 150, and Stob. *Ecl.* 142, 2, cited by von Arnim, *Stoicorum Veterum Fragmenta*, ii. 158, para. 482.

173. Plutarch, *On Common Conceptions*, 1079a. It has been held that in this passage it is, "clearly stated that the subset is equivalent to its set in the sense defined by the modern theory of sets." (S. Sambursky, *Thy Physics of the Stoics*, London, 1959, p. 97; cf. A. Wedberg, *Plato's Philosophy of Mathematics*, pp. 65, 130; W. K. C. Guthrie, *History of Greek Philosophy* ii, Cambridge, 1965, 290, has traced the assumption back to Anaxagoras.) But the Stoics themselves refused to say that any body or continuum consists of an infinite number of parts, so that we here deal with not an accepted theory of infinity, but one that the Stoics must have been compelled to reject. See H. F. Cherniss, *Plutarch's Moralia*, XIII, Part II, New York, 1976, p. 814, n. *a*.

174. Sir Thomas Heath once remarked: "The Greek geometers shrank from the use of such expressions as infinitely great or infinitely small and substituted the idea of things

greater or less than any assigned magnitude. Thus . . . they never said that a circle is a polygon with an infinite number of infinitely small sides; they always stood still before the abyss of the infinite and never ventured to overstep the bound of clear conceptions. They never spoke of an infinitely close approximation or a limiting value of the sum of a series extending to an infinite number of terms" (*Archimedes*, Cambridge, 1897, p. cxlii).

175.   Compare the use of τὸ ἐλάχιστον at 142e 4 and of σμικρότατα καὶ μέγιστα at 144b 5, cf. 2-3. See also the comparatives in 144b 7-8. On the other hand, Aristotle (*Phys.* IV 220a 26-33) refers to the smallest number: it is two. At *Phys.* III 206b 27-33, Aristotle ascribes to Plato the belief that one is the minimum number, and ten the maximum. There is, however, no evidence in Plato for either claim, the latter of which is contradicted by 144a.

176.   245a, trans. Cornford. Cf. *Theaetetus* 205a, *Parmenides* 157c-e.

177.   *Per contra*, cf. *Sophist* 244d-245a.

178.   *Phys.* IV 210a 25 ff. The relevance of this passage to the present one was pointed out by Simplicius (*in Phys.* 560.11-561.21 on *Phys.* 210b 18), who criticized Alexander for missing it.

179.   *Theaetetus* 204e-205d. The *Theaetetus*, it may be observed, does not recognize the existence of Ideas, and specifically the Idea of Wholeness, for which see *Sophist* 245c-d. Parmenides assumes that if a thing is a whole, it has a character distinct from all the parts, taken distributively.

180.   This is Simplicius' construction of the argument (*in Phys.* 561.1-2): a whole cannot be in itself in the primary sense. Cf. *Phys.* IV 210a 33.

181.   See also *Topics* VI 150a 15-21, *Phys.* I 185b 11-14.

182.   *Symposium* 211a-b, *Timaeus* 52a-b. The strongest statement of the proposition is at 151a 4: whatever (always) is must be somewhere.

183.   The same ambiguity in ἕν is found in the parallel proof in the First Deduction (139b-c); because nothing turns on it there, it has not been noted in the translation. The translation of this passage, however, has attempted to note the ambiguity, at the cost of some disfigurement. For the substantival use of ἕν without the article, see 143c 7 as a clear case. See also below, 149c 5-6.

184.   139e, 148a, cf. *Meta.* 1018a 15-17, 1054b 9-13, *PP* 125.

185.   *PP* 166 and n.1.

186.   *Topics* IV 121b 19-23, *Phys.* III 206a 18, *Meta.* XIII 1084b 1.

187.   Cf. *Meta.* XIII 1080b 28-30, *ACPA* pp. 15, 127-29, n. 81, *AM* i. 203-4.

188.   Burnet gave the doctrine to Plato (*Greek Philosophy: Thales to Plato*, London, 1914, pp. 32-323), and connected it with the doctrine that the line is generated from the point by a 'fluxion,' a ῥύσις στιγμῆς. This is refuted by Cherniss (*ACPA* n. 322).

189.   Incommensurability could be saved if it were possible to assume that there are minimal parts of different and incommensurable lengths; but it is impossible to assume this, since it implies that those lengths differ from each other by some length, and thus that they are not minimal. We speak here, of course, of geometrical rather than physical divisibility.

190.   Cf. *Parmenides* 140b-c, Euclid VII Def. 5.

191.   It is at least possible that the doctrine—if there was such a doctrine in the Academy—was meant, among other things, as an explanation of the fact of incommensurability, and specifically of the fact of successively diminishing rational approximations to irrational ratios (see *HGM* i 91-93). That the doctrine of indivisible lines was in some way connected with the fact of incommensurability would seem to be suggested by *De Lin. Insec.* 968b 5-22, 969b 6-12, 970a 1-3. It may have been supposed that the same infinitesimal parts might be reached by any principle of division, rational or irrational.

192.   Heath, *Archimedes*, pp. cxlii-cxliii.

193. Euclid VII. 37, 38.

194. *Meta.* XIII 1083b 37 - 1084a 9; see also *Physics* III 206b 7-9.

195. Thabit, the ninth century Arabic Platonist and mathematician, appears to have construed *Parmenides* 144a-b as implying an infinite number (see S. Pines, *Actes du XIe Congres International d'Histoire des Sciences,* 1957, p. 163), but the passage in fact only states that number is unlimited in multitude.

196. Cornford (*PP* 178 and n. 1), concerned to explain why the container is greater than the contained, suggests, "[I] f we consider the whole quantity as the sum of all the parts into which it *can* be divided, this sum will always be greater than the sum of any part into which it is actually divided. Thus the One as a whole will be greater than itself as all its actual parts." But to distinguish potential from actual parts is to make potential parts actual. Indeed, Aristotle knew this as an argument for an actual infinite: "For if a body '*can* be separated at the contacts' (as some thinkers express it), then, even though it has not yet been divided, it will be in a state of dividedness—since it can be divided, nothing inconceivable results" (*de Gen. et Corr.* 1 327a 12-14). If the infinite is genuinely potential, it would have no parts prior to the act of (physical or mental) division; and certainly there is no *sum* of parts into which Unity can be divided. Parmenides' inference is in fact a direct inference from the preceding proof of contact.

197. It is of interest to compare the historical Parmenides, who held that Being "was not in the past, nor shall it be, since is is now, all at once, one, continuous" (*DK* A 8.5). This seems to suggest a timeless present, distinct from the timeless Being of the *Timaeus* and the moving present of the *Parmenides.*

198. An interesting variation of this is to be found in the *Metaphysics.* At VII 1028a 30 - b 2, Aristotle distinguishes three senses in which substance may be said to be first, that is, ultimately prior: it is first in definition, first in the order of knowledge, and first in time. The reason for holding that it is first in time is that none of the other categories can exist independently except substance. This of course does not mean that substance begins temporally naked of categorical qualification and proceeds afterward to be vested with further determinations. The very fact that time is a category shows this to be impossible. The claim that substance is first in time is a claim of ontological priority, here presented as if it were temporal. It is difficult to suppose that Aristotle's choice of vocabulary does not have its roots in this section of the *Parmenides*: Unity is first logically (remembering always that Unity is a unity, 142d), and therefore ontologically, and therefore temporally. To be prior is to be prior in time.

199. The distinction recurs in Euclid. A number is part of a number, the less of the greater, when it measures the greater; but parts when it does not measure it (VII Defs. 3, 4, cf. V, Def. 1). Part means a submultiple or aliquot part; thus two is parts but not part of three, and part but not parts of 4. The resulting ratio of part to whole will always be that of one to a number when reduced to lowest terms; and one is always part but not parts of every number.

200. *TBEE* i 224. My thanks are due to Professor Marshall Clagett throughout this discussion, who is not, of course, responsible for its results.

201. *DK* B 2. Archytas' account of proportion certainly applied to numbers, but perhaps applied to any magnitudes, commensurable or incommensurable. There is no sufficient evidence to determine this point, but certainly Eudoxus' generalized theory of proportion, which is preserved in Euclid V, had antecedents.

202. Theon 22.10 - 23.3 (Hiller), Nichomachus II. xxiii (D'Ooge), Marshall Clagett, *Nichole Oresme and the Geometry of Qualities and Motions,* Madison, 1968, p. 611.

203. Should this be taken to imply that Plato has approximated, at least by way of negation, the concept of a mathematical limit, a concept not elsewhere found in Greek

mathematics? Presumably not, for the notion that Unity is continually becoming younger than the others appears to imply that if it could *reach* a limit, it could *pass through* the limit, and be younger than that than which it is older. This, indeed, explains Parmenides' emphasis on the fact that the sequence cannot terminate, that Unity is always becoming what it never can be.

204.   *In Parm.* 1287.11 (Cousin.)

205.   Aristotle, in one of his arguments against the possibility of a becoming of becoming, offers an account that may be related: "A thing which is capable of becoming is also capable of perishing: consequently, if there be becoming of becoming, that which is in process of becoming is in process of perishing at the very moment when it has reached the stage of becoming: since it cannot be in process of perishing when it is just beginning to become or after it has ceased to become: for that which is in process of perishing must be in existence." *Phys.* V 226a 7-10.

206.   *Phaedo* 70e ff., 102d-e et seq.

207.   *DK* B 51, after Kirk and Raven.

208.   *Meta.* IV 1010a 12-14, cf. I 987a 32 ff. Aristotle connects perpetual flux with the affirmation of contradiction, on the ground that perpetual flux implies that everything is true or nothing is true. Compare *Meta.* IV 1010a 6 ff. and 1012a 29ff.

209.   Cornford properly compares the list of physical, as distinct from psychical, motions at Laws X 893c ff. *PP* 197-99.

210.   *Phys.* VI 239b 5-9, cf. 30-32. See Ross *ad loc.*

211.   *Phys.* VIII 263a 4 - b 5, cf. Simplicius, *in Phys.* 1290.21-24 (Diels).

212.   *Ap.* Simp., *Phys.* 453.30. Cf. Ross, *Aristotle's Metaphysics* i. 170-71.

213.   *Meta.* I 991b 31. Cf. Ross *ad loc.*

214.   *Meta.* XIV 1091a 9-12; but see XIII 1084a 2-6.

215.   It is helpful to compare the following passages in serial order: 149e, 157d, 185b, c, 159e, 160c, 164d.

216.   See Russell, *Introduction to Mathematical Philosophy*, pp. 164, 171.

217.   *De Interpretatione* 20a 31-33.

218.   J. L. Ackrill, *Aristotle's Categories and de Interpretatione*, Oxford, 1963, p. 143 on *de Interp.* 19b 19.

219.   Cf. *Theaetetus* 190b-d.

220.   *PP* 223-24.

221.   Cf. *Categories* 11b 38 - 12a25.

222.   *De Interp.* 21a 32-33, trans. Ackrill.

223.   See, for example, *Euthydemus* 283e-284c, *Cratylus* 385b, *Theaetetus* 167a-d, 189a-b, *Sophist* 240d-241b.

224.   Cf. *Meta.* V 1024b 26-28 (along with IV 1011b 26-28): "A false account is the account of non-existing objects, in so far as it is false. Hence every account is false when applied to something other than that which is true." For Aristotle, truth and falsity of statement have to do with combination and separation in thought; this is essentially the account of the *Sophist*, which analyzes falsity in terms of difference (263b-d).

225.   Compare *Meta.* X 1054b 18-22: "'other or the same' can therefore be predicated of everything with regard to everything else – but only if the things are one and existent, for 'other' is not the contradictory of 'the same'; which is why it is not predicated of non-existent things (whereas 'not the same' is so predicated). It is predicated of all existing things; for everything that is existent and one is by its very nature either one or not one with anything else."

226.   The word ὄγκος may have been used by the historical Zeno: see *Phys.* VI 239b 34. Aristotle himself customarily uses the term to mean the bulk or volume of a body. Cf. *Phys.* 203b 28, 209a 3, 213a 17, 216b 6.

227.   For further introductory reading, see Courant and Robbins, *What is Mathematics?*

Oxford, 1963, 77-87, 108-12. An admirable summary of Cantor's work will be found in Kneale and Kneale, *The Development of Logic*, 438-43.

228. Cantor further showed that it is possible to construct an infinite sequence of transfinite numbers. The proof requires introduction of the notion of a power set. P is the power set of X if and only if P is the set of all sets included in X. It is to be observed that among the sets included in X is X itself, and ∅, the null set.

Given the notion of a power set, Cantor proceeded to prove that the power set of a set has a greater cardinal number than that set, whether the set is finite or infinite, and that for any set containing *n* members, the power set of that set will contain 2^n members. Whence it follows that, if infinity is an ocean, there are oceans of oceans.

229. *Meta.* XIII 1083b 37 ff.

Index Locorum

Index Locorum

PLOTINUS

Enneads

PLUTARCH

On Common Conceptions

Pericles

PORPHYRY

on Ptolemy's Harmonics

PROCLUS

(Proclus)

in Parmenides

Scholium in Parmenides

SIMPLICIUS

(Commentaria in Aristotelem Graeca, Vol. 9
(*Libros quattuor priores*), ed. Hermannus
Diels, Berlin 1882; Vol. 10 (*Libros quattuor
posteriores*), ed. Hermannus Diels, Berlin,
1895)

in Physics

R. E. Allen is professor of philosophy and classics at Northwestern University. He is the author of *Plato's Euthyphro and the Earlier Theory of Forms* and *Socrates and Legal Obligation,* the latter published by the University of Minnesota Press.